Strategic Command and Control

BRUCE G. BLAIR

Strategic Command and Control

Redefining the Nuclear Threat

THE BROOKINGS INSTITUTION

Washington, D.C.

Copyright © 1985 by

THE BROOKINGS INSTITUTION

1775 Massachusetts Avenue, NW, Washington, D.C. 20036

Library of Congress Cataloging in Publication Data

Blair, Bruce G., 1947–
  Strategic command and control.
  Includes bibliographical references and index.
  1. Command and control systems—United States.
2. Strategic forces—United States.   3. Military policy—
United States.   I. Title.
UB212.B5   1985   355.3′3041′0973   84-73164
ISBN 0-8157-0982-X
ISBN 0-8157-0981-1 (pbk.)

1 2 3 4 5 6 7 8 9

Foreword

AN ELABORATE system with daunting responsibilities has been created to operate the nation's strategic forces. Consisting of early warning sensors, communications, command posts, procedures, and people, this system must prevent unauthorized use of nuclear weapons while simultaneously permitting rapid execution of authorized orders.

Despite its intrinsic importance, the U.S. nuclear control system has remained on the periphery of analysis and policy debate in the West. Strategic forces themselves, rather than the means of their control, have dominated discussion of virtually all issues of nuclear security: strategic balance, crisis and arms race stability, arms reduction talks, nuclear strategy, and modernization of strategic arms. In this book, Bruce G. Blair explains why command-control is central to these issues. He provides an account of the structure and process of the U.S. nuclear control system as it evolved during the past twenty-five years and establishes its past and present weaknesses. His purpose is to assess the nuclear threat from a perspective that includes command-control and to indicate the adjustments to strategic thought and policy that are warranted by the assessment.

A research associate in the Brookings Foreign Policy Studies program when this book was written, Blair had earlier served in the Strategic Air Command as a Minuteman launch control officer and as a support officer for the SAC Airborne Command Post. After completing the draft manuscript for the book, he became project director for a study of strategic command and control undertaken at the Congressional Office of Technology Assessment. He recently moved to the Department of Defense where he continues to work on issues of command and control.

The author thanks the many present and former American military officers and government officials who consented to be interviewed during the project. These interviews were conducted with the understanding that their names would not be cited in the book.

Numerous individuals gave generously of their time to review the entire manuscript. The advice of these readers—Richard K. Betts, Garry D. Brewer, Ashton B. Carter, Robert F. Coulam, H. Dickinson, William H. Kincade, Michael Raskin, Martin Shubik, and H. Bradford Westerfield—is gratefully acknowledged.

John Baker, John Bassler, Bob Berman, Mike Evanisko, James Fesler, Rick Guzzo, Steph Haggard, Christine Helms, Gary Jusela, William Kaufmann, Jan Liss, Bill Mako, John Mearsheimer, Kenneth Moore, Ken Oye, Chae Pak, Barry Posen, and Bruce Russett offered helpful suggestions and encouragement. Paul Morawski spent long hours designing and programming computer models used in the research. Susan Nichols provided the secretarial assistance and typed the manuscript, and Louis Holliday and Mike Doleman helped in its production. James Schneider edited the book, Bruce Dickson and Alan G. Hoden checked its accuracy, Nancy Snider and Marilynn Imhoof proofread it, and Ward & Silvan prepared the index. For all these contributions, the author is deeply appreciative. He also thanks Judy Dunn and Bernice Plush for their many contributions along the way.

The author especially appreciated the assistance and unflagging support of Monica M. Yin and of John D. Steinbruner, director of the Foreign Policy Studies program. Generous financial assistance for the project was provided by the Ford Foundation throughout its duration and by the Carnegie Corporation in its final phases.

The views in this book are solely those of the author and should not be ascribed to the Ford Foundation, the Congressional Office of Technology Assessment, the Department of Defense, or to the trustees, officers, or staff members of the Brookings Institution.

BRUCE K. MACLAURY
President

March 1985
Washington, D.C.

Contents

Figures

Abbreviations and Acronyms

ABM	antiballistic missile
ABNCP	airborne command post
ADP	automated data processing
AFSATCOM	air force satellite communications
ALCC	airborne launch control center
ALCM	air-launched cruise missile
ANMCC	Alternate National Military Command Center
ASW	antisubmarine warfare
AWACS	Airborne Warning and Control System
BMEWS	Ballistic Missile Early Warning System
C³I	command, control, communications, and intelligence
CCPDS	Command Center Processing and Display System
CINCEUR	commander in chief, Europe
CINCLANT	commander in chief, Atlantic
CINCPAC	commander in chief, Pacific
CINCSAC	commander in chief, Strategic Air Command
COMSAT	Communications Satellite Corporation
DCA	Defense Communications Agency
DCS	Defense Communications System
DNA	Defense Nuclear Agency
DSCS	Defense Satellite Communications System
DTACCS	director of telecommunications and command control systems
DSP	defense support program
EAM	emergency action message
EMATS	Emergency Message Automatic Transmission System
EMP	electromagnetic pulse
ERCS	Emergency Rocket Communications System

FLTSATCOM	fleet satellite communications
GWEN	Ground Wave Emergency Network
HERT	headquarters emergency relocation team
ICBM	intercontinental ballistic missile
IDCSP	interim defense communications satellite program
IONDS	Integrated Operational NUDET Detection System
JCSAN	Joint Chiefs of Staff Alerting Network
JRSC	jam-resistant secure communications
JSTPS	Joint Strategic Targeting Planning Staff
LCC	launch control center
LES	Lincoln experimental satellite
MARISAT	maritime satellite
MCC	mobile command center
MEECN	Minimum Essential Emergency Communications Network
MGT	mobile ground terminal
MHD	magnetohydrodynamics
MIRV	multiple independently targeted reentry vehicle
NCA	national command authority
NEACP	National Emergency Airborne Command Post
NECPA	National Emergency Command Post Afloat
NMCC	National Military Command Center
NMCS	National Military Command System
NORAD	North American Air Defense Command
NUWEP	*Nuclear Weapons Employment Policy*
OSD	Office of the Secretary of Defense
PACCS	Post Attack Command Control System
PAS	Primary Alerting System
PARCS	Perimeter Acquisition Radar Control System
PPBS	planning, programming, and budgeting system
SAC	Strategic Air Command
SACCS	SAC Automated Command and Control System
SCF	satellite control facility
SLBM	submarine-launched ballistic missile
SLCM	sea-launched cruise missile
SLFCS	Survivable Low Frequency Communications System
SIOP	single integrated operational plan
TACSAT	tactical satellite
WWMCCS	World Wide Military Command and Control System

CHAPTER ONE

Command-Control
and Nuclear Capability

IMPORTANT open questions about national security in the nuclear age begin with the observation that the performance of command, control, communications, and early warning networks (C³I) is not a prominent issue in strategic assessment and debate. Analysis and advocacy alike dwell on weapons system characteristics and their implications for strategic balance, crisis stability, and deterrence. Nuclear bombers, submarines, and land missiles figure prominently in debate, while the physical and procedural arrangements created to operate those forces escape notice. This exclusion raises the basic question of whether standard measures of strategic capabilities are valid. Are the measures reasonably accurate indicators or do they bear only a marginal relationship to actual capabilities? Should decisionmakers rely on such limited calculations to formulate strategic policy, gauge the stability of deterrence, allocate resources, or set arms control priorities?

Although answers to these questions have not been supplied, assessments based solely on weapons system characteristics strongly influence perceptions of strategic strength. Debate over nuclear policy and strategic forces is clearly under the influence, if not the dominance, of such assessments. Witness the preeminence of the analyst who pits U.S. and Soviet nuclear weapons against each other in a statistical model of combat. Quantitative assessment of this kind, though lacking in consideration of organizational arrangements intended to provide coherent direction of strategic forces, speaks with great authority in policy discourse.

What accounts for the tremendous weight that standard enumeration carries in policy debates? One explanation is that the size and technical composition of U.S. and Soviet arsenals *are* relevant factors, and standard enumeration encompasses the number of weapons in the respective inventories and their explosive yields, accuracy, range, and reliability; their means of delivery; and a host of other variables ranging from the impact "footprints" of reentry vehicles to enemy countermeasures and defenses. Relevant targets also figure prominently: the number of enemy strategic bomber bases, missile silos, and submarines, the uncertainty of their location, and their ability to withstand the effects of nuclear explosions.

Another explanation for the popularity of standard calculations is that even the most sophisticated are easily performed. Although calculations of weapons vulnerability, for example, involve complex mathematical relationships, computers easily handle them. This ease of computation has swelled the ranks of expert strategic technicians to the point that very sophisticated discussions of, for example, missile silo vulnerability to blast effects are commonplace.

The sharp analytic edge of standard enumeration also permits policy issues to be cleanly dissected. Policy prescriptions are immediately suggested by estimates of the present and future vulnerability of missile silos, for example. Such estimates introduce clear, simple criteria for appraising the force structure, choosing among alternative weapons programs, and setting an agenda for nuclear arms control. They are thus valued for their role in simplifying choice, bridging divisions between policymakers, and forging a broad national consensus.

The absence of alternative measures lends added weight to measures tied to weapons system characteristics and a narrow definition of strategic capability. We settle for these indicators because no convincing set of measures that includes other dimensions, especially command performance and vulnerability, has been proposed and because policy decisions cannot be postponed indefinitely while analysts try to devise better ones. Even if pockets of ignorance exist, recommendations must be made and evaluated.

Although these explanations help account for the imbalance in the present state of analysis, they hardly dispel the suspicion that the strategic problem has been mispecified in a fundamental way. Dissatisfaction with the narrow focus of mainstream analysis occasionally surfaces, and users of analysis are occasionally reminded that standard calculations may be prone to serious error. But such misgivings and warnings are usually offered in a perfunctory spirit and relegated to obscure footnotes.

Laden with preconceptions and analytic conventions, standard assessments avoid heretical critiques and spurn alternative points of view. They not only reflect but reinforce the view that strategic capability depends on the size and technical composition of the respective force deployments.

The key limiting assumptions that underlie much strategic enumeration, particularly the assumption that weapons system characteristics are the key determinants of strategic strength, require more than a cursory examination and footnote. Although it is not unreasonable to exclude measures of command performance before they are seriously developed, it would be unreasonable to accept indefinitely the present imbalance in strategic analysis, to let a computational impasse discourage inquiry into the implications of nuclear weapons for command systems, or to allow the force of analytic habit to prevent assessments of command performance from taking their rightful place on the agenda for reviewing national security. Simple intuition suggests that omitting command parameters from consideration invites miscalculation. Such a practice is ipso facto grounds for contesting standard analytic conclusions and imposing a heavy burden of proof on them. And if the opportunity for miscalculation is as large as it seems, then much strategic enumeration is not only misleading but wrong. Command performance is quite possibly not just an important factor but the key determinant of real strategic capability.

The need to reexamine our assumptions is pressing. Strategic programs of unusual magnitude and consequence are being advocated under an extremely narrow definition of strategic capability. Analyses of the effectiveness of Soviet attacks aimed at U.S. forces indicate an incipient threat of Soviet nuclear blackmail and provide a justifying logic for investing nearly $250 billion between 1984 and 1988 to rectify the situation. The bulk of that sum is earmarked for modernizing offensive forces, whose three components all show signs of declining strength. The aging Poseidon missile submarines, the mainstay of one leg of the strategic triad, face forced retirement en masse. B-52 strategic bombers, the mainstay of another leg, have to contend with increasingly effective Soviet air defenses. And the Minuteman missile force appears to be severely and imminently threatened by its Soviet counterpart. Calculations indicate that it could be virtually negated as a retaliatory threat by existing Soviet weaponry.

Despite the probable survival of enough U.S. weapons to inflict severe punitive damage in retaliation to any postulated Soviet attack, many view current trends with alarm because significant force disparities favoring the Soviet Union are alleged to accompany them. Such asymmetry, should it be allowed to develop, would supposedly create a "window of vulnerability," an opening through which the Soviet Union could militarily maneuver into a position of exploitable bargaining dominance. A prevalent view is that Minuteman vulnerability alone raises the specter of nuclear blackmail. Unless remedied, this vulnerability leaves the United States without credible responses to limited nuclear attack.

The gloomy calculations provide stimulation and justification for massive investment in the strategic forces. But it is arguably our assumptions, not our forces, that are obsolete. If command performance is really the central question of national security, then heavy reliance on standard enumeration to gauge the Soviet threat and determine (or at least rationalize) the pattern of future U.S. investment incurs high costs in misplaced emphasis, unwise resource allocations, and unwarranted confidence. Strategic forces would be upgraded at the expense of the command system, an allocation that could prove wasteful and counterproductive no matter what the strategy or purpose behind it. It would be ironic if the modernization siphoned attention and resources from command programs to the point that stronger forces could not be directed to any deterrent purposes. No less bizarre would be an investment producing a force that was effectively geared to fighting a nuclear war (an ascendant theme of current defense policy guidance and the impetus for much of the programmed investment in strategic forces) but that failed to bring the command structure into close alignment with that purpose. Deficiencies in command performance could be cause for serious concern regardless of the resilience of the forces and the strategy to which they are subordinated. If command and control fail, nothing else matters.

This book argues that the risk of command and control failure has actually been high, and standard enumeration should be heavily discounted if not discarded. Deficiencies in U.S. C^3I systems have been so severe for so long that developments in the size and technical composition of the superpowers' arsenals have been practically irrelevant to the nuclear confrontation. It is hard to exaggerate the extent to which the omission of these deficiencies from strategic assessment has distorted the realities of this confrontation. Although standard assessment produces the comforting conviction that the United States could absorb the Soviets' maximum nuclear attack and inflict socially mortal damage in retaliation, the Soviet Union has actually posed a severe threat to U.S. retaliatory capabilities since the mid-1960s. In all likelihood Soviet strikes against C^3I systems would have severely impaired and possibly blocked U.S. retaliation. Building on the erroneous conclusion that the U.S. capacity for retaliation has long been assured, standard assessment compounded the error by arguing that crisis stability has been high. But the ability of Soviet forces to deliver a crippling blow to U.S. C³I systems long ago created strong incentives on both sides for launching a first strike or for launching a U.S. second strike on warning, incentives that have undermined crisis stability.

Standard assessment also fosters the impression and expectation that Soviet nuclear attack would be concentrated against our weapons. This targeting assumption then leads analysts to the worrisome but again defective conclusion that the Soviet Union could mount an attack that would increase its bargaining leverage over the United States during a protracted conflict. In reality, if damage limitation is the main objective of Soviet nuclear strategy, planners would concentrate their attack on U.S. C³I systems. Moreover, theoretical Soviet bargaining leverage could not be applied even if Soviet targeting doctrine conformed to the assumptions of U.S. standard assessments. Once deterrence fails, it fails completely; the rudimentary design and short endurance of our nuclear C³I system nullifies the whole conception of multiple, time-phased counterforce exchanges. The pursuit of a bargaining advantage by means of limited attack is a purely intellectual construction that has little or no relevance to present circumstances.

Finally, standard assessment assumes that nuclear war can be avoided through the threat of retaliation; Soviet attack will be deterred as long as the United States maintains an undeniable capacity to destroy the Soviet target base in a retaliatory strike. But avoiding nuclear war requires more than the ability to implement authorized strike plans. It also requires the ability to prevent unintentional attacks, including unauthorized attacks.

The need to reconcile the contradictions that flow from these alternative perspectives seems to have registered with recent administrations. In his 1983 annual report, Defense Secretary Caspar Weinberger observed that strategic analysis has been too narrowly focused in recent years. Although "survivable and enduring command, control and communications systems are decisive for deterrence and would be a critical force capability should deterrence fail," criteria used in analysis have nonetheless been "blind to command and control systems."[1] The report also notes

---

1. *Department of Defense Annual Report Fiscal Year 1983,* p. II-10.

that command system repair is essential and "perhaps the most urgently needed element" in the Reagan administration's overall plan for revitalizing the nation's strategic capabilities.[2] While certain features of that plan belie the secretary's words (force modernization will consume the lion's share of the total strategic budget, and standard analytic criteria continue to frame the discussion of this resource allocation), the administration does plan to spend additional billions of dollars on C³I improvements over the next five years and also considers the investment a precondition for modernizing the force structure. According to one authority, the $160 billion earmarked in 1981 for new strategic weapons was simply a waste of money unless the proposed investment in command structure development was also made.[3] To help ensure appropriation of the funds, the Pentagon assigned command, control, and communications elements associated with particular weapons a priority equal to the weapons themselves.[4] That equalization has been formally stipulated in National Security Directive 12 and reflected in C³ funding requests attached to major weapons proposals sent to Congress.[5]

These are positive signs. If the appearance is not deceiving, recognition of strategic command problems could be decisive because it would create a genuine demand for solutions and call forth greater tenacity of purpose in seeking them. Command deficiencies, however, have been chronic for reasons besides simple neglect. Present and future administrations must overcome powerful forces that will strongly resist any fundamental change in strategic priorities. Past administrations succumbed to them, and the Reagan administration is far from bringing them under control.

The scholarly literature on nuclear strategy and deterrence, for instance, has created and perpetuated major conceptual barriers to command system development. This voluminous literature has been enormously influential in molding strategic thought. But notwithstanding its many virtues, the literature has also helped erect two types of barriers, both of which are fundamental assumptions of deterrence theory. First, the theory rests explicitly on the assumption that nuclear weapons are

2. Ibid., p. I-39.

3. "DeLauer Calls New Strategic Plan 'Waste' Without C³ Improvements," *Aerospace Daily*, vol. 111 (October 14, 1981), p. 237.

4. *Department of Defense Annual Report Fiscal Year 1983*, p. III-77.

5. "Why C³I Is the Pentagon's Top Priority," *Government Executive*, January 1982, p. 14.

instruments of diplomacy, a means by which to influence an opponent's decisions. Implied is the assumption that an attacker would avoid the enemy's nuclear control apparatus and leadership so that diplomacy, negotiation, and coercion can play themselves out. Preservation of the enemy's command systems is a sort of theoretical imperative that assumes away or denies the possibility of deliberate assault on C³I systems. Deterrence theory thus ignores a critical scenario and slides past the prime justification for command structure development: command vulnerability could encourage deliberate, direct attack intended to achieve purely military rather than politico-diplomatic objectives.

The second assumption is that each government (including its strategic organization) behaves as if it were a single actor. Deterrence theory sees decisionmaking power concentrated in the hands of a very few who wholly determine the course of events. Command structure development obviously cannot proceed on this assumption. It is a staggering simplification that obscures the technical and organizational constraints that are the proper focus of development. Proper planning recognizes the diffuse and decentralized nature of actual operations. The decision process in situ involves hundreds and thousands of people, many with delegated powers. It involves standard operating procedures, rules of engagement, and a large number and variety of technical C³I components performing a wide range of functions at all echelons. The course of events would surely be affected, perhaps determined, by how these elements of the decision process operate. Even the decision to authorize the use of nuclear weapons, the decision most readily associated with the model of a single actor, cannot be profitably isolated from these elements. It is the decision of a single actor in only the most trivial sense.

Another barrier to command modernization is economic. During the past fifteen years the United States has invested an average of $1.5 billion a year (in constant dollars) in strategic command, control, communications, and tactical early warning. Though not a paltry sum, it still represents a tremendous underinvestment given the Soviet strategic force that has been deployed since 1970. President Reagan's C³I budget has been portrayed as a praiseworthy departure from this historical pattern, but the actual increase in this budget is modest in absolute terms and wholly inadequate to provide the degree of C³I sophistication that the president's nuclear policies demand. The president considers a modern command system as one that can survive a nuclear attack and continue to function for another six months.[6] Although estimates are inherently rough, the funds earmarked for strategic command modernization in the president's defense budget could not buy a survivable command system and would represent only a small down payment on an enduring one. The price tag on a survivable, enduring command system far exceeds proposed funding levels.

President Reagan's proposal at least enjoys a measure of political support. It is rare for any major strategic initiative to encounter as little opposition. Investment in C^3I is by far the least controversial item in the highly publicized strategic arms package unveiled in October 1981. No one denies that the command system has suffered from chronic neglect or that its repair deserves a high priority. Furthermore, few seem to regard the projected expense of repair as too great an economic burden to bear. No major defense programs would be sacrificed for the sake of command modernization. Therein lies the catch, however. Political support is not unqualified and could evaporate quickly if the endeavor proves more costly than the administration has predicted. The president's commitment to a survivable, enduring command system would be put to an especially severe test if the requisite investment threatened funding for major weapons systems such as the B-1 bomber.

The president himself would probably not scale down or forgo major weapons deployments in order to finance C^3I projects. For good reasons or bad, weapons programs like the B-1 and the MX missile are generally deemed essential to strategic revitalization; political risks would accompany any bold deviation from this entrenched position. MX retrenchment provoked the charge that he had scuttled his campaign promise to close the window of vulnerability at the earliest possible date. Further cuts in weapons investment would fuel criticism from the right. Reagan could possibly temper the criticism with reason—that command improvement more than compensates for cuts in weapons funding—but probably not. Command analysis is neither sufficiently developed nor sufficiently accepted to convince skeptics that money would be better spent on command modernization than force modernization. To many, the proposal would sound like a political maneuver that smacks of window dressing.

Present bureaucratic arrangements for managing resources also impede command modernization. Developing a viable system requires a broad view of the situation, a coherent overall plan, and central direction

6. James W. Canan, "Fast Track for C^3I," *Air Force Magazine* (July 1984), p. 45.

of the various projects undertaken. Today's management of C³I programs falls short of these requirements. It lacks focus, unity of purpose, and breadth of vision. And it is anything but centralized.

Decentralized resource management creates a two-pronged challenge. Besides the usual problems associated with excessive decentralization—bureaucratic inefficiency and error in problem definition, coordination of activity, and so forth—the absence of strong corporate management strengthens the hand of those officials who would oppose larger investment in command structure development. Such opposition is significant and is especially strong in the military services. First, the services attach overriding importance to weapons development and procurement. Along with ammunition, spare parts, and maintenance, C³I ranks low in priority. Second, many strategic C³I programs cut across service lines or extend upward to civilian rungs of the hierarchy; individual military services are loath to tap their own budgets to fund these collective goods. Finally, these programs often work to centralize control over force operations, and such centralization runs contrary to military traditions. Establishing a command system that provides for political authorization of a strategic campaign is fully accepted, but a system that permits national policy officials to manage the prosecution of that campaign in the detailed way that this (and the former) administration envisions is not countenanced.

Service opposition bodes grief for the administration's nuclear policies because it has not been disciplined. The services exercise enormous power over C³I programs and budgets, even though their main concerns and priorities lie elsewhere. They are reluctant to become serious partners in this endeavor, and without countervailing bureaucratic leverage, command improvement in all likelihood will continue to be stalled or otherwise fare poorly.

The prospects are not likely to improve soon; indeed, change for the worse seems more probable. In revising the Pentagon's planning, programming, and budgeting system, the administration gave the military services even greater leverage than they already have. Under the new arrangement, which the Pentagon calls "controlled decentralization," it will be harder than ever for C³I projects to survive the rigors of service review. The evidence is not yet in, but by all early indications the services are setting their sights much lower than the civilian officials of the Reagan administration.

There are also technical barriers to modernization. One of the civilian officials responsible for command modernization has said that the United States is "not prepared in a coherent fashion to spend $18 billion" on strategic command, control, and communications.[7] Though the remark brings to mind the bureaucratic problem mentioned above, the official was actually referring to the embarrassment of riches that stems from having too few promising technologies in which to invest newfound resources. Technical solutions to problems such as command vulnerability are not abundant. For all the sophistication of modern computer, communications, and sensor technology, the protection of a command network from the various measures that an aggressor might take against it is extremely difficult.

Nuclear policy has some very rough edges that need smoothing out before the technical implications for command and control can be clearly drawn. For instance, the requirement that the United States be prepared to fight a protracted nuclear war implies that the strategic command system must possess endurance; but disagreement exists over how long it must endure. Technical solutions are also elusive because convincing data and methods for measuring overall command performance are unavailable. Without good evaluation, decisions on where and how much to invest in repairs are little more than guesses. It becomes hard to say whether even extensive repair of numerous C^3I elements would actually aggregate to produce significant improvement in network performance. And technical solutions for certain known deficiencies associated with particular elements—command posts, satellites, and telephone switching centers, for example—are sometimes simply unknown. In some instances even the existence of a deficiency may not be known: the vulnerability of electronic components to electromagnetic pulses produced by nuclear explosions was unknown for many years.

Psychological barriers to confronting C^3I problems also exist. The gulf between the intrinsic importance of command performance and the lack of importance accorded it over the years suggests a deep-seated avoidance of the topic. Perhaps the system has been left massively underdeveloped out of fear of what deeper examination might reveal. Serious investigation could conceivably reveal, for example, that command vulnerability will not respond to treatment, regardless of the scale of investment, the efficiency of resource management, or the ingenuity of technicians. Protect-

7. "DeLauer Calls New Strategic Plan 'Waste' Without C^3 Improvements," p. 237.

ing a large, complex strategic organization from the destructiveness inherent in modern nuclear deployments might in the end seem futile.

Final recognition of the inherent vulnerability of command networks would shake confidence in our guiding principles for comprehending and managing the threat of nuclear destruction. These principles of deterrence assume that the nuclear decision process will function even under the most adverse conditions. If that assumption becomes untenable, strategies for deterrence become obsolete and in need of replacement. But there are no satisfactory replacements at the moment.

Do we dare entertain the possibility that command vulnerability is an insoluble problem and that the relevance of textbook principles of nuclear deterrence to the practical questions of national security has been vastly overstated? In the absence of alternative conceptions of national security in the nuclear age, the search for remedies to weaknesses in nuclear control may cause enough anxiety to inhibit that very search.

Scope and Purpose of the Study

Despite new efforts by the Reagan administration to elevate the priority of C^3I to a level the same as or higher than that of the forces, no dramatic shift in perspective or policy has occurred. Nor is it in prospect. The view that strategic capability turns on the size and composition of the opposing forces still prevails, and various elements exist to reinforce it powerfully. Under the circumstances, this narrow view will unquestionably continue to dominate debate over nuclear strategy and the pattern of future investment in strategic systems at a time when decisions of great consequence for modernization are being made.

We would seem lucky if sound nuclear policies emerged from a debate framed so narrowly and so bereft of insight into the command implications of nuclear weapons. That much is at least acknowledged. The relevance of command performance to the larger strategic debate and the need for a sensible program of modernization have not been lost on the debaters.

But adequate comprehension of the topography of the command problem is lacking. The Reagan administration has advanced a cogent argument for command modernization, one with strong intuitive appeal, but has not firmly grasped the complexity of the challenge it has set for itself.

Although the administration's assignment of equal priority to command and force modernization is a sign of heightened awareness and better understanding of the significance of command performance, it is also a symptom of imprecise calculations of the relative merits of investments in C^3I and in weapons modernization. Administration rhetoric gives the impression that its overall strategic arms package contains just the right mix of force and command ingredients, but there are no magic formulas.

There ought not be any illusions that either clarity or consensus on the question of C^3I performance has been achieved. Research did not begin in earnest until the late 1970s, and it would be unrealistic to impose extravagant expectations on such efforts any time soon. A good sense of direction, of appropriate and feasible objectives, of the proper balance between command and force development, are only beginning to crystallize. Meanwhile, command policies will be conceived under conditions of great uncertainty.

I hope this book will help expose the dangerously tenuous grasp of strategic reality that results from overreliance on theories and analyses that skirt the role of C^3I in nuclear confrontation. The means to this end, and the book's primary aim, is to provide an assessment of strategic command performance in the last twenty-five years. It describes in considerable depth the physical and organizational arrangements that exist to provide coherent direction to U.S. strategic forces. It traces the evolution of these arrangements, analyzes their strengths and weaknesses, and discusses their relationship to and effects on crisis stability, the overall strategic balance, the prevention of unauthorized, accidental employment of nuclear weapons, and U.S. policy on nuclear procurement and operations.

The implications of the deficiencies that have plagued the U.S. command system for twenty-five years cannot be fully understood without an appreciation of how mainstream theory views the strategic situation. Chapter 2 therefore presents a conventional view of the strategic situation, including the theory of deterrence, the evolution of national requirements, statistical models of combat between U.S. and Soviet forces, and policy prescriptions resulting from standard analyses.

Subsequent chapters are devoted to analysis of the command system and to a critical evaluation of mainstream treatment of the strategic problem. Chapter 3 presents an alternative perspective on the nature of strategic programs and operations. The limitations of the traditional model are gauged in chapters 4 through 7. Chapter 8 evaluates the president's modernization program. Chapter 9 makes policy recommendations, offering near-term and far-term goals for C³I development and discussing corresponding realignments in strategic operations and force procurement as well as the overarching requirement for redefining the nuclear threat.

The book omits or slights some important topics. It focuses on U.S. command systems that support single integrated operational plan (SIOP) forces and decisionmaking. Topics that deserve fuller treatment but that could not be accommodated here include Soviet and NATO C³I; war termination; nuclear "no first use"; bomber and cruise missile warning and defenses; and C³I for non-SIOP employment of U.S. strategic forces, for navigational and meteorological support of U.S. strategic forces, for ballistic missile defense, and for offensive and defensive antisatellite engagement.[8]

8. For a useful discussion of Soviet C³I, see Desmond Ball, "Can Nuclear War Be Controlled?" *Adelphi Papers,* 169 (London: International Institute for Strategic Studies, 1981); for NATO command systems, see Paul J. Bracken, *The Command and Control of Nuclear Forces* (Yale University Press, 1983). For no first use, see John D. Steinbruner and Leon V. Sigal, eds., *Alliance Security: NATO and the No-First-Use Question* (Brookings, 1983).

CHAPTER TWO

Mainstream Strategic Theory and Policy

THE DISTINGUISHING feature of mainstream strategic theory is its emphasis on rational choice by adversarial leaderships. The epicenter of decisionmaking is assumed to be the heads of state of the two superpowers, and the focus of theory and analysis is the range of options available to these adversaries under conditions defined by the capabilities and targeting plans of the respective forces.

According to the theory, modern strategic forces have limited rational choices to such an extent that their use for strictly military purposes would be irrational. As the two superpowers amassed weapons able to survive a first strike, prospects of overcoming enemy military strength by brute force diminished while the punishment for trying grew increasingly severe. When both sides stood to suffer massive damage and casualties, resorting to military force to defeat an adversary was no longer a rational alternative.

A first strike against an adversary's economy and population became no less irrational. The deployment of invulnerable forces able to decimate an aggressor's industry and cities in a second strike in fact hung like Damocles' sword over the superpowers. Nuclear attack on any scale against any target risked severe punitive retaliation. Increasingly, nuclear weapons appeared to serve only one purpose: to deter attack. Mutual deterrence based on mutual vulnerability became enshrined in strategic theory and has arguably rendered the threat of nuclear destruction comprehensible, manageable, and remote.

Conservative assumptions, however, did generate fears of asymmetrical situations in which the threat of full-scale retaliation might not deter limited attacks. Strategic theory acknowledged possibilities of limited war in which strategic weapons are brandished if not actually used to achieve exploitable bargaining dominance. Standard calculations that pit nuclear forces against each other in statistical models of combat to produce measures of counterforce effectiveness and postexchange residual capabilities are commonly used to gauge enemy potential to achieve such dominance. According to these calculations, the U.S. Minuteman force is highly vulnerable to Soviet attack, and U.S. forces as a whole compare unfavorably with Soviet forces in their ability to attack military targets. This alleged imbalance supposedly confers an exploitable advantage on the Soviet Union. To close this "window of vulnerability," the U.S. government has embarked on a course of strategic modernization that emphasizes weapons for prompt attack on military targets and command networks to control those weapons during a protracted conflict. Arms control remedies have been deemphasized by the Reagan administration.

Mutual Deterrence

The equivalent of 8 billion tons of TNT resides in the strategic arsenals of the two superpowers. U.S. strategic forces—missile submarines, manned bombers, and land-based intercontinental ballistic missiles (ICBMs)—carry about 3.5 billion tons. Soviet forces carry the rest.

The exact amount of potential destructive power that 8 billion tons of TNT represents is practically unknowable, but is roughly 640,000 times the explosive power of the atomic bomb dropped on Hiroshima, which killed 68,000 people and injured 76,000. The casualties from an all-out war now would undoubtedly dwarf the Hiroshima experience. It has been estimated and it is generally believed that only 0.4 billion tons—400 megatons in the parlance of nuclear strategists—exploded on urban and industrial targets in the Soviet Union would destroy two-thirds of that nation's urban population and three-fourths of its industrial capacity.[1] If used against the United States, 400 megatons would probably wreak even greater death and destruction.

Scholars in the United States between the end of World War II and the early 1960s created a body of theory about nuclear deterrence with which

1. Alain C. Enthoven and K. Wayne Smith, *How Much Is Enough? Shaping the Defense Program, 1961–1969* (Harper and Row, 1971), p. 207.

to comprehend and manage the dangers implied by these arsenals. Although it has not been subjected to normal scientific testing, the theory is coherent, well-developed, and built on a conceptual foundation that is accepted in Western culture. A solid consensus has been forged under the logic of deterrence, the basic perspective of which is based on the logic-of-choice tradition in economics and the decision sciences. As John D. Steinbruner notes, this tradition of rational analysis has provided the "clearest, most coherent, most developed conception of the decision process which is available at the moment."[2] It is not surprising that propositions about the prevention of nuclear war were cast from this mold.

Both rational analysis and deterrence theory see decisions as investment choices. Decisionmakers act to maximize gains or minimize losses under the limitations and threats faced. Whether advanced as a normative argument or a positive assumption about the nature of human decision-making, rationality connotes a procedure in which alternative courses of action are laid out, relevant costs and benefits of each option are calculated, and the alternative with the highest expected payoff or lowest cost is chosen. In the nuclear context the problem is usually structured in such a way that a rational decisionmaker will always choose not to attack the opponent. The choice is between two alternatives: attack or do not attack. Because it is usually assumed that neither side can disarm the opponent, choosing to attack risks nuclear retaliation; attack would thus be irrational and both sides are deterred. Nuclear stalemate exists despite the possibility that an aggressor might expect to destroy a large part of the opponent's forces and substantially weaken his resolve. Unless the probability of retaliation is vanishingly small, the expected costs of a first strike will always outweigh the benefits.

In its simplest version, deterrence theory thus eases the psychological burden of nuclear weapons by turning an apparent liability into a virtue—nations sharing a common fate, each averse to unleashing nuclear attacks because such attacks would result in mutual annihilation. All other determining factors in international conflict, whether deleterious or salutary, pale in significance. During periods of high tension when escalating confrontation threatens to elude resolution, this condition acts as a powerful restraint and stabilizing force. To its proponents, the underlying logic of deterrence theory is compelling, and the post–World War II ab-

---

2. "Beyond Rational Deterrence: The Struggle for New Conceptions," *World Politics*, vol. 28 (January 1976), p. 225.

sence of nuclear war lends credibility to its core argument. Mutual deterrence loomed large during the Cuban missile crisis of 1962, and Michael Mandelbaum likens that episode as well as the history of the nuclear age to two fencers on a tightrope, balancing precariously, "each fearing to thrust decisively because such a thrust would topple them both, attacker and victim, to mutual disaster."[3]

Though paradoxical, mutual vulnerability allays fear and even engenders a sense of invulnerability, provided of course that one's faith in rational assumptions is steadfast and that the condition of vulnerability applies to the population and economic infrastructure of nations and not to their respective nuclear forces.

Mutual deterrence dissolves when one or both sides can remove the opponent's ability to inflict severe damage in retaliation. In a crisis the side believing that an unacceptably large part of its retaliatory capacity could be suddenly nullified by the opponent's forces might be impelled to strike preemptively. The superior side also might be motivated to undertake the first aggressive actions. Regardless of its original intentions, the stronger side could plausibly imagine a siege mentality, a use-them-or-lose-them attitude, operating on the weaker side, and reason, rightly or wrongly, that it had better seize the initiative. A condition of vulnerability on both sides would further strengthen incentives for preemptive attack and pose an unacceptable risk of nuclear war. From the perspective of deterrence theory this is the worst of all hypothetical worlds.

This view is distinct from that of strategists governed by orthodox tenets, who would seek the capacity to neutralize enemy military capabilities, an achievement that would be termed unstable and undesirable by proponents of deterrence. Unlike traditional military strategy, deterrence strategy does not value military forces for their potential to defeat an adversary. In fact, the idea of military conquest is alien to deterrence. Instead, deterrence theorists value the capacity for violence, particularly nuclear violence, for its implied bargaining power. The ability to hurt the enemy forms the basis of a nuclear diplomacy oriented to influencing behavior rather than overcoming strength. Cast in this role, strategic forces are instruments of threat, coercion, and intimidation rather than of military victory.[4]

---

3. *The Nuclear Question: The United States and Nuclear Weapons, 1946–1976* (Cambridge University Press, 1979), p. 218.

4. The most thorough development of this basic theme is Thomas C. Schelling's *Arms and Influence* (Yale University Press, 1966).

Given the inherent destructiveness of nuclear weapons, the elevation of what Thomas Schelling calls the "diplomacy of violence" over orthodox military strategy was probably inevitable. Deterrence theory had its detractors, but a consensus quickly formed around it. There simply was no disputing one obvious fact: nuclear weapons could tear apart the social fabric and economic infrastructure of nations. They could inflict horrible pain on an unprecedented scale. Their potential as weapons of terror capable of structuring an opponent's motives and influencing his decisions could have scarcely been disputed. At the same time, their contribution to military victory was not evident. Meaningful victory would not be achieved if even a small number of opposing nuclear forces could survive a first strike and retaliate against cities. Victory required obliterating all of the enemy's nuclear capabilities. By the early 1960s, assurance of obliteration could no longer be provided, and under the technological conditions of the times, there were reasons to believe it would remain out of reach forever. In short, meaningful military victory in the modern nuclear era came to be regarded as unrealizable.

Although the logic of deterrence rejected the concept of military victory, it by no means implied that deliberate nuclear attack would never happen. But there emerged a strong belief that violence is most successful when held in reserve and made contingent upon the adversary's behavior. Nuclear diplomacy is the manipulation of latent violence—violence that can be withheld or inflicted in the future. It is also understood, however, that the power to hurt and the credibility of threats to do so may be communicated by some actual violence. This communication could involve attacks on opposing military forces, particularly if such attacks could be expected to improve the attacker's bargaining position. The nuclear scenarios commonly presented in recent years, for example, are readily folded into the logic of coercive diplomacy. The results of nuclear exchanges are projected in order to determine whether sharp shifts in relative bargaining power might result. Winning a war results from some limited strategic maneuver that allows one side or the other to achieve bargaining dominance. This is manifestly not the same thing as delivering a decisive blow against the opponent's forces.

Vestiges of orthodox military strategy still exist, however. Attacks geared to the objective of damage limitation, for example, continue to be programmed by U.S. nuclear planners who cannot know for sure whether nuclear diplomacy might break down.[5] Failure of deterrence could lead to sheer violence meant to demolish the enemy's capacity to fight a war and thereby limit the amount of damage that would be suffered from unilateral, "undiplomatic" use of brute force.

Nuclear attacks meant to influence decisions could be difficult to distinguish from nuclear attacks geared to damage limitation. Clearly, however, the aims are distinguishable. The former is intended to induce restraint and extort concessions, whereas the latter is meant to inflict the greatest possible damage on an enemy's military capacity in order to minimize one's own casualties. The corresponding attack strategies, too, would probably differ in some important respects. An attack strategy oriented to damage limitation might include destroying enemy command channels as well as individual force deployments, whereas a strategy linked to coercive diplomacy would surely not target enemy command channels, the very channels one wants to influence.

Policy Implications of Deterrence Theory

The basic policy prescription derived from the logic of deterrence is that adequate capabilities for retaliation must be provided in order to instill absolute certainty in the opponent's mind that nuclear attack would draw severe reprisal. By the same token the two superpowers have a stake in maintaining mutual deterrence; neither side should embark on a course that could severely undermine the other side's ability to retaliate. Military improvements on one side may increase confidence in its retaliatory posture but the opponent's posture might be eroded in the process, resulting in a net loss in overall stability. (In theory a successful grab for overwhelming strategic superiority would only create a hair-trigger problem that would reduce the security of both sides.) Or, if the opponent responds with improvements of his own, the result might be an open-

5. According to then Secretary of Defense Harold Brown, "U.S. strategic forces are not procured for a damage limiting mission. . . . However, should a nuclear war occur, our forces may be utilized to limit damage to the United States to the extent practicable in addition to being used to destroy resources which contribute to the postwar power, influence and recovery capability of the enemy." See *Fiscal Year 1978 Authorization for Military Procurement, Research and Development, and Active Duty, Selected Reserve and Civilian Personnel Strengths,* Hearings before the Senate Committee on Armed Services, 95 Cong. 1 sess. (GPO, 1977), pt. 1, p. 554.

ended arms race that raises the level of nuclear deployments but leaves neither side more secure.

The superpowers nonetheless routinely create new threats to each other's nuclear deterrent in apparent disregard for the effects on stability. Although stability requires deterrent capability on both sides, defense planners naturally concern themselves with their own side's deterrent strength. (A few like Albert Wohlstetter actually see more stability in unilateral advantage than in mutual deterrence and therefore advocate this stance.) Maintaining a strong credible threat of retaliation is a sine qua non of national security, one that takes clear precedence over the principle of mutual deterrence.

If the tenets of deterrence theory are not always adhered to, they are also not always good sources of practical guidance. Theory proves too abstract and general to offer concrete, specific advice on the kind and amount of destruction the United States must be able to inflict to deter an attacker or the particular military deployments that reflect these desiderata. These and other derivative policy choices—for instance, what arms control measures enhance strategic stability—require analysis that goes beyond the basic logic of deterrence. Given the paucity of valid, reliable data, however, analysis of these choices is intrinsically speculative and beyond empirical confirmation. And because there is a deeper conflict of values associated with most choices, a politico-bureaucratic bargaining process rather than rational analysis frequently determines the outcome.

At the same time, an analytical approach has proved to be a prime vehicle of consensus. Participants in the problem-solving process work with a common data base, common methods, and common problem parameters. They also share a common idiom in which to conduct debate and reconcile differences in the interpretation of results. Thus the groundwork for consensus exists, and indeed consensus is often achieved even when it comes to specifying conditions required to establish deterrence and specifying programs to meet those conditions. Again, analytic judgments frequently diverge, and, once delivered to the political arena, they may become sharply polarized and fester there indefinitely. Dissection of the issues is, however, ordinarily performed with sufficiently similar tools and surgical procedures that analytic judgments are naturally inclined to converge. Even when conflicting values and interests shape the debate, the parties involved often disguise their arguments as objective analysis, and at the very least this packaging promotes discourse and compromise.

The bases of consensus on nuclear policy are described in the next sections. The topics and the sequence of their discussion correspond to a series of steps readily associated with traditional rational analysis: establish the kind and amount of destruction needed to deter attack, estimate the damage expected from the opponent's maximum attack, determine whether residual U.S. destructive power satisfies the requirements established in the first step, and compare the merits of alternative remedies if current or projected capabilities fail to satisfy requirements.

Requirements: How Much Is Enough?

The one sacred cow in requirements for retaliation is known as "assured destruction." Strategists concluded long ago that the United States must be able to visit on an attacker a level of civil destruction that approaches the maximum amount that could be achieved under any circumstance. In specific terms this principle came to be defined during Defense Secretary Robert McNamara's term as the ability to destroy in retaliation to attack some 20 to 25 percent of the Soviet population and 50 percent of Soviet industrial capacity.[6]

Strategists reasoned that so stark a threat would dominate the calculations of any adversary, including one with barely any hold on rationality. Surely the capacity for reprisal on this scale "swamps all misperceptions arising, for example, from cultural differences, individual idiosyncrasies, and the complexities of internal politics."[7] Such, at any rate, was the rationale.

Widespread acceptance of this requirement has helped frame all subsequent discussion of nuclear policy and force procurement. But assured destruction has not solely or even primarily determined actual strategic deployments and targeting assignments. Force planners and political decisionmakers have established additional purposes and roles for the strategic forces that in turn demand a more differentiated targeting policy and a level of strategic deployment that exceeds the level required to achieve assured destruction alone.

One such role grew out of a political commitment to NATO, coupled with an apparent imbalance of conventional forces in the European theater. To fulfill its pledge to defend Western Europe against an invasion by

6. Enthoven and Smith, *How Much Is Enough?* p. 207.
7. Steinbruner, "Beyond Rational Deterrence," p. 227.

superior conventional forces of the Warsaw Pact, the United States extended an American nuclear umbrella over NATO in lieu of a full conventional counterweight. This umbrella is an integral part of the overall allied defensive strategy known as "flexible response." The strategy took shape in 1967 with the issuance of formal guidance MC-14/3 that envisioned a flexible posture based on the forces, the plans, and the control arrangements to execute, as necessary, a sequence of two distinct types of nuclear operations if direct defense of NATO territory with conventional forces fails to repel enemy invaders: escalation to the local use of nuclear weapons and, if required, resorting to general nuclear war.[8] Flexible response led to assigning some intercontinental U.S. nuclear forces to NATO's nuclear strike plan to supplement theater nuclear weapons under the command of allied commanders in Europe. These particular forces need not be, and under the envisioned circumstances are not expected to be, used in conjunction with attacks by U.S. forces under the single integrated operational plan. Attack strategy allows them to be decoupled from the SIOP and thus implicitly establishes a firebreak between theater and global nuclear conflict.

A sizable portion of the SIOP also is devoted to the defense of NATO. In the event of escalation to general nuclear war, these dedicated forces would cover the nuclear threat to Europe based in the Soviet Union, a threat that today consists primarily of SS-20 ballistic missiles and Backfire, Blinder, and Badger medium-range bombers.[9]

Besides being the linchpin for most thinking and analyses related to NATO and the defense of Western Europe, flexible response has been seized upon as an answer to a paradox that has long plagued the general nuclear war strategy of assured destruction.[10] The paradox is that if strategic deterrence based on the threat of unrestrained retaliation fails, then it would not be rational actually to carry out the threat. In the wake of Soviet attack, even large-scale attack, there would be a continuing necessity to influence the opponent's decision process to deter attacks by his residual forces or otherwise coerce restraint while attempts are made to negotiate a truce. In view of this necessity, leaders would have nothing substantial to gain and much bargaining leverage to lose by comprehen-

---

8. William W. Kaufmann, "Nuclear Deterrence in Central Europe," in John D. Steinbruner and Leon V. Sigal, eds., *Alliance Security: NATO and the No-First-Use Question* (Brookings, 1983), p. 22.

9. Kaufmann, "Nuclear Deterrence in Central Europe," p. 29.

10. Steinbruner, "Beyond Rational Deterrence," pp. 231–34.

sive retaliation. Moreover, the mass destruction of Soviet urban and industrial targets would be so disproportionate a response to limited nuclear attack as not to be credible. The threat of comprehensive retaliation thus might not deter low-level threats or attacks confined, for instance, to military facilities located in sparsely populated regions of the country.

The idea behind flexible response in the context of global nuclear war, then, is to prevent a situation in which the failure of strategic deterrence would be sudden, categorical, complete, and catastrophic and to replace it with a situation in which overall deterrence is strengthened by allowing for failure in stages. Since the enunciation of a flexible "no cities" doctrine in the early 1960s, the training, disposition, and operational plans of U.S. strategic forces have reflected this idea. National policy requires that nuclear strategy allow for selective attacks on the Warsaw Pact and Soviet target base, whether those attacks would be undertaken in defense of Western Europe or in response to Soviet attack on the United States. National authorities want options to attack target subsets of their choice, and in electing to respond in a limited fashion they would not wish to relinquish options to employ withheld forces later. Above all, the national leadership does not want to be confronted with a choice between all-out attack and surrender. Even after a large-scale attack on American urban and industrial targets, all-out retaliation may not be judged appropriate. Many argue that some strategic reserve forces should be withheld for an indefinite period on the theory that a reserve force could provide bargaining leverage even in the aftermath of a strategic exchange that destroys much of the populace and economic resources on both sides. Flexible response is thus seen as an important means of extending deterrence into war itself and of providing distinguishable firebreaks between levels of intercontinental nuclear warfare.

Although requirements associated with purposes other than assured destruction have long existed, their formal roots in U.S. strategic policy have remained shallow by comparison. As far as procurement policy (guidelines for acquiring weapons) is concerned, assured destruction has been the principal benchmark of sufficiency. If a strategic weapons program involved substantial investment and if it was directed to purposes other than assured destruction, it was prudent to promote it in terms of its contribution to basic deterrence. Without such justification, systems were more likely to stir controversy and opposition.

The need to show consonance with assured destruction may seem peculiar in light of long-standing political commitments to the nuclear defense of Western Europe, broad intellectual and political acceptance of the idea of flexible response, and the existence of war plans that put into operation principles of nuclear diplomacy and deterrence extended in time. It is not, however, as peculiar as it seems. In the first place, procurement decisions made during the late 1950s and early 1960s (before assured destruction became the predominant guideline for weapons acquisition) resulted in nuclear deployments that greatly exceeded the level needed to achieve the condition of assured destruction. This surplus could be devoted to other purposes such as covering military targets. Second, calculation of the forces required for assured destruction was based on such conservative assumptions that it automatically allowed for a large enough force to satisfy requirements for a wide range of missions. Finally, there was never a close relationship between procurement and employment policy (guidance for weapons assignment, targeting, option packages, and so forth). They were managed independently. Civilian officials in the executive branch and Congress, together with various American institutions such as the media, tended to bury themselves in the budgetary aspects of nuclear policy, limiting their involvement in formulating employment policy. And war planners were hardly bound by the criteria applied in weapons acquisition; they devised attack strategy and allocated existing and programmed surplus inventories with a broad range of purposes in mind.

After the early 1970s, forces to bring procurement and employment policies into closer alignment and to do so under broad guidance emphasizing purposes besides assured destruction gained strength. The Soviets' nuclear buildup and their extensive hardening of military facilities and forces generated this momentum. Changes in targeting partially addressed the emergent threat, but many saw the need for a new procurement policy that provided for proportionate U.S. retaliatory responses to certain kinds of options becoming available to Soviet leaders. Assured destruction was criticized on the grounds that it no longer automatically produced the surplus forces needed, for instance, to respond in kind to a Soviet attack aimed at U.S. strategic forces, including fixed-based missile silos. Although it still provided forces far in excess of realistic requirements for assured destruction, the technical composition of these forces made them mainly suitable for attacks on relatively soft targets. They were becoming less and less suited to such tasks as retaliating against time-urgent hard targets in the USSR.

The groundwork for a merger of procurement and employment policy based on a broader deterrent posture than assured destruction was laid in the early 1970s, and Secretary of Defense James Schlesinger deserves much of the credit. He stated that U.S. attack strategy was too rigid and too heavily oriented toward assured destruction.[11] But his advocacy, which seemed to be concerned with a particular issue of force utilization (the type of issue normally and routinely addressed by employment policy), transcended the particulars of flexibility and even the general issue of employment policy. A message of much broader and deeper import was conveyed: in modern nuclear circumstances there are purposes other than assured destruction at stake, and these purposes ought to be served by procurement as well as employment policy.

It is dangerous to ascribe motives and infer beliefs when they are not publicly expressed, but it does not seem likely that the nuclear war plans then in existence were, in and of themselves, the cause of Schlesinger's concern. He may actually have wanted to establish the legitimacy of principles besides assured destruction in order to pave the way for eventual approval within procurement channels of programs embodying such principles. He did not seek support for new weapons systems, but that logical consequence eventually did plant itself in discussions of acquisitions. The resulting ascendancy of rationales such as deterrence during war has had a profound effect on procurement policy. Today, force and command structure programs designed to serve such purposes as counterforce and protracted war-fighting are openly discussed in those terms. Programs need no longer be wrapped in pretenses of assured destruction to facilitate budgetary approval.

Formal guidance issued during Schlesinger's tenure was consistent with the departure from assured destruction. National security decision memorandum 242, signed by President Nixon in January 1974, and associated documents—*Nuclear Weapons Employment Policy* and *Policy Guidance for the Employment of Nuclear Weapons*—specify objectives for damage to the Soviet Union in terms of the percentage of economic, political, and selected military targets destroyed. The military targets reportedly include hardened missile silos and command and control facilities.[12]

11. *U.S.-USSR Strategic Policies,* Hearings before the Subcommittee on Arms Control, International Law and Organization of the Senate Committee on Foreign Relations (GPO, 1974).

12. See Desmond Ball, "Counterforce Targeting: How New? How Viable?" *Arms Control Today,* vol. 11 (February 1981), pp. 1–9; and *Fiscal Year 1978 Authorization for Military Procurement, Research and Development,* Senate hearings, pt. 1, p. 556.

Population is not targeted per se, but when escalation cannot be controlled, the guidance established a requirement for destroying 70 percent of the Soviet industrial base, which translates into attacks on perhaps 200 Soviet cities where one-third of the total Soviet population lives.[13] A strategic reserve force was also established.

The promulgation of countervailing strategy and memorandums issued by the Carter administration continued Schlesinger's policies; President Reagan's policy has advanced them further. U.S. strategy has become heavily oriented to fighting a nuclear war in a budgetary as well as an operational sense. The countervailing strategy and memorandums PD-53, PD-58, and PD-59, legacies of the Carter administration that have remained in effect, were concerned with controlled attacks on a target list that includes enemy missiles in hardened silos. A fiscal commitment to these goals was implicit, and there is reason to expect a continuation of this commitment during Reagan's second term.

Although the requirements established under the Carter and Reagan administrations have not been publicly spelled out in detail, they are generally thought to be similar to the requirements and plans outlined in national security decision memorandum 242. Basically, the United States must be able to absorb the enemy's maximum attack and still be able to destroy a specified percentage of Soviet economic, political, and military resources. Former Secretary of Defense Harold Brown determined that U.S. forces must continue to be able to destroy a minimum of 200 major Soviet cities.[14] The principle of assured destruction was thus retained, though again Soviet population per se is not targeted.[15] Beyond this, Brown proposed to cover Soviet missile silos, command bunkers, and nuclear weapons storage sites with at least one reliable warhead per target whose probability of destroying the target is substantial and to target Soviet general purpose forces, communication, command, and control facilities, and war reserve stocks necessary to the conduct of theater campaigns.[16] Furthermore, national leaders must be able to maintain control over this retaliatory capability for weeks or months if necessary. PD-53 (November 1979) required the national communications system to be

13. *Department of Defense Appropriations for 1978,* Hearings before a Subcommittee of the House Committee on Appropriations, 95 Cong. 1 sess. (GPO, 1977), pt. 2, p. 212.

14. *Department of Defense Annual Report Fiscal Year 1979,* p. 55; *Department of Defense Annual Report Fiscal Year 1980,* p. 77; and *Department of Defense Annual Report Fiscal Year 1981,* pp. 65, 79.

15. *Department of Defense Annual Report Fiscal Year 1982,* p. 42.

16. *Department of Defense Annual Report Fiscal Year 1980,* pp. 77–78.

able to ride out a Soviet attack and provide for central and flexible orchestration of U.S. attacks by forces that might be held in reserve for an extended time following the initial exchange.[17] PD-58 (June 1980) required improvements in the continuity of government with emphasis on protecting selected components during all phases of enemy nuclear attack. Protective measures include evacuation of key leadership and deployment of enduring command posts for key officials and communications systems.

The Reagan administration framed the discussion of nuclear requirements in terms that further deemphasized assured destruction. NSDD-13 (November 1981) endorsed NSDM-242 and PD-59 and placed more emphasis on providing nuclear options during protracted war. The first complete guidance prepared by the Reagan Pentagon went even further. *Fiscal Year 1984–1988 Defense Guidance* (March 1982), a classified document leaked to the press in 1982, outlined a comprehensive strategy for fighting a nuclear war. According to press accounts, the guidance said that if the Soviet Union mounts a nuclear attack against the United States, its forces, or allies, then U.S. nuclear capabilities "must prevail even under the condition of a prolonged war."[18] Should strategic nuclear war with the Soviet Union occur, the United States must "be able to force the Soviet Union to seek earliest termination of hostilities on terms favorable to the United States."[19] The document spells out the following specific requirements:

— "Forces capable, under all conditions of war initiation, of attacking a wide range of targets, even when retaliating to a massive strike received without strategic warning. . . ."

— "Employment plans that assure U.S. strategic nuclear forces can render ineffective the total Soviet, and Soviet allied, military and political power structure through attacks on political/military leadership and associated control facilities, nuclear and conventional forces and industry critical to military power. . . ."

17. "In support of national security policy, the nation's telecommunications must provide for: (1) connectivity between the National Command Authority and strategic and other appropriate forces to support flexible execution of retaliatory strikes during and after an enemy nuclear attack; and (2) responsive support for operational control of the armed forces, even during a protracted nuclear conflict." *Presidential Directive/NSC-53* (The White House, November 15, 1979), p. 1.

18. Richard Halloran, "Weinberger Denies Plans for 'Protracted' War," *New York Times,* June 21, 1982.

19. George C. Wilson, "Preparing for Long Nuclear War is Waste of Funds, Gen. Jones Says," *Washington Post,* June 19, 1982.

— "Forces that will maintain, throughout a protracted conflict period and afterward, the capability to inflict very high levels of damage against the industrial/economic base of the Soviet Union and her allies so that they have a strong incentive to seek conflict termination short of an all-out attack on our cities and economic assets." This offensive capability must ensure that the "United States would never emerge from a nuclear war without nuclear weapons while still threatened by enemy nuclear weapons."[20]

— Strategic forces and C³ systems capable of supporting "controlled nuclear counterattacks over a protracted period while maintaining a reserve of nuclear forces sufficient for trans- and post-attack protection and coercion. . . . " Communications systems "must provide the capability to execute ad hoc plans, even subsequent to repeated attacks . . . [and] these systems should support the reconstitution and execution of strategic reserve forces, specifically full communications with our strategic submarines."[21]

Although many such requirements existed in one form or another in the past and to some extent were met, they were not accorded the legitimacy that assured destruction enjoyed, and they were satisfied only indirectly. Now that the pendulum of official and informed public opinion has swung toward concern for fighting a nuclear war, it will likely become much easier to advance programs meant to serve these purposes in the event that serious deficiencies develop.

The growing interest in strategic counterforce does not initially seem to mean that a policy of military victory is resurgent. Advocates of U.S. war-fighting policies instead usually couch their arguments in terms of the weakening of deterrence that could result if Soviet capabilities are allowed to expand to the point that the Soviet bargaining position might be strengthened by undertaking some limited strategic maneuver. To deny the adversary the additional leverage that might otherwise accrue as a consequence of, say, attack against the U.S. Minuteman force, strategists are proposing countervailing measures. Principles of deterrence appear to lend strong support to the general aim if not the specific remedies proposed. The idea of military conquest is not supposed to be driving any of the planned investments.

20. Richard Halloran, "Weinberger Confirms New Strategy on Atom War," *New York Times,* June 4, 1982.
21. Richard Halloran, "Pentagon Draws Up First Strategy for Fighting a Long Nuclear War," *New York Times,* May 30, 1982.

Yet one cannot fail to notice connections between U.S. strategy and winning a war in the traditional sense of the term. While U.S. strategy is being coupled with the idea of nuclear diplomacy during a war, it is also being tied to the objective of damage limitation, which connotes purely military engagement and carries some suggestion of nuclear conquest. Damage limitation has assumed a degree of rhetorical emphasis not seen since the early 1960s. Among those who have helped restore its legitimacy is General Bennie L. Davis, commander in chief of SAC:

> In a comprehensive strategy of deterrence, our strategic forces are the controlling rods of escalation—if escalation can be controlled. If it can't be controlled, and ultimate degrees of nuclear weaponry are employed, the size and strength of our weapons and the comprehensive planning of target selection and weapon laydown will determine the extent to which it is possible for our society to emerge from such conflict with advantage and [be] able to control its destiny.[22]

A strategy for fighting nuclear war can be simultaneously geared for damage limitation, nuclear conquest, and nuclear diplomacy. And in view of the deep skepticism that exists toward the chances of nuclear diplomacy during a war, one might doubt the claim that nuclear diplomacy is the sole reason for shifting to a war-fighting posture. The familiar claims for the utility of war-fighting strategy in exerting influence on enemy decisionmaking and in terminating hostilities at an early stage ring hollow when informed opinion considers escalation to full-scale general war almost inevitable once the nuclear threshold is crossed. The specter of a total collapse of diplomacy shortly after the first intercontinental nuclear salvo begins is barely concealed in the speculations of observers of every political and ideological stripe.

This fatalism is sufficiently deep and wide that strategy for fighting a war is probably valued more for its contribution to damage limitation than to nuclear diplomacy. The possibility that damage limitation is gaining ascendancy and is rekindling interest in the notion of military victory seems strong.

Estimation of Damage

The procedure generally followed in assessing the adequacy of U.S. nuclear deployments is to calculate the amount of destruction that can be

---

22. Speech delivered to the Air Force Association, April 1982. Quoted in "Gen. Davis: Deterrence is More than Just Hardware," *Aerospace Daily,* April 13, 1982, p. 255.

visited on the attacker with a retaliatory strike and to compare this figure with the amount deemed necessary to achieve systematic coverage of the Warsaw Pact and Soviet military-urban-industrial base. The amount of destruction that can be unleashed depends on the effectiveness of the enemy's first strike and the effectiveness of defensive operations, which in turn depend in varying degrees on each side's weapons, organization, plans, geography, communications, intelligence and warning systems, and doctrines and beliefs about the conduct of war.

Sophisticated analyses can be performed on many of these factors. To reduce the problem to manageable proportions, though, analysts focus attention on the size and technical composition of targets and attacking weapons. Estimation has become almost synonymous with computer-assisted simulation of interaction between these elements.

Before describing what could be called the statistical-combat approach to estimation and discussing its limitations, the variables considered, and the major conclusions reached, it should be noted that estimation is a highly subjective exercise that is less a technical assessment than an attitude. The level of uncertainty U.S. planners and political decisionmakers are willing to live with in the interest of nuclear deterrence is the key factor in estimation. As a rule, little uncertainty is tolerated. The principle of assured destruction itself is a manifestation of risk aversion, as is the insistence that it be estimated very cautiously, "crediting only that damage which established knowledge renders both certain and calculable."[23] Only the immediate and direct damage from nuclear attacks on urban-industrial targets is counted; famine, disease, long-term environmental damage, "nuclear winter," and so forth are excluded.

Similarly, conservative assumptions underlie calculations of the vulnerability of U.S. nuclear deployments. For instance, the official yardstick of strategic sufficiency in the 1960s measured the capability of nuclear forces to inflict assured destruction after a Soviet attack that was *greater than expected.*[24] In a more recent example, calculations based on conservative assumptions predict that only a small fraction of the Minuteman force would survive the heaviest possible attack the Soviet Union could deliver in the early-to-mid 1980s. However, plausible changes in the underlying assumptions—for instance, assumptions about the operational reliability and accuracy of Soviet ICBMs—generate results that would

23. Steinbruner, "Beyond Rational Deterrence," p. 227.
24. Enthoven and Smith, *How Much Is Enough?* pp. 178–79, 208.

presumably dishearten a cautious Soviet planner. For instance, in the hypothetical case of a future Soviet threat consisting of highly accurate, highly reliable, medium-yield multiple independently targeted reentry vehicles (MIRVs), "even rather modest shifts in the pertinent assumptions are sufficient to change the apparent advantage from the attacker to the defender if a full first strike on land-based missiles is attempted."[25] In the same vein, former Defense Secretary Harold Brown cited the possibilities of fratricide, missile unreliability, loss of accuracy in operation, and the launch of American missiles before Soviet warheads arrived as reasons why the Soviets cannot be sure that they could destroy 80 to 90 percent of the Minuteman force in the mid-1980s.[26] In sum, application of the conservative planning principle by both sides produces almost diametrically opposite conclusions. On the one hand, in Brown's words, "we will not have much confidence that more than a small percentage of our silo-based missiles can survive a Soviet preemptive attack." On the other hand, again according to Brown, "the Soviets could not be at all confident of destroying the bulk of our missiles."[27]

Disparate U.S. and Soviet perceptions of the degree of strategic vulnerability on both sides could probably be found in virtually all areas in which comparisons are made, and the conservative planning principle is largely responsible. While estimates of the static strategic balance and the effects of marginal changes are usually discussed in terms of underlying numerical and technological realities, the calculations are substantially driven by an entirely subjective matter having to do with attitudes toward risk. Conservatism underlies the calculations and conclusions of standard assessment.

Statistical Combat

Calculators of U.S. retaliatory strength assume that the attacker is committed to the destruction of individual elements of U.S. forces. Soviet land-based and sea-based ballistic missiles are committed to attacks on bomber bases, submarine ports, and individual ICBM silos. Antisubmarine warfare forces strive to find and destroy missile submarines patrol-

---

25. John D. Steinbruner and Thomas M. Garwin, "Strategic Vulnerability: The Balance Between Prudence and Paranoia," *International Security,* vol. 1 (Summer 1976), p. 168.

26. *Department of Defense Authorization for Appropriations for Fiscal Year 1979,* Hearings before the Senate Committee on Armed Services, 95 Cong. 2 sess. (GPO, 1978), pt. 1, p. 539.

27. *Department of Defense Annual Report Fiscal Year 1979,* p. 106.

ling the oceans. And air defense systems attempt to bring down strategic bombers and cruise missiles headed toward targets inside Soviet and Eastern bloc territory.

Analysts estimate the effectiveness of the attacker's offensive and defensive operations for different political and military scenarios, including surprise attack, implausible as that may seem. In keeping with the principle of conservative planning, analysts assume that the element of surprise could be present because attack preparations go undetected or unheeded.[28] Indeed, this assumption is deeply ingrained in Pentagon assessment practices. As former Secretary Brown noted, American defense planners are "obliged to make the contingency of a Soviet surprise attack on our strategic forces the fundamental test of the adequacy of those forces and the main basis for our strategic nuclear planning."[29] U.S. strategic forces are thus assumed to be at or near peacetime levels of readiness, and the damage credited to sudden Soviet attack is higher than it would be otherwise.[30] This is the cost incurred when strategic warning fails.

The penalty for failing to provide tactical warning, warning of an actual rather than an impending nuclear attack, is also severe. If tactical warning is not provided, alert forces that depend on rapid dispersal for their survival would be subject to destruction, and the expected damage is once again higher than it would be otherwise.

Extremely conservative estimates of the vulnerability of forces assume warning failures of both types. In an earlier era this assumption would not have been so conservative. Until the mid-to-late 1960s, confidence in strategic and tactical warning systems was justifiably low, and operations that reduced reliance on advance warning to a minimum seemed called

28. See Richard K. Betts, *Surprise Attack: Lessons For Defense Planning* (Brookings, 1982). Betts's excellent and thorough examination of historical cases explains why this assumption should be made.

29. *Department of Defense Annual Report, Fiscal Year 1979*, p. 53.

30. Perhaps the least defensible assumption about the failure of strategic warning concerns standard calculations of bomber prelaunch vulnerability. In most analyses, bombers on ground alert come under heavy attack by as many as twenty Soviet missile submarines positioned in U.S. coastal waters, a massive departure from peacetime patrol practices that goes undetected. U.S. intelligence could hardly fail to detect deployments of this magnitude, and decisionmakers could hardly fail to respond with measures—increasing alert bomber readiness, bringing off-alert bombers to alert, dispersing aircraft to inland bases, and so forth—to reduce the force's vulnerability. Yet, conservative planners base their calculations on the assumption that no such steps would be taken.

for. Accordingly, among other responses, some strategic bombers were flown on twenty-four-hour airborne alert between 1958 and 1968.[31] Indeed, the major force structure programs of the 1960s can be understood as attempts to hedge against the possibility of warning failures. Diversification of the force structure followed, with massive investments in weapons systems that did not require advance warning. Submarines at sea, for instance, could not be readily found and targeted. Land missiles were placed in underground silos that were difficult to destroy. Thus long-range bombers no longer monopolized deterrent forces, and the bulk of the alert forces could ride out a surprise attack.

Confidence in the performance of warning systems, however, has since grown, largely because of satellite reconnaissance. The standard assumption today is that while notification of impending attack would not necessarily be received or acted upon, units would at least receive timely tactical warning of an attack in progress. In most analyses, bombers on ground alert would receive warning early enough to escape incoming weapons, but off-alert forces could not be brought to alert status before Soviet forces are launched. Off-alert bombers and submarines in port would thus remain highly vulnerable to surprise attack.

Alert submarines continue to be considered virtually immune to destruction without regard to warning, but the consensus on the vulnerability of land missiles is different from what it was fifteen years ago. Land missiles are considered endangered by new Soviet weaponry, and their survival would require that they be launched on tactical warning before being struck (see appendix A). Land missiles have thus become like bombers; tactical warning is essential to their survival. But unlike bombers, they cannot be recalled after launch, a fact that greatly diminishes their contribution to U.S. deterrence. Long-range bombers and missile submarines thus have become the mainstays of the U.S. forces. Fortunately, they are strong mainstays.

The open ocean is a sanctuary for alert missile submarines. Once at sea they cannot be readily detected, located, or attacked, given the current and foreseeable state of Soviet technology. Soviet antisubmarine warfare forces thus present little danger to U.S. submarines on patrol. Furthermore, by taking advantage of a forward base in Scotland the navy has managed to sustain a high alert rate. About half its missile submarines are

31. Declassified posture statement.

on patrol at any given time (about 80 percent of the Soviet missile submarines are in port under normal conditions).[32]

The retaliatory threat carried by these alert units is stark. In 1984 after
a surprise Soviet attack, they could have delivered about 300 missiles
capable of dispensing nearly 3,000 warheads with roughly 34,000 times
the explosive power of the bomb dropped on Hiroshima.[33] The level of
second-strike destructive power in 1984 was 30 percent higher than it was
in 1973; the expected number of survivable warheads rose by 31 percent
over the ten-year period (see appendix table A-4).

32. While there is a consensus that U.S. submarines on patrol are not in danger, some
analysts are concerned that communications antennas they trail could become susceptible to
detection by nonacoustic sensors such as spaceborne radar. The chances of detection would
still be remote, but analysts generally believe that even sporadic detections could furnish
Soviet antisubmarine forces with useful information about U.S. patrol patterns. Soviet capabilities are assessed by Bruce G. Blair, "Arms Control Implications of Anti-Submarine
Warfare (ASW) Programs," *Evaluation of Fiscal Year 1979 Arms Control Impact Statements:
Toward More Informed Congressional Participation in National Security Policymaking,* Report for the House Committee on International Relations (GPO, 1978), pp. 103–19.

Although U.S. antisubmarine warfare capabilities are more advanced than Soviet capabilities, assessments that seem valid today conclude that the ability of the United States to
mount a totally effective preemptive strike against Soviet SSBNs "is not practically achiev-
able." There is "no realistic prospect of being able to destroy in a sudden attack a major
part of the deployed Soviet force of missile-launching submarines, certainly not before they
could launch their missiles in retaliation." See *Fiscal Year 1978 Authorization for Military
Procurement, Research and Development,* Senate hearings, pt. 10, p. 6756. At the same time,
the United States does have "a good capability to destroy enemy submarines in a protracted
war at sea." See *Department of Defense Appropriations for Fiscal Year 1975,* Hearings before
the Senate Committee on Appropriations, 93 Cong. 2 sess. (GPO, 1974), pt. 1, p. 45.

There are clear indications that the Soviet Union worries about the survivability of its
submarines. The deployment of Delta-class SSBNs armed with long-range missiles (4,800
nautical miles) reflects this concern. Because Delta submarines can strike the United States
from home waters (for example, the Barents Sea), Soviet naval forces can better defend them
against Western antisubmarine forces. By the middle of 1978 the Soviet Union had several
hundred single-warhead missiles and sixty MIRVed missiles on Delta submarines and had
demonstrated some capability to protect those forces at sea. Soviet Yankee-class submarines
armed with relatively short-range missiles (1,500 nautical miles) still had to contend with an
impressive array of Western antisubmarine elements, however. Soviet submarines must follow a dangerous course to reach launch stations off U.S. coasts. For further discussion of
U.S. capabilities against Soviet SSBNs, see Blair, "Arms Control Implications of Anti-
Submarine Warfare (ASW) Programs."

33. The power of the relatively secure portion of the Soviet submarine deterrent was
smaller but still large by absolute standards. Assuming that 20 percent of the Soviet force
operated at sea at any time, approximately 46 submarines were vulnerable to surprise attacks aimed at coastal ports. Discounting Western antisubmarine capabilities entirely, the
remaining Soviet submarines could have delivered 365 warheads in retaliation, for a combined yield equivalent to 30,000 Hiroshima bombs.

Deterioration from age rather than any external threat is the primary source of concern about the future of the missile submarine fleet. All forty-one submarines in operation in 1978 were commissioned between 1960 and 1967. Ten were recently retired, and the remainder—thirty-one Lafayette-class boats (Poseidon)—will reach the end of their twenty-five-year operating cycle at a rate of ten a year beginning in 1988. All are expected to be retired by 1992.[34]

Analogous problems afflict the strategic bomber force, but they are not as serious. Although the force is mainly composed of B-52s delivered between 1956 and 1963, most problems associated with age can be corrected through modification and replacement of parts. Many aircraft have undergone structural surgery, and as long as such efforts continue, the present fleet should remain structurally sound through the remainder of this century.[35]

Unlike submarines, however, alert bombers face significant external threats. Although they are poised for quick getaway, detection and prompt notification of an attack are critically important. Aircraft must be aloft well before the arrival of incoming warheads launched from Soviet submarines positioned near the U.S. coasts. Even under the best of circumstances, a surprise attack by Soviet submarines would be expected, on the basis of conservative planning assumptions about missile flight times, to destroy perhaps 10 percent of the alert bomber force on the ground.[36] Some analyses calculate that at least 30 percent could be destroyed, but such estimates seem overly conservative.[37]

The Soviet Union does not appear to be pursuing a strategy based on large-scale submarine attacks on bomber bases. Notwithstanding recent increases in forward submarine deployments in retaliation for U.S. Per-

34. Lawrence J. Korb, "The FY 1981-1985 Defense Program: Issues and Trends," *AEI Foreign Policy and Defense Review,* vol. 2 (May 1981), pp. 40-41.

35. For a graphic projection of B-52 G/H, B-52 D, and FB-111A aircraft life expectancy, see *Hearings on Military Posture and H.R. 1872* before the House Committee on Armed Services, 96 Cong. 1 sess. (GPO, 1979), pt. 3, bk. 1, p. 629.

36. See appendix table A-4. Surprise attack by the United States would be expected to destroy virtually all Soviet long-range bombers because they are evidently maintained at a very low state of readiness. See Joseph J. Kruzel, "Military Alerts and Diplomatic Signals," in Ellen P. Stern, ed., *The Limits of Military Interventions* (Beverly Hills: Sage, 1977), p. 88. U.S. Poseidon submarines are apparently assigned Soviet bomber bases as targets. See *Department of Defense Appropriations for 1978,* House hearings, pt. 2, p. 186.

37. Although such calculations typically assume depressed trajectories and therefore shorter times of flight for the missiles, the Soviets have never tested any submarine-launched missile in a depressed trajectory.

shing II and cruise missile deployments in Europe, Soviet SSBN forces appear to be concentrated close to home ports, especially Murmansk, where they can be defended against Western antisubmarine forces. Missiles launched from the Barents Sea or other waters contiguous to the Soviet Union have enough range to reach the United States, but their flight times would be very long. The prevailing view is that alert U.S. bombers would be aloft long before these missiles (as well as Soviet ICBMs with approximately thirty-minute flight times) struck U.S. airfields.[38]

A more serious external threat to strategic bombers is the Soviet air defense system. In the 1970s these defenses could have destroyed perhaps 10 to 15 percent of the bombers that survived initial attacks on airfields (see appendix table A-4). Technical developments have since worked against present-generation penetrating bombers and are expected to continue to do so. Yet Soviet deployment of an effective operational defense against penetrating U.S. bombers is probably a long way off. Present terminal defenses, mainly surface-to-air missiles at fixed locations, can be easily avoided or suppressed by ICBMs, SLBMs, or short-range attack missiles carried by the penetrating bomber itself. And the Soviet Union lacks an effective interceptor system that enables fighter aircraft to detect and destroy low-flying bombers. As a result, U.S. bombers should have at least a 80 percent chance of successful penetration, and that is a conservative estimate. Furthermore, this penetration rate should decrease only marginally during the 1980s, though some concern exists that advanced Soviet fighters and surface-to-air missiles might pose a formidable threat by the end of the decade. It should also be noted that as Minuteman forces become more vulnerable, bombers will be less able to rely on them to suppress Soviet air defenses before bomber penetration.

Although the future of the present fleet of penetrating bombers—the oldest component of the force structure—is somewhat cloudy, its contribution to deterrence now and in the recent past is generally considered substantial. Even after allowing for surprise attack, significant pre- and postlaunch attrition, and an alert rate that is much lower than it could be (declining, as a result of policy decisions, from about 50 percent in the 1960s to 30 percent in the 1970s), the amount of destruction that bombers could visit on an attacker is still immense. Calculations for 1984 credit

---

38. Some potential Soviet submarine launch stations in polar regions, however, were not adequately covered by U.S. tactical warning systems during the 1970s.

bombers with a capacity to deliver 740 weapons with a combined yield of 264 megatons (see appendix table A-4).

Adding this capability to those of the ICBMs and missile submarines, U.S. retaliatory strength, estimated very conservatively, was about 1,000 megatons and 4,000 warheads in 1984. There was an overall decrease in second-strike warheads and a parallel decrease in cumulative explosive yield between 1973 and 1984 (see appendix table A-4). Deliverable megatons are spread fairly evenly among the three force components, and in absolute terms the figures are very large. If assured destruction requires 400 megatons, the strategic forces were more than adequate. Presumably, much of the remainder would have been available for use against military targets. And given the magnitude of this surplus—thousands of weapons and approximately 600 megatons—major operations could have been conducted against those targets. Thus it is reasonable to suppose that as of 1984 the U.S. nuclear deterrent was robust, stable, and broad, at least under the established technical definition of nuclear capability.

U.S. capabilities for prompt attack against hard targets in retaliation have decreased the most since 1973. Despite authoritative assurances that "even after riding out a Soviet first strike while on day-to-day alert the United States will be capable of attacking a comprehensive list of military and non-military targets,"[39] the ability of U.S. forces to cover such military targets as extremely hard silos and command bunkers in a second strike has declined considerably. Standard calculations indicate that a concerted effort is needed to restore confidence in the U.S. capacity for prompt, comprehensive retaliation.

A costly program of force modernization has been under way since the late 1970s. Both the Carter and Reagan administrations developed ambitious plans whose goals included assurance that the United States could absorb a Soviet counterforce first strike, retaliate against residual Soviet forces, and still possess reserve forces as powerful as those of the Soviet Union in terms of numbers and megatons.[40]

Standard Assessments of Nuclear Flexibility

The ability to achieve systematic coverage of a comprehensive enemy target base in retaliation for an attack is not the only subject of standard

39. *Department of Defense Annual Report Fiscal Year 1981,* p. 126.
40. See ibid., p. 125, for a graphic summary assessment of the impact of the Carter administration buildup on the strategic balance. The modernization program of the Reagan administration is discussed later in this chapter and in chapter 8.

analysis. Concern also extends to the ability of the United States to employ nuclear forces in a flexible manner. Assessments of this capability fall into three distinct categories: analyses that treat flexibility as a matter of force structure; attack plans, especially targeting policy; and studies of the performance of C³I networks.

FLEXIBILITY AND SURVIVABLE FORCES. The basic premise of analyses that define flexible response as a matter of force structure is that to have any meaningful political choice among options, forces associated with the options must be able to survive attack. If in a limited intercontinental war a selective Soviet attack avoids most large American cities but destroys large segments of the U.S. force, U.S. leaders are left with hollow options. If appropriate forces do not survive in sufficient numbers to execute a retaliatory attack against Soviet military targets, U.S. leaders would capitulate. Under the circumstances, rational leaders would rule out retaliation against Soviet cities and industry because that would only invite attacks on American cities and would also forfeit all bargaining leverage in the future. By denying U.S. leaders the option to launch an effective counterstrike against Soviet military targets while preserving the threat to Soviet cities, the Soviets would reduce the scope of U.S. flexibility to the point that surrender might be preferred.

This perspective on flexibility argues that the United States must ensure the survivability and versatility of its forces. Analyses thus focus narrowly on the size and technical composition of the respective forces to assess whether the Soviet Union could achieve exploitable dominance by means of selective counterforce attack. Models of statistical combat drive the assessments, but the interpretation of results emphasizes the latitude for politico-military choice that they imply. Statistical combat is thus embedded in a broader context of nuclear diplomacy, and the calculations are performed less for measuring military strength per se than for gauging the relative bargaining power of the two sides. For example, the calculations appearing in a 1981 Department of Defense annual report implied that forces programmed by the Carter administration for deployment during the 1980s would have provided the option to mount an effective counterattack against military targets and, in the wake of such an exchange, a residual force as powerful as the opponent's would have equalized bargaining power on both sides.[41] If these calculations are valid,

41. Ibid.

the United States would seem to need forces to expand the range of effective executive choice.

Under this approach actual war plans are not usually examined. Thus the model that produced the results cited above executes hypothetical attack options that do not correspond closely to actual target assignments. No allowance, for instance, is made for theater nuclear operations to which hundreds of U.S. intercontinental weapons have been provisionally committed. Similarly, the simulation almost certainly misrepresents the opponent's targeting policy. For instance, the model assigns all Soviet strategic forces to intercontinental operations, even though many observers believe a large fraction of them have always been committed to regional operations.[42]

The model also typically omits C^3I arrangements. Although an explicit assumption of the simulation is that an initial Soviet attack would include C^3I facilities among its targets, the results reflect none of the plausible adverse consequences of such an attack.[43] In the model, U.S. retaliation is carried out as if it were centrally authorized and fully coordinated. The model also simulates retaliation in kind, implying accurate characterization of the opponent's initial attack, and conveys the impression that any residual forces left on each side remain fully responsive for an indefinite period to direction by their respective national authorities. In other words, the analysis presupposes a sophisticated command system that performs ideally even though the model subjects C^3I to direct enemy attack.

Such a model is representative of a larger class of analyses that deemphasize the risk and consequences of deliberate attacks meant to paralyze an opponent's command structure. This deemphasis artificially preserves the traditional framework of nuclear diplomacy in which weapons represent a means of influencing an opponent's behavior rather than inca-

42. Soviet weapons usually included in strategic calculations but generally believed to have a regional or theater mission are the entire bomber force, SS-11 and SS-17 ICBMs in medium-range and intermediate-range ballistic missile fields, and most Yankee-class SSBNs. The wartime role of the SS-11 is considered in *Department of Defense Authorization for Appropriations for Fiscal Year 1979*, Senate hearings, pt. 9, p. 6554.

43. "A meaningful . . . way to assess the deterrent capability of our strategic posture is to examine how our forces might perform in response to a hypothetical Soviet attack on them and on command, control, and communications (C^3) facilities associated with the operational control and employment of these forces. . . . This assessment does not . . . reflect the uncertainties resulting from the attacks on our C^3 systems." *Department of Defense Annual Report Fiscal Year 1981*, pp. 123–24.

pacitating him. These major distortions, omissions, and artifices reduce the relevance of standard models to realistic conditions and call into serious question the validity of their findings. Assessments of flexibility are nevertheless usually based on these models as though decisionmakers' latitude for choice is essentially determined by the characteristics of weapons systems.

FLEXIBILITY AND TARGETING. Simplifying the problem of flexibility also characterizes analyses that treat the details of actual strategic war plans as prime concerns. In this view, nuclear diplomacy depends for its success on appropriate attack strategy, target priorities, and weapons assignments. War plans should threaten vital Soviet interests, targeting what they value most and exploiting their fears in order to provide maximum influence over their decisions. The plans must also be tailored to provide sensible options for a range of hypothetical circumstances, to allow deterrence to fail in stages, and to facilitate early termination of a war on acceptable terms.

Adapting targeting policy to changing strategic circumstances and to continuing assessment of Soviet vulnerabilities and fears has involved creating additional options as well as some significant changes in target priorities. It is worthwhile to recount some of this history.

Until the early 1960s the strategic war plan provided only for all-out attack, but in 1962 the United States adopted the "no cities" doctrine that allowed three options: full-scale attack on Soviet and Warsaw Pact military resources, massive attack on enemy economic and industrial resources, and massive simultaneous attack on both sets of targets. In the event of a conventional attack, theater nuclear war, or strategic nuclear attack on the West, authorities could have elected to launch large-scale retaliation against military targets while withholding forces assigned to industrial and economic targets.[44] This ability to withhold forces aimed at Soviet nonmilitary targets partly resolved the paradox of assured destruction.

In the next major revision, a set of options for limited attack was introduced in 1975 because full-scale attack against military targets was expected to cause very high collateral damage to the Soviet population and economy and, in James Schlesinger's words, was "virtually indistin-

44. *Authorizing Appropriations for Aircraft, Missiles and Naval Vessels,* Report prepared for the House Committee on Armed Services, 88 Cong. 1 sess. (GPO, 1963), p. 16.

guishable from an attack on cities."[45] The revised doctrine attempted to establish more salient stages of escalation and improve the chances of a war's early termination.[46] The revision also reflected reassessments of the deterrent effect of different targeting policies. According to Desmond Ball such policies had been under review since the early 1970s as part of a wide-ranging attempt to identify the threats regarded as most grave by the Soviet leadership.[47] Planners hoped to devise a targeting policy that exploited Soviet fears and achieved the optimum deterrent effect. The initial phase of the study effort led to NSDM-242 and *Nuclear Weapons Employment Policy*. The latter document sets out attack options, targeting objectives, and damage levels needed to satisfy political guidance contained in NSDM-242 and an associated document *(Policy Guidance for the Employment of Nuclear Weapons)*.

According to Ball, additional studies undertaken during the Carter administration analyzed Soviet views on fighting a nuclear war, their fears of China, the adaptation of targeting to encourage regional insurrection within the USSR, and the deterrent effect of targeting Soviet instruments of domestic and external political control, especially command centers used by the political leadership and KGB facilities. The conclusions were incorporated in PD-59, signed in 1980, which provided a framework for a strategic war plan containing four basic target groups: nuclear forces, conventional military forces, military and political leadership, and economic and industrial targets. The plan further recognized four categories of attack:

— Major attack options, discussed above.

45. *U.S.-U.S.S.R. Strategic Policies,* Hearings before the Senate Subcommittee on Arms Control, International Law and Organization of the Senate Committee on Foreign Relations, 93 Cong. 2. sess. (GPO, 1974), p. 9.

46. The role of limited options in controlling escalation was clearly set forth ten years before in a document issued under the signature of General Curtis LeMay. General nuclear war included three possible types of operations—attacks against industrial targets and full-scale and limited attacks against military targets. Limited operations could "vary from a single sortie against one military target to a number of diversified target sorties. . . . Their objectives are: (1) To demonstrate to the enemy through military action that the United States possesses both the will and the capability to fight at higher levels of intensity to attain the political values at stake. (2) To convince an enemy that prompt termination of the conflict and negotiations of the issues on reasonable terms are preferable to escalating the war to a higher intensity." See *USAF Basic Doctrine* (Department of the Air Force, August 1964), p. 3-1.

47. For this and the ensuing discussion of PD-59, see Ball, "Counterforce Targeting," pp. 2–7.

— Selected attack options: for example, to impair Soviet capabilities of projecting power in the Middle East and Persian Gulf, U.S. planners have reportedly developed the nuclear option to strike Soviet military bases and airfields inside the Soviet Union near Iran.

— Regional nuclear options: for example, to permit the destruction of the forward elements of an attacking force within a particular area of operations.

— Limited nuclear options involving a very small number of sorties that reportedly permit highly selective attacks on fixed enemy military or industrial targets.

U.S. planners also created special options for preemptive strikes if enemy attack is believed imminent and for launching Minuteman ICBM forces upon receipt of tactical warning of a Soviet strike.

Despite such tailoring and refinement, there will always be fundamental doubt about the appropriateness of particular war plans. Scenarios are speculative and gauging the deterrent effect of different strategies is subjective. Policies emerge without benefit of any solid empirical foundation, the absence of which unavoidably results in the elevation of theory, bald assumption, and hand-waving over data, fact, and scientific conclusion. Because of these limitations, the question of whether current war plans would effectively foreclose enemy options must remain speculative.

Nevertheless, most analysts believe that the proliferation of options has been an appropriate reaction to changes in the force balance and that rational responses to most wartime circumstances can be imagined. This proliferation does not imply, however, that available weapons inventories adequately flesh out the objectives of the options, and both the Carter and Reagan administrations asserted that force modernization is necessary. But modern forces and varied employment options offer scant flexibility if C³I arrangements can only support a spasmodic response. The Carter and Reagan administrations determined that the command structure was indeed deficient and that vast improvement was needed, and under the Reagan administration, command structure development has been assigned a priority equal to that of strategic force modernization.

FLEXIBILITY AND C³I NETWORKS. Although U.S. doctrine since the early 1960s has incorporated plans for flexible and graduated use of nuclear force, the public record lacks authoritative testimony that C³I networks could accurately assess the size and character of enemy missile raids or support time-phased operations over any significant period after the first enemy weapons had struck. Until very recently, the criteria used to evaluate the performance of these networks were derived from the less taxing objective of assured destruction. Under this objective, C³I networks need only meet minimum standards of performance: reliable detection of enemy nuclear attack and rapid dissemination of a go code releasing the entire arsenal in a comprehensive retaliation. But for the last two decades, established war plans have implicitly required that C³I networks provide for control through a series of exchanges, while formal imposition of requirements that exceed the minimum needed for assured destruction has been resisted. H. D. Benington, then a key official responsible for command development, exemplified this attitude. In his view, C³I networks designed to support flexible response would "merely add complexity at the possible expense of reliability." Like his contemporaries of the late 1960s, Benington concluded that "it is better to keep retaliation pure, simple, and as unsophisticated as possible."[48]

Now that the doctrine of flexible response pervades nuclear policy, C³I networks are being evaluated against a set of more stringent standards. Lieutenant General Hillman Dickinson, chief military architect of strategic C³I during the Carter administration, is the source of a proposed set of revised criteria: "To support a credible deterrence posture and warfighting capability, strategic C³ systems must provide tactical warning and attack assessment . . . strategic force control, execution, termination, and Strategic Reserve Force employment for extended periods after absorbing a well-coordinated attack regardless of U.S. force and alert posture."[49] No one inside or outside government seems sanguine about the performance of existing C³I systems when measured against such criteria. According to Desmond Ball, who assessed the performance of present U.S. C³I systems against a similar set of criteria, the controlled, flexible employment of current U.S. strategic forces is illusory:

It is most unrealistic to expect that there would be a relatively smooth and controlled progression from limited and selective strikes, through major counterforce exchanges, to termination of the conflict at some level short of urban-industrial attacks. . . . In fact, control of a nuclear exchange would become very difficult

48. "Can Vulnerability Menace Command and Control?" *Armed Forces Management,* vol. 15 (July 1969), pp. 41–43.

49. *Department of Defense Appropriations for 1981,* Hearings before a Subcommittee of the House Committee on Appropriations, 96 Cong. 2 sess. (GPO, 1980), pt. 7, p. 493.

to maintain after several tens of strategic nuclear weapons had been used, even where deliberate attacks on command-and-control capabilities were avoided.[50] Ball's analysis thus confirms an earlier assessment by John D. Steinbruner that "regardless of the flexibility embodied in individual force components, the precariousness of command channels probably means that nuclear war would be uncontrollable, as a practical matter, shortly after the first tens of weapons are launched. . . ."[51]

Reagan administration officials openly acknowledge that U.S. C³I systems have not kept pace with evolving strategy and enemy threats to those systems. Recent studies have apparently exposed serious shortcomings, many of which defy ready solution. To Donald Latham, the assistant secretary of defense for C³I, current deficiencies underscore what "a very difficult job" it is "to make a system endure and be a war fighting system in a protracted conflict."[52] It is apparent that in the official estimation current U.S. C³I systems lack "an enduring capability to counter the Soviet capabilities for protracted conflict."[53] Chapter 7 examines C³I capabilities for flexibility and endurance in detail, and chapter 8 discusses the Reagan administration's proposed correctives.

Remedies

Assessments clearly demonstrate that present U.S. nuclear capabilities do not satisfy the requirements of U.S. nuclear policy. Strategic modernization and arms control offer two avenues to achieving the goals of that policy.

Strategic Modernization

A Defense Department report contends that the United States must increase the number, destructiveness, endurance and responsiveness of U.S. strategic forces in order to convince the Soviet leadership that "there can be no circumstance in which it could benefit by beginning a nuclear

50. "Can Nuclear War Be Controlled?" *Adelphi Papers,* 169 (London: International Institute for Strategic Studies, 1981), pp. 35–36.

51. "National Security and the Concept of Strategic Stability," *Journal of Conflict Resolution,* vol. 22 (September 1978), p. 421.

52. *Department of Defense Appropriations for 1983,* Hearings before a Subcommittee of the House Committee on Appropriations, 97 Cong. 2 sess. (GPO, 1982), pt. 5, p. 4.

53. Richard D. DeLauer, *The Fiscal Year 1984 Department of Defense Program for Research, Development, and Acquisition* (Department of Defense, 1982), p. V-1.

war at any level or of any duration." U.S. defense officials fear that "the Soviets could envision a potential nuclear confrontation in which they would threaten to destroy a very large part of our force in a first strike, while retaining overwhelming nuclear force to deter any retaliation we could carry out." The report continues that U.S. forces must be configured to deny any such advantage; to hold at risk those political, military, and economic assets that Soviet leaders value most highly; and to allow for terminating a nuclear conflict and "reestablishing deterrence at the lowest possible level of violence."[54]

In October 1981, President Reagan outlined a modernization program that supposedly would prevent Soviet realization of strategic dominance. To arrest alleged destabilizing trends in the strategic balance, and in particular to offset the superior Soviet capability for prompt destruction of hard targets, U.S. strategic power would be revitalized by augmenting and upgrading strategic C^3I; modernizing the manned bomber force; deploying new, more accurate and powerful SLBMs; improving land-based missiles' accuracy, power, and survivability; and strengthening strategic defenses.

Augmenting and upgrading strategic C^3I takes precedence over the rest. In his fiscal year 1984 annual report, Secretary Caspar Weinberger states that the administration has given "highest priority to increasing the ability of our strategic force management systems not only to survive but to remain capable of performing their basic functions throughout a sustained sequence of Soviet attacks."[55] Dozens of programs are included in the modernization, selected key elements of which are described in chapter 8. The administration believes its C^3I plan, once implemented, "would deny the Soviets the option of either attempting a decapitation attack, or using protracted war tactics to exploit the limitations of our C^3I system, and would provide the U.S. with a C^3I system compatible with our strategy of deterrence [flexible response]."[56]

The next priority is to modernize the manned bomber force.[57] At the end of 1983 the number of operational U.S. strategic bombers was about 322 (266 B-52s and 56 FB-111s). Modernization of this force is deemed

---

54. *Department of Defense Annual Report Fiscal Year 1984*, pp. 51–53.

55. Ibid., p. 54.

56. DeLauer, *The Fiscal Year 1984 Department of Defense Program for Research, Development, and Acquisition*, p. V-5.

57. Congressional Budget Office, *Modernizing U.S. Strategic Offensive Forces: The Administration's Program and Alternatives* (GPO, 1983), pp. 7–8.

necessary to ensure weapon penetration in the face of improving Soviet air defense systems. Some B-52s are thus being refitted to carry air-launched cruise missiles (ALCMs) that can be delivered at long distances from the target. The first squadron of ALCM-equipped B-52G aircraft became operational in 1982. The administration further plans to deploy 100 new B-1B bombers in the 1980s, and to begin deployment of 132 advanced "stealth" bombers in the early 1990s. About 3,200 ALCMs will eventually be deployed on these newer aircraft as well as the older B-52 force, with perhaps half the total cruise missile inventory having stealth characteristics now under development.

The administration also intends to deploy new, more accurate and powerful SLBMs.[58] Construction of Trident submarines to augment and eventually replace the aging Poseidon fleet began in 1981 and has continued at a rate of one a year. Each submarine has twenty-four C-4 missiles. The navy's thirty-one Poseidons each carry sixteen C-3 or C-4 missiles. Ten Tridents have been authorized through fiscal year 1983, and it is expected that authorization for ten more will be requested in the years ahead.

Beginning in 1989, D-5 missiles will be deployed on Trident submarines. The D-5 is larger and more powerful and accurate than the C-4. With 75 percent more payload and accurate to within about 400 feet, the D-5 could be used "to attack any target in the Soviet Union, including their missile silos."[59] This capability allows for the first time the use of missile submarines to strike the complete spectrum of targets in the Soviet Union.[60]

Also, starting in 1984, submarine-launched cruise missiles will be deployed on attack submarine and surface ships to strengthen the strategic reserve force.[61]

Between 1986 and 1988, 100 MX missiles will be lowered into existing Minuteman silos if the president's plan to strengthen the land-based missile force is implemented.[62] The Minuteman force will be reduced to 900 launchers and the Titan force will be retired. The MX is twice as accurate as current missiles and can deliver up to ten warheads, compared to three

58. Ibid., pp. 9–11.
59. "Background Statement from White House on MX Missile and B-1 Bomber," *New York Times,* October 3, 1981.
60. DeLauer, *The Fiscal Year 1984 Department of Defense Program for Research, Development, and Acquisition,* p. V-7.
61. Ibid.; and "Background Statement from White House."
62. Congressional Budget Office, *Modernizing U.S. Strategic Offensive Forces,* pp. 2–7.

for Minuteman III and one for Minuteman II. These attributes, together with increased explosive yield, give the MX the capability to destroy increasingly hard Soviet targets.[63] Administration officials argue that MX would rectify an existing imbalance in prompt hard-target capability that is presently "the most dangerous feature of the current strategic situation."[64] MX forces will put hardened Soviet C^3 facilities at risk and "break the Soviet monopoly on prompt counter-ICBM capabilities."[65]

Housing MX missiles in Minuteman silos, however, does not enhance force survivability. The Reagan administration has therefore proposed to begin engineering design work on a small single-warhead ICBM popularly known as Midgetman. Full-scale development could begin as early as 1986, with initial deployment in the early 1990s. Midgetman may operate in a variety of fixed and mobile modes and yet prove to be accurate enough to destroy very hard targets. Other measures that might enhance ICBM survivability range from superhardening missile silos to launch under attack. Research on the former is under way and holds out some promise.

Launch under attack is in one sense a policy option that is already available. The president may simply decide to launch the strategic forces before the full weight of enemy attack is absorbed, thereby permitting more forces, particularly ICBMs, to escape destruction. In principle, the decision not to ride out an attack already rests with national authorities, but implementing it is not, practically speaking, easily performed. Technical and procedural adjustments are required to achieve high confidence in our ability to exercise this policy option (see chapter 7).

The Reagan administration also intends to close large gaps in coverage in the North American air defense network, replace obsolete air defense interceptor aircraft, pursue a vigorous research effort in the area of ballistic missile defense, and continue development of an operational antisatellite system.

Strategic Arms Control

The strategic modernization program could be fully implemented under either the provisions of the unratified SALT II agreements, to which

---

63. DeLauer, *The Fiscal Year 1984 Department of Defense Program for Research, Development, and Acquisition,* p. V-8.

64. *Hearings on Military Posture and H.R. 5968* before the House Committee on Armed Services, 97 Cong. 2 sess. (GPO, 1982), pt. 2, p. 62.

65. "Background Statement from White House."

both parties have adhered by informal understanding, or the provisions proposed by the United States during the initial rounds of the START negotiations. At the same time, the U.S. proposal at START calls for drastic reductions in the Soviet weapons that sparked the latest drive to modernize the American arsenal.

SS-18s and SS-19s are the focus of U.S. concern because they confer a large Soviet advantage in the ability to destroy hard targets. The Soviets have 308 SS-18s, which can carry ten warheads each, and 330 SS-19s, which carry six warheads each. Using less than half these weapons, they theoretically could knock out the Minuteman force in a first strike. The Soviet Union's 2,500 residual warheads capable of attacking hard targets would then be available for other uses. This residual capability alone exceeds the capability of all 1,000 Minuteman missiles for attacking hard targets.

The American proposal would reduce SS-18 and SS-19 launchers to 110 and 100, respectively, in exchange for reductions of 425 Minuteman launchers (to 575). Although the Soviet Union theoretically could still knock out the reduced U.S. Minuteman forces, the size of their residual SS-18 and SS-19 force following a two-on-one attack would be much smaller (500 instead of 2,500). Furthermore, that force would pale in comparison with the survivable, prompt hard-target attack capability in the U.S. arsenal after the president's modernization program has been implemented.

By all indications, the Soviet Union will not accede to the U.S. demand for deep cuts in their heavy land-based missile force. Despite signs of American willingness to accept a higher subceiling on SS-18 and SS-19 missiles, the positions of the protagonists seem too far apart for marginal compromises to bring them together. At present, U.S. policymakers do not expect arms negotiations to succeed in removing what they perceive to be the major source of instability in the strategic situation. They generally see strategic modernization of U.S. forces as the only promising remedy.

Summary

Nuclear strategy, crisis behavior, and investment policy are commonly understood to be the products of a rational decision process. The process is rational in the nontrivial sense of having definite goals in mind and reasons for choosing one policy alternative over another. Decisionmaking is patterned after and disciplined by a formal logic: identify costs and benefits, judge the expected results of alternative courses of action, and select the best alternative. Implicit in this characterization is the image of an individual or close-knit group steering the ship of state. Thanks to a well-oiled rudder that is strongly connected to the steering wheel, executive control is considered firm and positive. Subordinate units involved in procuring weapons, devising strategy, and operating nuclear forces respond quickly and smoothly to the manipulations of the steersman.

Within such a framework, the nuclear confrontation is rendered comprehensible and manageable. Rational analysis provides a conception of the strategic problem in which a condition of mutual deterrence exists. It leads to the conviction that this state of affairs is basically stable and offers diagnostic methods for pinpointing certain technological developments that might undermine this stability. Standard assessment performs sophisticated calculations of the strategic balance and of the potential contribution of new military systems to our deterrent posture.

Standard assessment, however, commits a serious error of omission. It concentrates on nuclear forces and neglects the strengths and weaknesses of the U.S. nuclear control system. Although this imbalance has recently been acknowledged, the nuclear command-control system has yet to receive full attention. As the system becomes better understood, basic conceptions of the nuclear problem will likely be transformed. Careful examination of C³I technology and procedures will expose the actual process by which nuclear weapons are controlled—a process not captured by models of rational decisionmaking.

CHAPTER THREE

Organization of Strategic Programs and Operations

A CRITIQUE of the model based on rational analysis begins with the observation that organizations with responsibilities for strategic programs and operations comprise a multitude of people and activities. These organizations are simply too large and cumbersome for a single person or committee to steer them in any detailed way. Coordination by means of exhaustive instruction from a central decisionmaker would be a monumental and futile undertaking.

People and activities are actually governed largely by decentralized forces: a diffuse authority structure, restricted and disaggregated streams of information, and specialized sets of low-order decision rules (standard operating procedures, rules of thumb, and so forth). Decentralization alleviates the workload at the center by shifting a considerable amount of decisionmaking power and responsibility to the periphery. The workload at the periphery and, for that matter, at all levels of command is further alleviated by built-in rules that trigger preprogrammed responses when certain predefined conditions appear.

Appreciation of significant decentralization in strategic organizations is not a radically new development, but it carries an important general implication that the model of nuclear decisionmaking by a central authority does not consider: ample scope exists for discontinuity between national policy intentions and actions taken at subordinate echelons.

This discontinuity is particularly relevant to the president's aim of creating a command system that allows for central, flexible direction (and ad hoc redirection) of strategic forces during a protracted nuclear conflict. Such a system is the operational linchpin for a nuclear war-fighting and bargaining strategy, which is the logical answer to the paradox of assured destruction. However, existing institutions involved in the design and funding of command systems are not adroit in creating central systems because the institutions themselves are decentralized. Furthermore, the president naively overestimated the potential responsiveness of combat organizations to central direction during war. Only so much flexibility and centralization can be accommodated, and the aspirations of the current policy appear to lie far beyond those limits.

Management of Programs and Budgets: Institutional Laissez-faire

Since World War II a diffuse process for making decisions has determined the physical and organizational configuration of C³I systems. Most systems have been shaped by and for suborganizations without much concern for integration and centralization. Decentralization has been literally wired into the strategic communications network, leaving national officials without the physical means they would need to bring strategic operations under firm central control. And the entire multibillion dollar investment, which in the words of one observer was made "without even the semblance of a conceptual rationale,"[1] resulted in an overall C³I infrastructure—called the World Wide Military Command and Control System (WWMCCS)—that stubbornly resists attempts at rewiring it to strengthen communication between central decisionmakers and subordinates.[2]

Before the Defense Reorganization Act of 1958, integration and centralization of C³I elements was effectively blocked by legislative barriers that had been erected by the National Security Act of 1947 and the amendment of 1949. These laws required that military departments be administered as individual executive entities by their respective secretaries; comparatively little authority was vested in the secretary of defense, whose mandate was to provide general direction and guidance.

1. William J. Broad, "Philosophers at the Pentagon," *Science,* vol. 210 (October 24, 1980), p. 412.
2. Department of Defense Directive 5100.30 (December 2, 1971) defines the World Wide Military Command and Control System as providing "the means for operational direction and technical administrative support involved in the function of command and control of U.S. Military Forces." WWMCCS thus encompasses virtually all C³ assets within the military.

Legislation thus sanctioned and tacitly approved a buildup of separate C³I networks in each military department.

The Defense Reorganization Act of 1958 relaxed the restrictive covenants. The Office of the Secretary of Defense was empowered, for instance, to place C³I programs under its purview. The act also gave assistant secretaries of defense considerable authority over the departments and their C³I programs. This legal inroad was not exploited, however, and OSD surrendered most of its C³I management prerogatives.[3] In dividing management responsibilities among four assistant secretaries, the director of defense research and engineering, and numerous OSD staff offices, the OSD mimicked the laissez-faire practices of the military departments. A report critical of this arrangement stated that "communications was not considered as a system requiring integrated and unified consideration and a corporate management. . . . These fragmented and overlapping responsibilities resulted in inefficient and ineffective communications management throughout the Department."[4]

Under the 1958 act the secretaries of the military departments were excluded from the chain of combat command, but they retained primary responsibility for the C³I networks used by combat commanders. The departments were to engineer, install, and operate these networks.

In part because of fragmented oversight at the OSD level, the C³I needs of these commands took precedence over the national command system, and even they were administered with prejudice by the military departments. The departments opposed, for instance, interservice consolidation of C³I channels within each of the unified commands (the Pacific, Atlantic, and European commands and the Strategic Air Command), even though the basic idea of a unified command is to fuse forces from two or more branches to permit joint operations within a particular geographic region. This opposition, attributed to service parochialism,[5]

3. See *Review of Department of Defense Worldwide Communications Phase I,* Hearings before the House Committee on Armed Services, 92 Cong. 1 sess., report May 10, 1971 (GPO, 1971), pp. 1–42. (Hereafter *Phase I Report,* May 10, 1971.)

4. Ibid., p. 20.

5. "While many of the Subcommittee witnesses expressed reservations about the wisdom of consolidation, their objections were not based on any operational degradation of the military communications system. On close analysis, their vague objections appear to be based more on jurisdictional rather than operational grounds. They are reluctant to share their communication facilities with the other services." See *Review of Department of Defense Worldwide Communications Phase III,* Hearings before the House Committee on Armed Services, 93 Cong. 2 sess., report February 7, 1975. See also *Review of Department of Defense*

meant that communications channels in the unified commands would remain separate (with the military departments providing support only for their affiliated forces), to the detriment of force coordination. The departments also gave higher priority to weapons than to C^3I modernization; the combat commanders lacked a strong voice in that trade-off as well as in the specifics of C^3I development. The nonbinding recommendations of the senior combat commanders were forwarded to the Joint Chiefs of Staff and to the military departments. The former was itself a weak voice in budgetary deliberations, while the latter pitted the recommendations against every other defense program request during the annual budgetary sweepstakes. In the end, C^3I programs fared poorly.

Two noteworthy but feeble efforts to promote integration and centralization of C^3I networks were made in the early 1960s. The first led to the creation of the Defense Communications Agency. Formed in 1960 to institute a common worldwide military communications system, DCA assumed responsibility for a newly designated network called the Defense Communications System (DCS). This system was intended to provide long distance, point-to-point communications from the national command level to the unified and specified commanders, from the unified and specified commanders to their respective component (as well as other subordinate) commanders, and among the various unified and specified commanders. Many of these same DCS channels were included in the National Military Command System (NMCS), the C^3I bridge between civilian authorities and military forces, to which DCA provided technical support. The agency's responsibilities extended to other critical NMCS elements besides communications channels: primary and alternate national military command centers, national emergency command post aircraft, and telecommunications and computer processing equipment at various joint war rooms in the Pentagon.

DCA's grant of authority, particularly budget authority, was wholly incommensurate with its sweeping mandate. The agency's charter stipulated that the secretaries of the military departments would have statutory control over the Defense Communications System. Although the departments' interests scarcely overlapped those of the agency, they funded the procurement of equipment, funded and constructed the facili-

---

Worldwide Communications Phase II, Hearings before the House Committee on Armed Services, 92 Cong. 2 sess., report October 12, 1972 (GPO, 1972). (Hereafter *Phase II Report,* October 12, 1972.)

ties, and supplied the personnel for engineering and installing equipment. The departments maintained and operated all of the resources "on loan" to the Defense Communications Agency.[6] DCA was further weakened by the requirement that it report to the Joint Chiefs of Staff, which lacked budgetary clout under the law and often let service parochialism interfere with its handling of defensewide pursuits. Finally, DCA involvement in the development of tactical communications and intelligence systems was forbidden. The agency could not, therefore, facilitate progress toward centralization and integration of these systems, some of which provided early warning data or linked nuclear weapons commanders to higher authority. Thus legal and bureaucratic constraints enfeebled DCA and compromised its independence, virtually guaranteeing that the agency would perpetuate, not solve, the command problems that motivated its creation.

The other effort to promote centralization of C³I networks occurred in 1963 when the Office of the Secretary of Defense decided to stress the importance of meeting national as well as subordinate C³I requirements. Instead of giving DCA more power or expanding its own role in the supervision of C³I programs, however, OSD issued DOD Directive 5100.30, which amounted to little more than advice and exhortation. Although the directive emphasized, for example, that tactical networks ought to be made responsive to the needs of national decisionmakers, it stopped short of compelling compliance. The authority of the military departments was unaffected. And because OSD offered them no incentive to alter priorities, the logic and pattern of investment in developing the command structure were not affected. The parochial interests of the individual departments and their affiliated combat forces continued to take precedence.

This subordination of programs with defensewide applications was illustrated in an interview with a former American Telephone and Telegraph manager. About 1967 it was becoming increasingly apparent that DCA's AUTOVON network could offer a more survivable means of telephone communications with Strategic Air Command forces than the main system providing this service at the time. SAC possessed dedicated landline circuitry, the Primary Alerting System (PAS), which utilized AT&T transcontinental underground cables. A complementary cable

6. *Phase I Report* (May 10, 1971), pp. 18–20, 22–26.

running from Massachusetts to Florida was installed in 1969,[7] and additional cable and microwave augmented the cross-country backbone. AUTOVON also used the AT&T cable and microwave network but interconnected virtually all U.S. military bases as well as national command centers. Furthermore, AUTOVON featured a unique switching system for rerouting transmissions over surviving circuits. With some effort—for example, modest design modifications and improved automation of the circuit-switching process—AUTOVON could have far surpassed PAS in terms of survivability.

SAC was the sole proprietor of PAS, however, while AUTOVON was accessible to all, and the Defense Communications Agency, which key SAC personnel viewed with considerable disdain, was not a welcome partner in any prospective joint venture to modify strategic communications. Thus SAC simply enjoined the agency from any involvement in upgrading voice communications for SAC combat operations. DCA was in no position to contest such matters, and the idea of developing AUTOVON as the primary means of SAC communications was dropped. SAC continued to rely almost completely on PAS for strategic voice communications in spite of diminishing confidence in its survivability.[8]

By the end of the 1960s, fragmented management of programs had been responsible in no small measure for numerous worrisome conditions, operational inefficiencies, and misfortunes. There were thirty-three telecommunications centers on the island of Oahu alone. The commander in chief Pacific, and the army, navy, and air force Pacific commanders maintained separate telecommunications centers within a few miles of each other near Honolulu.[9] At over fifty-five sites worldwide, two or more

7. "Closer Military-Industry Relationship Seen Helping Command and Control," *Aerospace Daily,* vol. 106 (November 7, 1980), p. 33.

8. The transcontinental cables PAS used were laid in sections about 150 miles long and joined together at these intervals by manned maintenance facilities. A single break in the cable or the destruction of a single manned site would have had a disastrous effect on overall PAS performance. Two or three strategically aimed weapons probably would knock the system out completely. When PAS was originally designed, it was considered relatively survivable because analysts presumed that Soviet planners would not be willing to commit the forces needed to destroy it. The system was thus designed to sustain only collateral damage. By the mid-to-late 1960s, however, Soviet missile accuracy and deliverable warheads had increased to the point that a direct nuclear attack on PAS could no longer be discounted.

9. *Phase II Report* (October 12, 1972), pp. 16, 498.

military branches maintained independent telecommunications centers.[10] Within the Pentagon itself, the army and air force each operated three centers, and the navy operated two.[11] Because of technical incompatibility, neither telecommunications nor automatic data processing systems in operations around the world could bridge traditional service boundaries.

Communications had often broken down during crises. Communications malfunctions were the primary cause of the mishandling of several international incidents, including the attack on the USS *Liberty* (1967), the seizure of the USS *Pueblo* (1968), and the shooting down of a U.S. EC-121 aircraft (1969) by North Korea. Autopsies of these incidents pointed up how difficult it was for messages originating at the national level to find their way into the capillaries of military communications networks. Many were misrouted, misinterpreted, and even misplaced. Most arrived too late or never reached their intended destinations. Similar problems beset attempts at communications from the bottom to the top of the command hierarchy.[12]

Finally, in the late 1960s serious deficiencies also surfaced in the Minimum Essential Emergency Communications Network, described as "a last-ditch communications network which the president would use to pass emergency action orders to the military forces during and after a nuclear attack."[13] MEECN was a nominal system that was not well integrated, and many elements assigned to it were becoming incompatible because the services were designing without regard for forcewide compatibility. Defense Department research and engineering was unable to resolve the problem. Particularly, very low frequency radio equipment, the key component of MEECN, was under separate development by the navy and air force, and could not be coordinated.[14]

10. *Phase III Report* (February 7, 1975), p. 6.

11. In addition, the Pentagon housed a communications center for the Defense Intelligence Agency and the National Military Command Center, for a grand total of ten centers within the Pentagon alone. See *Phase II Report* (October 12, 1972), pp. 16, 498.

12. See *Phase I Report* (May 10, 1971), pp. 6–17.

13. *Department of Defense Appropriations for 1974,* Hearings before a Subcommittee of the House Committee on Appropriations, 93 Cong. 1 sess. (GPO, 1973), pt. 9, p. 1165.

14. See "Internetting to Enhance Survivability of Strategic Command and Control" and "Can Vulnerability Menace Command and Control?" *Armed Forces Management,* vol. 15 (July 1969), pp. 40–43; Lee M. Paschal, "WWMCCS—Nerve Center of U.S. C³," *Air Force Magazine,* vol. 58 (July 1975), p. 55; *Department of Defense Appropriations for 1970,* Hearings before a Subcommittee of the House Committee on Appropriations, 91 Cong. 1 sess. (GPO, 1969), pt. 4, pp. 861–62, and pt. 3, p. 1125; *Fiscal Year 1972 Authorization for Military Procurement, Research and Development, Construction and Real Estate Acquisition*

The impulse to reform management practices once again surfaced in the early 1970s. Concern about the lack of institutional focus, particularly on the part of then Deputy Secretary of Defense David Packard, led first to the creation in 1970 of the Office of Assistant to the Secretary of Defense for Telecommunications. The office was elevated in January 1972 to the level of assistant secretary of defense in a move to further unify OSD activities in this field. The WWMCCS Council was formed with a view to lending prestige and authority to the assistant secretary and to accelerating work on important strategic projects, such as new national command post aircraft and strategic satellite communications.[15] Packard also directed DCA to coordinate MEECN engineering and integration work, hoping this would steer the divergent research and development programs in the navy and air force onto parallel technological paths.[16] Finally, Packard attempted to rectify a decade of misplaced emphasis within the combat commands and military departments by designating the national military command system as the priority component of WWMCCS.[17] In Packard's words, "instead of the local commanders now having as their first priority to design their command system to meet the requirements of their mission, they first have to have a design to meet the requirements of the national command system and second, to meet the requirements of their mission."[18] DOD Directive 5100.30, reissued in 1971, not only elevated the priority of the national command system, but also downgraded the importance of the unified and specified commanders in the chain of command for execution of the strategic war plan. The Joint Chiefs of Staff was assigned responsibility for ensuring compliance with the provisions of this mandate.

The fatal weakness in this effort to consolidate management of C³I programs was that budget authority remained diffuse. In fact, as the disjunction between the national command system and the military com-

---

for the Safeguard IBM, and Reserve Strengths, Hearings before the Senate Committee on Armed Services, 92 Cong. 1 sess. (GPO, 1971), pt. 4, pp. 2759-61; *Fiscal Year 1973 Authorization for Military Procurement, Research and Development, Construction and Real Estate Acquisition for the Safeguard IBM, and Reserve Strengths,* Hearings before the Senate Committee on Armed Services, 92 Cong. 2 sess. (GPO, 1972), pt. 4, pp. 2628-29; and *Department of Defense Appropriations for 1974,* House hearings, pt. 6, p. 1705, and pt. 9, pp. 1165-66.

15. Members included the deputy secretary of defense, the chairman of the Joint Chiefs of Staff, and two assistant secretaries (for intelligence and telecommunications).

16. See footnote 14.

17. Department of Defense Directive 5100.30 (December 2, 1971).

18. *Congressional Record,* vol. 117 (October 29, 1971), p. 38381.

mand networks became more important to defense planners and as more centralized, coherent arrangements for supervising C³I projects began to coalesce, program and budget control in the Defense Department was being further decentralized. Packard himself was partially responsible for loosening OSD's reins on specific programs and budgets and for creating a modus operandi (called participatory management) that inhibited initiative at the OSD level. As a result of management practices instituted during Melvin Laird's tenure, the Office of the Secretary of Defense mainly exercised veto power over specific programs. It did set overall budget ceilings, prohibited service reprogramming of funds earmarked for certain special projects (particularly surveillance programs), reviewed programs requested by the services, and reserved the right to cancel programs or veto program objective memorandums submitted annually by the services. But it played a mostly passive or reactive role in setting internal budget priorities and seldom created or pushed ideas of its own.

Its authority was especially weak in telecommunications, where its activism was especially unpopular among the uniformed services. A congressional subcommittee report published in 1975 describes the circumstances in which OSD's Telecommunications Office (James Schlesinger downgraded the assistant secretary position to the level of director of telecommunications and command control systems, or DTACCS, in 1974) found itself:

> [The subcommittee views] the responsibility of the Telecommunications Office as the management of all telecommunication resources of the Department so as to provide the maximum communications capability at minimum costs from the viewpoint of the overall mission of the Department of Defense, while insuring adequate support for each of the military departments in carrying out their individual defense missions. In attempting to carry out that responsibility, however, the Telecommunications Office almost inevitably comes into conflict with the military services which either own or lease all of the Department's communication resources. Each of the services has established an independent communications system designed to satisfy its peculiar requirements in carrying out its defense mission. Because of that identity of their communications systems with defense missions, the services tend to regard any action of the Telecommunications Office which would result in reduction or alteration of those systems as an interference with their responsiveness to their mission responsibilities. Accordingly, the proposals of the Telecommunications Office . . . have been strenuously resisted by the armed services . . . [and] the Telecommunications Office has not had sufficient authority to overcome such resistance. . . .[19]

19. *Phase III Report* (February 7, 1975), p. 5.

Richard H. Schriver, the head of DTACCS in 1976, candidly acknowledged his lack of direct budget authority, though he gave the impression that his veto power conferred substantial indirect control: "The fiscal control is not direct. I think it is important to understand that the way we function is primarily through a veto power in order to have the services fund projects that may not be totally in the service interests but are in the JCS and OSD interests."[20] The hearings indicated, for instance, that this leverage enabled OSD to persuade the air force to spend an additional $63 million on the Defense Satellite Communications System (a program that is managed by DCA and supports the national command system) in fiscal year 1977. However, this was the only telecommunications item in a consolidated budget of approximately $4 billion that had not been originally requested by the services. OSD initiated few proposals and infrequently exercised, or threatened to exercise, its right of veto. Pressure was applied in a few exceptional cases, such as in securing service support for the E-4 national command aircraft, but it was seldom brought to bear when smaller, though often important, items were at stake. For instance, between 1976 and 1978 the head of WWMCCS engineering at DCA recommended acquisition of ten different types of communications and command equipment to improve capabilities for rapid reaction to urgent contingencies.[21] They were intended to provide national officials with better means of managing tactical engagements involving conventional forces, particularly forces deployed to areas where they normally did not operate.[22] The items, such as transportable satellite earth terminals, were relatively inexpensive. But the services declined requests to fund them,

20. *Department of Defense Appropriations for 1977,* Hearings before a Subcommittee of the House Committee on Appropriations, 94 Cong. 2 sess. (GPO, 1976), pt. 6, p. 33.

21. Department of Defense Directive 5100.79 (November 21, 1975) established within DCA an engineering office to design a command network according to IBM Corporation studies and plans for WWMCCS through 1985. IBM placed primary emphasis on the need to handle such contingencies as the Cambodian seizure of the *Mayaguez* and hence on investment in rapidly deployable C^3 equipment.

22. The idea was to be able to operate anywhere in the world in the manner of the "tree-cutting" operation in the Korean demilitarized zone, when the national military command center in Washington, the Pacific commander in chief in Hawaii, and the commander of the United Nations forces in Korea were able to set up a conference and maintain continuous control of the operation. *Fiscal Year 1978 Authorization for Military Procurement, Research and Development, and Active Duty, Selected Reserve, and Civilian Personnel Strengths,* Hearings before the Senate Committee on Armed Services, 95 Cong. 1 sess. (GPO, 1977), pt. 10, pp. 6793-96.

and senior OSD officials did not threaten to veto service programs in order to gain support of the communications engineer's proposals.

The participatory management system instituted by Melvin Laird and institutionalized by his successors was not the only reason for OSD's deferential, passive role. The office did not, for instance, believe it necessary to undertake any ambitious new programs to develop strategic command capabilities. Few if any OSD personnel took issue with the official position that "the ability to execute the nuclear force in the large general war case was adequately provided for by the programmed systems,"[23] a conclusion that fostered complacency and averted a clash between the office and the services over budget priorities. A different conclusion would have generated demands on the services to divert resources from weapons programs to C³I programs, which they generally eyed with disfavor. The Office of the Secretary of Defense, notably the director of telecommunications and command control systems, and the Defense Communications Agency had in fact acquired a reputation for undervaluing survivability measures in their quest for greater efficiency in peacetime communications networks. This reputed tendency is blamed, for instance, for the low protection against nuclear effects afforded satellites. The DSCS satellites, for example, were deployed without significant protection during the mid-1970s (the cost of a fully hardened satellite is approximately 10 to 15 percent above that for a nonsurvivable satellite).[24]

Furthermore, OSD officials apparently believed that the protection of individual weapons deserved a higher priority than the protection of the C³I systems that stand behind the forces. Thomas Reed, for example, who as DTACCS during the mid-1970s was responsible for basic communications policy, defended a proposal to construct a vulnerable system for communicating with submarines on the grounds that not only would it increase the stealth of the submarines by eliminating their need to trail antennas near the ocean's surface, but also that its vulnerability would not matter because missile submarine survivability was what really counted. When asked whether he favored a transmission grid that could survive a direct nuclear attack, Reed replied, "it is not clear to me we ought to try to build a surface survivable anything in this era . . . because

23. *Fiscal Year 1978 Authorization for Military Procurement, Research and Development,* Senate hearings, pt. 10, p. 6795. This "official position" was actually that of the WWMCCS plan developed by the IBM Corporation. Ultimately the conclusion was rejected by the Carter administration.

24. *Department of Defense Appropriations for 1984,* Hearings before a Subcommittee of the House Committee on Appropriations, 98 Cong. 1 sess. (GPO, 1983), pt. 8, p. 504.

the submarines are what really provide the stability in case of some worldwide difficulties."[25]

This reasoning is consonant with the traditional perspective on strategic stability. The overriding importance of protecting the weapons was also invoked by the navy in justifying the vulnerable Seafarer communications system.[26] The rationale seemed to run as follows: because Seafarer enhances the survivability of submarines, it increases the number of nuclear weapons available for use in a second strike and hence strengthens deterrence; because bolstering deterrence lessens the risk of a Soviet first strike, there is that much less cause for concern about the vulnerability of Seafarer itself. However dubious this reasoning may seem, it was nothing more or less than an articulation of the conventional wisdom that discouraged investment in C³I survivability. Given that communications and weapons compete for the same scarce resources, and given that the most economical C³I systems tend to be the least survivable, organizations that value weapons more than communications or cost-effective C³I networks more than survivable ones would not be inclined to challenge this wisdom.

Formal defense planning guidance perpetuated the imbalance between the development of command systems and weapons. Even the WWMCCS Council, the high-level oversight group that presided over all military C³ programs, stated that its policy, "as expressed in DOD planning guidance, is that command, control, and communications . . . should not constrain the flexibility or survivability of the weapons systems themselves."[27] Requirements for C³I survivability and interoperability were

25. *Hearings on Military Posture and H.R. 3689* before the House Committee on Armed Services, 94 Cong. 1 sess. (GPO, 1975), pt. 4, p. 4024.

26. Admittedly, program justifications serve rhetorical and political purposes and do not necessarily indicate any deep-seated view of strategic stability or anything else. In fact, until 1975 the navy insisted that a survivable communications system (then called Sanguine) was essential: "The whole idea behind Sanguine is to produce a means of communicating with our missile-launching nuclear submarines which is so sure and so survivable under any conditions including nuclear attack that any enemy would be most hesitant to attack us knowing our retaliatory capability is assured. In other words, having Sanguine as one of our defense systems will, hopefully, prevent a nuclear attack on the United States." Letter of Rear Admiral Jon L. Boyes, director of naval telecommunications, submitted in *Fiscal Year 1975 Authorization for Military Procurement, Research and Development, and Active Duty, Selected Reserve, and Personnel Strengths,* Hearings before the Senate Committee on Armed Services, 93 Cong. 2 sess. (GPO, 1974), pt. 6, p. 3207.

27. *Fiscal Year 1977 Authorization for Military Procurement, Research and Development, and Active Duty, Selected Reserve and Personnel Strengths,* Hearings before the Senate Committee on Armed Services, 94 Cong. 2 sess. (GPO, 1976), pt. 12, p. 6802.

conspicuously absent from written directives. Formal planning guidance explicitly incorporated them only recently.

The issues of C³I vulnerability and program management lay dormant until President Carter took office. The new administration rejected the Ford administration's contention that employing U.S. nuclear forces in the wake of a massive Soviet first strike was adequately provided for by the C³I budget. There were reasons to believe that was not so under any responsible definition of adequacy, and there were no illusions that the C³I budget adequately supported the strategy for fighting a nuclear war advanced by the Carter Pentagon.

This policy turnabout resulted in part from a series of studies that exposed serious C³I vulnerabilities and operational deficiencies and in part from the Carter administration's move to raise the standard of C³I performance. With concern swinging away from assured destruction and toward flexible response, the administration saw a need for greater endurance, survivability, flexibility, and centralization in C³I networks, a need reflected in PD-53, PD-58 and PD-59. Key combat commanders in chief, notably SAC Commander General Ellis, shared this assessment and strongly backed the administration's effort. Throughout Carter's term, however, attempts at overhauling C³I management and acquisition practices failed to wrest resource control from the military departments, leaving the Office of the Secretary of Defense and the combat commanders in chief without sufficient influence on C³I budgets and programs.

The most noteworthy and the earliest of these attempts began when a Defense Science Board task force was commissioned to reevaluate the process by which OSD and the military departments designed and procured command systems. Completed in the summer of 1978, the task force report confirmed what everyone already knew: "The nation is failing to deploy command and control systems commensurate with the nature of likely future warfare, with modern weapons systems, or with our available technological and industrial base."[28] The report went on to say that fundamental improvements were needed to allow U.S. forces to respond appropriately under the careful control of national authorities at all levels of conflict and to avoid unnecessary escalation.

To remedy the situation, the task force called for the creation of a new agency with statutory authority "to manage the design and acquisition of

28. *Command and Control System Management* (Office of the Under Secretary of Defense Research and Engineering, July 1978), p. 1.

command and control systems . . . which cut across Service boundaries or are of major concern to OSD, JCS or the National Command Authority."[29] The task force also recommended that the combat commanders in chief be provided with sufficient funds and personnel to modernize their command systems within the guidelines established by the new agency. Finally, the report recommended that combat commanders' capabilities for evaluating their command systems should be strengthened.

Because of President Carter's general policy forbidding the creation of new government agencies and because of powerful opposition from the military departments, these recommendations were watered down as they passed through successive stages of bureaucratic review. Instead of a new agency, the Defense Communications Agency would be expanded and assigned the new responsibilities. Then it was determined that DCA's statutory authority should extend only to interservice systems strictly defined, which excluded such key elements of the strategic network as E-4 airborne command posts, TACAMO submarine communications relay aircraft, and strategic early warning networks. Ultimately no statutory control at all passed to the agency. The Joint Chiefs of Staff and the services unanimously and effectively opposed it on the grounds that "service prioritization of command and control systems among other programs in the planning, programming, and budgeting system would be lost if statutory control of them was given to an agency."[30] The proposed restructuring not only threatened the services' control over C³I expenditures but also indirectly threatened their control over the allocation of resources to other programs. From their standpoint this was an intolerable proposition, not to mention a circumvention of the law under the 1958 Defense Reorganization Act. The task force had found no other solution. In the end the Defense Science Board review led only to the creation of a new office within the Joint Chiefs of Staff headed by a senior general officer. Under the direction of Lieutenant General Hillman Dickinson, this office—Command Control Communications Systems (C3S)—vigorously pursued President Carter's C³I goals, but it lacked the necessary authority to fulfill them.

Following the inauguration of President Reagan, several senior officials who had been deeply involved in command system development

29. Ibid., p. 2.
30. Gerald P. Dinneen, "C³ Systems Management," *Signal,* vol. 34 (September 1979), p. 18.

reflected on the circumstances in which they found themselves. The usual complaints were voiced. H. L. Van Trees, acting assistant secretary of defense for C³I, noted the perennial OSD struggles—identifying the things that needed to be done, getting the services to put the needed C³ programs in their budgets, and making sure that the funds were not moved to support some other program—and advocated establishing stronger control of resources within OSD.[31] General Ellis, who would soon retire from his post as commander in chief of SAC, also recommended further centralization of budget authority and suggested placing a C³I advocate at the deputy secretary level (two notches higher than usual) to ensure OSD budget control.[32] Ellis also lamented that although a high-level Joint Chiefs of Staff office had finally been created for the purpose of giving the combat commanders a stronger voice in C³I affairs, the office in question (C3S) lacked the budget and program authority needed to implement the recommendations. Lieutenant General Dickinson, then director of C3S, summed up, "in general, the development and programming and procurement process throughout the Government is not designed to handle C³-system problems."[33]

Under the Reagan administration the situation improved in some respects and deteriorated in others. James Wade, principal under secretary for research and engineering, galvanized the Pentagon, formed working groups to address the command problem, and generated a master plan meant to rectify the long-standing imbalance in investment and ensure a coherent modernization effort. But the Carter administration's Office of the Assistant Secretary of Defense for C³I, which lacked sufficient leverage vis-à-vis the services according to Richard DeLauer, the undersecretary for research,[34] was replaced by an office of even lower rank—deputy under secretary for C³I (the ASDC³I position was not reinstated until 1983). Headed by Donald Latham, this office enjoyed exceptional managerial talent and technical expertise, but had insufficient influence on the

31. *Department of Defense Authorization for Appropriations for Fiscal Year 1982,* Hearings before the Senate Committee on Armed Services, 97 Cong. 1 sess. (GPO, 1981), pt. 7, p. 4225.

32. Ibid., p. 4226. At this hearing Ellis also noted that "strategic C³I has not received cohesive management attention nor the funding support commensurate with the job it has been asked to do. This deficiency is a direct threat to the effective employment of our strategic forces. . . . My thought is that we establish at the Secretary of Defense level an office reporting directly to him in which all of the responsibilities reside" (pp. 3792, 3803).

33. Ibid., pp. 4226–27.

34. "Why C³I Is the Pentagon's Top Priority," *Government Executive* (January 1982), p. 14.

Defense Resources Board. At the same time, the Pentagon's revision of the budget system, featuring controlled decentralization, further consolidated the services' tight control of the C³I budget. Programs and budgets continued to be driven by diffuse interests. OSD still functioned within the participatory management framework built by Melvin Laird and therefore lacked the power to bring the services' programs into line with OSD interests. The prospects for fundamental reform of the sort recommended by the task force remained as remote as ever. Without such reform, which probably involves revising the law, the president's promise to create a command system that allows for central, flexible direction of strategic forces during a protracted conflict will surely remain unfulfilled.

Management of Force Operations: Illusion of Central Control

Although changes in programming, planning, and budgeting are essential to effective modernization of the U.S. nuclear control system, certain goals for C³I modernization would remain beyond reach. Better management of resources probably could bring the control system into alignment with a simple strategy of assured destruction, but there is no realistic prospect of aligning C³I with a strategy that demands highly centralized, flexible operations over a long time. The direction of forces is not and cannot be nearly as central, flexible, or precise as the nuclear strategy of the Reagan administration requires.

Like programs and budgets, force operations do not correspond to the prevailing conception. In both cases, activities are better understood as products of a diffuse, decentralized decision process than as intentional choices of rational decisionmakers pursuing definite goals.

Low-order decision rules and standard operating procedures are the key regulating mechanisms of force operations. Their regulation of the peacetime activities of strategic forces is extensive. At this moment the alert bomber crews, submarine commanders, land missile launch crews, and the warning and C³ units that support them are following standard routines that account for practically all their behavior. Routines determine the location, disposition, and readiness of the units assigned to the strategic mission. Routines selectively focus on certain aspects of the operating environment to simplify it, they channel energy to simplify operations on the environment, they provide ready-made solutions to the ordinary problems they encounter, and they coordinate a diversified, far-flung, and large-scale military machine with a minimum amount of interaction between units. Programmatic activity stabilizes a potentially dangerous operation and does so without constant or even frequent direct supervision by high-level civilian or military officials.

The programmatic decision process that accounts for such stability operates on simple principles.[35] It requires focused reception of preselected data on an environmental variable. The data are then compared with a desirable range of values for that variable. If the data fall outside this predefined interval, minor adjustments (a programmed response) are made until they fall within tolerances. When these adjustments succeed, the system can be said to have adapted to environmental disturbances. Gain adjustments to radio receivers used by strategic units to monitor communications illustrate a simple version of this process. Such adjustments are made when environmental forces—especially changing atmospheric conditions—perceptibly reduce the strength of radio signals. If gain adjustments fail to restore adequate reception—in abstract terms, if the monitored data remain outside defined tolerances after a simple programmed response is made—other programmed responses—frequency switching, reorientation of antennas, and activation of backup receivers— are triggered sequentially until reception is restored or the repertory of responses exhausted.

Such responses, each of which operates in a characteristic way upon receipt of information, increase the adaptive capacity of the system. As long as the environment does not undergo radical change, an entity consisting of nothing more than a set of built-in decision rules, which apply to only a small domain of environmental conditions and are capable of invoking only a limited range of responses, can possess high adaptive capacity. Such capacity can exist even in a complex environment where the pertinent variables and combinations of variables are numerous. The capacity for ultrastability in a complex environment is gradually acquired

35. For a thorough treatment of programmatic decision processes, see John D. Steinbruner, *The Cybernetic Theory of Decision: New Dimensions of Political Analysis* (Princeton University Press, 1974). Other particularly relevant sources include Graham T. Allison, *Essence of Decision: Explaining the Cuban Missile Crisis* (Little, Brown, 1971); Richard M. Cyert and James G. March, *A Behavioral Theory of the Firm* (Prentice-Hall, 1963); Richard R. Nelson, "Issues and Suggestions for the Study of Industrial Organization in a Regime of Rapid Technical Change," in Victor R. Fuchs, ed. *Policy Issues and Research Opportunities in Industrial Organization* (National Bureau of Economic Research, distributed by Columbia University Press, 1972); Karl Weick, *The Social Psychology of Organizing* (Addison-Wesley, 1969); and John D. Steinbruner, "Beyond Rational Deterrence: The Struggle for New Conceptions," *World Politics,* vol. 28 (January 1976), pp. 223–45.

through evolutionary changes in rule structure. As the environment reveals its variety and as established sequences of action prove to be inappropriate enough that system instability results, the maladaptive rules and procedures are modified or dropped. This process of trial and error appears to have a better chance of restoring equilibrium through eliminating or modifying routines than through elaborating or overhauling them. Attempts at major restructuring, which may be based on rational analyses, are seldom made in any case.

Virtually all aspects of nuclear operations are programmed in a manner analogous to the example above. Programmed activity is so much a part of the operations that the behavior of the forces requires no further explanation. One need not introduce central decisionmakers' (or anyone else's) goals or calculations, for example, to explain the activity. In fact, general policy goals may be rationalizations of existing patterns of behavior rather than the other way around. Goals are tied more closely to past activities than has been realized and frequently are better understood as summaries of previous actions. Much of an organization's work does not seem to be directed toward achieving a goal, nor is it influenced by rational analysis. Instead, it can be understood more readily as actions performed with a primitive orderliness, which is enhanced after individuals review what has come to pass as a result.

This view that organization is an agent of simplification rather than maximization and that it seeks stability rather than goals obviously runs contrary to the rational choice model. The view is strongly supported, however, by the observation that operating routines and the environmental conditions that produce them are not well understood, let alone devised, at the national level. It is further strengthened if one recognizes that national strategy has not greatly influenced the development of the channels providing the highly specific information that triggers operating routines. A decentralized bureaucracy dominated by service interests has let evolve a collection of information channels individually tailored to the narrow missions, specific environments, and unique procedures of relatively low-level actors. As the discussion of institutional laissez-faire showed, the development of a national military command system geared to central control was retarded as a consequence.

This is not to say there is no connection between choice and operating routines. Connections exist in some instances, and at times operational policy—for example, alert rates—is set at a high level. But even for those instances, the policy decisions usually include little specific operational guidance, leaving myriad details to be worked out by people and suborganizations not under the close supervision of central authorities. Some suborganization interprets the policy, generates the criteria for choice, performs the analysis, and adjusts procedures. If policymakers did influence the original pattern of operations, it was probably later transformed through adaptation to unforeseen or changing circumstances without the benefit of further review or guidance. In time, the original reasons for many operating routines are lost and new rationalizations are invented to explain them.

These propositions generally apply to emergency as well as peacetime operations. Although crises or wartime circumstances are especially apt to evoke the image of a central steersman taking personal charge of the diplomatic and military components of American policy, the steering wheel remains loosely connected to the rudder. During such tensions, the decision process is still diffuse and programmatic. It has to be. A central authority simply cannot be aware of all that is relevant. Even if channels could provide all the data needed to make decisions, no individual or small group could assimilate the information (such channels have not been well developed in any case). And if authorities could assimilate it, they could not attend to all the details of a military response. Conditional rules—do A if event one occurs, B if event two occurs—exist to prevent the overload of decisionmakers at all levels. Depending upon the information from the environment, rules alert the decisionmakers and the forces, trigger attack preparations, and coordinate nuclear strikes.

While the nature of the decision process does not change from situation to situation, rules salient during peacetime differ in important ways from those salient during national emergencies. Under normal peacetime circumstances, strategic forces and the supporting C^3I systems follow routines that maintain *negative control,* defined as the prevention of accidental or unauthorized launch of nuclear weapons.[36] Negative control, embodied in various rules and standard operating procedures, appears to be the dominant peacetime intent of nuclear organizations. Units function so as to minimize the risk of inadvertent war, which takes precedence over all other objectives.

Those other objectives can be grouped under the heading of *positive*

36. John D. Steinbruner, "Nuclear Decapitation," *Foreign Policy,* no. 45 (Winter 1981–82), p. 23.

control, defined as the authorization and coordination of attack preparations or actual strikes or both. In a diffuse and decentralized fashion, nuclear organizations begin to shift their priorities from negative to positive control as tensions mount during a crisis. Positive control would take priority in the event of war, particularly a Soviet first strike.

If the nature of the decision process is as programmatic and decentralized as the earlier characterization suggests, then both negative and positive control are largely epiphenomenal outcomes. Neither is simply a matter of organizational compliance with orders issued by a central authority but rather a coincidence of programmed behavior and national policy objectives. Control is achieved when diffuse organizational reactions accomplish aims that corrrespond to national purposes salient at the time.

Thus control during national emergencies depends less for its success on C³I networks that give central authorities access to large amounts of information and allow them to issue detailed operating instructions than it does on careful attention in peacetime to the self-organizing properties of large organizations: the conditional rules and the information channels needed to implement the rules. Subjecting the programmed repertory of organizations and the supporting information channels to intensive scrutiny and periodic modification is an attempt at preordination that complements and simplifies efforts by central authorities to keep national policy objectives and military operations aligned during crises or war. Specific instructions would not suffice. Central authorities cannot reasonably expect military organizations simply to carry out orders, however rational the orders may be. Organizations are not that pliant. Any attempt to assert positive or negative control in a way that requires major abrupt changes in operating procedures, a situation more likely to occur if operating routines escape attention in peacetime, would invite confusion and disorder. To disrupt established routine is to court either organizational paralysis or severe disjuncture between national objectives and military operations. As General Power, former commander in chief of SAC, once put it, "You cannot coordinate a plan after you have been told to go to war. It all has to be part of a well-thought-out, well-worked-out plan. And there is one basic law you must follow: Do not change it at the last minute."[37]

37. *Department of Defense Appropriations for 1961,* Hearings before a Subcommittee of the House Committee on Appropriations, 86 Cong. 2 sess. (GPO, 1960), pt. 7, p. 88.

The Limits of Organization

While it is important to recognize that programmed rules and not special instructions issued by central authorities primarily govern military operations, it is also important to realize that no one can confidently judge whether the rules ensure that military operations and national purposes will dovetail.

Preordination requires unusual exertion on the part of national policy officials. This means active civilian participation in decisions traditionally reserved for military planners, many of whom resist the involvement, regarding civilians as interlopers. Legend has it that when General Curtis LeMay was commander in chief of SAC, he alone knew the exact manner in which the nuclear forces under his command would fight.[38] The role of the national authority in positive control was basically confined to providing political authorization to unleash the forces. An authorization message would have been sent without detailed knowledge of the plan SAC would actually implement. Furthermore, SAC did not integrate its war plan with the plans of the other services until 1960, when Secretary of Defense Gates established (despite strong protests from one of the service chiefs) a joint strategic target planning staff under the direction of the SAC commander in chief. Before that there was no formal mechanism for coordinating long-range nuclear strike plans developed by SAC and the navy, much less a mechanism for including civilians in the planning process.[39]

Today, civilian access to the military's contingency plans is much freer. On occasion, national policy officials even participate in formulating preprogrammed options. Without exception, however, the detailed planning is delegated and delegated again. Timing, targeting, execution procedures (including procedures for authenticating messages), and measures devoted to negative control are revised by subordinates to create rule structures far more complex than the menu of options would suggest.

As a result, authorities, particularly national authorities, cannot fully comprehend many aspects of the nuclear policies and plans they inspire: the extent to which rule structure limits the kinds of responses that au-

38. David Alan Rosenberg, " 'A Smoking Radiating Ruin at the End of Two Hours': Documents on American Plans for Nuclear War with the Soviet Union, 1954–55," *International Security*, vol. 6 (Winter 1981/82), p. 25.

39. Alain C. Enthoven and K. Wayne Smith, *How Much Is Enough? Shaping the Defense Program, 1961–1969* (Harper and Row, 1971), pp. 3, 171.

thorities may call forth, the exact character of a programmed response, and the complexity of the organizational reactions triggered and what can go wrong during implementation. Authorities probably do not realize, for example, that even without damage to the command network, current organizational arrangements do not permit them significant personal control over the implementation of any given option. They could trigger implementation of an option, but they could not impose conditions on the firing of weapons assigned to that option. Suppose that authorities wanted to order that no weapons be fired until most commanders have acknowledged receipt of orders to fire. Or that no weapons will be fired until all commanders have copied the correct targeting instructions and aimed their weapons accordingly. Or that commanders who find themselves unable immediately to launch some of their weapons (those not deliberately withheld) will withhold those weapons until further notice. These conditions could not be imposed; no provisions exist to accommodate them. And an attempt by central decisionmakers to impose them in an ad hoc way would only invite confusion. These are minor conditions that pertain to the implementation of a prepackaged attack option. It is easy to imagine the confusion that would result from attempts to make major changes in operating procedures.

Yet lack of experience in nuclear crisis or wartime environments precludes assurance that major changes would be unnecessary. Whereas peacetime routines are at least susceptible to direct observation and appropriate modification, routines followed during war can only be simulated. In peacetime, adverse consequences caused by inappropriate routines often induce, albeit over an extended time, appropriate adjustments. But rules and technologies devoted to both positive and negative control during national emergencies have not profited from any such evolutionary learning process, nor could they profit from it during an emergency. The environment of major crisis or war changes much more rapidly than the peacetime environment. Even without damage to information channels, adaptation would have less chance of success.

Planners rely heavily on exercises to compensate for this lack of experiential learning. Insights from simulation and exercise data do often suggest appropriate changes in operating routines and physical C³I arrangements, but these insights are relevant to only a narrowly defined set of plausible situations. Even then, war games and exercises only partially illuminate the physical and procedural modifications needed to ensure positive and negative control. The learning process is completely artificial; modifications stem from dissatisfaction with the performance of units thrust into a world of make-believe. The lessons drawn are no less hard to validate than the representativeness of the fictional environment in which exercises are conducted.

Until the early 1980s, exercises were manifestly unrealistic. SAC exercises, for instance, were conducted with communications intact, as though outages would not occur or would not matter in the event of nuclear war. The Joint Chiefs of Staff now requires greater realism in exercises, though in the end all circumstances contrived for exercises are basically fictitious and may not even faintly resemble those encountered in actual mobilization or war. In the absence of experience and a solid empirical foundation, planners cannot be confident that nuclear organizations would operate according to appropriate decision procedures. No rational analysis, study, or exercise could justify high confidence.

This lack of experience and the limited capacity of highly structured organizations to adapt well to radically disturbed environments justifies several theses: the consequences of triggering rules cannot be fully anticipated, the repertory of preprogrammed responses will prove inappropriate, major changes in the repertory will be warranted, and major changes during crisis or wartime operations could not be made by either executive fiat or organizational adaptation. To the extent that these are valid theses, intense nuclear confrontation or war creates a significant risk that military operations will diverge from and may not accomplish national objectives. Breakdowns of positive control, negative control, or both would happen.

The historical record lends support to this general argument. Various accounts of the Cuban missile crisis of 1962, for instance, conclude that the navy's aggressive pursuit of its antisubmarine mission in the North Atlantic, though consistent with the general political construction that national officials set on the course of events, diverged from the formulated intention of policymakers. This bold campaign, undertaken as a normal operational measure in support of the blockade, reduced if not removed the nuclear threat posed by Soviet cruise missile submarines. Its success greatly bolstered U.S. defenses against nuclear attack and could have been a decisive factor in a nuclear war with the Soviet Union. But neutralizing this particular component of Soviet nuclear capability was never an explicit aim of policy officials. The navy's actions did seem to have followed the general political signals of policymakers, whose actions and pronouncements painted the gloomiest of prospects. The possibility of immediate nuclear war with the Soviet Union was hanging over the entire incident, and aggressive preparations seemed warranted and consistent with the tenor of the confrontation. Nevertheless, the navy's campaign not only escaped the attention of the president and his advisers until well into the crisis but also "constituted extremely strong strategic coercion and violated the spirit of the Executive Committee policy. It is not unreasonable to suppose that American ASW activity in the North Atlantic was in fact the strongest message perceived in Moscow in the course of the crisis, and if that is true, then the efforts to bring American policy under central direction must be said to have failed."[40] National authorities are increasingly moved to try to bring military operations under their direct supervision. During the Cuban missile crisis, political leaders tried to give specific instructions directly to local commanders of destroyers stationed along the quarantine line. Since then direct civilian supervision of crisis military operations has been attempted on numerous occasions, especially after the advent of communications satellites. The evacuations of Lebanon and Saigon, the tree-cutting operation along the Korean demilitarized zone, the *Mayaguez* rescue, and the abortive mission to rescue American hostages held in Tehran can be cited as examples. But remote control over these special operations was neither absolute nor generally successful (witness the delay in stopping bombing raids on Cambodia during *Mayaguez;* U.S. military forces conducted those raids more than thirty minutes after the president ordered them to cease following the release of the ship's crew).[41] These episodes are special cases that might not support generalization, but the record contains little evidence that military operations of the sort associated with U.S.-Soviet nuclear confrontation could be brought under the strict control of a central authority. Given the scale, diversity and geographic dispersion of the weapons systems, objectives, risks, and stakes involved, nuclear operations would appear even less tractable than *Mayaguez*-type operations.

The cases might be similar in at least one important respect: central direction runs contrary to military tradition. Direct civilian supervision of local operations bruises the sensibilities of uniformed professionals who respect the principles of hierarchy, decentralization, and conformity to

40. John D. Steinbruner, "An Assessment of Nuclear Crises," in Franklyn Griffiths and John C. Polanyi, eds. *The Dangers of Nuclear War* (University of Toronto Press, 1979), pp. 38–39.

41. John D. Steinbruner, "National Security and the Concept of Strategic Stability," *Journal of Conflict Resolution,* vol. 22 (September 1978), p. 424.

preestablished plan as virtues as well as necessities. This tension was in evidence during the Cuban missile crisis when political leaders communicated instructions directly to U.S. ship commanders. Graham T. Allison characterizes this encroachment as "unique in naval history and, indeed, unparalleled in modern relations between American political leaders and military organizations." He goes on to point out that establishing a direct command channel from the White House to local commanders, made possible by advances in the technology of communications, created "enormous pain and serious friction." Similarly, a stormy exchange took place when Robert McNamara demanded of Admiral Anderson, chief of naval operations, precise information on the navy's procedures for intercepting Soviet ships that might attempt to pass through the blockade.[42]

A wealth of anecdotal evidence suggests that what could be called institutional ethos is a source of tension and that it affects the interaction of national policy and military operations. One story tells of Defense Secretary Donald Rumsfeld monitoring, from the national military command center in the Pentagon, the 1976 evacuation of Americans from Lebanon. Some military officers are said to wince at the part of the story in which Rumsfeld maintains direct, instant voice contact with the boatswain's mate in charge of the landing craft that transported evacuees to a waiting navy ship.[43] Another story told by a former senior official in the Office of the Secretary of Defense concerns the navy's role in the evacuation of Saigon. The ranking navy officers near the scene transported themselves from ships in direct communication with Washington to those without that capability in order to gain local autonomy in directing the evacuation. This same official summed up the attitude of many navy officers toward a 1972 OSD directive (5100.30) removing the shore-based unified commanders from the chain of command for executing the strategic war plan: "they believe strategic communication runs to and stops at the shore." In other words, national authorities should provide only initial communication of nuclear authorization to unified commanders, and both the traditional chain of command and the operational autonomy of local ship commanders (in this case, missile submarine commanders) ought to be preserved.

The prevailing ethos is clearly at odds with the idea of central manage-

42. *Essence of Decision,* pp. 127, 128, 131–32.

43. Benjamin F. Schemmer, "Strategic C³: The Satellite Arena," *Armed Forces Journal International,* vol. 115 (February 1978), p. 18.

ment. It works to restrict direct communication between national officials and commanders on the scene, and it inhibits full disclosure of operations in progress. It also promotes conformity with preprogrammed operational measures in support of prearranged contingency plans, discourages national authorities from changing plans at the last minute, and encourages aggressive pursuit of established missions by military commanders. And it resists the imposition of more stringent safeguards against the accidental or unauthorized use of nuclear weapons by local commanders.

This assessment is not meant to insinuate that military commanders are overzealous, that they question the authority of their civilian superiors, or that anyone intentionally undermines national policy. Nor does the assessment imply that resistance to centralization necessarily detracts from either military effectiveness or the achievement of broader national policy objectives. To the contrary, a strong argument can be made that control depends heavily on decentralized implementation of existing plans in accordance with standard operating procedure. Improvisation on the part of central authorities invites massive disruption of established routine, especially during large-scale operations, and could increase rather than reduce the potential for discontinuity between national policy intentions and force behavior.[44]

If institutional ethos promotes decentralization of crisis or wartime operations, by the same token it opposes changes in C^3I that would enhance the ability of civilian authorities to control those operations. Thus the services and combat commanders avoid designing command systems to be optimally responsive to national authorities and instead design them to meet the narrower requirements of their own missions. The Office of the Secretary of Defense periodically struggles to balance these priorities without much success. As a later chapter notes, at least one senior OSD official concluded that this imbalance in command system development has been so extreme that even the most rudimentary form of positive control—the initial communication of presidential authorization to retaliate—might not be possible in the event of a Soviet first strike against the U.S. command system.

44. To the extent that effective improvisation is possible in a rapidly changing environment, it is probably best left to local commanders. Attempts at centralized improvisation perhaps only undermine the ability of local commanders to respond with the necessary speed and flexibility. An instructive case study and theoretical discussion is Dan Horowitz, "Flexible Responsiveness and Military Strategy: The Case of the Israeli Army," *Policy Sciences*, vol. 1 (Summer 1970), pp. 191–205.

Implications

The secondary applications of rational logic—proportionate retaliation and intrawar strategic bargaining—advanced as an answer to the paradox of assured destruction, appear to require drastic alteration of the existing structure of military organizations. The activities of these organizations, which range from C³I procurement to war planning to force operations, are not regulated by axioms of deterrence or by specific instructions from national policymakers. Attempts at developing a command structure that allows for central, flexible direction of strategic force operations will be frustrated. Military traditions that oppose centralization will create barriers. A decentralized budget process, affirmed by law, that assigns low priority to C³I modernization and even lower priority to programs designed to meet national command requirements will create obstacles. And military organizations, highly decentralized and heavily structured by low-order rules, operate according to fundamentally different principles of control.

Unusual efforts on the part of national policy officials would be required to bring nuclear operations into closer alignment with national purposes and strategy. The amount of control that central leaders could potentially exercise once hostilities begin depends in large part upon the degree of their involvement in contingency planning. With time in the missile age measured in minutes and hours, operation plans must be worked out in detail and in advance. To have a choice of striking or not striking certain targets, for example, the target list must at least be divided into preplanned option packages to which specific forces have already been assigned and readied. Provided such preparations have been made and information channels have been properly configured, national authorities could order the forces to release the entire arsenal in a comprehensive attack or to release portions of the arsenal. But programmed crisis and wartime operating procedures had better be understood and approved by central leaders before hostilities erupt because otherwise there will be little scope for review and ad hoc changes.

The degree of control that can be achieved also depends on the survivability of information channels associated with implementating a strategy or set of operating procedures. Whether national authorities are in or out of a particular programmed decision procedure, the destruction of channels that carry information to those who must carry out decisions would obviously impair their ability to perform. These channels just as obviously need protection from attack.

The services, however, have historically allocated too little funding to C³I protection. National policy officials would have to take extraordinary and unpopular steps to ensure that protection. They would probably have to strip the services of control over C³I resource allocations and transfer statutory control elsewhere.

There is no doubt that such a move would be necessary if we want to include national authorities in more decisions. But the greater the responsibility of central leaders to analyze information and instruct forces in what strategy to follow and the greater the complexity of national strategy, then the greater the need for developed survivable C³I networks that tie into the national command level. Once again, however, unusual effort would be required to effect such development. Past attempts at establishing the national military command system as the most important component of WWMCCS have not succeeded.

Central leaders are not inclined to devote the effort needed to make these difficult adjustments, and even if the adjustments were made, control would be far from assured. Significant decentralization of operating procedure and information channels cannot be avoided. Significant vulnerability of command centers and communications links cannot be eliminated. Pertinent details of nuclear operations will inevitably escape notice. The exact nature and degree of organizational constraints on executive decisionmaking cannot be fully determined. The consequences of triggering the diffuse organizational reactions associated with mobilization or attack cannot be precisely anticipated. In sum, an irreducible risk of discontinuity between national purpose and military operations will always exist.

The scope for such divergence is sufficiently large that the paradox of assured destruction has not been resolved in practice. Carefully calibrated retaliation and strategic bargaining plans provide more academic than operational answers. Any large-scale Soviet nuclear attack, even one strictly designed to inflict maximum damage on military forces, would cause sufficient damage to C³I networks to make war uncontrollable, regardless of calculations U.S. political leaders might make and irrespective of retaliatory options created for this very contingency. Soviet nuclear attack would trigger diffuse organizational reactions that, in conjunction with damage to C³I networks, almost guarantee the breakdown of positive and negative control and a quick departure from any preferred course of action.

Questions can also be raised about the ability of central leaders to manage crisis operations. Would diffuse organizational reactions to information from political leaders and the external environment produce results that coincide with the intentions of national policy officials? Many have come to believe that even without damage to the command system, positive control of crisis operations could break down. John D. Steinbruner, for example, concludes that "the most serious threat of war under current circumstances probably lies in the possibility that organizationally and technically complex military operations might override coherent policy decisions and produce a war that was not intended."[45]

Finally, the primary application of rational logic—deterrence based on the threat of assured destruction—is a matter of some doubt. Positive control in this context simply means that operating procedures geared to prompt nuclear retaliatory attacks on a massive scale would be triggered and successfully performed once assured destruction becomes the objective of national security. While we are reminded that it would not be rational to actually carry out a strategy of massive retaliation, the capacity to do so is considered to be the essence of nuclear deterrence.

With so much attention focused recently on secondary questions of intrawar nuclear deterrence and bargaining, one might suppose that all problems related to the elementary requirement of assured destruction have already been solved. We do indeed have some grounds for believing that arrangements for positive control are adequate and would allow massive retaliation. Senior defense officials assure us of this, just as they have repeatedly assured us since the missile age dawned. But whether the confidence they express has actually been warranted depends in part on command performance, and analysts of U.S. second-strike capabilities have usually skirted the issue. Historical assessment of U.S. deterrence strategy has been based almost entirely on calculations of the vulnerability of individual weapons deployments. The following chapters demonstrate that these calculations and the conclusions drawn from them appear erroneous or misleading.

45. "National Security and the Concept of Strategic Stability," p. 424.

CHAPTER FOUR

Command Performance
in the Mid-1960s

In 1960, General Thomas Power, commander of SAC, said, "If you are going to attack a nation, you have to attack its control centers." But to the student schooled in the theory of rational deterrence, preserving or destroying the opponent's command structure appears to be the most critical, difficult, and controversial of choices. Thomas Schelling, a leading developer of the theory, stated, "Here is a point where the distinction between the straightforward application of brute force to block enemy capabilities and the exploitation of potential violence to influence his behavior is a sharp one."[1] It is a distinction with a dilemma. On one hand, an attack on command structure seems inconsistent with the idea of exploiting nuclear force for political effect. The diplomacy of violence could not be practiced if decisionmakers on either side instructed their forces to follow a strategy that would leave the opponent's decisionmaking and bargaining apparatus fractured or that would severely impair his ability to maintain control over surviving forces. Nuclear diplomacy, the primary purpose of nuclear weapons, might well be defeated by such a strategy. On the other hand, a strategy based on destruction of politico-military control might be an effective deterrent threat and might also offer the most attractive solution to the problem of limiting damage from enemy attacks if deterrence fails. If the judgment is made that nuclear war probably cannot be avoided, then attacking the opponent's command structure, as General Power asserted, could be a plausible defensive act. The choice of strategy, then, depends on "whether the enemy's command

---

1. *Arms and Influence* (Yale University Press, 1966), p. 214.

structure is more vital to the efficient waging of war or the effective restraint and stoppage of war, and which of the two processes is more
important to us."[2]

Whether Soviet strategy is geared to destroying U.S. control centers
and communications channels is an open question. Soviet strategy may
have evolved much like its American counterpart, becoming increasingly
oriented to selective attacks with options to withhold forces aimed at
population and command centers. But Soviet strategists have historically
treated attacks on command structure with utmost seriousness. This is
evident in their extensive efforts to protect their own command structure
from nuclear attack[3] and in their doctrinal writings, which strongly suggest that in wartime they intend to exploit weaknesses in U.S. C³I. One
apparently representative Soviet author stated, "The targets of destruction will now include . . . in the first instance the economies of the bellig-
erents . . . the strategic offensive nuclear weapons . . . the system of
governmental and military control and the main communications centers."[4] Others go so far as to suggest that disruption of C³I networks could
lead to the defeat of the opponent.

Under conditions of a nuclear war, the system for controlling forces and weapons,
especially strategic weapons, acquires exceptionally great significance. A disruption of the control over a country and its troops in a theater of military operations
can seriously affect the course of events, and in difficult circumstances, can even
lead to defeat in a war. Thus, areas deserving special attention are the following:
knowing the coordinates of stationary operations control centers and the extent of
their ability to survive; the presence of mobile command posts and automatic
information processing centers; the communications lines' level of development
and, first of all, that of underground and underwater cable, radio-relay, ionospheric and tropospheric communication lines; field communication networks
and duplicate communication lines; communication centers and the extent of
their facilities, dispersion and vulnerability.[5]

Besides betraying a keen awareness of the potential decisiveness of
attacks against command structure, Soviet military literature reveals an

2. Ibid., pp. 212–13.

3. John D. Steinbruner, "Nuclear Decapitation," *Foreign Policy,* no. 45 (Winter
1981–82), p. 19; and Desmond Ball, "Can Nuclear War Be Controlled?" *Adelphi Papers* 169
(London: International Institute for Strategic Studies, 1981), pp. 44–45.

4. V. D. Sokolovskiy, *Soviet Military Strategy,* Harriet Fast Scott, trans. and ed. (Crane,
Russak, 1975), p. 242.

5. Quoted in Joseph Douglass, Jr., and Amoretta Hoeber, *Soviet Strategy for Nuclear
War* (Stanford: Hoover Institution Press, 1979), p. 78.

appreciation of the significance of rather esoteric nuclear effects such as atmospheric ionization. One author has been quoted as saying that "a nuclear explosion in the 50 [megaton] range of force at an altitude of 80 km can lead to a complete loss of ordinary ionospheric radio communications over an area radius of 4,000 km."[6] The Soviets also understand the importance of electromagnetic pulse: "a considerable threat to the intercontinental ballistic missiles are powerful nuclear explosions set off at great altitudes, because the impulses of electromagnetic energy created by such explosions can put out of commission not only the on-board missile equipment, but also the ground electronic equipment of the launch complexes."[7]

A widening audience of U.S. analysts and senior policy officials has lately recognized the apparent Soviet determination to suppress the U.S. command structure in wartime. Fritz W. Ermarth characterizes Soviet strategy as placing "a high premium on seizing the initiative and imposing the maximum disruptive effects on the enemy's forces *and* war plans. By going first, and especially disrupting command and control, the highest likelihood of limiting damage and coming out of the war with intact forces and a surviving nation is achieved, virtually independent of the force balance."[8]

Many senior U.S. military and civilian officials share this view of Soviet strategy. Gerald Dinneen, former assistant secretary of defense for C³I, said the Soviets "believe that by neutralizing part of our command, control, and communications by electronic countermeasures and striking part by direct firepower, they will disrupt our control effectiveness. . . . That this doctrine is being implemented is demonstrated . . . almost daily."[9] General Alton D. Slay, then commander of the Air Force Systems Command, noted, "the Soviets, as a matter of doctrine, treat destruction or disruption of our C3 systems as an integral part of their force planning and execution. . . . The range of exploitation is wide, ranging from physical destruction to electronic disruption and deception. In other words, C3 systems are targets just like aircraft, airfields, and supply cen-

6. Ibid.

7. Ibid., pp. 49–50.

8. "Contrasts in American and Soviet Strategic Thought," *International Security,* vol. 3 (Fall 1978), p. 152.

9. *Department of Defense Appropriations for 1978,* Hearings before the House Committee on Appropriations, 95 Cong. 1 sess. (GPO, 1977), pt. 3, p. 639.

ters."[10] In 1978, Daniel J. Murphy, deputy under secretary of defense for policy, added, "At the moment it is possible that he does think . . . he could attack our Minuteman forces . . . take out our NCA . . . destroy a major part of our population and industry, and suffer no retaliation in turn because he had knocked out our communications."[11]

Former Defense Secretary Harold Brown also stressed in a speech that Soviet strategic forces were aimed at U.S. command and warning elements.[12] In all likelihood, he said, these elements had always been targeted. For instance, in the past the Soviets "almost surely targeted" 200 SS-9 ICBMs against 100 underground launch centers that directly control the U.S. Minuteman force.[13] If so, it suggests that Soviet planners believed that, at least as far as this particular force was concerned, the control system rather than the individual missile emplacements constituted the target of greatest opportunity. Might it not also suggest that Soviet planners determined C³I was America's primary nuclear vulnerability and concluded that attacks on it would have a far better chance of parrying retaliation than would attacks on the individual weapons themselves?

If damage limitation has been set forth as the main objective of the Soviet nuclear war plan, if operational strategy has been that an attack on C³I networks serves this purpose better than an attack designed to inflict maximum damage on individual force deployments, and if C³I networks have in fact constituted the weakest component of the U.S. strategic forces, then popular accounts of trends in U.S.-Soviet strategic capabilities distort historical realities. Inasmuch as these accounts usually either rest explicitly on standard calculations of weapons vulnerability or emphasize the same set of variables that such calculations include, they may overstate and perhaps greatly exaggerate the amount of damage that the United States could have inflicted since the 1960s on an aggressor.

A reconsideration of strategic history begins in this chapter. To provide context and a basis for comparing the vulnerability of forces and C³I,

10. *Department of Defense Authorization for Appropriations for Fiscal Year 1979*, Hearings before the Senate Committee on Armed Services, 95 Cong. 2 sess. (GPO, 1978), pt. 5, pp. 3799–800.

11. *Department of Defense Authorization for Appropriations for Fiscal Year 1979*, Senate hearings, pt. 9, p. 6439.

12. "Our National Security Position," speech delivered before the Council on Foreign Affairs, September 13, 1978, *Vital Speeches*, vol. 45 (October 15, 1978), p. 27.

13. Richard Burt, "Brown Says Soviets Long Sought Way to Knock Out U.S. Missiles," *New York Times*, May 31, 1979.

assessments based on enumeration that exclude measures of command performance are woven into the discussion. However, in most areas, strict comparisons cannot be made for want of a common unit of measurement; unlike individual weapons, C³I networks generally do not lend themselves to quantitative assessment. But weaknesses and vulnerabilities can be sufficiently appreciated that meaningful comparisons with force structure vulnerabilities are not precluded; they are simply more difficult and qualitative.

The Golden Age Revisited

Although it was generally believed that the United States possessed overwhelming nuclear superiority in the mid-1960s, senior U.S. defense officials realized as early as 1961 that vital segments of the command network lacked adequate protection from missile attack. Of the problems that were identified shortly after Robert S. McNamara became secretary of defense in 1961,

perhaps the most critical vulnerability . . . lay in the U.S. high-level command structure, which was located in a comparatively small number of points on or near Strategic Air Command (SAC) bases or major cities, all of which were themselves prime targets for enemy attack. Most of the facilities were soft, and most of the communications links were vulnerable. A well-designed Soviet attack . . . would have deprived our forces of their authorized commands to proceed to targets.[14]

In debunking the mythical missile gap that had earlier projected Soviet missile superiority, government officials reaffirmed the overwhelming superiority of the United States at the end of 1961 but neglected to point out that the vulnerability of U.S. command centers remained a severe problem.

At McNamara's behest, measures designed to reduce this vulnerability were briskly implemented.

Several alternative national command centers were established, including some maintained continuously in the air. New procedures, equipment, and safeguards were introduced to make certain that only authorized national authorities could release nuclear weapons. Steps were taken to improve the survivability and reliability of communications systems, and all such systems were merged into a new National Military Command System.[15]

14. Alain C. Enthoven and K. Wayne Smith, *How Much Is Enough? Shaping the Defense Program 1961–1969* (Harper and Row, 1971), pp. 166–67.

15. Ibid., p. 169.

Although McNamara's program has been described as extensive, this overstates its actual scope. The revolutionary implications of the nuclear missile age for negative and positive control had scarcely been thought out. Testifying before Congress in 1963, by which time the main steps in his initiatives had been taken, McNamara acknowledged that there was still substantial vulnerability in the U.S. command and control system. He mentioned in particular the vulnerability of the Strategic Air Command and national-level communications systems.[16] He did not cite, but surely anticipated, serious problems with missile submarine communications.

In that same appearance, McNamara reported that the Defense Department had hardly begun to study the command and control system, particularly the communications system. The United States had already deployed a large intercontinental missile force. Several hundred land-based missiles were operational, and several hundred more were under construction. Polaris missile submarines had been introduced in November 1960. By 1963, operational submarine launchers numbered about 200 and their number would double by 1965. If the management of nuclear forces was as poorly understood as McNamara suggested, then it seems fair to say that the rapid and large-scale deployment of raw nuclear power held the highest priority during the early 1960s. The implications of the nuclear buildup for command and control were only slowly dawning.

Minuteman Vulnerability

Initial deployments of Soviet ICBMs did not put land-based Minuteman missiles at risk. According to standard calculations that estimate damage from nuclear blast, the strategic rocket force of the Soviet Union, even if fully committed, could have destroyed only a small fraction of the Minuteman force. At least two conditions deemed necessary for comprehensive damage to the force were absent: approximate numerical parity, permitting the Soviet Union to assign at least one weapon to each target, and pinpoint missile accuracy. The absence of these conditions was apparently responsible for repeated assurances by U.S. officials that the Minuteman force was invulnerable.

As late as 1966 a first strike involving the entire Soviet land missile

16. *Department of Defense Appropriations for 1964,* Hearings before a Subcommittee of the House Committee on Appropriations, 88 Cong. 1 sess. (GPO, 1963), pt. 1, p. 407.

Table 4-1. *U.S. and Soviet Land Missile Characteristics, 1966*

Country	Missiles deployed	Type	Yield (megatons)	Accuracy[a] (nautical miles)	Hardness[b] (psi)	Reliability[c] (percent)
United States	54	Titan II	5	0.7	300	75
	800	Minuteman I	1	0.7	300	75
	80	Minuteman II	1	0.3	300	75
Soviet Union	150	SS-7	5	1.5	5	75
	70	SS-8	5	1.5	100	75
	110	SS-9	25	0.7	100–300	75
	10	SS-11	1	1.0	300	75

a. Accuracy is measured by CEP (circular error probable), the median miss distance in nautical miles; 50 percent of the missiles are expected to fall within a circle whose radius is the CEP, and 50 percent are expected to fall outside.

b. Hardness is the amount of overpressure in pounds per square inch (psi) that a missile silo can withstand.

c. Reliability is the product of the individual probabilities that the missile will not malfunction during each stage of countdown, launch, and flight.

force would have destroyed only about 10 percent of the numerically superior American force.[17] Table 4-1 gives the assumptions that underlie this estimate, which is not very sensitive to changes in the assumptions. For example, if under the principle of conservative planning the reliability of Soviet missiles is raised from 75 percent to 90 percent, the expected damage increases from 10 percent to 12 percent of the U.S. force. Similarly, more conservative assumptions about Soviet missile accuracy only marginally change the results. Under all plausible conditions, a Soviet attack aimed at American missile silos would have been ineffective and self-disarming. Thus, to the extent that American confidence in its land-missile deterrent rested on standard calculations of force structure vulnerability, high confidence was warranted.

Such confidence however, might have been questioned because one dimension of the problem was excluded by standard calculations. Before conclusions about the retaliatory capability of the Minuteman force in 1966 can be stated, one must consider the performance of the manned underground facilities that maintained remote launch control over the

17. According to my calculations, the theoretical kill probability of an SS-7 or SS-8 missile was 10 percent. Given the availability of 220 of these missiles, the Soviet Union could have expected to destroy 22 American silos in a first-strike attack in 1966. The SS-9 missile force with a kill probability of 64 percent and the SS-11 missile force with a kill probability of 8 percent could have attacked 120 missile silos and destroyed 71 of them. Thus Soviet land missiles threatened only 93 of 934 U.S. silos.

missiles.[18] An interesting comparison emerges between the results calculated for an attack aimed at these launch control centers and an attack aimed at the silos.

The key physical aspects of this particular problem concern the number of attacking Soviet missiles in 1966, their ability to disable individual launch control centers, and the amount of redundancy existing in the Minuteman launch control system. The Soviet ICBM force, though too small to attack many silos, was large enough to have aimed at least one high-yield SS-9 missile at each of the eighty-eight operational LCCs.[19] The estimated yield and accuracy of SS-9 missiles were sufficient to generate powerful blast overpressure near the centers, threatening destruction of most. The probability of LCC survival depended on hardness, which may have been as low as 250 pounds per square inch (psi) of blast overpressure. If that were the case, a control center would have had only an 11 percent chance of surviving an attack by an SS-9 missile with perfect reliability.[20]

The most severe vulnerability problem was that the communications linking the launch control centers to higher authority were far more susceptible to damage from nuclear weapons effects than was the LCC structure itself. SAC's Primary Alerting System, the main medium of strategic communications, employed a voice link akin to an ordinary telephone that was vulnerable to modest overpressure (10–150 psi for the various PAS components) despite its subsurface deployment. The SAC Automated Command and Control System (SACCS), a teletype connection, depended on surface land lines vulnerable to overpressure of about 5 psi. Backup channels consisted of radio systems, only one of which was designed to withstand nuclear attack. This system, however, featured underground pop-up antennas intended to receive high frequency radio transmissions, and the antennas were not heavily protected. Once deployed, their vulnerability to blast effects would have been acute. Even in their

18. At least three miles separates unstaffed missile silos from staffed launch control centers. Hardened underground cables, and in some instances radio links, connect the centers to the silos.

19. Under the Minuteman program, 10 missile silos were deployed for every launch center; 1,000 silos and 100 centers were eventually constructed.

20. The estimated probability of LCC survival against nuclear blast effects was approximately 15, 20, 24, 29, and 33 percent for a one-on-one attack by missiles with corresponding reliabilities of 95, 90, 85, 80, and 75 percent. Some estimates of LCC hardness range as high as 1,000 psi, however, in which case a launch center had at least a fifty-fifty chance of survival.

underground sheaths, they were not expected to withstand overpressures exceeding 50 psi. All the communications equipment was also vulnerable to fields of electric and magnetic energy that would have been generated by SS-9 surface detonations.

The launch of Minuteman forces required the active participation of LCCs. Backup centers provided considerable though limited launch redundancy. Not every center was interconnected with every missile in the force. Instead, the forces were organized into squadrons of fifty silos and five LCCs.[21] The squadrons were independent of each other; it was physically impossible for launch centers in one squadron to fire missiles belonging to another. However, within a given squadron, arrangements were such that any two functioning centers could fire all fifty missiles. A single center could also fire them, but the countdown to lift-off would have been extended by half an hour or perhaps longer. To avoid this delay, two centers had to perform the launch procedures.

The destruction of all five LCCs within a squadron would have removed all launch capability for that unit. Calculations of the expected damage to LCCs can thus be converted to an estimate of the unusable portion of the Minuteman force following the initial Soviet strike: fifty fewer missiles for every squadron deprived of launch control. Estimates of the unusable portion of the Minuteman force do not tell the whole story, however. Partial damage to a squadron would also have impaired performance. Apart from launch delays caused by destruction of four LCCs, there are conditions that could have caused problems of intrasquadron coordination among two or more surviving centers, and the attendant lowering of unit performance could have been serious. As chapter 3 argued, the consequences of following preprogrammed routines cannot be fully anticipated, and this general proposition is borne out when one attempts to predict the results of LCC operations under conditions of partial damage. Although launch control operators are instructed to follow well-defined procedures and may do so to the letter, remarkably little

21. Basic LCC configuration and operations have not changed much since their initial deployment. For recent descriptions that would be valid for the mid-1960s except for discussions of airborne launch control (which was not operational in 1966), see *Department of Defense Authorization for Appropriations for Fiscal Year 1979*, Senate Hearings, pt. 9, pp. 6465–67; *Hearings on Military Posture and H.R. 10929* before the House Committee on Armed Services, 95 Cong. 2 sess. (GPO, 1978), pt. 3, bk. 1, p. 342; and *Fiscal Year 1978 Authorization for Military Procurement, Research and Development, and Active Duty, Selected Reserve, and Civilian Personnel Strengths*, Hearings before the Senate Committee on Armed Services, 95 Cong. 1 sess. (GPO, 1977), pt. 10, pp. 6845–47.

is known about the results the process can generate under various conditions. But aided by a computer program that models the squadron procedures, it has been possible to simulate at least some of the unfolding interactions that appear to have adverse effects on performance.[22]

Before describing illustrative interactions and their consequences, I will summarize calculations of the unusable portion of the Minuteman force. The immobilization of entire squadrons is estimated on the basis of expected damage from blast overpressure and electromagnetic pulse. Because degradations resulting from problems of intrasquadron coordination are excluded from the calculations, the results should be interpreted as the minimum expected damage from a Soviet attack dedicated solely to the destruction of Minuteman LCCs. For sample calculations and details of resulting assessments see appendix B.

Damage from blast overpressure depends on assumptions about target hardness, Soviet missile accuracy and reliability, and Soviet attack strategy. But in practically every case the estimated damage from blast effects alone exceeds that which an all-out Soviet attack on missile silos inflicts. In most cases the difference is significant (see appendix tables B-1 to B-9).

Contrary to then-prevailing opinion, the size and accuracy of the Soviet missile force did not preclude a major threat to Minuteman. If these two are taken to be the only pertinent parameters, then in 1966 an SS-9 missile attack aimed at launch centers rather than individual silos might have virtually neutralized the Minuteman force.

There are of course other relevant parameters that must be taken into account. Missile reliability and reprogramming capabilities, for example, are shown in table B-1 to be important determinants of the effectiveness of a Soviet attack on LCCs. Closer examination of the Soviet missile force would probably conclude that the capability for extensive reprogramming was lacking in 1966 and that SS-9 missile reliability was far from perfect. Nevertheless, cautious planning assumptions would probably credit the SS-9 with an overall reliability of 80 to 85 percent, in which case a significant risk (≥ 10 percent) existed that one-half to two-thirds of the Min-

22. The Brookings model of the operation of a Minuteman II squadron developed by Paul Morawski and me incorporated complex rules that embodied negative and positive control procedures governing the operation of the missiles. For discussions of the model and the results it produced, see Paul Morawski, "A Computer Simulation of Launch Procedures for a Squadron of Minuteman II ICBMs," *Simulation* (July 1983), pp. 16–24; and John D. Steinbruner, "Launch under Attack," *Scientific American,* vol. 250 (January 1984), pp. 37–47.

uteman force would have been incapacitated even without any repro-gramming of the attacking forces. (According to standard calculations, a comparable threat based on attacks against silos did not develop until recently.) Presumably, a risk-averse American planner would also have found cause for worry if missile reliability were much lower but repro-gramming capabilities could not be ruled out. Even if reliability were only 70 percent, a highly significant risk (≥ 20 percent) existed that reprogram-ming the attack would have resulted in the loss of launch control over three-fifths to three-quarters of the Minuteman force.

The reasoning behind these estimates is that the Minuteman force was at least as vulnerable as the LCCs that controlled it, and the centers were at least as vulnerable as the communications that linked them to higher authority. For table B-1 the destruction of that link at a given LCC was assumed to occur if blast overpressure exceeded 50 psi, the estimated tolerance of the hardest communications system. Tables B-2 and B-3 show the results when this threshold is raised to 100 and 150 psi, respec-tively.

Structural damage rendering LCCs (not just communications) inoper-able is associated with blast overpressures of 250 to 1,000 psi. A strategy designed to destroy the LCC structures themselves while still attempting to destroy the maximum number of squadrons would have forced Soviet planners to allocate at least ten missiles per squadron (at least two for each center). Calculations summarized in tables B-4 to B-9 (except for B-6) assume such a strategy, which, owing to limited Soviet SS-9 re-sources, precludes attacks on many squadrons in order to double up on others. The results assume no reprogramming.

The result of these computations is that a Soviet attack using nuclear blast effects against a very restricted part of the U.S. nuclear command system offered, at least on paper, a good chance of disabling the bulk of the Minuteman force, and the expected damage exceeded by a wide mar-gin the damage that could have been expected from an attack on missile silos, at one-third the number of Soviet missiles expended. Although in most of the cases considered the odds against disarming the Minuteman force by such means were overwhelming, the Soviet SS-9 force could have substantially reduced U.S. land missile strength, and there was an outside chance that the damage would have been very great indeed.

The standard analytic conclusion that Minuteman was an invulnerable force also completely discounted possible damage from a nuclear weapons effect known as electromagnetic pulse.[23] Originating with the interaction of released gamma rays and air, EMP is a brief but intense energy wave that can induce tremendous voltage and current surges in cables, antennas, power and telephone lines, buildings, and aircraft. These collectors can then deliver the power surge to electronic components, causing temporary or permanent damage to such systems (see appendix C for further information).

After a high-yield nuclear explosion above the earth's atmosphere, the gamma rays released would travel long distances before colliding with air. As a result, the pulse would cover a large area of the earth. A single high-yield explosion sixty miles above the United States would blanket all missile silos and LCCs located within the six operational Minuteman fields with a pulse of 20,000 to 50,000 volts per meter (figure 4-1). For ground or near-surface bursts, which electrify both the air and the ground, the pulse would be at least an order of magnitude greater than the peak pulse observed at the surface from a high-altitude explosion,[24] but its peak strength would have a radius of only five miles. Pulse strength dissipates rapidly with increasing distance from the burst point.

Given Soviet missile accuracy in 1966, Minuteman LCCs (and some nearby silos) would have been exposed to strong electromagnetic fields. But each SS-9 explosion would not necessarily have exposed a launch control center to high blast overpressure. Missiles falling well within seven-tenths of a mile from their targets would have subjected the centers to extreme overpressure, but those falling, say, two miles from their targets would not have. Blast overpressure and electromagnetic pulse are thus separate and independent threats to the LCCs. Bursts near the surface generate both phenomena, either of which might damage the target. Compounding the problem, any exoatmospheric explosions could have blanketed the entire area in which centers and silos were deployed.

Vulnerability to EMP cannot be measured precisely, but it appears to have been appreciable in 1966. Regarding missiles and their support equipment inside their silos, Defense Department testimony reveals that "in the early 1970s, we began an extensive EMP assessment of Minuteman silos to determine their hardness to high altitude and ground burst EMP. We found that, although there was some EMP hardness inherent in

23. For further references and discussion of EMP, see appendix C; see also Samuel Glasstone and Philip J. Dolan, eds., *The Effects of Nuclear Weapons*, 3d ed. (Department of Defense and Department of Energy, 1977), chapter 11, pp. 514–40.

24. See Glasstone and Dolan, *The Effects of Nuclear Weapons*, pp. 517–19.

Figure 4-1. *Area of Exposure to Electromagnetic Pulse*

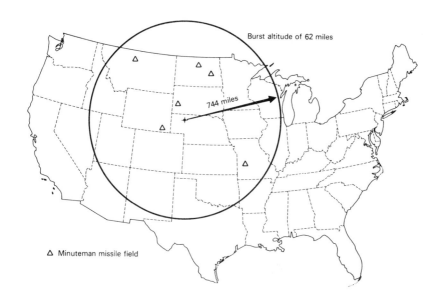

existing Minuteman silos, additional EMP hardening was required to provide greater assurance that Minuteman silos were not vulnerable to EMP."[25]

Launch control centers also appeared vulnerable. Because each LCC is a large, distributed, and redundant electrical system with cables, transmission lines, and antennas to collect the energy from electromagnetic fields, voltage and current surges could have entered along many paths. And in 1966 the LCCs lacked any special protection against EMP. Disabling a single critical element—the main computer or the communications receivers—could also have rendered an LCC inoperable, even though other critical components suffered no damage. Finally, theoretical and experimental studies of the vulnerability of electrical systems similar to those found at launch centers suggest that they were prone to damage or serious disruption from a typical high-intensity pulse. High-frequency antennas, for example, can "collect many thousands of amperes and ex-

25. *Department of Defense Authorization for Appropriations for Fiscal Year 1979,* Senate hearings, pt. 9, p. 6538.

hibit voltages well in excess of their normal voltages."[26] Another study determined that the surges induced in antennas and transmission lines could exceed 1 million volts and 10,000 amperes.[27] The values suggest the magnitude of the problem for communications. Appendix C analyzes the vulnerability of computers at launch control centers.

The method used in appendix B to calculate SS-9 damage to the Minuteman force can accommodate probabilistic representations of EMP threat. Various levels of threat, ranging from 0 to 90 percent probability that a single pulse would disable an LCC exposed to it, were combined with expected blast damage to estimate the compound damage to the Minuteman force from an SS-9 attack in 1966. The results in appendix C indicate that unless the LCCs were not very susceptible to damage from EMP effects, a Soviet attack in 1966 offered a good chance of reducing the effective retaliatory capacity of American land missiles to low levels. They do not establish the actual vulnerability of exposed LCCs, but they raise that as an important question. It is a hard question, much more so than the question of vulnerability to blast effects. But the very fact that damage from electromagnetic pulse cannot be assessed with analytical precision or high confidence is a story unto itself. It casts fundamental doubt on the standard approach to analysis of strategic vulnerability.

Many problems of both a technical and organizational nature are not reflected in these assessments of LCC damage from blast or EMP. Technical problems that probably would have been encountered include, in particular, severe degradation of communications reception at surviving centers. Restoring communications would have been difficult and slow in the event that telephone and other unprotected communications systems broke down under attack (a virtual certainty).

Erecting an antenna to receive high frequency transmissions would have been attempted with fingers crossed (an explosive charge wired to LCC controls was supposed to propel the antenna out of its underground sheath into position). If the antenna were successfully deployed, the launch center would once again become dependent upon exposed and easily destroyed equipment. Furthermore, while high frequency radio

26. *DNA EMP Awareness Course Notes* (Chicago: I.I.T. Research Institute, September 1973), DNA 2772T, p. 263. The report notes that "EMP energy collection tends to be maximized within the HF band."

27. J. H. Marable, R. Barnes, and D. B. Nelson, "Power System EMP Protection," ORNL–4958 (Oak Ridge National Laboratory, May 1975), p. 2.

normally confers the benefits of long-distance communications, the adverse effects of nuclear explosions on wave propagation are pronounced at this wavelength. A nuclear burst could produce sufficient atmospheric ionization to cause signal blackout, and with some direct effort—for instance, a high-altitude detonation—"blackout may persist for many hours over regions thousands of miles in diameter."[28] The Defense Nuclear Agency reported to Congress in 1976 that it had restudied the data from atmospheric nuclear tests conducted in 1962 and had "reconfirmed that high frequency band radio is grossly degraded in a nuclear environment."[29] While it is uncertain whether nuclear explosions would have totally blacked out the frequency range within which the only semisurvivable means of receiving instructions from higher authority operated in 1966, disruption of high frequency radio reception at surviving launch control centers was virtually certain to be severe.

Other adverse effects on squadron performance could have resulted from interactions among human, technical, and procedural factors. Suppose that a Minuteman squadron after a Soviet attack had three LCCs destroyed, one damaged, and one undamaged. An undamaged LCC is defined as one that remains internally functional and that maintains normal control over the squadron's fifty missiles and normal contact with higher authorities. A damaged LCC is defined as one that remains interconnected by underground cable to the squadron's missiles but that lacks a communication link to both higher authority and the undamaged LCC in its squadron.

Under these circumstances, established operating procedures would have prevented retaliation, even though the silos had escaped damage altogether and the squadron had a normally functioning LCC with a line of communications to higher authority. The inability to launch missiles would have been caused by procedures that governed actions by the damaged isolated LCC. This center and the undamaged center would have worked at cross-purposes. Upon receipt of valid war commands from higher authority, the undamaged center would have sent commands to arm, target, and fire to all fifty missiles in the squadron. But the damaged center, though it could not receive emergency action messages from

28. Glasstone and Dolan, *The Effects of Nuclear Weapons*, p. 485.

29. *Fiscal Year 1977 Authorization for Military Procurement, Research and Development and Active Duty, Selected Reserve and Civilian Personnel Strengths,* hearings before the Senate Committee on Armed Services, 94 Cong. 2 sess. (GPO, 1976), pt. 6, p. 3906.

higher authority, would not have remained passive while its companion initiated the launch sequence. It would have canceled the arm, target, and fire commands. Because it would have been able to monitor squadron missile status, the damaged center would have detected an apparent attempt to fire without authorization. It could have, and if it adhered to preestablished safeguard procedures would have, successfully prevented the countdown.[30]

In the above example, it is assumed that the undamaged launch center would have validated the execution message and initiated the launch sequence. But the decision to treat the message as authentic normally required confirmation from another squadron LCC, and in the absence of such information, the undamaged center would not necessarily have exercised its conditional grant of authority to initiate the launch sequence on its own. To have done so, it must have satisfied itself that the message was apparently authentic and then exhausted every possible means of obtaining confirmation from an outside source. At what point, if ever, would the LCC have decided that it had availed itself of every possible means of obtaining confirmation, that the effort was futile, and that the proper course of action was to launch the squadron's weapons?

The rules of authentication were (and doubtless still are) ambiguous enough that the final decision could have gone either way. It is reasonable to guess that under many imaginable circumstances an LCC would have never abandoned the effort to make outside contact, in which case there would not have been any arm, target, or launch commands for the other surviving but isolated center to cancel. Thus if the isolated LCC had been destroyed too, removing the capability of preventing a successful launch by the sole surviving LCC, missiles might not have been dispatched even despite the receipt of an authentic execution message by the survivor. It is further conceivable that under established procedure no missiles would have been launched even if all five LCCs had survived attack and all had received an apparently authentic execution message but each had been isolated from the others and persistently sought outside confirmation to no avail.

Positive control could have also been impaired by the destruction of mechanisms that help correct errors committed during the launch sequence. Intrasquadron computer and voice communication links provided the primary means of error correction, and if they were damaged,

30. *Fiscal Year 1978 Authorization for Military Procurement, Research and Development,* Senate hearings, pt. 10, p. 6845 and passim.

the chances of recovering from mistakes in time to avoid, for example, execution of the wrong attack plan or execution of the right plan at the wrong time would have been diminished.[31]

Outcomes like these might not be foreseen in advance of actual conflict, but they would come as no great surprise to analysts who view strategic organizations as operating in accordance with a programmatic decision process that has benefited little from experience. Although standard models of strategic conflict exclude both operational detail and human error in control systems, such factors do exist and their effects on performance can be significant.

The ability of the Soviet Union to impair performance would have depended on the inherent tension between two priorities that determined the behavior of Minuteman squadrons. Much of the established procedure within the squadron (and any other strategic unit) was devoted to negative control and much to positive control. Launch control vulnerability intensified the trade-off between them. In this instance, procedures devoted to negative control were predominant, and the interaction resulted in failure to execute an authorized launch. Positive control broke down.

Our hypothetical cases can be modified to illustrate the degradation of negative control. Suppose that a sole surviving LCC had received an invalid execution message, but that it could not determine validity unless it could talk to an external unit. If it failed to make contact yet proceeded to launch squadron missiles as was allowed by established procedure, then negative control would have broken down.

A complete, unmitigated breakdown of negative control would have occurred if LCCs had launched forces on their own accord, without receiving an execution message at all. In that event the destruction of all launch center communications links to higher authority would not have negated squadron retaliation (as the previous calculations assumed). The physical ability to launch the squadron's missiles would have existed in 1966 as long as at least one LCC survived the attack. The possibility that surviving centers would have engaged in unauthorized operations cannot be categorically ruled out.

Negative control is clearly a relevant criterion for assessing the performance of strategic organizations, but it is also a complicating factor.

31. A specific example would be dialing the wrong attack option into the LCC computer for transmission to silos. See ibid., p. 6846 and passim.

For current purposes, consider that positive and negative control are embodied in rules and procedures that determine the behavior of strategic units, that the two priorities are intertwined, that an unresolved trade-off exists between them, and that command system vulnerability intensifies this fundamental tension.

Further degradation of overall command performance would have been incurred in both positive and negative control in the event Soviet forces had attacked other parts of the command structure. Primary targets may have included national command centers, high-level military headquarters, early warning sensors and assessment centers, and the communications channels by means of which execution messages would have been disseminated to the bomber and submarine forces as well as to Minuteman LCCs. These C³I elements constituted a relatively small set of potential targets, and none were more vulnerable than those used to manage missile submarine operations in 1966.

Missile Submarine Vulnerability

In 1966 the Soviet Union had no proven, effective ability to detect, locate, or attack U.S. missile submarines deployed at sea. But this nuclear weapons system, the least vulnerable to enemy attack, was at the same time the least manageable. Strong evidence indicates that with some concentrated effort the Soviets could have detached the submarine fleet from external command channels and that the force would have remained isolated.

Organizational arrangements as well as physical configuration created this vulnerable state. The chain of command for executing the strategic war plan ran from the national command authorities to the unified and specified commanders, and then to the executing missile submarines (and bomber and land missile forces under the jurisdiction of the SAC commander in chief, the specified commander). This arrangement meant that, for instance, national leaders would call the commander in chief Pacific, who would then pass the order to the forces.[32] But this also implies that

32. *Department of Defense Appropriations for 1977,* Hearings before a Subcommittee of the House Committee on Appropriations, 94 Cong. 2 sess. (GPO, 1976), pt. 6, p. 47. Statement by Lieutenant General Lee M. Paschal, director, DCA. Admiral Burke, questioned as to where Polaris submarines would get their firing orders in the event of general nuclear war, testified in 1961 that "any submarine at sea would get them from the unified commander." See *Military Posture Briefings,* Hearings before the House Committee on Armed Services, 87 Cong. 1 sess. (GPO, 1961), p. 967.

successful attacks on CINCPAC and CINCLANT (commander in chief Atlantic) would have removed a vital link in the command hierarchy and isolated Pacific- and Atlantic-based missile submarines under these respective unified commands.

The primary command centers of the unified commanders were fixed ground-based facilities in Honolulu and Norfolk. They could not have withstood attacks directed against them. Located nearby were fixed emergency alternate command centers that were either unhardened or only partially protected. One of the best protected command posts, CINCPAC's alternate facility in the Kunia tunnel, probably was vulnerable in a practical sense to direct attack.

This vulnerability was partially mitigated by the deployment of an EC-135A airborne command post to satisfy a CINCPAC requirement established in 1965.[33] The aircraft was maintained on ground alert and would be launched upon receipt of tactical attack early warning or earlier if circumstances warranted. Its weaknesses included lack of protection against EMP, dependence on an unreliable tactical early warning network for prelaunch survival, and limited range and endurance. The EC-135A aircraft also possessed extremely limited communications capabilities. It probably could not have established direct contact with either alert missile submarines or higher authorities based in the continental United States.

The main communications channels connecting national authorities with missile submarines employed vulnerable land lines, undersea cables, and fixed coastal radio stations. Emergency action messages sent from the national command authority would have been routed via land line to CINCLANT and via land line and undersea cable to CINCPAC (before 1964, when the transpacific cable was laid, communications with CINCPAC relied on high frequency radio to span the Pacific). The unified commanders would have then passed the message to dispersed shore-based radio stations for transmission to alert submarines. Attacks against CINCPAC and CINCLANT headquarters could therefore have destroyed critical communications as well as command nodes.

The radio stations and transmitters were of course more numerous and widely scattered than the facilities in Honolulu and Norfolk that coordinated their use. Radio stations at sixty or more shore locations worldwide

33. *Department of Defense Appropriations for 1966,* Hearings before a Subcommittee of the House Committee on Appropriations, 89 Cong. 1 sess. (GPO, 1965), pt. 2, p. 372.

were dedicated to the fleet broadcast system, and radio transceiver capabilities on hundreds of surface ships augmented this system. Although
even conventional explosives could have destroyed any given shore-based
station,[34] including any one of the handful of very low frequency (VLF)
transmitters that were key to submarine communications,[35] many in the
early 1960s contended that the large number of transmission facilities on
land and at sea ensured adequate communications following an attack.
Admiral William Raborn told Congress,

Practically all military and civilian shore communications stations in all countries
of the world are vulnerable to nuclear attack. . . . Hardening such facilities for
protection against thermonuclear bombs would be a tremendously expensive undertaking. POLARIS communications reliability will not be governed by the vulnerability of any single shore radio station. It is a fact that a large amount of
dispersed U.S. Navy communications equipment and stations exist today in the
United States, at sea in every Navy ship, and in friendly countries which would
survive an attack due to sheer numbers. Any or all of these facilities can and will
be commanded quickly to act as communication stations for POLARIS as the
need arises. The sheer multiplicity of radio stations will almost assure with certainty an adequate number of surviving stations capable of communicating with
the POLARIS submarine.[36]

34. Such facilities are "only as hard as a handgrenade or a single conventional weapon."
Hearings on Military Posture and H.R. 5068 before the House Committee on Armed Services, 95 Cong. 1 sess. (GPO, 1977), pt. 3, bk. 2, p. 1878.

35. VLF has always been the primary mode of communication with missile submarines.
Using a high-powered transmitter, VLF signals propagate thousands of miles and can still
penetrate seawater down to about thirty feet. Reception requires a submarine to position an
antenna within a few feet of the surface.

The propagation characteristics of VLF inspired the construction of strategically located
transmitters for use by the unified commanders and the equipping of submarines with towed
buoy and buoyant wire antennas for underwater reception (receive only). Construction was
begun in the late 1950s, with stations already in existence providing an interim capability
until the better-situated and higher-powered transmitters became operational. Sites
planned, operational, or under construction during the mid-1960s were located at Cutler,
Maine; Jim Creek, Washington; North West Cape, Australia; Hawaii; United Kingdom;
Japan; and Balboa, Canal Zone. See *Department of Defense Appropriations for 1964,* Hearing
before a Subcommittee of the House Committee on Appropriations, 88 Cong. 1 sess. (GPO,
1963), pt. 5, pp. 819–20; "Navy Emphasis Swings Toward Strategic Command and Control," *Armed Forces Management,* vol. 15 (July 1969), pp. 62–64; and "Navy: A Theory of
Evolution," *Armed Forces Management,* vol. 16 (July 1970), pp. 4–42. The Cutler and North
West Cape (later renamed Harold E. Holt) stations served virtually the entire globe, with
remaining VLF sites providing backup. If the two main sites and backup sites were lost,
operational procedure required submarines to monitor low frequency broadcasts (approximately twenty stations) and then high frequency broadcasts (thirty stations) if all else had
failed.

36. *Department of Defense Appropriations for 1961,* Hearings before a Subcommittee of
the House Committee on Appropriations, 86 Cong. 2 sess. (GPO, 1960), pt. 5, p. 359.

Former Secretary McNamara echoed this appraisal in an appearance before a congressional committee in 1963.

MR. FORD.   What about your very low frequency communications with POLARIS submarines? Are these transmitting stations secure?

SECRETARY MCNAMARA.   I am told [by Admiral Anderson, then chief of naval operations] that they are probably secure, but that, to the extent they might be destroyed, the redundancy in our total naval communications system is such that beyond any reasonable doubt we could communicate with the POLARIS submarines.[37]

This was wishful thinking. In the first place, these assessments did not acknowledge the full range of physical threats to missile submarine communications. Besides being vulnerable to the blast effects of nuclear and conventional explosives, radio stations were susceptible to electronic countermeasures, especially jamming. The U.S. Navy's radio broadcast system possessed few antijam capabilities. Until and unless suppressed by Western forces, Soviet jammers probably could have substantially reduced the effective range of HF radio transmissions from shore and ships at sea. Among other key stations potentially subject to such interference were the VLF shore stations, some of which could not radiate enough power to overcome even modest jamming and all of which lacked the special antijam equipment needed to achieve maximum effectiveness from available power.[38] Because authoritative public information is lacking, however, the Soviet Union's ability to jam VLF communications is unknown.

Other physical threats not sufficiently weighted in the official assessments include the effects of EMP. High-altitude bursts could have caused widespread damage not only to shore stations but to ships as well; neither had been hardened against EMP. The leased commercial telecommunications channels that linked higher authorities to radio stations also lacked this protection. Finally, messages broadcast over LF and VLF were susceptible to distortion from nuclear effects in the ionosphere, and long-

37. *Department of Defense Appropriations for 1964,* House hearings, pt. 1, p. 407.

38. The lack of antijam features in fixed VLF stations is noted by the then deputy assistant chief of naval operations, in "Navy: A Theory of Evolution," p. 41. Mention of ongoing efforts to obtain adequate VLF antijam capability is found in *Department of Defense Appropriations for Fiscal Year 1969,* Hearings before a Subcommittee of the Senate Committee on Appropriations, 90 Cong. 1 sess. (GPO, 1968), p. 2150. The program name for these efforts is "Verdin." Verdin did not begin operating until the late 1970s. Power upgrading of the fixed VLF network was still under way as late as 1972; see *Fiscal Year 1973 Authorization for Military Procurement, Research and Development,* Senate hearings, pt. 5, p. 2834.

distance HF radio communications might have been blacked out for very long periods.[39] Loss of high frequency would have severely impaired navy communications because most shore stations and all ships relied on HF radio transmissions for long-distance communications.

The official conclusion also had not recognized that successful propagation of messages through a partially damaged and loosely coupled network requires elaborate and coherent operating procedures to coordinate the actions of individual units. Recent experience indicates that such procedural factors rather than technological factors impose the sharpest constraints on performance. In 1979, when the navy finally began serious investigations of various schemes for using ships at sea to relay messages to missile submarines, it found that sheer numbers do not ensure reliable communications. Testimony by Admiral Kaufman, then director of navy command, control, and communications, is instructive:

> The Navy is currently refining the means for using ships to relay communications to submarines with High Frequency radio equipment already installed in the fleet. Exercises conducted in the Atlantic . . . further tested a concept we call Mobile HF. Under this concept, ships monitor selected frequencies [deleted] and relay them over several frequencies according to predetermined schedules to avoid interfering with each other. This results in a chain reaction effect in the High Frequency spectrum with many messages, on many frequencies, from many sources leading to a high probability these messages will be received by a submarine. Preliminary results from the January tests are encouraging, but a complete analysis must await the return from sea of the submarines involved in the exercise.[40]

Because the planning required to organize a functional network involving ships and other general purpose communications stations had not even been initiated by the mid-1960s, the official assessment of their contribution to postattack communications with missile submarines was overly optimistic.

The official conclusion was vulnerable on one last score. Redundancy was not really a distinguishing feature of the overall naval communications system. Many transmitters were geographically collocated, and those that were not in close physical proximity were functionally tied into

---

39. Interference with signals transmitted in these frequencies may last for hours. See Glasstone and Dolan, *The Effects of Nuclear Weapons,* pp. 482–86; Michael A. King and Paul B. Fleming, "An Overview of the Effects of Nuclear Weapons on Communications Capabilities," *Signal,* vol. 34 (January 1980), pp. 59–66; and *MX Missile Basing* (Washington, D.C.: Office of Technology Assessment, September 1981), pp. 298–99.

40. *Department of Defense Authorization for Appropriations for Fiscal Year 1980,* Hearings before the Senate Committee on Armed Services, 96 Cong. 1 sess. (GPO, 1979), pt. 6, p. 3403.

common command centers or communications facilities. The existence of critical nodes and the considerable interdependence among shore-based elements suggest that redundancy was actually minimal. And as far as command redundancy was concerned, practically none existed at all. The destruction of the two unified command headquarters would probably have produced such a severe concussion to the command system that it would have been impossible to exercise positive control over the missile submarine force.

How authority over submarine operations would have devolved and what problems of negative control may have arisen if enemy attacks had ruptured the command system are matters of speculation. But we at least know that submarine crews, like LCCs, possessed the physical capacity to launch nuclear weapons on their own.[41] Unlike LCCs, however, submarine crews might have operated under formal guidance that permitted the firing of missiles without the personal command of higher authorities. Under some circumstances, the exact nature of which remain secret, a conditional grant of launch authority evidently extended to the lowest rung of the submarine command hierarchy. That nuclear launch authority might have been delegated to submarine commanders is suggested by the following colloquy in congressional hearings held in 1963:

MR. FLOOD.   What I have in mind is a Buck Rogers situation where you have 18 of your POLARIS on station waiting for the signal to fire.

Somehow, somewhere, in some way the enemy has cut your communications with the 18. You don't know about it and the submarines don't know about it.

You give the order with the red button and nothing happens.

(Discussion with Admiral Galantin deleted)

Then the situation I pose is most unlikely within the rule of reason?
ADMIRAL GALANTIN.   That is right.
MR. FLOOD.   Then there is a point and time under certain circumstances in which the ship commander is authorized to open up?
ADMIRAL GALANTIN.   Yes sir.
. . .

MR. FLOOD.   There never has been the need to exercise that right? The need has never occurred?
ADMIRAL GALANTIN.   That is right.[42]

41. This capacity is authoritatively confirmed in testimony given as early as 1960 and as late as 1976. See *Department of Defense Appropriations for 1961,* House hearings, pt. 5, p. 367; and *First Use of Nuclear Weapons: Preserving Responsible Control,* Hearings before the Subcommittee on International Security and Scientific Affairs of the House Committee on International Relations, 94 Cong. 2 sess. (GPO, 1976), p. 94.

42. *Department of Defense Appropriations for 1964,* House hearings, pt. 5, p. 817.

This testimony may be misleading, but we can be reasonably sure that military commanders at relatively low echelons in the missile submarine command hierarchy operated with the knowledge that their links with higher authority were tenuous indeed and that retaliation might have to be executed without the personal command of their civilian or military superiors.

Bomber Vulnerability and Additional LCC Vulnerabilities

By 1966 SAC had made considerably more progress than the navy toward establishing a viable command channel for controlling its strategic forces. SAC operated a ground network with an airborne backup that provided a degree of genuine redundancy and survivability. Under the principle of conservative planning, Soviet calculations might have estimated that the overall system, in spite of its many deficiencies, was sufficiently robust to have delivered execution messages to large segments of SAC's forces. But by the same token, U.S. planners had cause for serious concern about the system's performance in a nuclear environment.

Cautious planners on both sides could have quickly concluded that even small-scale attacks would neutralize the ground network. Individual ground-based command centers and communications lines had little chance of surviving the blast effects of direct nuclear attack, and too little redundancy (except for LCC redundancy) existed to offset this vulnerability. And there was a critical node in the network. Authorization of nuclear strikes would have been passed from the national command authority to the specified commander, who would have relayed the message (after translating it into SAC message formats) to the executing forces. Thus the destruction of SAC headquarters in Omaha would have severely impaired the performance of the ground network. And destruction was likely if the headquarters had been directly attacked; the command center was underground but "not in any secure way," as former Secretary Robert McNamara once put it.[43]

Assuming that SAC headquarters survived, the go code authorizing nuclear attack would have been transmitted simultaneously over several ground-based systems to subordinate units. These systems included the Primary Alerting System (PAS); a teletype channel known as the SAC Automated Command and Control System (SACCS); and leased com-

---

43. *Military Procurement Authorization, Fiscal Year 1964,* Hearings before the Senate Committee on Armed Services, 88 Cong. 1 sess. (GPO, 1963), p. 56.

mercial land line communications, particularly AUTOVON/AUTODIN. All except PAS used surface land lines and were liable to suffer severe impairment even from collateral damage. Although PAS featured modest protection from blast effects and thus might have withstood collateral effects, no system was protected from the effects of EMP. All lines went to the three numbered air force headquarters in the United States, the Minuteman and Titan LCCs, wing command posts at primary SAC bomber bases, and other units at home and abroad. With the exception of the LCCs, none was built to withstand nuclear attack.

The soft numbered air force headquarters located at Barksdale AFB, Louisiana; March AFB, California; and Westover AFB, Massachusetts, were particularly important in exercising positive control over SAC bombers in flight. Collocated with these bases as well as with SAC headquarters itself were HF antennas used for long-range communications with bombers en route to their targets.[44] This system, then called Short Order and now called Giant Talk, was an integral part of an operation known as Positive Control Launch. Upon receiving early warning of actual Soviet attack (tactical warning), standard operating procedure called for SAC headquarters to order bombers to fly to designated points outside enemy territory, loiter for awhile, and automatically return to home bases unless they received an execution message.[45] Short Order was the primary means of delivering the execution message. But the transmitters could not have withstood attack and might not have withstood EMP effects, while the transmission signals were susceptible to high frequency blackout and enemy jamming.

A collection of ground radio stations called Green Pine sites, located on an arc between Alaska's Aleutian Islands and Iceland, augmented Short Order.[46] Beyond the Green Pine arc, HF signals transmitted from stations in the United States were unreliable even in peacetime. The sig-

44. *Development of Strategic Air Command 1946–1976* (Headquarters Strategic Air Command, March 21, 1976), p. 84. System characteristics are described in *Department of Defense Annual Report July 1, 1959 to June 30, 1960,* pp. 323–24.
45. *Development of Strategic Air Command 1946–1976,* p. 84.
46. Kenneth J. Stein, "Realtime Data Aid SAC Mission," *Aviation Week & Space Technology* (May 10, 1976), p. 49. Authoritative references to the Green Pine network are few and far between. The closest thing to official acknowledgment of its existence during the mid-to-late 1960s is the mention of "forward area UHF sites, which have as their purpose to communicate with the B-52 bombers." *Department of Defense Appropriations for 1970,* Hearings before a Subcommittee of the House Committee on Appropriations, 91 Cong. 1 sess. (GPO, 1969), pt. 3, p. 1125.

nals were also susceptible to interference from enemy jamming, and in a nuclear environment Short Order might have been blacked out completely. If an execution message could have been delivered to Green Pine sites, they could have relayed it via UHF radio to bombers en route to their loiter areas. Assuming these backup sites were not destroyed by Soviet attacks, they could have communicated to any bomber within line-of-sight range (approximately 200 miles) without risking serious disruption from jamming or nuclear effects. Once the bombers had traversed the arc and flown out of UHF range, however, further communications would have become problematical.[47]

The central postattack problem, though, lay in reaching Green Pine sites in the first instance. In peacetime, SAC headquarters or numbered air force headquarters or both could have sent the go code over leased land lines and HF radio. But neither the communications media nor the originating command centers were survivable. Postattack communications with Green Pine sites would have been no less difficult than wartime communications with the bombers themselves.

Although the ground segment of SAC's command network would have disintegrated under attack and could not have been employed to trigger retaliation, it nonetheless served some important control functions, especially during the critical period between the launch and impact of enemy weapons. One of its prime purposes was rapid dissemination of orders from SAC headquarters to launch ground-alert bombers under the policy of positive control. Getting bombers off the ground and a safe distance away from home bases within minutes after detecting incoming warheads was essential to bomber survival. Given that tactical warning of ICBM attack could have been as short as fifteen minutes from detection to impact at the northernmost bases in the continental United States, or shorter still if the performance of the Ballistic Missile Early Warning System (BMEWS) was less than its theoretical best, and given that bomber crews on day-to-day alert required about fifteen minutes from the

47. A fairly recent assessment applies equally to earlier circumstances: "After the aircraft have passed beyond line of sight of our ground based radios, we presently rely on high frequency communications to pass execution or recall orders to the bombers. . . . However, the high frequency radio has an availability of about 90 percent under benign conditions; worse than that over polar or aural [sic] regions and can have extended outages under conditions of nuclear perturbation of the ionosphere." Statement of Major General Robert L. Edge in *Department of Defense Appropriations for 1977*, House hearings, pt. 6, pp. 82, 85.

time they received notice of the attack until the time they put a safe distance between themselves and their home base, SAC could not afford even short delays in implementing a positive control launch.[48]

CINCSAC was in the best position to expedite this procedure. Attack indications picked up by BMEWS sensors would have been sent to North American Air Defense (NORAD) Command headquarters in Colorado, and promptly relayed from there to SAC headquarters. A message directing a positive control launch would have originated in Omaha and traveled over PAS to wing command posts and other locations. Using an automated patching system, SAC headquarters would have sounded a klaxon alarm at these remote bases, cueing the alert crews to scramble to their aircraft, and would have transmitted the message via radio patches directly to the aircraft, triggering the launch of the bomber force to predesignated points outside Soviet territory.

The ground segment also generated the airborne command system (the Post Attack Command Control System) before the impact of incoming weapons. SAC maintained EC-135 command aircraft on fifteen-minute ground alert at its numbered air force headquarters and kept one EC-135, called Looking Glass, on twenty-four-hour airborne alert near Omaha.[49] Looking Glass served as the alternate command post for SAC headquarters. SAC also deployed EC-135s with radio-relay missions to Lockbourne AFB, Ohio, and Ellsworth AFB, South Dakota, where they were maintained on fifteen-minute ground alert.[50] Upon detection of Soviet launches, EC-135 aircraft on ground alert would have been flushed into the air by means of the same communications channels used to launch the bomber force. Under established procedures for a positive control launch,

48. "The BMEWS warning time is about fifteen minutes, about half the transit time of an ICBM." *Military Procurement Authorization, Fiscal Year 1966,* Hearings before the Senate Committee on Armed Services and the Subcommittee on Department of Defense of the Committee on Appropriations, 89 Cong. 1 sess. (GPO, 1965), p. 1158. An experimental complex of over-the-horizon, forward-scatter radars, designed to provide an additional ten minutes of warning, had been installed in Asia and Europe in December 1965, but the system did not become operational until 1968 (see discussion in chapter 5).

Testimony also noted the availability of "some 900 bombers, well dispersed, half of them on 15-minute alert and backed up by an improved warning system" (ibid., p. 950).

49. Locations of EC-135 deployments are identified in *Development of Strategic Air Command 1946–1976,* pp. 84, 93, 102. The alert status of fifteen minutes is my estimate. For a Soviet view of the U.S. airborne command system, see Colonel V. Lebeder, "Control From the Air," *Voyennaya misl',* vol. 6 (1967), pp. 79–84.

50. *Development of Strategic Air Command 1946–1976,* p. 123.

EC-135s would have occupied predesignated airborne stations inside U.S. territory, forming a network similar to the present-day net depicted in chapter 5 (figure 5-5).

PACCS employed UHF radio for line-of-sight communications with launch centers, wing command posts at bomber bases (from which alert bombers would have already been launched), and outbound bombers within UHF range. High frequency radio was the sole means for long-range communications. It provided the only direct link from PACCS aircraft to remote Green Pine relay sites and far-flung strategic bombers in flight, and was relied on substantially for communications between PACCS aircraft. (Note that the network depicted in chapter 5 is more compact and allows for UHF interconnection between all aircraft adjacent to one another. This tight UHF serial linkage resulted from a restructuring of PACCS in 1970, when command aircraft at numbered air force headquarters were relocated to bases in the Midwest. In 1966, when key command aircraft were stationed in Massachusetts, California, and Louisiana, PACCS was widely dispersed, and consequently reliance on HF radio for intra-PACCS communications was much greater.)

Reliance on airborne high frequency radio systems for long-distance communications was a major liability because the adverse effects of nuclear explosions on radio signal propagation are severe at that wavelength. Furthermore, the transmitting power of airborne radios could not match the strength of ground-based transmitters and could not perform as effectively if stressed by enemy jammers. Consequently, even without direct damage to PACCS, reliable communications with strategic bombers that were beyond UHF range (400 nautical miles) could not be safely assumed by cautious U.S. planners, at least not for a nuclear environment. Nor could completely reliable communications among PACCS aircraft themselves be taken for granted. And for that matter, communications from PACCS aircraft to LCCs may have been difficult. Although EC-135s operated within UHF range of many Minuteman complexes, the best-protected receiving antenna at the launch centers operated at the HF bandwidth, a much less stable frequency than UHF in a nuclear environment.

Nor were PACCS aircraft immune to direct damage. There was some risk that alert aircraft would have been destroyed on the ground, perhaps because of sluggish tactical warning of ICBM attack or undetected attacks by submarine missiles launched from waters contiguous to coastal EC-135 bases. Soviet Golf-class and Hotel-class missile submarines that periodically patrolled the Eastern Atlantic in 1966 posed a potential threat to the command aircraft based in Massachusetts, for example. Sensors designed to detect submarine-launched ballistic missiles did not become operational until 1968 (see chapter 5).

The effects of electromagnetic pulse probably posed a greater threat to PACCS, however, Aircraft exposure to EMP was virtually certain, and the resulting currents flowing through the plane could have reached very high levels (a problem analyzed further in chapter 5). Under conservative planning assumptions, PACCS aircraft and their communication suites probably would have suffered significant damage from EMP.

In sum, Soviet attacks aimed at SAC's command structure would have greatly undermined positive control over bombers and ICBMs. SAC could have used the soft ground network to flush ground-alert bombers and PACCS aircraft before the impact of incoming weapons (provided that tactical warning information arrived in time), but it relied heavily on an airborne command network to deliver execution messages to its nuclear forces, and the postattack capability of this network was questionable.

The failure of primary ground and airborne communications would have left SAC with one last-ditch means of strategic communications: the Emergency Rocket Communications System (ERCS), which was made up of Blue Scout rockets deployed in an unprotected configuration on Wallops Island just off the Virginia coast. An execution message could have been recorded on a tape device inside a missile before launch. After launch the message could be transmitted over UHF by the missile's communications package. The idea was to exploit the altitude, range, and velocity of a missile so that a message could be quickly disseminated over a large area using a frequency that would not be drastically distorted by nuclear explosions. In principle, any SAC unit within line of sight of any portion of the missile's trajectory could have received the message. In practice, ERCS was a troubled system. It was not well integrated into any nuclear command hierarchy, and technically it was a thin reed to lean on. Its reliability, transmitter power, and prelaunch survivability were such that cautious planners would not have counted on it at all. Design improvements and better protection for ERCS deployments were in fact in store. Minuteman missiles would be equipped with communications packages and operationally deployed in silos in Missouri in 1967 (see chapter 5).

All these deficiencies in SAC's command structure could only have aggravated the problem of negative control, especially in the case of LCCs. The isolation of bombers from higher authorities did not present as serious a problem. Established procedures required them to turn back in the event authorization to attack was not received. This guidance was unambiguous. Yet, it is likely that bombers, like LCCs and submarines, lacked physical safeguards against unauthorized retaliation. If safeguards were consistent across all three force components, then strategic bombers did not need to receive enabling codes from higher authority before weapons could be unlocked and armed. The public record, however, does not sustain any firm conclusions about negative control over bombers in the 1960s.

National Command Vulnerabilities

In 1966, national command authorities had access to four primary national command posts from which nuclear operations could have been managed. Components of the National Military Command System (NMCS), they are listed in descending order of vulnerability: the National Military Command Center (NMCC) located inside the Pentagon; the Alternate National Military Command Center (ANMCC) located near Fort Ritchie, Maryland, about seventy-five miles from Washington; the National Emergency Command Post Afloat (NECPA), a navy cruiser deployed in the Atlantic near the coast; and the National Emergency Airborne Command Post (NEACP), an EC-135 aircraft maintained on fifteen-minute ground alert at Andrews AFB, Maryland, just outside Washington.[51]

The NMCC, a soft facility with a direct communications link to the White House situation room, obviously had no chance of surviving a nuclear attack directed against it. It could have been destroyed with no more than twenty minutes of advance notice if attacked by Soviet ICBMs. If attacked by submarine missiles, it might have been destroyed without warning.

The ANMCC had been in operation since 1953 when the Soviet nuclear threat consisted of atomic weapons delivered by bombers.[52] The

51. Entities are enumerated in Library of Congress, Legislative Reference Service, *United States Defense Policies in 1963*, 88 Cong. 2 sess. (GPO, 1964), H. Doc. 335, p. 32. See also J. H. Wagner, "NMCS: The Command Backup to Counterforce," *Armed Forces Management*, vol. 9 (July 1963), pp. 23–25.

52. *Department of Defense Authorization for Appropriations for Fiscal Year 1979*, Senate hearings, pt. 9, p. 6447.

underground facility has recently been rated as "moderately hard,"[53] which probably means that in the mid-1960s the structure itself stood a good chance of surviving submarine missile attack and a reasonably good chance of surviving ICBM attack. Backward extrapolation of information would also suggest that a small number of people manned the facility around the clock (with additional personnel on standby) and that it maintained constant communications with the NMCC.[54] Data bases were kept up-to-date by means of reports submitted by the NMCC, NORAD, and other major commands.

The ANMCC and the NMCC were connected by landline telephone and teletype systems with the unified and specified commands among others, and a radio communications link to NEACP was also provided by the ANMCC.[55] Not surprisingly, all these links were "vulnerable in any practical sense" according to testimony by Robert McNamara in 1963.[56] This vulnerability necessitated that the ANMCC perform a transition function by which transfer of control from the ground facilities to airborne command posts could have been effected in an orderly fashion during the brief period between the detection of an ICBM attack and weapons impact.

Because of its mobility, the NECPA ship deployed in the Atlantic was less vulnerable to attack than the ground facilities. In 1966, however, the ship was restricted to waters within troposcatter communications range of a single shore facility in Delaware.[57] This restriction probably put it at greater risk. During the Cuban missile crisis NECPA operated in the

53. *Hearings on Military Posture and H.R. 5068*, House, pt. 1, p. 1055.

54. *Hearings on Military Posture and H.R. 12564* before the House Committee on Armed Services, 93 Cong. 2 sess. (GPO, 1974), pt. 4, p. 3605; and *Department of Defense Authorization for Appropriations for Fiscal Year 1979*, Senate hearings, pt. 9, p. 6409.

55. Emergency voice communications traveled through the Joint Chiefs of Staff Alerting Network (JCSAN), and emergency teletype communications were transmitted through the Emergency Message Automatic Transmission System (EMATS). See Wagner, "NMCS: The Command Backup to Counterforce," p. 24; and also *Hearings on Military Posture and H.R. 10929* before the House Committee on Armed Services, 95 Cong. 2 sess. (GPO, 1978), pt. 3, bk. 1, p. 308. Both JSCAN and EMATS used AT&T terrestrial communication lines. For radio communications, see *Department of Defense Appropriations for Fiscal Year 1976*, Hearings before the Senate Committee on Appropriations, 94 Cong. 1 sess. (GPO, 1975), pt. 1, p. 850.

56. *Department of Defense Appropriations for 1964*, House hearings, pt. 1, p. 407.

57. *Department of Defense Appropriations for 1968*, Hearings before a Subcommittee of the House Committee on Appropriations, 90 Cong. 1 sess. (GPO, 1967), pt. 5, pp. 237–38; and "Electronic Systems," *DMS Market Intelligence Report* (DMS Inc., September 1969), NMCS, p. 5.

Chesapeake Bay. More importantly, the shore facility could easily have been lost to Soviet attack.

The national command aircraft had a better chance of surviving nuclear attack than any of the others. Secretary McNamara had decided in 1961 to station EC-135 aircraft at Andrews AFB. Three were deployed in 1962, one on ground alert.[58] National officials had the option to board NEACP in time of crisis, but ground-based facilities were more suitable for managing a crisis because they provided ample space for advisers, unlimited prewar endurance, immediate and direct access to main communications and intelligence networks, and greater capacity to handle larger amounts of data. Nevertheless, NEACP did provide an option, and if it were exercised well in advance of Soviet attack, chances of the survival of national officials would have been much improved.

NEACP survival was by no means assured, however; Soviet planners did not lack strategies to attack aircraft in flight. A single high-altitude explosion would have blanketed a large area of airspace with EMP, and NEACP was almost certain to be within it. The aircraft's flight pattern was in fact likely to have been confined to a small area where approximate coordinates probably could have been predicted with fair accuracy. Two requirements and a condition combined to impose sharp limits on NEACP's flexibility. The first requirement was to maintain continuous communications with the ANMCC before and during an attack, as long as that was possible, in order to receive early warning and other vital information being fed to the ANMCC from NORAD, SAC headquarters, and other combat commands. The second requirement was to establish communications with adjacent aircraft in the PACCS network. The relevant condition was the limited communications range of the EC-135 aircraft then in service. Until EC-135J aircraft replaced them in 1968, NEACP's range allowed it to tie into only "one or two sole points on the ground."[59] This constraint and the requirement to be interconnected with PACCS aircraft limited NEACP's operational flexibility.

If national authorities chose to remain on the ground during a crisis, as seems likely, NEACP could have been launched and maintained on airborne alert for up to ten hours without refueling. In the event of a sudden attack on Washington-area command posts, NEACP's primary responsibility, if no execution message had been issued before the president's

58. *Fiscal Year 1973 Authorization for Military Procurement, Research and Development,* Senate hearings, pt. 3, p. 1462.

59. *Department of Defense Appropriations for 1968,* House hearings, pt. 5, p. 238.

death, would have been to contact a constitutionally designated successor and feed any orders from the new authority into the PACCS network. There was some chance that the initial attack would have been detected in time to permit the NCA to escape in helicopters, in which case it might have been possible to coordinate a rendezvous with NEACP at one of the many airstrips in the Washington area.[60]

An alternative would have kept NEACP on maximum ground alert, standing by to receive national officials and take off minutes before incoming ICBMs arrived. A helicopter flight from downtown Washington to Andrews AFB would have taken perhaps eight minutes, and additional minutes would have elapsed before and after this flight. But BMEWS was expected to provide fifteen to twenty minutes' warning, which might have been just enough time to permit the successful launch of NEACP with national officials on board. During a period of tension, NEACP could also have been relocated to any of several airstrips near Washington to confound Soviet intelligence and targeting. National authorities may have been able to rendezvous with NEACP and take off with more time to spare because of such covert deployment.[61]

Maintaining NEACP on ground alert, however, would have increased the risk of its destruction. Undetected attack by missile submarines was not impossible. BMEWS malfunction, official indecision, and a host of other causes of delay potentially fatal for both the NCA and NEACP can also be imagined. Whether the added risk of a ground-alert posture would actually have been taken for the sake of keeping NEACP accessible to national authorities is of course a moot question.

Under normal peacetime conditions, protection of the NCA would have been much more difficult. In the event of a surprise attack, national authorities would not have been in the best position either to escape or ride out the attack. NEACP's chances of survival were doubtless better if BMEWS performed at its theoretical best and if the aircraft had standing orders to launch without the NCA upon receiving tactical warning. Still, the margin of error would have been narrow for an aircraft maintained on

---

60. For more recent discussions of this procedure, see *Department of Defense Appropriations for 1980*, Hearings before a Subcommittee of the House Committee on Appropriations, 96 Cong. 1 sess. (GPO, 1979), pt. 6, p. 187.

61. Such an operation appears to be included in more recent contingency plans. *Department of Defense Appropriations for 1976*, Hearings before a Subcommittee of the House Committee on Appropriations, 94 Cong. 1 sess. (GPO, 1975), pt. 2, p. 66.

fifteen-minute ground alert. Under the best of circumstances for a surprise attack, NEACP had only a few minutes to spare.

Thus given the technical conditions of the mid-1960s, it was not possible to protect fully either the president, his successors, or the four national command posts from sudden attack, not even during an extreme national emergency when precautions to reduce vulnerability could have been taken. Protection of the communications required to connect national authorities with subordinate echelons was even more difficult.

This situation once again raises questions about predelegating authority and possible attendant problems of preventing accidental or unauthorized missile launches. The issue of predelegation is succinctly stated in a report prepared by the Congressional Research Service:

> The realities of command and control in the nuclear age would seem to increase the necessity for prior delegation under certain carefully defined conditions. For example, in the event that the president were disabled in a surprise attack and his lawful successor were not immediately accessible, a contingency plan, containing a delegation of authority to order the use of nuclear weapons under certain conditions, would seem to be a logical and prudent precaution—perhaps necessary to national survival.[62]

The president's right to delegate his authority to use nuclear weapons is generally unquestioned: "Under existing law, the president alone has the basic authority to order the use of nuclear weapons. This authority, inherent in his constitutional role as Commander-in-Chief, may be delegated to subordinate officers in the chain of command virtually without limitation."[63] In one instance, at least, that authority has been delegated to a military command. In a prepared statement presented to a congressional subcommittee in 1976, a former senior military officer disclosed that "no . . . U.S. or NATO field commander has been delegated authority to use U.S. nuclear weapons without express approval of the President of the United States, with one exception . . . the North American Air Defense Commander, who has been delegated such authority only under severe restrictions and specific conditions of attack."[64] Although the "specific conditions of attack" were not defined, the severe restrictions consisted mainly of a requirement that the NORAD commander persist in trying to

---

62. *Authority to Order the Use of Nuclear Weapons,* 94 Cong. 1 sess. (GPO, 1975), pp. 3–4.

63. Ibid., p. 1.

64. House Committee on International Relations, *First Use of Nuclear Weapons: Preserving Responsible Control,* p. 55.

reach civilian authority until the last possible moment.[65] This requirement is reminiscent of procedures followed by an isolated LCC, which was to make every effort to get independent confirmation of the authenticity of an execution message. Unlike a launch control center, however, the NORAD commander could have initiated nuclear operations (the passage quoted above presumably refers to air defense nuclear weapons, not intercontinental offensive weapons) without ever having received an emergency action message from higher authority.

Others besides the NORAD commander probably were predelegated authority under some formal guidance. During congressional hearings held in 1960, General Power, commander in chief of SAC, suggested that he possessed conditional authority to unleash SAC's nuclear arsenal. While it is not very specific nor necessarily indicative of arrangements in the mid-1960s, the testimony seems germane:

MR. MAHON. You cannot tell where the President might be. He might be, at the time of a surprise attack, in South America, in Russia, in India, or he might be some other place. Since you are the man who is charged with the responsibility of commanding the Strategic Air Command and launching our retaliatory force, has a system been worked out that would enable you to get going with your intercontinental ballistic missiles or your intermediate-range ballistic missiles or your airplanes?

GENERAL POWER. Yes, there is a very adequate system. But again, you have to go through and verify that you are actually under attack. [Testimony deleted.] In other words, no one is going to make that hasty a decision. It would not be right to do it. You might start a war accidentally, and you cannot afford to do that. Mind you, we are talking about a matter of minutes. Let us say you see, at its apogee, a missile coming over. This gives you 15 minutes' warning. You will not have to be particularly bright when those 15 minutes have passed to know if they are real missiles; they will be going off in this country. Therefore, we are talking about a very short time period.[66]

Predelegation of basic authority to order the use of nuclear weapons facilitates the exercise of positive control in the event of NCA or NMCS incapacitation and hence presumably weakens the enemy's motivation to attack them in the first place. Predelegation of basic authority does not, however, remove all incentive to neutralize the NCA and the NMCS. The destruction of the highest levels of the nuclear command hierarchy would probably cause considerable loss of attack coordination, an important

65. Ibid., p. 79.
66. *Department of Defense Appropriations for 1961*, Hearings before a Subcommittee of the House Committee on Appropriations, 86 Cong. 2 sess. (GPO, 1960), pt. 7, p. 69.

aspect of positive control. Coordination requires detailed advance preparation of operational units, a process that unavoidably decentralizes many significant aspects of control. And the appropriateness of diffuse, preprogrammed rules and procedures does limit the amount of coordination theoretically attainable. But central authority must be exercised in order for the theoretical optimum to be reliably achieved.

Strategic planners assume that central authorities would at least be able to designate a pattern of attack and the exact time at which that attack would be launched. The coordination of target assignments and firing schedules of the established war plans are predicated on this necessary integration to achieve systematic and efficient coverage of the enemy target base. National authorities are in the best position to provide these simple but basic instructions through the NMCS. Their inability to do so would leave SAC and missile submarine units without a common frame of reference. By extension, the inability of the unified and specified commanders to provide such instructions to their forces would result in further impairment. Coordination would clearly be minimal if commanders of individual weapons were completely isolated from each other as well as higher authority. Although extensive predelegation of basic authority to launch weapons would ensure retaliation, it would not ensure systematic coverage of the enemy target base. The level of destruction visited upon the Soviet Union could be immense, but certain classes of targets might escape damage altogether.

What has been called institutional ethos, however, possibly could act as an invisible hand directing the expectations and behavior of isolated units and creating greater force coordination than random chance would suggest. Because of role playing in war games and exercises, indoctrination, familiarity with existing attack options, and even informal interaction within professional military circles, key personnel may come to share assumptions about the course of action each is apt to pursue. If there had been extensive predelegation in 1966, the standard massive counterforce option would probably have been seized upon by a large number of units and attacks would have generally conformed to that plan in spite of the fact that such intentions and behaviors could not have been overtly communicated. Still, this invisible hand could not have resulted in the most efficient coverage of Soviet military targets, and it could have resulted in minimal coverage of urban-industrial targets.

Of course, contingency plans may not only have predelegated basic authority but may also have specified rules for choosing an attack plan and execution time. Such instructions would have removed much of the uncertainty that would have otherwise undermined positive control. But there are reasons to suppose that specific instructions were not endorsed by national policy officials. Resistance to elaborate qualification could have been politically motivated: unambiguous instructions would dilute the effective power of the president.[67]

The Strategic Situation: 1966

The concerns raised in this chapter fall outside the scope of the established conception of the strategic problem, whose narrow compass directed attention to such issues as the emergent SS-9 ICBM threat to Minuteman silos. These issues appeared to be few, understandable, and resolvable. But such appearances dissolve under a broader definition of strategic capability, and appropriately so. Although the narrower, simpler focus generated valuable technical comprehension of certain aspects of the situation, it excluded consideration of the vulnerability of communications and command systems. As a consequence, the Soviet threat was underestimated, and the policy conclusions derived from these miscalculations were unsound.

U.S. Second-Strike Capabilities and Strategic Balance

Analysis of the adequacy of force structure and command structure generate divergent assessments of the strategic balance. If the standard calculations are to be believed, a first strike by the Soviet Union would have been ineffective and self-disarming if directed against U.S. strategic forces. For this reason, and because a U.S. first strike could have destroyed much of the Soviet strategic force, the United States was generally believed to possess overwhelming strategic superiority. But analysis of U.S. arrangements for exercising positive control over retaliatory forces alters this judgment. An attack strategy with a much higher probability of blunting U.S. retaliation would have been based on destruction of key command and communications nodes. From both U.S. and Soviet standpoints, conservative planning assumptions leave little doubt that this strategy would have been far more effective than a strategy based on

67. John D. Steinbruner, "National Security and the Concept of Strategic Stability," *Journal of Conflict Resolution,* vol. 22 (September 1978), p. 419.

massive attack against alert U.S. forces. And to conservative U.S. planners, this strategy ought to have been seen as a very serious threat to U.S. capabilities for assured destruction.

Thus analyses of command structure refute the idea that during most of the 1960s the balance of strategic power greatly favored the United States. It is difficult to regard these as halcyon days of American nuclear supremacy when the strategic organizations responsible for the conduct of war were liable to disintegrate under the weight of enemy attacks.

Crisis Stability

The Soviet Union did not have an opportunity to strike with impunity. The destructive power of the U.S. force was immense, and conservative Soviet planners undoubtedly expected much of it to be expended in the wake of a Soviet attack. In spite of the tenuous U.S. command and communications channels, Soviet confidence in their ability to paralyze those channels should not have been very high. The U.S. nuclear posture was surely a powerful deterrent.

Nevertheless, the situation during these years was less stable than has been commonly believed. Standard calculations did not impart an adequate appreciation of Soviet incentives to strike quickly and first in a crisis. The creaky condition of the command structure created these incentives. This condition also created incentives for early use of U.S. forces. The difference between the effectiveness of an attack executed while the command structure was still coherent and one executed after absorbing the full weight of the opponent's strike would have been stark. In the second case, retaliation would have been much slower to develop, and the magnitude and coordination of the attack could have been drastically reduced. There was also a distinct possibility of unauthorized retaliation by isolated U.S. forces. National policy officials might therefore have preferred to authorize attacks early if they sensed a growing loss of control and if further delay risked a loss of influence over the counterattacks finally mounted.

Force Components and Strategic Stability

Most analysts equate the vulnerability of each force component with its contribution to strategic stability. Alert missile submarines were considered invulnerable to attack, and hence their deployment was viewed as a stabilizing factor. Silo-based ICBMs seemed more vulnerable than submarines or bombers and were the least stable component of the force structure. Alert bombers occupied an intermediate position; they were considered less stabilizing than submarine deployments but more so than ICBM deployments.

A reversal of this order results when the components are differentiated with respect to the viability of their C³ systems. In 1966, missile submarines would have been the least manageable component both before and after a Soviet attack, especially an attack aimed at the U.S. command network. Prestrike and postattack control of ICBMs would have been good by comparison and better than for bombers.

ICBMS AND COMMAND STABILITY. In 1966 a command network with significant redundancy regulated land missile operations. Although no individual ground communications link or command node could have been expected to survive a direct nuclear attack, the ground segment provided timely and reliable two-way communications in peacetime and in the prestrike phase of conflict, and the airborne segment, though dependent upon the prestrike performance of the ground network (including early warning facilities) had some chance of establishing communications with many of SAC's dispersed strategic forces. During peacetime and periods of high international tension, the ground structure kept the ICBM force under firm authoritative direction. Direct and instantaneous transmission of directives was possible, and each element in the chain of ICBM command could acknowledge receipt of such messages almost instantly. Direct land line communications also enabled SAC headquarters to monitor ICBM alert status on a near real-time basis. Thus if, for instance, a certain missile aimed at a high priority target went off alert for maintenance, SAC could and did authorize coverage of that target by another missile. Once the maintenance was completed, SAC received immediate notification of the retargeting, as did higher authorities, including the NMCC and ANMCC.

The fixed location and availability of both landline and radio communications facilitated control of ICBM forces. Transmitters and receiving antennas were confined within the continental United States where atmospheric conditions play less havoc with signal propagation than is the case at higher latitudes, and any problems of signal propagation could yield to simple telephone instructions to change frequencies. The launch control centers did not move, and as a result the orientation of antennas with respect to ground-based transmitters remained constant and optimal. The relatively close proximity of radio transmitters and receivers made communications less susceptible to deliberate interference from jamming, and unless land lines were attacked as well, the resulting degradation of command performance would not have been serious. Fixed locations, access to supplies, and the availability of maintenance personnel facilitated, under normal circumstances, the repair of landline and radio communications systems. Interested parties could be quickly notified of a problem affecting any portion of the communications system, and work to correct serious malfunctions could proceed on a priority basis. Under combat conditions, the restoration of ground-based communications would have been unlikely, but the prospects would have been far worse if the system terminated at imprecisely known, inaccessible locations.

After a large nuclear attack on the American command structure, control of ICBM launch centers would have depended heavily on the functioning of SAC's airborne command network, which in many respects did not measure up to very high standards. Individual aircraft lacked adequate protection from the effects of EMP. The range for communications, particularly in a nuclear environment, was too limited. Aircraft were subject to inherent limits on endurance—a maximum of ten hours in the air without refueling. The warning time provided by BMEWS was barely enough to ensure their prelaunch survival. The survival and smooth interaction of a network of such aircraft was questionable.

Still, PACCS did provide a redundant link to ICBM launch centers that was far more survivable and coherent than the ground-based and ship-based network used to control missile submarines. The destruction of SAC headquarters and subordinate command units on the ground would not have isolated SAC forces, whereas attacks on the unified commands would have severed the main arteries through which information flowed to missile submarines. Continuity of command over the submarines would have probably been lost if the navy's ground elements had been attacked.

MISSILE SUBMARINES AND COMMAND STABILITY. Although missile submarines were generally less amenable than bombers and ICBMs to pre- and postattack control, their communications gear, launch mechanisms, and crew were invulnerable. The Soviet Union could have targeted every LCC in the Minuteman force, but missile submarines at sea were virtually immune. The favorable comparisons end there, however.

During peacetime, as a security precaution, no one except the crew itself knew the exact location of a missile submarine on patrol (the commander drew up his sixty-eight-day patrol plans after leaving port).[68] Once deployed, a submarine observed strict radio silence, never engaging in two-way communications (except when it could not perform its primary mission) so that intercepted signals would not compromise location. Ordinarily, then, higher authorities could not monitor the status of the submarine.

Missile submarines could receive communications during routine patrols only with some difficulty. The primary means of communications, fixed VLF shore stations, frequently encountered adverse atmospheric conditions. Submarine reception was especially variable in the North Atlantic and the Mediterranean. Reception also depended on the trailing antenna's orientation with respect to shore-based transmitters, and fluctuations could result from changes in heading.[69] Signal-processing equipment in missile submarines also left room for substantial improvement, and underpowered shore-based transmitters aggravated the problem. In general, circumstances varying from changes in signal pulse strength to interference from fishing nets frequently required "urgent excursion to shallow depths to regain communications."[70]

Given the submarines' total dependence on radio, routine maintenance or mechanical difficulties greatly reduced their responsiveness, while similar problems had very little effect on SAC forces. This was true for malfunctions at both ends of the communications channel. At the transmitting end, equipment downtime interrupted the flow of information from higher authorities. At the receiving end, problems such as the loss of towed buoys (the lines sometimes snapped) interrupted reception. And communications malfunctions at the receiving end had to be repaired without outside assistance or supplies, which in practice meant that some repair work had to await return to port.

During peacetime many missile submarines at sea were exempt from a national requirement to maintain twenty-four-hour communications re-

68. *Fiscal Year 1978 Authorization for Military Procurement, Research and Development,* Senate hearings, pt. 1, p. 6631.

69. A recent report notes that problems of reliability have historically plagued the towed buoy antenna. As a result, commanding officers have generally employed the buoyant wire antenna, which is bidirectional and thus cannot receive signals throughout a full 360 degrees. General Accounting Office, *An Unclassified Version of a Classified Report Entitled "The Navy's Strategic Communications Systems—Need for Management Attention and Decisionmaking,"* PSAD-79-48A (May 2, 1979), pp. 17, 37.

70. *Fiscal Year 1977 Authorization for Military Procurement, Research and Development,* Senate hearings, pt. 12, p. 6821.

ception. Submarines in transit, for example, followed modified alert procedures that called for periodic rather than continuous reception of messages broadcast from shore.[71] They often operated at depths and speeds that were not conducive to signal reception using trailing antennas at or near the ocean's surface. Only periodically would a missile submarine in transit slow down, float an antenna, and monitor broadcasts.

An intense international crisis would have tended to magnify these command and communications problems. The surging of port-bound missile submarines to protect them from a Soviet first strike and to bring them within striking range of Soviet targets would have substantially increased the number in transit; many would not have been in the best position to receive information on a continuous basis, nor would higher authorities have known their location and status. In the absence of two-way communications, no one could have determined which had arrived on station, which were prepared to fire, which had received the latest emergency action and intelligence information, which were experiencing problems with communications, or which were engaged with Soviet anti-submarine forces. In the event of detection, harassment, or attack, the submarine commander's main responsibility was to escape, using force if necessary. All the while, he could not have informed authorities of the incident nor awaited instructions on course of action. Indeed, trailing an antenna would have been impractical while the submarine undertook evasive action. Interruption of reception was both necessary and permissible under such circumstances.[72]

By all indications, arrangements for postattack control of submarines were in disarray. Ground communications provided a precarious link, and an embryonic airborne system had not yet achieved significant operational capability. The navy had not deployed anything that satisfied even minimal requirements for postattack control. With a small but concentrated effort the Soviets could have isolated the entire force from higher authorities, a state of affairs that was not acknowledged at the time. Official assessments were reassuring: the sheer multiplicity of survivable radio stations at sea and on land would, they said, compensate for the vulnerability of primary shore-based elements. But it was no simple matter to sustain a chain reaction that successfully relayed messages

71. General Accounting Office, *The Navy's Strategic Communications Systems*, pp. 2–3.
72. *Fiscal Year 1978 Authorization for Military Procurement, Research and Development*, Senate hearings, pt. 10, p. 6734.

through an ancillary network to submarines. Planning, practice, and the tuning of procedures are prerequisites; none of this had been done during the 1960s. Furthermore, several episodes of crisis management during the 1960s raised serious doubts about the performance of even undamaged naval communications networks. The official position was more assertion than fact. Whatever potential redundancy did exist in the naval communications system could not have been effectively exploited in wartime.

STRATEGIC BOMBERS AND COMMAND STABILITY. Strategic bombers on ground alert were like ICBMs in terms of command stability, while bombers on airborne alert were more like missile submarines.

In peacetime, bombers stationed at primary SAC bases remained under the firm control of higher authorities. SAC knew their exact location at all times, and monitored their readiness by means of automated command and control system (SACCS) reports submitted by local wing command posts.[73] Established procedures allowed bomber readiness to be stepped up in a timely and orderly fashion, though not without some impairment of control during and after major transitions such as the dispersal of bombers from primary to secondary bases to reduce their vulnerability. The Primary Alerting System provided a direct, reliable link to send alert messages out and accept returning acknowledgments. SACCS and PAS, however, did not extend to many of the dispersal bases.

A substantial impairment of control would have accompanied a launch; at some early point, bombers would have maintained communications silence to avoid detection. Their ability to receive instructions would have steadily decreased as they flew farther from SAC radio stations. Receipt of a recall order, a go code, or a go-code cancellation would have become increasingly difficult. Receipt could not be acknowledged, and attack by Soviet fighter interceptors also could not be reported. At some point in their flight toward the Soviet Union, all communications with the force would have been lost.[74]

Soviet attacks on fixed command centers and communications channels would have compounded these problems. In all likelihood, the

73. SACCS provided CINCSAC and the NMCC with an automated system for monitoring the status of all SAC forces. Terminals were located at SAC headquarters, the three numbered air force headquarters, and all SAC bomber bases and missile launch centers within the continental United States. SACCS became fully operational in 1965. It used unprotected land lines to interconnect the terminals.

74. *Fiscal Year 1978 Authorization for Military Procurement, Research and Development,* Senate hearings, p. 6816.

PACCS airborne network would have assumed primary responsibility for the control of strategic bomber operations, but it would have been hard-pressed indeed to fulfill this responsibility. PACCS itself was not invulnerable to attack, and even an intact network could have reached only a small fraction of the bomber force once it had flown beyond line-of-sight range of PACCS aircraft. The chances of reaching the far-flung bombers by means of emergency communications rockets were even more remote.

Negative Control

Insight into the problem of negative control, a topic ignored by standard assessment, begins with an appreciation of its close relationship to positive control. Physical and procedural arrangements serve both priorities, but a physical condition—vulnerability to attack—creates a trade-off between them that has not and probably cannot ever be resolved fully.

Under the technical conditions of the mid-1960s, full protection of both the president and the physical means by which he would have authorized employment of nuclear weapons (a small but important aspect of positive control) could not be provided; therefore, absolute negative control could not have been achieved without risking Soviet neutralization of the entire nuclear arsenal by a sudden attack on the NCA or the National Military Command System. To dispel any Soviet notion that surprise attack could be successful, military organizations possessed the physical capability and possibly some form of conditional authority to employ nuclear weapons without the personal command of the president or his Constitutional successors.

Despite unusual secrecy, open and credible sources indicate that in the early 1960s nuclear attacks might have been launched under conditions ranging from communications blackout to verification of nuclear explosions within U.S. territory. These sources also suggest that procedures for dispatching forces without the personal participation and approval of national officials had been spelled out clearly. As a matter of principle, precise guidance would seem necessary to ensure proper and smooth procedure. Ambiguous definitions of the necessary circumstances, the authorities involved, and the actions permissible would have invited confusion (though such ambiguity might have been effective as a deterrent to a Soviet first strike against U.S. command centers).

However, because unambiguous definitions would have eroded the effective power of the president, military commanders probably operated under significant ambiguity of authority.[75] Logically, vertical predelegation of this ambiguous authority ought to have been extensive. The unified and specified commands, though less vulnerable than the NCA by virtue of greater numbers, dispersion, mobility, and readiness, had not been provided protection comparable to that afforded subordinate units, especially commanders of individual bomber, submarine, and ICBM units. It seems reasonable to suppose, therefore, that the only foolproof hedge against decisive decapitation was predelegation of authority to low-level units. But if such authority cascaded to the bottom of the chain of command, it was probably very ambiguous authority. Formal, unambiguous guidance at the bottom would have so compromised the power of national leaders that it was surely not provided.

Ambiguous authority cuts two ways, however. It avoids troublesome political implications, and it might preserve the effective power of the president during communications outages of significant duration, but at some point clear definitions and precise guidance could preserve it better. Decisionmakers presumably do not have an unlimited tolerance of uncertainty. We cannot realistically expect ambiguity of authority to be endured with aplomb for an indefinite period.

How might the uncertainty be resolved in the absence of formal guidance? What has been called institutional ethos—the attitudes, traditions, and beliefs prevalent in military organizations—would arguably have the most systematic effect on behavior. It may well be the key determinant of the behavior of American nuclear forces in wartime under conditions in which authority is ambiguous. I believe that nuclear commanders have a

75. The following passage develops a pertinent argument that also has historical relevance: "A responsible president . . . would presumably never determine in advance that a failure of communication between the White House and SAC lasting more than five minutes would automatically confer on the SAC commander full authority to take any military action deemed necessary. Such a rule would remove the president from the chain of command under so many imaginable circumstances that even if it were to be stated in an apparently authoritative manner a judicious SAC commander would hardly believe it. Under many of these circumstances, a president with communications restored would clearly be expected to reassert control and would not appreciate aggressive, extensive exercising of power during the interim. An attempt at elaborate qualification could produce more credible rules of procedure; but it is precisely because increased credibility would increase the real effect on presidential power that the political implications would also become more difficult. As a consequence of this dilemma we must expect that modern strategic forces operate with the knowledge that there are conditions under which strategic operations might have to be undertaken despite ambiguous authority to do so." See Steinbruner, "National Security and the Concept of Strategic Stability," pp. 419–20.

sense of duty and beliefs about American nuclear policy in the event of Soviet nuclear attack and that these would eventually drive isolated commanders to dispatch their weapons.

Reliance on Tactical Warning

Analysis suggests that airborne command posts, the most survivable components of the command structure, could not have absorbed the full weight of a Soviet nuclear attack without timely advance warning and fast reaction. This reliance on tactical warning is usually understated. Although standard calculations of bomber vulnerability include assumptions about tactical warning, calculations of the overall strategic strength of the United States leave a wrong impression that early warning became less important once the United States shifted from total reliance on bombers to reliance on diversified forces, two components of which, ICBMs and missile submarines, seemed capable of riding out a surprise attack. In reality, tactical warning became indispensable because the United States failed to develop a strategic command network that could survive sudden attack without it. With the exception of Looking Glass, the command system provided no hedges against intelligence failure and early warning malfunction. Instead, the United States depended on controlling nuclear retaliation by means of a system that employed ground-alert aircraft and generated its capacity in anticipation of Soviet nuclear attack.

The highest echelon of the command hierarchy was not exceptional in this respect. In 1966 the national command post with the best chance of escaping attack unscathed was an EC-135 aircraft normally maintained on fifteen-minute ground alert near Washington. Without sufficient warning from BMEWS radar, the national command aircraft as well as all PACCS aircraft except for Looking Glass could have been caught on the ground and destroyed. The vulnerability of the two ground-based and one ship-based national command posts, particularly their communications, meant that prompt notification of attack and immediate reaction by command aircraft were essential to the control of U.S. retaliatory forces.

Policy Implications in Retrospect

During the mid-1960s, nuclear explosive energy was being deployed much faster than it was being harnessed for the national purposes it was intended to serve. The capacity of the United States to manufacture and deploy weapons outstripped its capacity to impose the organizational and physical controls needed to bring them and the threat of retaliation they carried under strict control in wartime. To rectify this imbalance, the rate of deployments should have been slowed, and marginal dollars in protective investment should have been channeled into command structure. Missile submarines were the worst offenders in terms of command stability; their deployment should have been sharply curtailed pending development of more viable arrangements for their control. Other areas of underinvestment doubtless included tactical warning, the performance of which determined whether command channels would have been capable of triggering retaliation. And improvements in tactical warning systems notwithstanding, expenditures that reduced dependence of command channels on early warning would have represented a prudent investment.

That the strategic policy actually pursued at the time incurred high costs in unwarranted confidence, misplaced emphasis, and unwise resource allocations is a judgment that enjoys the benefits of hindsight. In fairness to the consensus responsible for that policy, many of the problems that posed potentially severe threats to the strategic command network could not have been well appreciated at the time. For example, the generation of electromagnetic pulse by nuclear bursts in the exoatmosphere was not discovered until the Teak-Orange atmospheric nuclear tests were conducted in 1958. The phenomenon was not confirmed until the Fishbowl nuclear tests of 1962. Rigorous scientific assessment of the field strength of EMP as well as the potential damage it could cause to communications systems was established between 1962 and 1965. That few parts of the U.S. command structure had been deliberately protected against EMP through 1966 can be blamed on the vicissitudes of scientific discovery in the nuclear field. (The only major C³I system to be protected before 1966 was NORAD headquarters.) Similarly, the performance of strategic organizations turned on small procedural details that defied earlier comprehension because of their complex interaction. Full comprehension of the consequences of the programmatic decision process in strategic organizations was in fact beyond reach. It still is.

A sharp shift in strategic priorities could not have been effected regardless of the store of available knowledge. The policy commitment to large-scale deployments of ICBMs and missile submarines, made at the expense of C³I, could not have been replaced by a commitment to a program reflecting balanced priorities unless the machinery to manage such a program existed or could have been instituted quickly. The machinery did not exist. Management of C³I programs was decentralized, diffuse, and fragmented. And the prospects of bringing the relevant programs under any strong, corporate direction must have seemed too remote to warrant the attempt. In any case, it would have taken many years to introduce the necessary machinery.

In spite of this institutional intractability, some significant C³I programs were initiated during the early 1960s and several came to fruition. Innovative solutions to certain problems were found and applied. Though they were not treated as prime concerns, the problems of negative and positive control certainly were not shrugged off as ones of minor significance. Given the established conception of the nuclear problem at the time, the command problem received more attention than one would have expected.

The arguments that can be made in defense of an ill-conceived policy during the initial period of nuclear deployments cannot be carried over to succeeding periods, however. The United States embarked on a fixed course, and too few paused to review what had come to pass. Analysts retreated into the abstract and mechanistic world of standard strategic enumeration, where it was almost axiomatic that capabilities turned on the size and technical composition of the respective weapon deployments, even though that same view of the world had created a policy that left glaring deficiencies in the means by which those weapons would be managed in wartime. Instead of correcting these deficiencies as well as the basic policy responsible for them, for the next fifteen years analysts anchored themselves even more firmly to the conception of the strategic problem that treated nuclear weapons as instruments of prewar and intrawar diplomacy, a means by which to influence the opponent's decisions, and that in effect denied the possibility of an attacker deliberately striking an opponent's command system. This conception made preservation of C³I a sort of theoretical imperative and fostered the belief that the only way a nuclear war might be won was by maneuvering into a position of bargaining dominance through attacks on enemy forces.

CHAPTER FIVE

Command Performance in the Early 1970s

ALTHOUGH the second half of the 1960s witnessed a dramatic surge in the number of Soviet intercontinental nuclear missile deployments, the confidence of the United States in its nuclear capabilities remained high. In their annual reports, defense secretaries repeatedly stressed the reliability and survivability of U.S. strategic forces and asserted without reservation that the threat of retaliation could not be removed by a Soviet first strike. Furthermore, the public was informed that "even if the Soviets attempt to match us in number of strategic missiles we shall continue to have, as far into the future as we can now discern, a very substantial qualitative lead and a distinct superiority in the numbers of deliverable weapons and the overall combat effectiveness of our strategic offensive forces."[1] Even extremely conservative assessments of retaliatory capabilities during the early 1970s struck reassuring notes. Paul Nitze, for example, applied worst-case assumptions and a measure of capability (strategic vehicle "throw weight") that biases calculations in favor of the Soviet Union and still concluded that the United States enjoyed a margin of superiority.[2]

The conventions of strategic thought and analysis that produced these assurances also continued to guide strategic planning and formal arms control negotiations. Planning emphasized protecting offensive forces

---

1. *The 1970 Defense Budget and Defense Program for Fiscal Years 1970–74* (Department of Defense, 1969), p. 46. See also *Fiscal Years 1972–76 Defense Program and the 1972 Defense Budget* (Department of Defense, 1971), p. 63; and *Annual Defense Department Report FY 1973*, p. 67.

2. "Assuring Strategic Stability in an Era of Detente," *Foreign Affairs*, vol. 54 (January 1976), pp. 207–32. Nitze's calculations, however, pointed to a precipitous reversal of that situation in the near future.

from attack and bolstering their ability to penetrate enemy defenses. The emergent SS-9 ICBM threat in particular stimulated efforts to protect Minuteman missiles with extra layers of defense, both passive (silo hardening) and active (antiballistic missile deployments). Penetration of enemy defenses was enhanced by equipping intercontinental and sea-launched ballistic missiles with multiple independently targeted warheads.

The conceptual and analytic conventions applied to force planning also spilled over into the strategic arms limitation talks, in which antiballistic missile (ABM) and Soviet SS-9 deployments became focal issues. The initial impetus to engage in formal arms negotiations arose from small-scale Soviet ABM deployments that U.S. observers feared might lead to a nationwide system capable of shielding Soviet people and industry from a U.S. counterattack. Because such defenses would be profoundly destabilizing, the U.S. delegation sought to constrain the deployments even though large-scale ABM defense of Minuteman would have to be abandoned as a consequence.

Although the antiballistic missile treaty precluded any major effort to deploy active systems to defend Minuteman silos, the aim of protecting Minuteman was pursued in negotiations devoted to offensive arms limitation. In fact, this goal was paramount. U.S. negotiators were unyielding in their insistence that a sublimit of about 300 SS-9 launchers was the sine qua non of any comprehensive agreement to limit offensive systems. The sublimit was a bone of contention until the eleventh hour of the two-year-long negotiations. John Newhouse chronicles the events surrounding the issue:

As SALT recessed briefly for Christmas [December 1971], the Soviets were still balking at the sublimit, the Americans still pushing, but without much hope. A failure to get the sublimit was among the gloomiest of prospects. Signing a SALT agreement bereft of this his highest priority could have cost Nixon the support of the American military and perhaps other parts of the government, as well. No one can say whether he'd have taken the risk.[3]

This was high drama because the continuing expansion of the SS-9 force could have eventually put the Minuteman force at great risk.

A Divergent Assessment

Against this background, it was unusual for someone in David Packard's position to be immersed in the management of strategic C³I pro-

3. *Cold Dawn: The Story of SALT* (Holt, Rinehart and Winston, 1973), p. 238.

grams. While he was the deputy secretary of defense from 1969 to 1972, Packard personally reviewed strategic C³I capabilities and became a forceful advocate of modernization. Packard had come to believe that command and control was the most serious question that needed attention within the Defense Department and that the greatest requirement, the greatest shortage, was for improvement in the U.S. airborne command and control system.[4] He considered the program deserving the highest priority within the Defense Department as a whole to be the development of a survivable airborne command post to replace the EC-135 aircraft used in the NEACP and Looking Glass operations.[5]

The priority he assigned to the E-4 program reflected a deeper concern: the United States might not be able to respond at all to a Soviet nuclear attack because of weaknesses in postattack control over strategic forces.[6] Variations on the theme of command vulnerability also filled pages of congressional hearings on defense supplemental requests submitted just after Packard's resignation. Secretary Melvin Laird, for example, citing serious deficiencies in strategic C³ survivability and reliability, told Congress that it was the most vulnerable single element in our strategic deterrent and that repair was a matter of extreme urgency.[7]

The command system of the early 1970s seemed almost designed to collapse under the weight of attack. Table 5-1 evaluates the primary ground-based command nodes and communications links relied on in 1971–72. Virtually every element lacked adequate protection from one or more effects of a nuclear attack. And mutual dependence among the elements was such that the destruction of only a few critical nodes would have severely impaired the entire ground network. The airborne backup network, although more likely to survive than the ground component, was certainly far more vulnerable than the weapons themselves. Also, the effectiveness of the airborne network depended critically on the performance of the ground-based network during the early phases of conflict.

---

4. Statement by Robert C. Moot, assistant secretary of defense, *Department of Defense Appropriations for 1973*, Hearings before a Subcommittee of the House Committee on Appropriations, 92 Cong. 2 sess. (GPO, 1972), pt. 2, p. 17; see also pt. 4, p. 987.

5. *Fiscal Year 1973 Authorization for Military Procurement, Research and Development, Construction Authorization for the Safeguard ABM, and Active Duty and Selected Reserve Strengths,* Hearings before the Senate Committee on Armed Services, 92 Cong. 2 sess. (GPO, 1972), pt. 3, p. 1463.

6. See Orr Kelly, "Ready for Doomsday," *Washington Evening Star-News* (February 28, 1973).

7. *Department of Defense Appropriations for 1973*, House hearings, pt. 2, p. 18, and pt. 4, p. 510.

Table 5-1. *Vulnerability of Ground C³ Segments, Early 1970s*

Ground segments	Redundancy			EMP vulnerability			Blast vulnerability			Atmospheric change vulnerability		
	Low	Medium	High	Low	Medium	High	Low	Medium	High	Low	Medium	High
Command centers												
National Military Command Center (NMCC)	x					x		x				
Alternate NMCC	x					x		x				
CINCSAC headquarters	x					x			x			
Numbered air force headquarters	x					x			x			
CINCLANT/CINCPAC headquarters and alternates		x				x			x			
SAC wing command posts	x					x			x			
Launch control centers			x				x					
North American Air Defense (NORAD) headquarters	x			x			x					
Communications												
Land lines and switching centers			x			x[a]			x			
Transoceanic cables	x			x[a]					x			
Navy main shore terminals for communications worldwide	x					x			x			
Navy LF/VLF stations	x					x			x	x		
Navy HF stations		x				x			x			x
SAC LF/VLF stations	x					x			x	x		
SAC HF stations			x			x			x			x
SAC UHF Green Pine sites	x					x			x	x		
SAC UHF emergency communications rockets	x					x		x			x	
Satellite control centers	x					x			x	x		

a. Vulnerable to magnetohydrodynamic effects of high-altitude nuclear explosions.

One of Packard's last official acts was to issue Department of Defense Directive 5100.30 in December 1971, which sought to reduce C^3I vulnerability by eliminating some critical nodes in the command structure. For instance, it modified the chain of command for executing the strategic war plan so that in principle national authorities could direct nuclear forces in the absence of the unified and specified commanders. The aim was not to eliminate intervening command nodes but rather to be able to bypass them if they were destroyed. Some physical and organizational restructuring along the lines set forth in the directive occurred, but not until the late 1970s.

Another element with patent deficiencies that attracted Packard's attention was the Minimum Essential Emergency Communications Network. MEECN was supposed to provide a last-ditch means by which the president could pass execution messages to the strategic forces during and after a nuclear attack, but the network was merely a collection of ground and airborne communications elements that appeared to be the least susceptible to direct attack, jamming, or other adversities. These elements were mainly LF and VLF radio systems being operated or developed to meet special mission requirements of the unified and specified commanders rather than the requirements of the national command authority.[8] MEECN thus consisted of a very restricted set of subnetworks that for technical reasons were not generally interoperable. The SAC and navy VLF subnetworks, for example, were basically incompatible; an execution message that found its way into one of the navy's VLF MEECN channels would not have been propagated outside this channel, so SAC forces would not have received it.

To bring the purpose and the performance of the MEECN network into closer alignment, Packard expanded its scope to include elements besides LF and VLF transmitters, and he assigned responsibility for the system to the Defense Communications Agency and the Joint Chiefs of Staff. During the early 1970s, however, MEECN remained a nominal system. After compiling a data base and identifying elements that could be made compatible to provide an initial survivable system, DCA forwarded an initial set of recommendations to the Joint Chiefs of Staff and the secretary of defense in December 1971.[9] In congressional testimony

8. *Hearings on Military Posture and an Act (S. 3293)* before the House Committee on Armed Services, 90 Cong. 2 sess. (GPO, 1968), pp. 8684–85.

9. *Department of Defense Appropriations for 1974,* Hearings before a Subcommittee of the House Committee on Appropriations, 93 Cong. 1 sess. (GPO, 1973), pt. 9, p. 1166.

the official responsible for the program said of its status in 1972 that "we have made substantive progress in learning more about the network as it is, in defining some of its deficiencies, laying out a program that is aimed at improving some of these deficiencies, and in turn we have made some progress in laying out longer range program objectives and efforts."[10] These remarks were made exactly ten years after Robert McNamara's testimony that the Defense Department had hardly begun to study the communications system on which U.S. retaliatory capabilities depended. The implications of the missile age for communications were scarcely any clearer in 1972 than they had been a decade earlier.

Packard had also become concerned about the command system's vulnerability to EMP. This threat still had not been confronted squarely even though theoretical breakthroughs achieved during the early 1960s had given rise to some dire speculation.[11] Senator Barry Goldwater recalled that in Senate hearings in the mid-1960s, "the theory was discussed . . . that a [deleted] megaton device detonated [deleted] miles above Kansas City would destroy all of our communications ability for most of the United States. And it was generally conceded that that was true. And at that time I know that they started hardening the entire communications system."[12] The effort to harden communications was insignificant, however. Contrary to Goldwater's impression, funding went almost exclusively for increasing protection of individual offensive and defensive weapons (NORAD headquarters was the notable exception). Between 1965 and 1972, research on the vulnerability of command systems to this esoteric phenomenon languished; it was still languishing long after the missile force had been hardened.

A modest effort to assess the EMP vulnerability of general purpose communications systems had been started about 1969,[13] but the research

10. *Fiscal Year 1973 Authorization for Military Procurement, Research and Development,* Senate hearings, pt. 4, p. 2628.

11. Seminal theoretical development is associated with the work of W. J. Karzas and Richard Latter, for example, "Detection of the Electromagnetic Radiation from Nuclear Explosions in Space," *Physical Review,* vol. 137 (March 8, 1965), pp. B1369–B1378.

12. *Military Construction Authorization Fiscal Year 1977,* Hearings before the Subcommittee on Military Construction of the Senate Committee on Armed Services, 94 Cong. 2 sess. (GPO, 1976), p. 551.

13. The main study effort sought to produce by 1979 a data base for high-altitude EMP vulnerability of the principal elements—leased landline telephone (AUTOVON) and teletype (AUTODIN) switches and military satellite ground terminals—of the defense communications system. See *Department of Defense Appropriations for 1974,* House hearings, pt. 9,

conducted through 1972 produced results that many considered inconclusive. According to the director of the Defense Communications Agency, tests on some of the relays and switches of AUTOVON, for example, "did not prove conclusively that there would be damage to the system."[14] In another test conducted about 1970, DCA in effect wrapped an electronic cocoon around an entire AUTODIN switching center to simulate EMP attack. Temporary outages lasting less than a minute resulted, but the findings once again suggested that the center would recover, and the DCA spokesman remarked, "we just are not going to worry about it any more."[15] Some observers questioned the validity of such findings, however, noting that the building housing the switch point was not the problem (though later tests of the switch point itself did uncover considerable vulnerability).[16] Conclusive results could only be obtained from tests of the total circuit—the switch point and the hundreds of miles of EMP "collectors" (communications cables and power lines) converging on it.[17]

Observers also challenged those who maintained there was no cause for concern unless test results proved conclusively that a problem existed. Such an attitude conflicted with the principle of conservative planning. Testifying in 1972, John A. Northrop, former deputy director of the Defense Nuclear Agency and a conservative planner, shed some light on the status of EMP research and the divisions of opinion that had affected progress.

We have gone through a period of some years now in which our major strategic systems have indeed been hardened against this electromagnetic pulse threat. This is the Poseidon and the Minuteman, and our strategic defense systems Sprint and Spartan.

---

p. 1151. For a description of AUTOVON, AUTODIN, and related networks, see *Fiscal Year 1976 and July–September 1976 Transition Period Authorization for Military Procurement, Research and Development, and Active Duty, Selected Reserve, and Civilian Personnel Strengths,* Hearing before the Senate Committee on Armed Services, 94 Cong. 1 sess. (GPO, 1975), pt. 1, pp. 152–53.

14. *Research, Development, Test, and Evaluation Program for Fiscal Year 1971,* Hearings before the House Committee on Armed Services, 91 Cong. 2 sess. (GPO, 1970), pt. 2, p. 8453.

15. Ibid. AUTODIN is a teletype network using commercial land lines. The Emergency Message Automated Transmission System (EMATS), the primary teletype system for disseminating launch messages to nuclear forces, employed some AUTODIN channels.

16. EMP tests of an AUTOVON switching center conducted in 1975 reportedly caused extensive damage. See William J. Broad, "Nuclear Pulse (II): Ensuring Delivery of the Doomsday Signal," *Science,* vol. 110 (June 5, 1981), p. 1116.

17. *Hearings on Military Posture and H.R. 12604* before the House Committee on Armed Services, 92 Cong. 2 sess. (GPO, 1972), pt. 2, p. 10763.

Now, the one issue that we identified last year in our testimony that we were beginning to address, however, was the effect of the electromagnetic pulse on communications systems. . . . Programs to harden this system to the other nuclear effects of radiation blast, blackout, and fallout are available and present no unknowns in their solution. The EMP research has not progressed to the same status. This supplemental fund request is intended to provide the initial effort to evaluate the effects of threat level, high altitude EMP on elements of the C^3 systems, and will be the first step toward providing a C^3 system with balanced hardness. . . .

When we presented Dr. Foster and the staff last year the proposal that there should be, frankly, a major escalation in the funding level to attack this problem, it was basically a question of whether we could prove the problem existed, whereas from our point of view the question was could we prove it did not exist.

In our initial studies it was hoped that we could identify that the problem would not be a continuing one—that is that the problem would go away. I think what has happened here is the final recognition that the problem appears to continue to be a potential hazard that must be addressed, and that our initial studies were not successful in making it go away.[18]

Among the studies that failed to make the hazard go away were laboratory tests that exposed small electronic components to a simulated EMP environment. Secretary Laird reported in 1972 that the tests "are now far enough along to cause grave concern about the effects on all our electronics systems unless special protective measures are taken and verified."[19]

Virtually no special protective measures were taken, however, for the ground segment of the command structure, including computers and power supply systems as well as communications. First, the cost of replacing all old systems with new ones designed to operate in EMP environments would have been prohibitive, and it was never seriously proposed. In addition, high-confidence protection of networks already in use could not be provided without a detailed assessment of the vulnerabilities peculiar to each, and in most cases such diagnoses were impractical. The experiments that a thorough assessment demanded entailed either atmospheric nuclear testing (banned by treaty) or the simulation of EMP fields over large areas (technologically infeasible). Like others, therefore, the Defense Science Board concluded that "the effects of EMP on the enormously complex leased telephone circuits are not (and, in our opinion, cannot be) understood well enough to assess with reasonable confidence the extent of their vulnerability to EMP."[20] Third, the likely conclusions

18. Ibid., pp. 10746, 10751, 10762.

19. *Department of Defense Appropriations for 1973*, House hearings, pt. 2, p. 18.

20. Cited in *Military Construction Authorization Fiscal Year 1977*, Senate hearings, p. 574.

of a thorough assessment might have aided the Soviet Union more than the United States; some may have found in this risk a reason not to undertake the assessment.

Full protective shielding for nuclear command posts and strategic communications was also not initiated because it could have cost billions of dollars, an expense the services did not want to bear. But the most important reason was that the blast effects of a direct attack against ground facilities could have wrought havoc in any case, and protection against the effects of EMP would not have removed that threat. Extensive EMP hardening thus appeared a dubious investment except for the already blast-resistant Minuteman silos and LCCs.[21] EMP protection would, however, be built into certain future procurement items. This investment would mitigate vulnerability to EMP, but only partially; most critical systems such as the leased land lines linking the various elements would remain unhardened indefinitely.

Nor would terrestrial communications be protected against magnetohydrodynamics, another esoteric effect of high-altitude explosions, whose significance came to light soon after Secretary Laird testified on the EMP problem. Solar emissions of unusually high intensity bombarded the earth throughout the summer of 1972. On August 4 the solar storm reached such proportions that it created a severe anomaly in the earth's magnetic field and caused a major outage in AT&T's newly installed L-4 transcontinental telephone cable. By altering the earth's magnetic field, the storm generated about seven volts per kilometer in the earth's crust, which was sufficient to trigger the automatic protective shutdown of a segment of the cable. An underwater cable between England and Dover was also shut down.

The susceptibility of cables to magnetic storms had been known before 1972. Earth potentials exceeding fifty volts per kilometer and fifteen volts per kilometer were recorded during storms in 1940 and 1958, respectively.

21. Minuteman silos were hardened against EMP beginning in 1972, with completion expected by late 1979; see *Department of Defense Authorization for Fiscal Year 1979,* Hearings before the Senate Committee on Armed Services, 95 Cong. 2 sess. (GPO, 1978), pt. 9, p. 6538. Hardening included installing sensors to detect an oncoming pulse and setting critical circuits to a passive mode during the pulse. Surge protection devices were installed to isolate all lines that penetrated the silo; see *Fiscal Year 1977 Authorization for Military Procurement, Research and Development and Active Duty, Selected Reserve and Civilian Personnel Strengths,* Hearings before the Senate Committee on Armed Services, 94 Cong. 2 sess. (GPO, 1976), pt. 11, pp. 6485–86. Some EMP hardening was also provided for launch centers; see *Military Construction Authorization Fiscal Year 1977,* Senate hearings, p. 574.

These storms caused telecommunications outages over large areas of northern Europe and North America. It was also known that high-altitude nuclear detonations caused magnetic field disturbances and corresponding earth potentials on cables. Geomagnetic disturbances roughly equal in magnitude to the 1972 storm were recorded during the Argus and Fishbowl nuclear tests over a decade earlier. During these tests, earth potentials were observed on at least one cable system, even though neither the tests nor the data measurements were designed for MHD analysis.

The L-4 outage in 1972 was geographically limited and short-lived. The only segment affected was a stretch of cable between Illinois and Iowa, and service was restored in thirty minutes by manually resetting circuit breakers and restoring power to the cable. The equipment suffered no physical damage. Nonetheless this outage revealed a weakness potentially greater than vulnerability to the effects of EMP. Because the L-4 had been identified as a candidate for interleaving communications among Safeguard ABM sites, studies were undertaken to determine whether high-altitude nuclear explosions would cause earth potentials of greater magnitude than the shutdown threshold of the L-4 cable. They apparently concluded that nuclear-induced potentials are much larger. According to one estimate, the potentials would be tens of volts per kilometer, which substantially exceeds the estimated threshold of four to eight volts per kilometer at which loss of L-4 service results.[22]

L-4 vulnerability was especially serious in view of the fact that the transcontinental underground cable was and still is the backbone of the operational communications network, tying together the nation's main nuclear command centers and forces. The L-4 cable is relied on to carry early warning data from sensors to command centers, to conduct emergency telecommunications conferences between national political and senior military authorities, and to deliver emergency action messages to strategic force and C^3I units before incoming missiles strike.

Apparently the vulnerability of ground communications to direct attack—the realization that their preservation or destruction had become a Soviet wartime prerogative—led Packard to examine carefully the airborne segment, the only alternative means of providing information to strategic forces in the wake of nuclear attack. He became certain that a major program to upgrade its capabilities was needed. The command

22. *DNA EMP Awareness Course Notes,* DNA 2772 T (Chicago: I.I.T. Research Institute, September 1973), p. 14.

aircraft then deployed, and the network they constituted, inspired so little confidence that Packard embarked on a personal crusade to hasten the replacement of EC-135 aircraft with advanced E-4 airborne command posts. An unmistakable sense of urgency surrounded congressional hearings and other public discussions of airborne capability in general and that of the National Emergency Airborne Command Post in particular. The EMP hazard for NEACP was addressed with special seriousness, and protection was assigned high priority. Although for several years after Packard's departure it was given less consideration, high priority was restored during the Carter administration, and the necessary protection was ultimately provided. In the early 1970s, however, the entire airborne network was exposed to the effects of EMP.

A host of reasons were given to justify replacing EC-135 aircraft. The E-4 would provide additional space for national policy officials. NEACP's endurance would be extended from ten hours to sixteen hours without refueling and from twenty-four hours to seventy-two with refueling. The E-4 would be able to store and process more data, and it would also have longer-range and more effective communications. But the overarching justification was simply that the United States had clearly staked its ability to control retaliation on an airborne system, and the EC-135 was pitifully outmoded. The time had come to deploy a command aircraft that would have a reasonably good chance of carrying this burden. In the words of Secretary Laird,

[The] Advanced Airborne Command Post is an urgent program if we are to retain a credible and realistic deterrent in the future. . . . Our current airborne command system is severely deficient in survivability and capacity and cannot fulfill our essential needs in the event of nuclear attack on our country. It lacks the survivable secure communications needed for control and execution of the forces. . . .[23]

Central Command Vulnerabilities: Reliance on Airborne Systems Grows

Simple extrapolation of the baseline conditions described in chapter 4 would give a reasonably good idea of conditions existing in the early

23. *Department of Defense Appropriations for 1973,* House hearings, pt. 2, p. 7. This testimony contrasts with the milder words of Laird's annual report: "Our current airborne command and control system is deficient in that it lacks capacity for added communications and data processing equipment. We need to improve the survivability of the system, and to provide the more secure communications needed for control and execution of the forces"; see *Annual Defense Department Report FY 1973,* p. 73.

1970s. The situation was not static between 1966 and 1973, though, and it is useful to review some of the changes.

Circumstances in the early 1970s were in part the result of two internal decisions, both of which increased reliance on the airborne network. In 1970, the navy terminated the National Emergency Command Post Afloat (NECPA) program, which had been expanded during the late 1960s to include two ships and several shore-based troposcatter stations along the Eastern seaboard.[24] The decision, for which the navy invoked fiscal austerity as justification, irritated many OSD officials concerned with the survivability of the national command authority and the National Military Command System. They took particular umbrage that they were not consulted and that the navy scrapped NECPA while retaining all its own command ships. Nevertheless, the decision was allowed to stand. Under the decentralized budgetary procedures followed at the time, reversing the decision would have involved high-level intervention and bureaucratic infighting that OSD officials did not care to instigate.

The second decision concerned protective investment in fixed, ground-based command facilities. In the mid-1960s, Secretary McNamara advanced the principle of complementarity: neither a survivable airborne command post nor a survivable ground-based command post would by itself adequately serve C^3 purposes after an attack.[25] Contending that positive control required both, McNamara recommended construction of a deep underground center for SAC to back up its vulnerable Omaha headquarters and complement its short-endurance airborne network. Under the same principle, provision of like facilities for use by national officials would have been advisable, and it is likely that plans to build a deep subterranean shelter for the NCA were drawn up.

Had such plans gone forward, construction would have probably been completed by the early 1970s. The installations almost certainly would have become obsolete soon thereafter, but for a while conservative Soviet planners probably would have concluded that the facilities could not be destroyed with high confidence. The plans were disapproved or shelved,

24. *Department of Defense Appropriations for 1968,* Hearings before a Subcommittee of the House Committee on Appropriations, 90 Cong. 1 sess. (GPO, 1967), pt. 5, pp. 237–38; *Department of Defense Appropriations for 1970,* Hearings before a Subcommittee of the House Committee on Appropriations, 91 Cong. 1 sess. (GPO, 1969), pt. 3, p. 668; "Electronic Systems," *DMS Market Intelligence Report* (September 1969), p. 5; *Research, Development, Test, and Evaluation Program for Fiscal Year 1971,* House hearings, pt. 2, p. 8058.

25. *Military Procurement Authorization Fiscal Year 1964,* Hearings before the Senate Committee on Armed Services, 88 Cong. 1 sess. (GPO, 1963), pp. 55–56.

however, leaving SAC and the National Military Command System without survivable ground-based facilities. The Alternate National Military Command Center was thought at least partly survivable by many in 1966, but by 1972 technical judgment considered that it could not withstand a determined missile attack.[26] A senior military officer summarized how Packard and other members on the newly formed council of the World Wide Military Command and Control System viewed the situation at the time: "members were concerned about the eroding survivability of the underground command post [near Ft. Ritchie]. We could find ourselves in a position where it was impossible to guarantee the survivability of the National Command Authority."[27]

The obsolescence of the ANMCC was not only preordained by the Soviet commitment to deploy a large force of modern ICBMs by the end of the 1960s but also by Soviet deployment of a new generation of missile submarines. By 1970, Yankee-class submarines armed with more reliable, accurate, and longer-range missiles than their predecessors were operating in the Atlantic within striking range of Washington and the ANMCC.[28] The submarines added a new dimension to the vulnerability of command posts because of the short flight times of missiles launched at relatively close range and because reliable, timely detection of launches was problematic. Ground-based national command facilities could thus be destroyed or isolated before command and control could be transferred to NEACP.

The more serious consequence of Yankee deployments was the new threat posed to NEACP itself. The command aircraft were routinely maintained on ground alert at Andrews AFB near Washington in the early 1970s, and according to the air force, there was a very serious risk that "an SLBM 'launch without warning' attack could destroy NEACP aircraft . . . when Red submarines are in close proximity to U.S. shores."[29] But as the air force hastened to add, there were circumstances in which

26. *Fiscal Year 1973 Authorization for Military Procurement, Research and Development,* Senate hearings, pt. 3, p. 1973.

27. *Department of Defense Appropriations for Fiscal Year 1973,* Senate hearings, pt. 4, p. 988.

28. Richard T. Ackley, "The Wartime Role of Soviet SSBNs," *U.S. Naval Institute Proceedings* (June 1978), p. 36. According to Ackley, Yankee-class submarines were also patrolling the Pacific within range of the continental United States by 1971.

29. *Fiscal Year 1973 Authorization for Military Procurement, Research and Development,* Senate hearings, pt. 3, p. 1975.

the aircraft might survive because calculations were sensitive to a range of assumptions, particularly about the capabilities of tactical warning systems in operation then.

SLBM Early Warning Capabilities

Before mid-1972 the United States lacked a respectable system for detecting submarine missiles launched from waters contiguous to its shores. The only system in operation consisted of seven height-finder radars deployed along the East and West coasts and the Gulf of Mexico, augmented by a somewhat more advanced radar maintained on standby status at a station on the East Coast. The seven sites employed antiquated dish radars originally designed for defense against enemy aircraft.[30] Their range was inherently restricted by line of sight; a missile launched from 1,200 nautical miles at sea on a westerly trajectory, for instance, would have reached an altitude of 200 miles before radar could possibly have detected it. While the total flight time over this distance would have been fourteen minutes, the climb to altitude, which the radar could not see, would have accounted for three to four minutes. More significantly, the effective range of the radars was no greater than about 750 nautical miles[31] and perhaps considerably less, so that even a missile within line of sight could have escaped detection for several more minutes. That translates into a maximum warning time of six to eight minutes.

Some warning time, furthermore, would have been consumed by activities that intervened between initial sensor detection and aircrew reaction. Data flowed automatically from the radar sites through NORAD

---

30. See "Sea-Launched Ballistic Missile Warning Net Development Set," *Missiles and Rockets* (January 24, 1966), pp. 16–17; Otis C. Moore, "No Hiding Place in Space," *Air Force Magazine* (August 1974), p. 45; "Electronic Systems," *DMS Market Intelligence Report* (December 1968), 474N (SLBM), p. 2; and *Annual Defense Department Report FY 1973*, p. 75. The more advanced radar located in New Jersey was deactivated in 1974 for environmental reasons. A more advanced phased-array radar located in Florida was activated about the same time to provide extensive coverage of the Caribbean area. *Jane's Weapon Systems, 1982–83*, AN/FPS-49 (2509.153) and AN/FPS-85 (2546.153), p. 505; Phillip J. Klass, "FPS-85 Radar Expands to Cover SLBMs," *Aviation Week & Space Technology* (February 19, 1973), pp. 61–66; and *Department of Defense Appropriations for Fiscal Year 1975*, Hearings before the Senate Committee on Armed Services, 93 Cong. 2 sess. (GPO, 1974), pt. 1, p. 516.

31. The estimate is from John J. Hamre, Richard H. Davison, and Peter T. Tarpgaard, *Strategic Command, Control, and Communications: Alternative Approaches for Modernization* (Congressional Budget Office, October 1981), p. 10.

headquarters to the major command posts—NMCC, ANMCC, CINC-SAC, CINCPAC, CINCLANT, and CINCEUR headquarters—which in turn manually alerted aircrews under their jurisdiction after first evaluating the indications of attack. Even if these intermediate steps took no time at all—that is, aircrews were alerted the instant the missiles were detected—aircraft on ground alert at coastal locations still had virtually no chance of escape, and the odds were not very much better for aircraft on high alert.

The successful launch of early warning satellites brought a dramatic improvement in submarine missile detection.[32] In 1971 a satellite was placed in stationary orbit over the Indian Ocean at an altitude of 22,300 miles, where its sensors monitored Soviet ICBM missile launches in the eastern hemisphere. Because of the high altitude, almost all of the Soviet Union, China, and other potential missile launch and test areas were within view (figure 5-1). This satellite thus complemented BMEWS as well as the foreign-based, over-the-horizon (OTH) radar network that had become operational in 1968.[33] A second satellite launched in 1972 was positioned in a stationary orbit over Panama to monitor areas of the Atlantic, Pacific, and Caribbean that Yankee submarines patrolled (figure 5-1). Like the satellite over the Indian Ocean, it reportedly carried both thermal infrared and visible light detectors.[34] The infrared devices could

32. "Additional Warning Satellites Expected," *Aviation Week & Space Technology* (May 14, 1973), p. 17; *Annual Defense Department Report Fiscal Year 1973*, p. 75; *Annual Defense Department Report Fiscal Year 1974*, p. 63; and Bruce G. Blair and Garry D. Brewer, "Verifying SALT Agreements," in *Verification and SALT: The Challenge of Strategic Deception*, William C. Potter, ed. (Boulder, Colo.: Westview Press, 1980), p. 28.

33. The so-called forward-scatter radars, code-named 440L, transmitted HF radio waves across the Soviet landmass from foreign-based transmitters. Distant receivers detected a missile during its vertical boost through the ionosphere by measuring the resulting disturbance in the received radio signal and relayed the data to NORAD; see *Department of Defense Appropriations for Fiscal Year 1973*, Senate hearings, pt. 4, p. 649. An experimental 440L warning system was installed in late 1965, successfully tested in 1966, further developed and expanded during 1967, and completed in early 1968. See *Military Procurement Authorization for Fiscal Year 1967*, Hearings before the Senate Committee on Armed Services and the Subcommittee on Department of Defense of the Committee on Appropriations, 89 Cong. 2 sess. (GPO, 1966), p. 873; *Department of Defense Appropriations for 1968*, House hearings, pt. 5, p. 601; *Jane's Weapon Systems, 1979–80*, Ground Radar (1948.153), p. 528; *The 1970 Defense Budget and Defense Program for Fiscal Years 1970–74*, p. 64; and Edgar Ulsamer, "Strategic Warning, Cornerstone of Deterrence," *Air Force Magazine* (May 1974), pp. 42–43.

34. *Department of Defense Appropriations for Fiscal Year 1975*, Hearings before the Senate Committee on Appropriations, 93 Cong. 2 sess. (GPO, 1974), pt. 4, p. 591.

Figure 5-1. *Maximum Coverage of Early Warning Satellites Positioned over the Indian Ocean and over Panama*

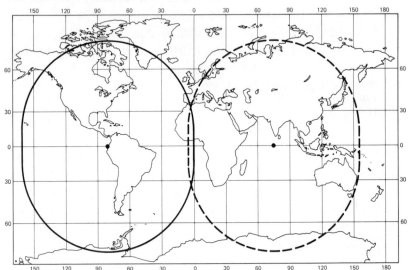

sense the radiated energy of the missile's plume during its relatively slow climb to altitude. A missile may have been detectable only thirty seconds after breakwater, depending on cloud conditions and other factors.

These early warning satellites have been credited with the ability to provide thirty minutes of advance warning of ICBM impact (compared to twenty-five minutes for OTH radar and fifteen to twenty minutes for BMEWS)[35] and a manifold improvement in tactical warning of missile submarine attack. Performance, however, was subject to a variety of constraints, and closer examination of the technical details uncovers deficiencies. For example, sun glint and glare from clouds and the ocean surface occasionally triggered false alarms and created blind spots that impaired coverage,[36] although the time of these occurrences and the areas affected were fairly predictable because they tended to be correlated with seasonal

35. *Military Procurement Authorization Fiscal Year 1966,* Hearings before the Senate Committee on Armed Services and the Subcommittee on the Department of Defense of the Committee on Appropriations, 89 Cong. 1 sess. (GPO, 1965), p. 1158.

36. Barry Miller, "U.S. Moves to Upgrade Missile Warning," *Aviation Week & Space Technology* (December 2, 1974), pp. 17–18; and *Department of Defense Appropriations for Fiscal Year 1975,* Hearings before the Senate Committee on Appropriations, 93 Cong. 2 sess. (GPO, 1974), pt. 1, pp. 116, 516.

changes. The problem was not much alleviated until the launch of a companion satellite in 1973. The coverage of the two extensively overlapped, but they were spaced far enough apart that blind spots normally would not coincide. False alarms continued to plague surveillance, however.[37] Satellite receiving stations were affected by unpredictable computer malfunctions and communications outages.[38] Readout stations associated with ICBM and SLBM launch detection, sited near Woomera, Australia, and at Buckley Airfield, Colorado, respectively,[39] experienced problems with communications, and data processing equipment evidently caused intermittent breakdowns in service as well as false alarms.

Another technical limitation was the field of view of the satellite sensors. Figure 5-1 shows the total surface area within line-of-sight range of a particular satellite, not the specific area actually under surveillance at any given instant. A satellite positioned over Panama, for instance, could not have monitored both oceans simultaneously, nor could it have simultaneously monitored all possible launch points within either ocean. A Yankee submarine SS-N-6 missile with a range of 1,300 nautical miles could have hit Washington from an area of the Atlantic one million miles square, but the satellite over Panama probably had less than one percent of this area in view at any given time.[40] Full coverage of the area required the satellite sensor to scan portions of the surface methodically, bringing one part of the ocean into view as another left it. There would have been at least a slight delay in initial detection, and during inclement weather a missile burn of short duration might have escaped confirming detection during subsequent scans. There was a significant risk that the satellites would fail to detect the leading missile of a salvo or would give a false alarm. For multiple launches such errors were less likely to occur.

The basic physical limitation imposed on the satellites' range by the earth's curvature also proved significant once the Soviets deployed Delta submarines armed with SS-N-8 missiles. Tested toward the end of 1972 and deployed soon afterwards, SS-N-8s had a range in excess of 4,300 nautical miles and were easily capable of flying undetected over U.S.

37. As late as 1980 many satellite infrared signals proved not to be associated with a missile launch. *Recent False Alerts from the Nation's Missile Attack Warning System,* Hearings before the Senate Committee on Armed Services, 96 Cong. 2 sess. (GPO, 1980), p. 4.
38. *Department of Defense Appropriations for 1974,* House hearings, pt. 6, pp. 1688, 1691.
39. Miller, "U.S. Moves to Upgrade Missile Warning," p. 16.
40. Estimate based on Miller, "U.S. Moves to Upgrade Missile Warning," p. 18, which reports that the sensor contained many infrared elements, each capable of subtending an angle corresponding to two square miles of surface area.

coastal radar.[41] They could have been launched from points in the Pacific, North Sea, and Arctic that were beyond the line of sight of early warning satellites in geosynchronous orbit.[42] Some parts of these regions were also behind BMEWS and hence outside its area of coverage. A senior military officer testified in 1973 that the SS-N-8 posed a new threat to U.S. strategic forces, including land-based warning systems, command and control centers, and SAC bomber bases,[43] a view reinforced by the deputy secretary of defense, who reportedly asserted in 1973 that "all points in the continental United States are now subject to SLBM attack without warning. . . ."[44]

The warning elements themselves were also exposed to nuclear attack. All the radar sites used in early warning were vulnerable to blast or the effects of EMP and MHD, as were the landline communications that fed radar sensor data to NORAD headquarters, the focal point of and critical node within the radar network. A granite mountain protected the underground operations center itself but not the communications entering it, and even the underground center was unlikely to survive an ICBM attack directed against it. Regarding satellite early warning, the two readout stations were the least survivable components of the system;[45] they had very little protection. The long-haul terrestrial and undersea communications lines linking satellite readout stations with NORAD were also enormously exposed to blast effects and to EMP and MHD effects. Finally, all communications lines linking the sensors and NORAD with SAC, the National Military Command System, and the unified commanders were vulnerable to these same effects.

These vulnerabilities undermined but did not necessarily preclude advance warning of an attack in progress. A major strike against the warning system would almost certainly have been detected by that same system before its destruction, unless it were sabotaged in advance. Furthermore, the inexplicable loss of particular warning sensors might have

41. *Department of Defense Appropriations for 1975,* Hearings before a Subcommittee of the House Committee on Appropriations, 93 Cong. 2 sess. (GPO, 1975), pt. 4, p. 936, and pt. 7, pp. 1328–30.

42. John W. Finney, "Pentagon Seeks Funds for Radars," *New York Times,* December 4, 1973; *Department of Defense Appropriations for Fiscal Year 1975,* Senate hearings, pt. 7, p. 116; and *Department of Defense Appropriations for 1975,* House hearings, pt. 4, p. 936.

43. *Department of Defense Appropriations for 1974,* House hearings, pt. 6, p. 1691.

44. Finney, "Pentagon Seeks Funds for Radars."

45. *Department of Defense Appropriations for 1975,* House hearings, pt. 4, p. 935.

been interpreted as an indication, albeit ambiguous, that an attack was under way.[46] In short, warning to aircraft on ground alert was not necessarily jeopardized by the vulnerability of the warning system. For purposes of estimating the prelaunch survivability of the NEACP and other airborne command posts, this vulnerability will be ignored.

Organizational arrangements for the dissemination of satellite warning data improved upon the scheme devised for BMEWS and the SLBM radar detection network. All data from radar sensors were funneled into NORAD headquarters before spreading out to other users. By contrast, operators at satellite readout sites transmitted data directly to SAC headquarters and the NMCC and the ANMCC as well as to NORAD.[47] The Joint Chiefs of Staff had also included the unified commanders among the units designated as users of satellite data,[48] but these commanders evidently received information via NORAD rather than directly from the readout stations.

Despite this attempt at streamlining the warning process, the network remained complex; data still flowed through numerous communications nodes before reaching final destinations. The process remained elaborate in other respects. Optimal performance required, for example, a working relationship between the navy and NORAD in which the navy was to track Soviet submarines and report their location to NORAD. For operations involving sensors with limited range, field of view, and so forth, information on known or suspected submarine locations would have been valuable both for sensor operation and data interpretation.

Organizational complexities like these, together with the technical constraints, suggest that such simplifying assumptions as ninety seconds elapsing between missile breakwater and klaxon alarm at airbases can be misleading. And these assumptions underlie most strategic analyses—

---

46. The minute BMEWS goes out, a former SAC commander in chief once speculated, "I am liable to launch the ground alert force." *Department of Defense Appropriations for 1961*, Hearings before a Subcommittee of the House Committee on Appropriations, 86 Cong. 2 sess. (GPO, 1960), pt. 7, p. 76.

47. It is easy to infer from numerous sources that NORAD was a critical node for relaying all sensor data except for early warning satellite data. Apparent corroboration of this point is found in *Recent False Alerts from the Nation's Missile Attack Warning System*, Senate hearings, p. 3, which notes that satellites and PAVE PAWS radars are the only two systems that feed data directly to major command centers besides NORAD. (PAVE PAWS radars were not deployed until the late 1970s.)

48. *Department of Defense Appropriations for Fiscal Year 1975*, Senate hearings, pt. 4, p. 591.

for instance, calculations of the prelaunch survivability of U.S. strategic bombers on ground alert.[49] I too resort to simplifying assumptions about tactical warning in order to assess the prelaunch vulnerability of airborne command posts. My calculations and conclusions probably are optimistic.

In spite of the tendency to gloss over many aspects of tactical warning operations to simplify calculating the threat, few analysts failed to appreciate the possibility that overlooked or slighted details could have grave implications for wartime performance. For all the technological marvel of modern early warning satellites, many cautious planners eschewed on principle heavy reliance on any tactical warning. The opportunities for technical and organizational error were too numerous, and the allowable margin of error was too slim. Tactical warning could not be a precondition for the success of operations. Dependence on it for generating the retaliatory capability of the strategic bomber force became widely regarded as a major liability, and missile submarines won praise for being able to ride out attacks without any warning whatsoever.

This principle, however, was not applied to command system development. Tactical warning became indispensable, and strategic warning became increasingly important. The prelaunch survivability of NEACP and other command aircraft within striking range of Soviet missile submarines depended as much on anticipation of imminent Soviet attack and on knowledge of the movements of Soviet submarine deployments as it did on the performance of tactical warning networks. Even if systems dedicated to detecting attack performed at their theoretical optimum, aircraft at normal alert readiness could not have coped with surprise attacks; their reaction times were too slow. Prelaunch survival therefore depended on anticipating attack and on correspondingly increased vigilance and alert readiness. Similarly, movements that brought Soviet submarines closer to U.S. air bases warranted precautionary U.S. responses—for instance, an increase in the readiness of aircraft on ground alert to compensate for the reduction in flight time of the submarine missiles.

This dynamic is partially captured by the estimates that follow. They serve illustrative purposes only. They may not be completely relevant to realistic conditions because it is hard to know what changes in the disposition of command aircraft were likely to be triggered by strategic warn-

49. See, for example, Alton H. Quanbeck and Archie L. Wood, *Modernizing the Strategic Bomber Force* (Brookings, 1976), especially pp. 46–47.

ing indications, changes in submarine patrol patterns, and so forth. The alert status of command aircraft may not have been geared, for example, to the disposition of Soviet missile submarines, although the public record strongly suggests a preoccupation with monitoring the submarine threat to U.S. strategic bombers on ground alert. Because of the small scale of enemy deployments during peacetime, this threat did not seem serious even when submarines moved to positions near U.S. coasts. But under this definition of the threat the implications for the security of command aircraft would not be noticed.

Prelaunch Vulnerability of NEACP and Other Aircraft

In one respect the estimates that follow are conservative. The analysis rests on the assumption that a significant risk existed if the probability of a successful attack on ground-alert aircraft exceeded 10 percent. In other respects the estimates are optimistic because they are based on unusually favorable conditions that existed for only a brief time in 1972. Before 1972 the prelaunch vulnerability of command aircraft, including NEACP, was almost certainly much greater. Warning satellites for detecting submarine attack had not yet been orbited, and key Post Attack Command Control System aircraft were deployed near the coast (SAC did not begin to transfer the command aircraft at Westover AFB, Massachusetts, for example, to inland bases until the middle of 1970). After 1972, SS-N-8 missiles launched from certain ocean areas might have avoided both radar and satellite detection.

Other assumptions used in the analysis work to inflate the chances of aircraft survival. Submarine missile launches are assumed to be detected without fail, and all aircraft receive takeoff orders only two minutes after missile breakwater. This is an optimistic view of the technical and organizational performance of the early warning system. Blast is also assumed to be the only effect that can cause aircraft damage. Vulnerability to EMP attack is excluded, even though a strategy based partially on high-altitude EMP attack could have been employed to reduce effective warning time (EMP instantly radiates 700 miles from the burst point) and exploit the vulnerability of aircraft that are exposed while still on the ground (currents induced in aircraft on the ground are estimated to be several times higher than those induced in flight). Similarly, the analysis does not consider the possible effects of EMP or MHD damage to the ground-based communications circuits that carry sensor data to command centers and

Figure 5-2. *Flight Times and Ranges for Three Submarine-Launched Ballistic Missile Trajectories*

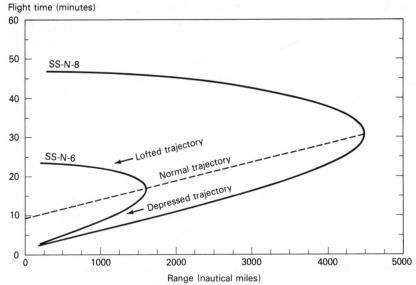

takeoff instructions to ground-alert aircraft. (A threat postulated in recent years that could just as easily have been proposed in the early 1970s imagines a submarine missile launched at close range and detonated at high altitude during the upward portion of its trajectory, creating EMP pulses and MHD effects that cause massive outages of primary communications channels only a few minutes after missile breakwater. The concern is that this precursor high-altitude attack would delay the launch of ground-alert command aircraft long enough to permit followup Soviet SLBMs and perhaps ICBMs to inflict blast damage on them.)

Notwithstanding these optimistic assumptions, ground alert aircraft were acutely vulnerable to surprise attack. Enemy submarine missiles launched against EC-135 aircraft on day-to-day alert could have caught them on the ground or immediately after takeoff and destroyed them because the flight time of the attacking missiles was shorter than the reaction time of the aircraft. Flight times are shown in figure 5-2. The slope of the dotted line relates flight time to range. For instance, the elapsed time between SS-N-6 breakwater and weapon impact over distances of 500 and 1,000 nautical miles would have been eleven and fourteen minutes, respectively. Even the longer flight time is shorter than the normal reaction time (the time between missile breakwater and aircraft brake release) of ground-alert command aircraft.

How much shorter is not a matter of public record because actual reaction times of aircraft are classified, but available evidence indicates that the reaction time of aircraft maintained at a normal state of readiness was about fifteen minutes, allowing for warning delay, crew scramble, engine start-up, taxi, and other procedures preceding takeoff. Pertinent testimony reveals, for example, that EC-135 engine start-up took about three minutes and that an aircraft could be airborne about six minutes afterward.[50] An additional six minutes, for a total of fifteen, would have plausibly been lost to warning delay and crew scramble. (It seems certain that no less than two minutes would have elapsed between missile breakwater and the receipt of tactical attack warning at the airbases and that crews would have taken several minutes to scramble from their alert facilities to their aircraft.) Primary-alert EC-135s operated by the commanders in chief of the European, Pacific, and Atlantic commands were reported to be on fifteen-minute alert (CINCLANT did not deploy an airborne command post until 1973).[51]

The actual flight time of Soviet SS-N-6 missiles is also not clear, owing to uncertainty about the location of enemy submarines at the time of launch. But in all circumstances in which submarine missiles were assumed within firing range of the target, the flight time would have been sufficiently short that destruction of the target would have been highly probable. Even if an SS-N-6 missile were fired at maximum range, 1,600 nautical miles from the target, an aircraft on fifteen-minute alert could not have put enough distance between itself and its airbase (the assumed aimpoint) to survive the blast effects. The flight time of the missiles would have been no more than seventeen minutes (and perhaps as little as sixteen if they flew a direct east-to-west trajectory to exploit the earth's rotation). Aircraft brake release for takeoff occurs, in this example, only two minutes before the incoming weapon explodes, and the aircraft

50. *Research, Development, Test, and Evaluation Program for Fiscal Year 1973,* Hearings before the House Committee on Armed Services, 92 Cong. 2 sess. (GPO, 1972), pt. 3, p. 11054.

51. *Department of Defense Appropriations for 1974,* House hearings, pt. 5, p. 1655. This testimony indicated that each command maintained those aircraft with the primary and secondary on fifteen-minute and sixty-minute ground alert, respectively.

Figure 5-3. *Distance Flown by EC-135 Aircraft as a Function of Time after Brake Release*

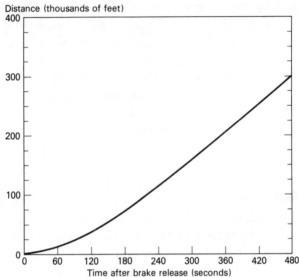

Distance (thousands of feet)

Time after brake release (seconds)

Source: Author's estimates based on unclassified data and Alton H. Quanbeck and Archie L. Wood, *Modernizing the Strategic Bomber Force* (Brookings, 1976), p. 48.

would have flown only 42,000 feet from the runway (see figure 5-3). The lethal radius of a Soviet SS-N-6 missile was itself 42,000 feet (assuming a weapon yield of one megaton and aircraft hardness of two psi of blast pressure). Thus destruction was virtually certain unless the attacking missile proved unreliable.[52]

Figure 5-4 maps the patrol areas in the Atlantic from which Soviet Yankee submarines armed with one-megaton weapons posed a serious

52. Formal calculation of the probability of safe escape can be performed using the equation,

$$P_s = 1 - r_m (R_L/R_U)^2, \text{ for one weapon,}$$

where P_s is the probability of safe escape, r_m is the missile reliability, R_L is the lethal radius of the weapon, and R_U is the distance between aircraft and aimpoint at the moment of detonation. Assuming missile reliability to be 85 percent, the chance of safe escape for an aircraft whose reaction time and escape speed places it 42,000 feet from the aimpoint at the moment of weapon detonation equals $1 - 0.85 (42,000/42,000)^2$, or 15 percent. Two or more incoming missiles spaced to strike around the aimpoint would further reduce an aircraft's chance of safe escape. In the hypothetical example given above, the probability of safe escape for aircraft during an attack by two weapons is $(0.15)^2$, or 2 percent. See Quanbeck and Wood, *Modernizing the Strategic Bomber Forces*, especially the appendixes.

Figure 5-4. *Soviet Submarine Zones Threatening U.S. Command Aircraft on Ground Alert*

threat to the various EC-135 elements of the PACCS network.[53] Theoretically, the firing of a single reliable SS-N-6 missile from any of the Atlantic zones—marked A, A-B, and A-B-C—would have destroyed the national command aircraft stationed at Andrews AFB under normal day-to-day alert conditions. In 1972 NEACP alone was within firing range of a Soviet submarine stationed in zone A (CINCLANT's airborne command post came under the same threat when it was deployed in 1973 at Langley AFB, Virginia), but enemy submarines could move progressively closer to the U.S. shoreline to bring other elements of the PACCS network within range. From zone A-B, a submarine firing two reliable missiles would, in addition to NEACP, have destroyed PACCS aircraft on ground alert in Indiana. From zone A-B-C, a submarine posed an equivalent threat to PACCS aircraft stationed at Offutt AFB, Nebraska. Finally, a submarine on patrol in zone A-B-C together with one in zone D-E could have destroyed NEACP and all other ground-alert elements of PACCS in a surprise attack.

53. The PACCS network comprises NEACP and SAC EC-135 aircraft as shown in figure 5-5, but formally excludes NEACP and EC-135 aircraft assigned to the unified commanders. Except for Looking Glass, all the orbits shown in figure 5-5 would have been occupied by EC-135 aircraft normally maintained on ground alert. *Department of Defense Appropriations for 1974,* House hearings, pt. 5, p. 1655.

The significance of this theoretical vulnerability is debatable. Many observers reject the danger of surprise attack on the grounds that signs of enemy preparation would appear before the actual attack, that such indications would be correctly read, and that military organizations would react in time to avoid the worst consequences. In this view, command vulnerability to surprise attack, however acute, does not merit serious concern as long as organizations are prepared to take steps—dispersing PACCS aircraft, reducing aircraft reaction times, and instituting airborne alert—to complicate enemy targeting, provide more escape time, and otherwise protect the command structure. Emergency measures would presumably be taken in a crisis and would presumably work to thwart enemy exploitation of peacetime vulnerabilities.

To conservative U.S. planners, however, the scope for intelligence failure, political indecision, and sluggish organizational response is sufficiently large that surprise attack is not implausible.[54] U.S. nuclear forces have been designed to accomplish their mission despite nearly total surprise because a surprise attack has long been considered a serious contingency by American military planners. Extreme prelaunch vulnerability of PACCS aircraft on normal ground alert is therefore a pertinent fact, and in light of the key role these aircraft play in postattack strategic control, it is an important fact.

Opinion can also split over the related issue of the effectiveness of programmed responses to crisis. Whether implementing emergency protective measures would have substantially reduced PACCS aircraft vulnerability depends on a complex of factors, many of which were excluded from earlier calculations. Pertinent considerations include the threat of sabotage, the effects of electromagnetic pulse, and the ability to sustain airborne alert operations throughout a prolonged crisis. The analytic approach applied earlier shows that while the prelaunch vulnerability of aircraft placed on a higher-than-normal ground alert during a crisis would not have been acute, it would have still been significant. Depending on the disposition of enemy submarine deployments and U.S. PACCS aircraft, particularly NEACP, high confidence in the prelaunch survivability of EC-135s would not have been warranted under many circumstances.

54. Numerous historical cases reveal that aggressors usually achieve military surprise in the initial phase of war. See Richard K. Betts, *Surprise Attack: Lessons for Defense Planning* (Brookings, 1982).

Consider a hypothetical situation in which a planned response to crisis would have reduced NEACP's reaction time from fifteen minutes to seven. SS-N-6 missiles launched from a distance of, say, 500 nautical miles would have arrived about four minutes after brake release, allowing the aircraft to put 123,000 feet between itself and the runway before detonation. But the risk of NEACP destruction in this case is still 10 percent (0.85 $[42,000/123,000])^2$. In the event of attack by four missiles, the estimated risk is 40 percent, and these risk assessments are optimistic because they pertain only to blast effects.

To achieve a very high level of confidence (over 90 percent) in NEACP's survival against nuclear blasts from a large attacking force (for example, four enemy missiles) with short flight times (eleven minutes), the reaction time of the aircraft had to be reduced to four minutes or less because seven minutes were needed to fly a safe distance away from the barraged area (an area centered on the airbase, assuming optimally spaced and timed detonations). In other words, to be highly survivable the aircraft had to be positioned at the end of the runway, engines running and ready for immediate takeoff upon receipt of tactical warning. Beyond the practical difficulties of maintaining this level of readiness during a prolonged crisis, there would have been virtually no margin for error or delay in processing tactical warning information, but it would not have been prudent to expect flawless performance.

Soviet deployment of submarine missiles capable of flying on depressed trajectories would have further diminished the benefits that emergency measures were intended to provide. The following table shows the reduction in SS-N-6 flight time that might have been achieved if depressed trajectories could have been flown.

Range (nautical miles)	Normal trajectory (minutes)	Depressed trajectory (minutes)	Time reduction (minutes)
500	11.50	5.00	−6.50
750	12.75	7.00	−5.75
1,000	14.00	8.50	−5.50
1,250	15.25	11.00	−4.25
1,500	16.50	14.00	−2.50

The implications of such short flight times can be illustrated by comparing the prelaunch vulnerability of NEACP to attack by normal and depressed-trajectory missiles. NEACP's probability of survival against four missiles fired at a range of 500 miles and in normal trajectories would have been 90 percent if the aircraft's reaction time were four minutes. If depressed trajectories are postulated, however, a single SS-N-6 fired from 500 nautical miles away would have had an 85 percent chance of destroying NEACP; from a distance of 750 miles, the probability would have been 25 percent. Conversely, NEACP's probability of survival ranged between 15 and 75 percent for a single missile launched from a distance of 500 to 750 miles. In the event of attack by four missiles, the probability of survival declines to between 0 and 20 percent.

Although Soviet missiles evidently had not been flight tested in depressed trajectories, and testing almost certainly would have been conducted before weapons designed to operate in that mode were fielded, the calculations do illustrate that certain tactics could have at least partially offset the additional margin of safety that increased alert readiness was supposed to provide. (It is also worth noting that standard calculations of force vulnerability, and in particular bomber vulnerability, usually include depressed-trajectory missile attacks among the cases considered.)

The main conclusion of these illustrative calculations is that the limited deployment of Soviet missile submarines in 1972 was very significant. From the standpoint of alert-bomber survivability, the Soviet missile submarine threat was a token one. Yankee-class submarines nonetheless put command aircraft at considerable risk. If genuine strategic surprise were achieved, neither NEACP nor any other major elements of the airborne command network on ground alert would have been successfully launched. If genuine strategic surprise were not achieved and aircraft alert readiness was higher than normal, as seems likely in many crisis circumstances, the prelaunch vulnerability of command aircraft would not have been acute. But the successful launch of NEACP before submarine-launched weapons arrived would have been questionable under certain plausible circumstances even if tactical warning systems performed flawlessly. And given the extreme sensitivity of aircraft vulnerability to tactical warning performance, significant risk was inherent in the situation. These risks applied to all command aircraft on ground alert, not just NEACP.

The above illustrations also reveal that SAC stood a better chance of surviving a dedicated attack on the command structure than key national entities did. It enjoyed greater geographic insulation from enemy submarines on patrol, operated an alternate command post on round-the-clock airborne alert, and normally maintained additional command aircraft on ground alert. By contrast, geography did not favor the prelaunch survivability of national command aircraft. For various reasons the maximum precaution against sudden attack—continuous airborne alert—could not be taken, and backup alert aircraft were not normally provided.

Postlaunch Capabilities of NEACP and PACCS

The airborne command network was reorganized in 1970. EC-135 command aircraft located at the three numbered air force headquarters in Louisiana, Massachusetts, and California were transferred to bases in the Midwest. These reassignments reduced the vulnerability of ground-alert aircraft to missile submarine attack and provided for a more compact network that could be serially interconnected by UHF line-of-sight radio communications. Backup systems for communicating beyond line-of-sight range included HF and newly deployed LF radio, neither of which worked as well as UHF in a nuclear-disturbed atmosphere.

Once launched under emergency wartime procedures, the airborne network would have extended from Washington to the far west Minuteman missile complexes. Figure 5-5 shows a hypothetical network of eight airborne stations.[55] Line-of-sight communications to ground missile units limit the orbits of Looking Glass and three airborne launch control centers. Looking Glass is also restricted to a flight pattern allowing continuous line-of-sight radio communications with SAC headquarters in Nebraska. The easternmost orbit, occupied by NEACP, is assumed to be confined to a region within line-of-sight range of ground-entry points and national command posts near Washington. Additional constraint is imposed on these five orbits and the remaining three occupied by a radio relay aircraft and two auxiliary command aircraft to reflect the loss of flexibility that results when line-of-sight communications between all adjacent aircraft must be continuously maintained.

An attack strategy based on EMP effects probably offered the best chance of damaging these aircraft. In the event of a high-altitude burst

55. The existence of eight airborne stations is acknowledged in *Fiscal Year 1976 and July–September 1976 Transition Period Authorization,* Senate hearings, pt. 6, p. 2751. A total of thirty-two aircraft supported PACCS (three national command aircraft, five Looking Glass aircraft, nine SAC auxiliary command aircraft, nine airborne launch control aircraft, and six SAC communications relay aircraft); see also *Department of Defense Appropriations for 1973,* House hearings, pt. 2, p. 28.

Figure 5-5. *Hypothetical Postattack Airborne Network*

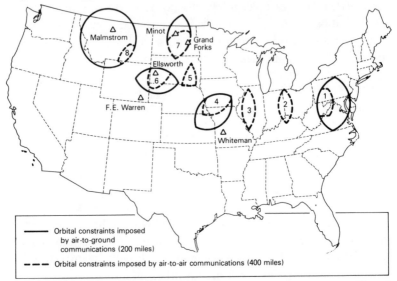

Note: Function/orbits (and home base) are 1. NEACP (Andrews AFB, Virginia); 2. Relay aircraft (Grissom AFB, Indiana); 3. East auxiliary (Offutt AFB, Nebraska); 4. Looking Glass and ALCC/ERCS for Whiteman missile complex (Offutt AFB, Nebraska); 5. West auxiliary (Ellsworth AFB, South Dakota); 6. ALCC for F. E. Warren and Ellsworth missile complexes (Ellsworth AFB, South Dakota); 7. ALCC for Grand Forks and Minot missile complexes (Minot AFB, North Dakota); 8. ALCC for Malmstrom missile complex (Minot AFB, North Dakota).

above the center of the country, exposure to EMP was virtually certain, and the loss of only one or two aircraft in the linkage could have been very costly. This will become clearer when I discuss the specific functions performed by the constituent parts of the network.

That the entire airborne command network might be vulnerable to EMP was a possibility worrying many defense officials during the early 1970s. Although the performance of aircraft exposed to EMP fields had not been assessed with scientific precision, theoretical refinements of the mid-1960s strongly suggested that aircraft would be highly vulnerable unless special protective measures were taken. Analysts realized not only that EC-135 aircraft (and EC-130 TACAMO submarine communications aircraft discussed later) lacked such protection,[56] but that they were also being equipped with transistors and semiconductors that were more susceptible to damage than vacuum tubes.

These predictions would be validated later. Analyses and test simulations would show that EMP could induce very large currents on the exterior and interior of aircraft exposed to a full-threat (50,000 volts per meter) pulse. The following table provides estimates of exterior currents

56. *Department of Defense Appropriations for 1973,* House hearings, pt. 2, p. 38.

for an aircraft.[57] While these values have been taken from a study of the B-1 bomber and therefore may not reflect actual values for NEACP and other aircraft in the airborne command fleet, they probably do not over-estimate current levels for EC-135 and EC-130 TACAMO aircraft. Given the configuration of most airborne command posts and radio relay air-craft—for instance, their use of a trailing antenna several miles long—the applicable values would probably be even higher than those shown.

Configuration	Peak current (amperes)
Cockpit	
Airborne	5,600
Ground	12,700
Air refuel	26,700
Fuselage, center	
Airborne	8,850
Ground	25,000
Fuselage at wing	22,600

Experience indicates that basic fuselage construction allows about one-tenth of the exterior current to flow on the inside of an airframe.[58] Thus, interior current flow might range between 560 and 2,670 amperes. In the case of the B-1, hardening plans called for extra shielding to reduce these currents to less than 10 amperes. Internal communications and avionics equipment would also have been protected against current surges on the order of 10 amperes. In the case of the unprotected EC-135 and EC-130 aircraft deployed in the early 1970s, one could reasonably expect hun-dreds or thousands of amperes to flow inside, potentially coupling into sensitive equipment that had damage thresholds far below this level. Un-less this diagnosis severely distorts the realities of the problem, NEACP and the rest of the airborne command network were never the robust linchpin that they were considered during these years.

By the early 1970s, this threat loomed large indeed because NCA au-thorization of retaliation hinged on the performance of NEACP. In Dep-uty Secretary Packard's opinion, so much was riding on outmoded air-craft that a crash program to modernize the airborne network deserved the highest priority. He advocated accelerating the schedule to develop and deploy the E-4, a militarized jumbo jet hardened against EMP, par-tially on the grounds that the high vulnerability of the operational aircraft

57. L. W. Ricketts, J. E. Bridges, and J. Miletta, *EMP Radiation and Protective Tech-niques* (John Wiley, 1976), p. 291.
58. Ibid., pp. 291–92.

then assigned to NEACP and Looking Glass missions should be eliminated as soon as possible. The air force responded to Packard's personal
intervention with a proposal to deploy E-4 aircraft to support NEACP
and SAC on an accelerated schedule, and Secretary Laird pursued his
recommendation by directing the air force secretary to initiate the E-4
program immediately.[59]

As part of the supplemental budget request for fiscal year 1973 submitted in recognition of the need to accelerate the E-4 program, funds
were also sought for "an EMP simulator of sufficient size to test adequately avionics in full-size aircraft at close to the EMP threat level."[60]
According to the air force project officer, the simulator would be available
by 1975 to test equipment at the level of fifty kilovolts per meter that was
expected to exist and to ensure that the E-4 "does in truth have the
protection against EMP that our current systems [EC-135s, EC-130s] do
not have."[61] Soon after Packard's resignation, however, the air force qui-
etly dropped its plans to design the E-4 to be less vulnerable to EMP; the
aircraft were retrofitted to provide this hardness at the insistence of officials in the Carter administration.

A barrage attack depending on blast effects to destroy command aircraft also could have been attempted, and with some chance of success.
This concern surfaced in the early 1970s and became part of the rationale
for deploying an E-4 fleet. Supporters argued that the E-4B would be able
to use random flight patterns and evasive manuevers without losing communications with strategic forces, thus adding to the enemy's intelligence
and targeting problems. Although the Soviet Union did not have any
known capability to conduct real-time surveillance of PACCS aircraft in
flight, Soviet planners could have studied details of the network—home
bases, missions, communications capabilities, and so forth—and deduced
a fair amount of information about probable flight patterns in wartime.[62]

59. The history of the E-4 program, beginning in 1964, is traced in *Fiscal Year 1973
Authorization for Military Procurement, Research and Development*, Senate hearings, pt. 3,
pp. 1461–64. Packard has been given full credit for reversing past failures in having the
E-4 program assigned sufficient importance for it to compete with other service priorities;
see *Department of Defense Appropriations for Fiscal Year 1973*, Senate hearing, pt. 4,
pp. 986–88.

60. *Department of Defense Appropriations for 1973*, House hearings, pt. 2, p. 8.

61. *Fiscal Year 1973 Authorization for Military Procurement, Research and Development*,
Senate hearings, pt. 3, p. 1945.

62. Operators of TACAMO, the airborne submarine communications system, actually
filed flight plans with the proper civil aviation authorities according to one official interviewed for this study.

A surprise barrage attack aimed at Looking Glass operating on routine alert in peacetime may have had an even better chance of success. Peacetime practices were not as covert, and Soviet planners doubtless had the benefit of accumulated intelligence gathered over many years. They knew the home base of operations, and they could easily have discovered that much of the operation proceeded like clockwork. The schedule for take-offs and landings, for instance, was fixed, repetitive, and predictable. Using ferret satellites or other collectors of signal intelligence or intercepting routine communications between Looking Glass and SAC headquarters probably was possible.[63] Such intelligence might have readily discovered that Looking Glass normally flew around one or another of the ground-entry points located at Fairview, Kansas, and Lyons, Nebraska, that served as the primary interfaces between its radio communications and the SAC-wide Primary Alerting System that utilized AT&T underground cables. (Alternative interfaces were provided by the ground-entry points located at Lamar, Colorado, and Hillsboro, Missouri.) The peacetime orbit parameters of Looking Glass around these points were in fact unclassified. In short, Soviet planners surely knew where to direct a barrage attack.

For purposes of illustration, let us suppose that Soviet planners determined that Looking Glass typically stayed within line-of-sight radio communications range of both the Lyons, Nebraska, ground-entry point (near SAC headquarters) and the Minuteman complex in Missouri. Figure 5-6 shows the area of operations that would allow for such simultaneous links from an aircraft flying at an altitude of about 32,000 feet. UHF radio communications from spots outside this perimeter would not have been as effective because those spots lie over the horizon from Lyons or the Minuteman complex or both. The constrained area measures 49,000 square miles. For obvious reasons the air space above some 9,000 square miles within and immediately around the Minuteman sites is excluded from the orbit.

The probability that a barrage attack of varying intensity would destroy Looking Glass is shown in the table below. These estimates assume

63. Since 1967, Soviet electronic reconnaissance satellites as well as certain communications satellites have probably played a role in monitoring the airborne program. Soviet ferret satellites routinely passed over the airborne orbit shown in figure 5-6. Those with an inclination of 74°, a period of 95 minutes, and a circularized altitude of about 340 miles transversed the aircrafts' operating region twice daily. The Soviets did not allow the orbit to drift during successive passes, implying strong interest in that specific region.

Figure 5-6. *Potential Peacetime Operating Region for SAC Airborne Command Post*

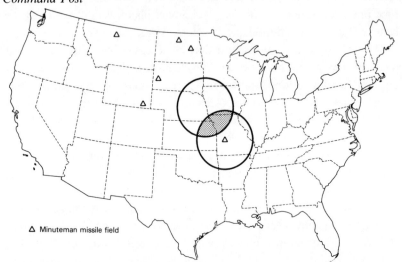

△ Minuteman missile field

Note: The region is defined by the intersection of two circles, one centered on Lyons, Nebraska, and the other centered on the Whiteman Minuteman complex in Missouri. The radius of each circle is 200 miles, which is about the range limit of line-of-sight communications for aircraft at an altitude of 6 miles.

an altitude of 32,000 feet for both the target and the explosions, aircraft hardness of one or two psi, missile reliability of 80 percent, and the commitment of ten to fifty SS-9 ICBMs.[64] Under these assumptions, the risk of destruction is significant. To a conservative planner, it is very significant if a large-scale barrage (thirty or more missiles) is postulated. Actually, the risk would be much greater if calculations included airborne hazards associated with coterminous attacks on ground targets in the vicinity of the orbit. Radioactive clouds, turbulence, or particulate matter might have destroyed or severely impaired the Looking Glass aircraft, its crew, or such communications equipment as trailing antennas.

64. These estimates have been scaled to account for the attenuating effects of altitude on blast overpressure. For instance, the overpressure generated by an SS-9 against a target thirteen miles away varies from 3 psi for a target altitude of one mile to 1 psi for a target altitude of six miles. Against a target nine miles away, overpressure varies from 6 to 2 psi for target altitudes of one and five miles, respectively. Because the lethal radius of a single SS-9 burst is thirteen miles against an aircraft flying at 32,000 feet and hardened to withstand 1 psi, the probability of destroying the aircraft, which could be anywhere within a 40,000 square mile expanse, is 1.54 percent. The lethal radius against an aircraft hardened to 2 psi is nine miles; the probability of destruction is 0.79 percent.

Soviet missile reliability (percent)	Aircraft hardness (psi)	Probability of destroying aircraft by number of missiles targeted (percent)				
		10	20	30	40	50
80	1	11	21	32	43	53
80	2	05	10	15	21	26

The underlying assumptions for this illustration are not arbitrary. The results depend mainly on the parameters of the aircraft's orbit, and the parameters used in the analysis can be justified on the grounds that they appear to define an optimal area of operations. If Looking Glass were to maintain continuous, direct radio communications with SAC headquarters via the ground-entry point at Lyons, it could monitor the disposition of SAC forces until the ground network came under attack. Under pre-attack conditions, the ground network could also have relayed early warning, execution, or other emergency messages sent via land lines from NORAD and the NMCS. In the event of attack, SAC headquarters could have immediately notified Looking Glass or delegated CINCSAC authority to it. It would also have been prudent for Looking Glass to operate within line-of-sight range of Minuteman units in Missouri. This practice would have facilitated direct, timely, and survivable radio communications, avoiding vulnerable land lines, to the ICBM force in Missouri as well as to the Emergency Rocket Communications System missiles also deployed there. Through ERCS, Looking Glass had some chance of reaching the rest of SAC's forces, including far-flung manned bombers. A requirement to operate within communications range of ERCS would seem further warranted in light of the limited airborne endurance of Looking Glass and the possibility that an attack could occur any time during a normal eight-hour shift. Without aerial refueling, the aircraft would have had enough fuel to fly for only two hours if an attack occurred at the end of its regular shift.

Looking Glass could use ground-entry points other than that at Lyons to tie directly into SAC's primary alerting system, however. This capability did expand its freedom of movement beyond the limits defined above. Nevertheless, Looking Glass entry points were few (figure 5-7). (Alternative ground-entry points also expanded NEACP's freedom of movement; their number and exact location are not publicly known, but there were

Figure 5-7. *Ground-Entry Points for SAC Airborne Command Post*

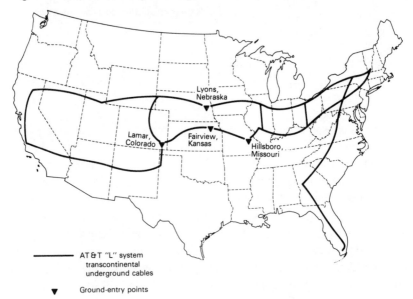

not very many of these either.)[65] Furthermore, the sudden disruption of ground communications channels was an ever-present danger, and hence Looking Glass could not stray too far from an orbit that would allow direct radio contact with ICBM units, nor could it have roamed too freely if it hoped to be in a position to link up quickly with other PACCS aircraft over UHF, which offered both voice communications and relative immunity to jamming and disruptive atmospheric effects.

The workload of Looking Glass was potentially so great that in 1962 SAC deployed auxiliary command aircraft to provide assistance in wartime.[66] Nine such aircraft existed in 1972, two of which were kept on ground alert at all times. One, the west auxiliary airborne command post stationed at Ellsworth AFB, South Dakota, would have positioned itself

65. Congressional testimony later disclosed the existence of fourteen ground-entry points that NEACP and SAC command aircraft can use to tie into terrestrial communications channels; see *Department of Defense Authorization for Appropriations for Fiscal Year 1980,* Hearings before the Senate Committee on Armed Services, 96 Cong. 1 sess. (GPO, 1979), pt. 1, p. 390. See also figure 6-2.

66. *Department of Defense Appropriations for 1977,* Hearings before the House Committee on Appropriations, 94 Cong. 2 sess. (GPO, 1976), pt. 6, p. 10.

after launch between Looking Glass and missile-launching aircraft to the west. The east auxiliary airborne command post was based on ground alert at SAC headquarters. Time permitting, the SAC commander in chief and the Joint Strategic Targeting Planning Staff would have boarded and assumed a flight position between Looking Glass and the east communications relay aircraft.[67] The SAC airborne battle staff and the workload would have thus been spread over three aircraft interconnected serially by UHF line-of-sight radio communications. But the workload was still considered too great. Using manual methods of data processing, battle staffs would have been saturated with incoming information during exercises[68] and unable to process incoming data while at the same time making nuclear war decisions.

Communications equipment aboard these EC-135C aircraft consisted of UHF radio for line-of-sight voice transmissions and HF and LF radio for longer-range voice and low-speed teletype communications, respectively. Assuming an intact, eight-station PACCS network, UHF links provided access to all Minuteman launch centers. Looking Glass could communicate directly with LCCs in Missouri complexes via air-to-ground UHF radio and indirectly with LCCs at other Minuteman complexes via air-to-air UHF links running through the west auxiliary aircraft and missile-launching aircraft. In the other direction, communications from NEACP were relayed to Looking Glass by the east communications relay aircraft and the east auxiliary aircraft. All four aircraft in this chain used UHF air-to-air radio as the primary means of interconnection.

Looking Glass and its auxiliary aircraft were assigned responsibility for controlling outbound bombers (launched on tactical warning) as well as the ICBM force. Communications with far-flung bombers were still problematical, however, because reliance on HF radio was still very great. Since 1966 SAC twice had tried and failed significantly to enhance long-range communications with bombers. The first effort was made as part of a major teletype communications program called the Survivable Low Frequency Communications System (SLFCS). In 1968 SAC deployed two SLFCS radio transmitters on the ground and equipped launch centers, bomber base wing command posts, and Green Pine facilities to receive

67. The deployment of the Joint Strategic Targeting Planning Staff in a command aircraft is corroborated in *Department of Defense Appropriations for 1973,* House hearings, pt. 2, p. 47.
68. *Research, Development, Test, and Evaluation Program for Fiscal Year 1973,* House hearings, pt. 3, p. 10929.

the transmissions. SAC command post aircraft and NEACP were equipped with SLFCS transceivers used in conjunction with a trailing antenna that extended about two miles from the tail of the plane.[69] The idea behind both the ground and air segments of SLFCS was to exploit the superior propagation characteristics of the low frequency radio bandwidth in order to increase the reliability of long-range communications, especially with LCCs and Green Pine sites, in a nuclear environment.[70] Ionization of the upper atmosphere caused by nuclear explosions can black out HF but not LF signals. Another important characteristic was the ability of low frequency signals to penetrate the earth to considerable depths, which could improve communications to LCCs. The burial of SLFCS antennas at launch centers greatly increased the resistance of the centers' communications to blast effects.

The ground portion of SLFCS worked well, but it was extremely vulnerable. The fixed transmitters in Nebraska and California could not withstand attack, and the Green Pine receiving stations that would have relayed messages to nearby bombers were also exposed. The airborne systems were basically immune to attack, but were plagued by technical problems ranging from insufficient transmitter power to inefficient antenna design and antenna reel-out jams. Even in a benign environment the airborne command posts could not have reliably reached the Green Pine sites to relay messages to bombers. Their ability to reach such closer units as EC-135C command post aircraft in PACCS and Minuteman launch centers, which were equipped for receiving LF transmissions in 1968, was also questionable. In a benign environment the equipment reliability and signal range of SLFCS was such that NEACP probably could have reached Looking Glass, which in turn probably could have reached launch centers at all six Minuteman wings. But the overall probability of getting a message through this network using SLFCS was perhaps no better than 50 percent under favorable conditions and worse in a nuclear environment.

Early recognition of the deficiencies of the airborne SLFCS and the growing vulnerability of Green Pine facilities led to a program to develop a long-range, very low frequency system. Initiated in 1967, the special purpose communications program was a one-way, antijam (seven words per minute) system that employed a very long trailing antenna for trans-

69. *Department of Defense Annual Report for Fiscal Year 1968*, pp. 397–98; *Department of Defense Appropriations for Fiscal Year 1973*, Senate hearings, pt. 4, p. 985; and *Department of Defense Appropriations for 1970*, House hearings, pt. 4, pp. 862–63.
70. *Department of Defense Appropriations for 1970*, House hearings, pt. 3, p. 1125.

mission to bombers and tankers equipped with VLF receivers and short antennas. In 1969, a spokesman for the air force promoted the project on the grounds that it might be the difference between success and failure in getting the message through to bombers.[71] By 1971, plans to equip bombers and tankers with receivers and EC-135 aircraft with transceivers were shelved because of fiscal belt tightening. Development of transceive VLF capabilities for command post aircraft proceeded independently under the E-4 program.

As a result of cutbacks in the special purpose communications program, the systems available in the early 1970s for long-range communications from command post aircraft to strategic bombers included HF radio, which was unreliable in a nuclear or heavy jamming environment; SLFCS, which was unreliable, lacked sufficient range, and depended on relay by Green Pine sites; and the Emergency Rocket Communications System, a last-ditch element that had become fully operational in 1967. SAC would rely on these tenuous channels for the duration of the decade, while pursuing a solution based on satellite communications.

About 1963 Robert McNamara initiated the development of a system for launching Minuteman missiles by airborne remote control. Successful tests of an EC-135 were completed in early 1967, and the Airborne Launch Control System was declared operational.[72]

Besides Looking Glass, which may have doubled as an airborne launch control center as well as a command post, SAC possessed nine dedicated missile launching aircraft in 1972. Three of them, along with air crews and launch control personnel, were stationed on ground alert at all times. An airborne launch control center based at Ellsworth AFB, South Dakota, had responsibility for 150 Minuteman ICBMs at Ellsworth and 200 at F. E. Warren AFB, Wyoming. One of two ALCCs based at Minot AFB, North Dakota, had responsibility for 200 missiles at Malmstrom AFB, Montana. The other was responsible for 150 missiles at Minot and 150 at Grand Forks AFB, North Dakota.

ALCC aircraft backed up the underground launch centers and could gain control over a missile or group of missiles if they had become iso-

71. *Department of Defense Appropriations for 1970,* House hearings, pt. 4, pp. 861–64.
72. *Hearings on Military Posture and H.R. 13456* before the House Committee on Armed Services, 89 Cong. 2 sess. (GPO, 1966), p. 7352; *Department of Defense Annual Report for Fiscal Year 1967,* p. 364; and *Fiscal Year 1973 Authorization for Military Procurement, Research and Development,* Senate hearings, pt. 3, p. 1462. Deployment of LF ground receivers probably extended past 1967; see *Department of Defense Appropriations for Fiscal Year 1973,* Senate hearings, pt. 4, p. 985.

lated from all five LCCs in a squadron. Missiles normally received a continuous, computer-automated stream of signals from the launch centers. Cessation of these signals from the destruction of all five centers or the severance of LCC-missile communications links would have spontaneously activated a radio receiver at each isolated silo to monitor computer-coded transmissions from any airborne control center in the vicinity. ALCCs could transmit all the target, arm, and launch commands that a ground center could. Unlike LCCs, however, the airborne centers could not monitor missile status before, during, or after the transmission or commands. A radio link from the silo to the ALCC did not exist.[73]

Several silos at Whiteman AFB, Missouri, housed missiles equipped with a tape recorder and a UHF radio package instead of a warhead. These Minuteman Emergency Rocket Communications Systems had been successfully tested in 1966 and declared fully operational in late 1967,[74] replacing earlier ERCS variants such as Blue Scout rockets. Looking Glass could transmit voice messages to the missiles before launching them,[75] though airborne launch control was once again contingent upon the loss of LCC control (not to mention the survival of ERCS silos and associated communications, both of which were at least as vulnerable as standard Minuteman silos).[76] Functional ERCS missiles could record an execution message sent by Looking Glass (or by LCCs), play it back to permit launch crews to check its completeness and accuracy, and broadcast the message during a flight along either a northwest or northeast trajectory.[77] These trajectories would have positioned the missiles to broadcast, for no more than thirty minutes (the flight time of a Minuteman missile), single integrated operational plan execution messages to Minuteman and Titan LCCs, wing command posts at bomber bases, stra-

73. *Department of Defense Appropriations for Fiscal Year 1981*, Hearings before a Subcommittee of the Senate Committee on Appropriations, 96 Cong. 2 sess. (GPO, 1980), pt. 4, pp. 917–18.

74. *Department of Defense Annual Report Fiscal Year 1967*, p. 364; and *Department of Defense Annual Report Fiscal Year 1968*, p. 397. ERCS missiles have never been fired from their operational silos, and other tests of their components have been restricted in order to prevent enemy identification of the silos.

75. " 'Looking Glass' Capabilities Improved," *Aviation Week & Space Technology* (May 10, 1976), p. 57.

76. *Fiscal Year 1978 Authorization for Military Procurement, Research and Development, and Active Duty, Selected Reserve, and Civilian Personnel Strengths*, Hearings before the Senate Committee on Armed Services, 95 Cong. 1 sess. (GPO, 1977), pt. 10, p. 6845.

77. The first tests of the playback capabilities of operational Whiteman systems were not conducted until 1976, according to a defense official interviewed. The tests revealed complete failures of the playback mechanisms associated with certain silos.

tegic bombers in flight, and any other SAC unit that was tuned to the proper UHF frequency and within range.[78] Range was subject to the limitations imposed by the earth's curvature, the transmitting power of the ERCS communications package, and the effects of atmospheric scintillation on the UHF signals. Nuclear explosions in the upper atmosphere could have blacked out such transmissions (see chapter 6).

Navy nuclear units such as TACAMO aircraft likely also listened for ERCS transmissions. The prevailing expectation, however, was that CINCLANT and CINCPAC would pass execution orders down to the TACAMO and the missile submarine fleets. Thus TACAMO was probably less than fully integrated—procedurally if not technically—into the ERCS channel. If it had been, SAC would have been in a position to dispatch nuclear forces under the jurisdiction of non-SAC commanders.[79]

Within SAC itself, procedural arrangements were such that under certain conditions the attempt to launch either ERCS or nuclear missiles by means of command aircraft would have failed. A Soviet attack aimed at underground launch centers could have destroyed or temporarily disrupted their communications while they remained interconnected with missiles in their squadron. This isolation from higher authorities and ALCCs could have created internal procedural contradictions that would have prevented execution. The LCCs could not have received execution messages, and the ALCCs could not have exerted remote control because as long as even a single underground launch center continued to be connected to the squadron missiles, airborne access to them was blocked. There was a procedure whereby surviving underground centers could deliberately relinquish control of the missiles (accomplished by turning off all LCC computers) to permit an ALCC to assume control, but it re-

78. *Department of Defense Appropriations for Fiscal Year 1974,* Hearings before a Subcommittee of the Senate Committee on Appropriations, 93 Cong. 1 sess. (GPO, 1973), pt. 4, p. 480; and General Russell E. Dougherty, "SAC Command Control," *Signal* (March 1975), p. 49.

79. Minuteman and B-52 forces are the only components identified in testimony as potential receivers of ERCS signals; see *Research, Development, Test, and Evaluation Program for Fiscal Year 1973,* House hearings, pt. 3, p. 11009. In principle, however, the Minimum Essential Emergency Communications Network included ERCS, and under the MEECN concept, ERCS transmissions would be used by strategic forces of all services; see *Department of Defense Appropriations for Fiscal Year 1974,* Senate hearings, pt. 4, p. 481. More recent hearings disclosed that the signal from ERCS rockets flying over open ocean in both the Atlantic and Pacific may be received by TACAMO or by submarines directly; see *Department of Defense Authorization for Appropriations for Fiscal Year 1980,* Senate hearings, pt. 6, p. 3346. This testimony notes that submarines must have antennas at the surface to receive the signals.

quired coordination between the underground and the airborne centers, and coordination required communications. Furthermore, this procedure would not have applied unless a launch message had already been received and acted upon by an underground launch center. Its purpose was to enable an airborne center to send a second launch vote to missiles in squadrons that contained only one surviving LCC. The launch vote from this LCC would have begun the delayed launch countdown; a second vote from an ALCC would have eliminated the delay, resulting in immediate liftoff.

The priority of negative control explains the absence of a procedure whereby underground centers would turn off their computers if they lost communications with higher authorities. To have done so would have facilitated positive control in that their missiles would have automatically switched to receive ALCC launch commands, but negative control would have been impaired. LCCs that shut down their computers cannot monitor their own missiles or those of companion launch centers in the squadron. An unauthorized launch command sent by a companion LCC would have escaped notice.

Established procedure thus emphasized negative control at the expense of positive control. In the situation described here the launch of ICBMs and ERCS missiles by ALCC aircraft would have been stymied, and positive control would have been further impaired. ERCS, the most survivable method of message dissemination, would not have been activated.

This particular predicament would not have arisen if at least one LCC maintained communications with higher authorities, or if all five had been destroyed, allowing for automatic access to missiles by ALCC aircraft. Yet some loss of positive control would have still been incurred, especially upon destruction of all five LCCs. Like LCCs, airborne centers could have executed the launch sequence, but unlike LCCs they could not have confirmed that the proper commands had been received and processed. As defense spokesmen put it, airborne missile control crews launched "in the blind" without knowledge of missile availability or control over missile targeting.[80] ALCC aircraft could not have determined, for example, whether a nuclear detonation in the region had interfered

80. *Department of Defense Appropriations for Fiscal Year 1981,* Senate hearings, pt. 4, p. 918; *Hearings on Military Posture and H.R. 5068* before the House Committee on Armed Services, 95 Cong. 1 sess. (GPO, 1977), pt. 1, p. 1039; and *Hearings on Military Posture and H.R. 10929* before the House Armed Services Committee, 95 Cong. 2 sess. (GPO, 1978), pt. 3, bk. 1, p. 343.

with the radio signals carrying target instructions to the missiles. If the radio command did not reach the missiles in proper code, the ALCC launch command that followed could have hurled the wrong number of missiles at the wrong targets at the wrong time. Coded launch signals might also have failed to register at numerous silos housing missiles that were supposed to be launched, and the resulting need to retransmit the signals might not have been apparent to airborne launch crews.

Delay in launching the retaliatory forces is another form of impaired positive control. Some delay was inevitable, given that ALCC aircraft or ERCS missiles or both would have been used to relay execution messages to surviving LCCs or to fire missiles at isolated silos. The length of the delay would have depended on factors such as aircraft locations and readiness. For instance, an hour or more could easily have elapsed between the time that NEACP and PACCS aircraft were flushed into the air and the time that they were positioned to establish fully coherent UHF communications. By this time, ERCS deployments themselves could have been destroyed by Soviet ICBMs. The loss of ERCS would have spelled isolation for large numbers of bombers. It would also have left TACAMO aircraft isolated and thus broken communications with large numbers of submarines.

Despite reassurances from personnel who portrayed the navy's ground-based radio broadcast network coupled with shipborne radio communications as a reliable means of control over missile submarines after an attack, Secretary McNamara became convinced of the need to fortify communications links from the NCA to those forces. In 1965 he placed an alert EC-135 airborne command post in Hawaii at the disposal of CINCPAC. In 1967 he established the navy's Special Communications Project Office, which was given responsibility for developing programs to satisfy an "urgent need" to ensure "effective communications at all times from the National Command Authorities and Commanders in Chief to the deployed FBM [fleet ballistic missile] forces . . . during and after heavy nuclear and electronic jamming attack."[81]

In the late 1960s after McNamara's departure from government, the navy's airborne VLF radio relay program, TACAMO, became operational, providing the most survivable communications link to missile submarines. A second project, Pilgrim, enabled Pacific-based missile subma-

---

81. *Fiscal Year 1973 Authorization for Military Procurement, Research and Development,* Senate hearings, pt. 5, p. 2844.

rines and TACAMO aircraft to receive messages broadcast over navigation radios operated by the U.S. Coast Guard.[82] Several such radios, so-called Loran-C stations located in the Western Pacific, were capable of rebroadcasting launch messages by superimposing information onto the navigation signals emitted in the VLF range.[83] The navy thus added to its missile submarine communications network radio stations that transmitted on a frequency superior to LF and HF in range, jam resistance, and vulnerability to ionization effects produced by nuclear explosions. This expansion, however, was of minor significance. The enlargement and modernization of the Soviet strategic arsenal rendered Pilgrim vulnerable before it was even put in operation. By 1972 the United States could not rely on fixed communications stations to trigger submarine retaliation.

The United States had come to depend almost totally upon airborne command posts and TACAMO communications relay aircraft for post-attack control over the submarine force. A spokesman for the Special Communications Project Office, which had overall responsibility for the TACAMO program, described the aircraft as "the only operational survivable element that the Navy has today [March 9, 1972] and most likely will have until the latter part of the 1970s."[84] While it testifies to the questionable effectiveness of other available systems—notably, shore-based and ship-based radio communications—the statement warrants strong qualification. TACAMO by no means ensured a secure, reliable link between higher authorities and submarine commanders. The system featured propeller-driven (280 knots an hour cruise speed and 4,530 mile range), unrefuelable EC-130 aircraft outfitted with VLF transmitters and trailing antennas,[85] and its sole purpose was to relay nuclear war orders to missile submarines. In accordance with the joint strategic objectives plan, EC-130s operated in the Pacific and Atlantic.

TACAMO consisted of twelve aircraft when it became operational in 1969. Four were assigned to the Pacific and eight to the Atlantic.[86] For various reasons, the program never did satisfy formal requirements for maintaining one aircraft on continuous airborne alert in each sector:

82. Ibid., pp. 2846–47. Also see *Fiscal Year 1975 Authorization for Military Procurement, Research and Development,* Hearings before the Senate Committee on Armed Services, 93 Cong. 2 sess. (GPO, 1974), pt. 6, p. 3225.

83. *Department of Defense Appropriations for 1974,* House hearings, pt. 7, pp. 775–77.

84. *Fiscal Year 1973 Authorization for Military Procurement, Research and Development,* Senate hearings, pt. 5, p. 2836.

85. *Hearings on Military Posture and H.R. 10929,* House, pt. 2, p. 625.

86. *Department of Defense Appropriations for 1974,* House hearings, pt. 6, p. 603.

about fourteen operational aircraft—seven in each ocean—were needed to achieve this objective.[87] Training demands and periodic maintenance raised the necessary inventory to eighteen. In 1972 twelve aircraft were authorized and only nine were available for duty; one had crashed in January 1972 and two were being modified.[88] Consequently, the navy was forced to cut back the Pacific contingent in order to sustain operations in the Atlantic. Airborne alert in the Pacific was intermittent; it was probably maintained at the rate realized in 1980, about 25 percent of the time.[89] Although the rate in the Atlantic was much higher, continuous airborne alert was not achieved until late 1973.[90] In both oceans the navy evidently tried to maintain backup aircraft on thirty-minute ground alert.[91]

The technical sophistication of TACAMO communications left much to be desired. Aircraft transmitters radiated only about fifty kilowatts of peak power, and efficient use of this power was difficult to achieve because of design and operational problems associated with the trailing antenna.[92] TACAMO's effective range probably did not exceed several hundred miles under the best of circumstances, and hence only a fraction

87. *Department of Defense Appropriations for 1980,* Hearings before a Subcommittee of the House Committee on Appropriations, 96 Cong. 1 sess. (GPO, 1979), pt. 6, p. 142.

88. *Department of Defense Appropriations for 1974,* House hearings, pt. 6, p. 603.

89. *Department of Defense Appropriations for 1981,* Hearings before a Subcommittee of the House Committee on Appropriations, 96 Cong. 2 sess. (GPO, 1980), pt. 7, p. 554.

90. *Department of Defense Authorization for Appropriations for Fiscal Year 1982,* Hearings before the Senate Committee on Armed Services, 97 Cong. 1 sess. (GPO, 1981), pt. 7, p. 4048.

91. *Department of Defense Appropriations for 1976,* Hearings before a Subcommittee of the House, Committee on Appropriations, 94 Cong. 1 sess. (GPO, 1975), pt. 5, p. 903.

92. The peak power of shore-based VLF transmitters provides a suggestive comparison. The transmitter at Cutler, Maine, for example, radiated over 1,000 kilowatts, or roughly twenty times the power of operational TACAMO systems and five times that of a 200 kilowatt TACAMO transmitter under test and development. It is also important to note that antenna verticality determines signal range and seawater penetration, and achieving proper verticality using long antennas trailed from a moving platform represented no small feat. The Cutler power rating is given in *Fiscal Year 1978 Authorization for Military Procurement, Research and Development,* Hearings before the Senate Committee on Armed Services (GPO, 1977), pt. 10, p. 6706. The development of a higher-power TACAMO VLF transmitter and plans for its deployment (the TACAMO IV program) in the mid-to-late 1970s are disclosed in *Research, Development, Test, and Evaluation Program for Fiscal Year 1971,* Hearings before the House Committee on Armed Services, 91 Cong. 2 sess. (GPO, 1970), p. 8053; and *Fiscal Year 1973 Authorization for Military Procurement, Research and Development,* Senate hearings, pt. 5, pp. 2837, 2846–47, 2851. The 200 kilowatt power rating for TACAMO IV VLF transmitters was provided in *Department of Defense Authorization for Appropriations for Fiscal Year 1979,* Senate hearings, pt. 9, p. 6721. The importance of antenna verticality for signal range is noted in General Accounting Office, *An Unclassified Version of a Classified Report,* PSAD-79-48A (GPO, May 2, 1979), p. 46.

of the widely dispersed alert submarines could be reached at any given time. Communications performance would have been even poorer under conditions of heavy jamming.[93] Nuclear effects might also have limited TACAMO signal propagation, a point made by a defense official who said that the aircraft had "insufficient communication range in a nuclear environment."[94] Under either of these conditions the aircraft might not have been able to communicate successfully with alert submarines unless they were close to them, but the aircraft probably would have run out of fuel long before they could have delivered an execution message, particularly to submarines stationed in the North Atlantic and Mediterranean.[95] In all likelihood, only a few submarines could have been served during the aircrafts' time on station. Furthermore, neither TACAMO nor higher authority could confirm the successful delivery of a message because missile submarines normally would not and could not acknowledge receipt.

No one had good reason to believe that TACAMO would work. It was declared operational in the late 1960s even though the chief of naval operations stated that its effectiveness had not been established, and the navy did not begin a scientific assessment of its effectiveness in relaying messages until 1976.[96]

Limitations on range discouraged basing alert TACAMO aircraft in the continental United States; they were normally forward-based at locations such as Wake Island, Guam, Bermuda, and Western Europe. As a result, they were more susceptible to detection and more vulnerable than were U.S.-based PACCS aircraft, for example, which served Minuteman and bomber units. An authoritative assessment during the late 1970s probably would be valid for the earlier period: "a ground-alert TACAMO within range of submarine launched ballistic missiles (SLBMs) is clearly vulnerable to destruction."[97] This high prelaunch vulnerability probably stemmed in part from their inaccessibility to timely tactical early warning data. Although aircraft on airborne alert obviously

93. *Fiscal Year 1975 Authorization for Military Procurement, Research and Development,* Senate hearings, pt. 6, p. 3311.

94. *Department of Defense Appropriations for 1973,* House hearings, pt. 4, p. 759.

95. The fact that SSBNs operated in the Mediterranean is from *Department of Defense Appropriations for 1976,* Hearings before a Subcommittee of the House Committee on Appropriations, 94 Cong. 1 sess. (GPO, 1975), pt. 5, p. 904.

96. General Accounting Office, *An Unclassified Version of a Classified Report Entitled "The Navy's Strategic Communications Systems—Need for Management Attention and Decisionmaking."* Report PSAD-79-48A (May 2, 1979), p. 28.

97. *Department of Defense Appropriations for 1979,* Hearings before a Subcommittee of the House Committee on Appropriations, 95 Cong. 2 sess. (GPO, 1978), pt. 4, p. 650.

would have been much less vulnerable to nuclear blast, air mobility did not preclude exposure to EMP, and these aircraft had not been afforded any protection against it.[98]

Forward deployment also entailed some risk that TACAMO aircraft would be detected and tactically engaged by Soviet fighters. The overt character of normal TACAMO operations—crews often filed their flight plans with civil aviation authorities, for instance—compounded this risk. TACAMO did take precautions to counter enemy pursuits of this sort, however. Like the submarines they served, the aircraft maintained virtual communications silence during patrols.[99] But the absence of routine two-way communications between TACAMO and other units kept higher authorities and submarine commanders from knowing whether the aircraft were fulfilling their role. Neither the status of alert submarines nor the condition of the most survivable communications link to those forces could have been ascertained by higher authorities.

Compounding the uncertainty about submarine responsiveness was the continuing problem of communications in transit, which TACAMO did not ameliorate. Missile submarines that were not on high alert in their patrol areas—usually 50 percent of those at sea—only periodically positioned themselves to copy radio transmissions.[100]

Tenuous communications channels connecting higher authorities to TACAMO further reduced confidence in the effectiveness of the system. In peacetime, TACAMO could reliably receive information from many sources, including LF and HF shore stations scattered around the globe. Certain land-based LF and HF transmitters were dedicated to the TACAMO mission.[101] The main link to aircraft on airborne alert in the Atlantic, for instance, evidently consisted of HF transmitters at various locations that were keyed at CINCLANT fleet headquarters in Norfolk.[102] But in wartime, the reliability of communications could have been drasti-

98. In the early 1970s, testing and evaluation of TACAMO vulnerability to EMP were being planned for the mid-to-late 1970s; see *Fiscal Year 1973 Authorization for Military Procurement, Research and Development,* Senate hearings, pt. 5, p. 2847.

99. *H.R. 8390 and Review of the State of U.S. Strategic Forces,* Hearings before the House Committee on Armed Services, 95 Cong. 1 sess. (GPO, 1977), p. 207; and General Accounting Office, *Unclassified Version of a Classified Report,* p. 45.

100. If recent figures are any indication, twenty-three submarines were at sea, of which twelve were on station on full alert. Eleven were at sea but not fully alert. These estimates are based on a fleet of forty-one submarines, an at-sea rate of 55 percent, and a full alert rate of 30 percent; see General Accounting Office, *Unclassified Version of a Classified Report,* p. 2.

101. Ibid., p. 45.

102. *Department of Defense Appropriations for 1980,* House hearings, pt. 6, p. 146.

cally reduced. Soviet attacks on land-based transmitters and their nodal keying facilities, which cautious planners would have expected to occur, would have severely affected communications from higher authorities, probably isolating TACAMO from its critical sources of information— U.S.-based command aircraft such as NEACP and Looking Glass lacked communications capabilities to span the great distances separating them from TACAMO units (and from CINCPAC's command aircraft).

Deficiencies of major proportions plagued all three of the interconnecting circuits: HF radio, LF radio, and ERCS-borne UHF radio. HF radio was susceptible to blackout in a nuclear environment. It is also doubtful whether common high frequencies between TACAMO and other key command aircraft such as Looking Glass were used. TACAMO normally monitored HF transmissions from navy sources, and it seems unlikely that they would have switched channels to listen for SAC broadcasts unless required to do so by the Joint Chiefs' MEECN plan, which did not include HF radio in the early 1970s. Thus intercommand compatibility of HF communications probably did not exist.

The effectiveness of the Survivable Low Frequency Communications System (SLFCS), which constituted a major portion of MEECN, was also questionable. Technical incompatibilities, cited earlier, evidently reduced the potential for TACAMO reception of LF transmissions from SAC aircraft, despite demands from the Joint Chiefs of Staff for complete interoperability among MEECN components. Furthermore, U.S.-based EC-135 command aircraft used SLFCS equipment that could not effectively or reliably broadcast messages over very long distances. Had it been available, even an E-4 command aircraft equipped with modern LF/VLF communications would have had difficulty reaching forward TACAMO units. Testimony in 1980 indicated, for instance, that LF/VLF systems designed for the E-4 would permit NEACP to reach Looking Glass in an adverse environment and Pacific-based TACAMO in a benign environment.[103] If such ranges approach the limit of feasible E-4 capabilities, then the less advanced LF communications equipment carried by U.S.-based EC-135 aircraft during the early 1970s clearly lacked the range needed to reach TACAMO units. These older systems employed far less efficient antennas and could generate only one-tenth the transmitter power of an E-4 system (20 kilowatts versus 200). As a consequence, the chances were slim that the SLFCS equipment aboard NEACP, Looking Glass, or any other EC-135 aircraft could have success-

103. Ibid., p. 179.

fully transmitted messages to any forward-deployed TACAMO unit or to CINCPAC's airborne command post. NEACP had the best chance of reaching Atlantic-based TACAMO aircraft because its assigned orbit would have been the closest to TACAMO's operational area on the Atlantic side. However, NEACP's home base was also the closest to enemy missile submarines, and its prelaunch vulnerability made it the least survivable of the command aircraft.

Whether the emergency rocket communications system could have prevented TACAMO's potential isolation from command channels is difficult to know. The available unclassified information on the strengths and weaknesses of this rather exotic system is meager and inconclusive. Optimists saw many virtues in ERCS, among them that communications missiles were deployed in protective silos capable of withstanding large blast overpressures. ERCS missiles could also have been deployed in sufficient numbers to ensure the survival of at least two (one each for Atlantic and Pacific trajectories). But the system's liabilities were as numerous. It required complicated launch operations and was susceptible to signal distortion caused by atmospheric scintillation from high-altitude bursts. In addition, nuclear fireballs between an ERCS missile and the receiving unit would have blacked out the signal. (This presented a severe operational problem for communications with Minuteman LCCs but only a minor problem for communications with bombers and TACAMO aircraft. Multiple fireballs in the Minuteman fields were expected.) More significantly, the vulnerability of ERCS silos to blast effects would have been much greater than standard calculations suggested if Soviet intelligence had discovered their locations. Even if only the particular squadron within which ERCS missiles were deployed had been identified, preferential targeting could have destroyed them all in a three-on-one attack by SS-9s. Considering other real or apparent deficiencies in addition—the vulnerability of ERCS silos to EMP, for instance—the ERCS communications link to TACAMO aircraft was of dubious value. Conservative U.S. planners could not have counted on ERCS to perform this vital function.

The Strategic Situation: 1972

By 1972 the perspective that saw strategic capability as determined by the size and technical composition of force deployments was beginning to yield to a broader view encompassing organizational performance as well.

A cadre of analysts and senior defense officials led by David Packard had come to believe that excluding either dimension from strategic assessments invited miscalculation and distortion of defense priorities. Packard and others also concluded that past attitudes toward C³I had indeed weakened U.S. security. They seriously doubted the ability of command channels to keep nuclear operations aligned with coherent national purposes in the wake of a Soviet first strike on C³I.

Nevertheless, the implications of large-scale nuclear weapon deployments for positive control were only dimly understood in most quarters. The strategic agenda of the Nixon administration continued to treat the number, technical characteristics, and economics of nuclear weapons and delivery systems as the central considerations of national security. The elaborate physical and procedural arrangements for managing those forces were overshadowed by issues of force structure and by arms limitation talks, which were also dominated by issues of force structure. This imbalance between strategic analysis and the security agenda led to gross misunderstanding of the actual strategic balance and obscured other important aspects of the strategic situation.

U.S. Second-Strike Capabilities

Popular calculations based on weapons characteristics indicated a strong U.S. nuclear posture and a significant advantage in overall strength. Although the overwhelming superiority supposedly enjoyed in earlier years had evaporated as a result of the Soviet arms buildup of the late 1960s and early 1970s, analysts believed the United States still maintained an advantage. Only the most conservative projections had the Soviet Union drawing even with or overtaking the United States in the near future. Popular calculations, however, obscured the fact that Soviet attack on the U.S. command structure could have blunted or blocked retaliation.

The major problem was preserving control in the wake of a surprise attack. The consequences of intelligence failure or inadequate response to indications of impending attack could have been severe. With the deployment of Yankee-class Soviet submarines, the United States became exposed to nuclear strikes that could have virtually destroyed the most survivable portion of the U.S. command system, the fleet of ground-alert C³ aircraft. The national emergency airborne command post was especially vulnerable to submarine missile attack, which meant that the national command authority could be destroyed or the military command system through which a surviving NCA would have unleashed the forces could be lost, or both. Such events would have been decisive if retaliation required the personal authorization of the president. NEACP vulnerability also meant that one of the two key communications links (the other was ERCS) to Atlantic-based TACAMO aircraft controlling the response of missile submarines was tenuous. Most other C³ aircraft were practically as vulnerable as NEACP. Consequently, a surprise Soviet first strike might have shut down communications with 70 to 100 percent of the U.S. nuclear weapons on alert.

More than half the total number of alert weapons might have been isolated even if the U.S. command system had fully anticipated the attack. Advance strategic warning followed by command mobilization would have greatly enhanced the survivability of the airborne command system, but survivability was not by itself sufficient to guarantee delivery of launch messages to the forces. Direct radio communications between the airborne C³ elements and the forces were too tenuous, and the performance of missile-borne communications too uncertain to warrant high confidence in the ability of the command network to trigger coherent, systematic retaliation, particularly by submarines (via TACAMO relay) and strategic bombers outside the line-of-sight UHF range of C³ aircraft.

In short, standard estimates of U.S. second-strike capabilities were misleading. The number of survivable U.S. weapons exceeded the number of controllable second-strike weapons by a factor of two or more. The Soviet threat was much greater than generally believed.

Crisis Stability

Unleashing a nuclear strike on the basis of calculations showing that attacking the U.S. command structure might succeed would have defied reason so long as Soviet leaders could still summon hope that general war with the United States could be avoided. Success was not guaranteed, and the consequences were sufficiently unpredictable that the influence of this consideration on Soviet decisionmaking ought to have been marginal.

Attacks against command structure risked failure in many ways. Soviet missile submarines, which presumably would have been central to such a strategy, did not lend themselves well to coordinated attacks on time-urgent targets; cautious Soviet planners surely discounted, and heavily, their effectiveness. And even if high performance was expected of these forces, modest changes in assumptions about, for example, the reaction times and hardness of U.S. C^3 aircraft on crisis alert would have drastically reduced expectations of an effective attack. The advantage could have easily shifted from the attacker to the defender. Neither could Soviet planners predict the effects of electromagnetic pulse on U.S. C^3I equipment, the extent and duration of radio communications degradation caused by nuclear explosions in the atmosphere, and the inherent range constraints and other limitations of U.S. communications systems. An attack on U.S. command structure would thus be a gamble. Given the stakes, rational leaders would have exhausted all diplomatic means of crisis resolution and finally abandoned all hope for staving off general war before they would have resorted to attack.

Having said this, the fact remains that U.S. command vulnerability and little else was responsible for creating a situation in which Soviet nuclear attack could have been a rational act, albeit an act of last resort. Command vulnerability was the main potential source of instability in a nuclear confrontation, and it represented a potential catalyst for intentional escalation on the part of both sides, given the powerful incentive to strike first.

On the American side, command vulnerability was the only factor that could have seriously undermined confidence in U.S. second-strike capabilities. The uncertainties that caused Soviet doubts about the effectiveness of an attack on U.S. C^3I were, under the principle of conservative planning, cause for U.S. decisionmakers to harbor fears that such an attack might actually succeed. Pressures to release the forces would have mounted as hope for a diplomatic resolution of the crisis waned. With diplomacy on the verge of collapse, incentives for preemption could have grown strong on both sides, despite mutual expectations that opposing forces would survive. Once diplomacy collapsed, and assuming successful Soviet preemption, pressure to unleash U.S. forces immediately upon detection of an attack would have been overwhelming. In this respect, strong incentives for launch-on-warning existed long before Minuteman vulnerability pushed this dangerous tactic into the spotlight of policy debate.

Negative Control

For the period from 1966 to 1973 the unclassified literature is virtually devoid of information on safeguards against accidental or unauthorized use of strategic weapons. It is hard to know whether negative control became more stringent or more relaxed, if it changed at all. However, tension between attempts to improve positive and negative control increased. Soviet missile submarine deployments in the Western Atlantic created a new threat to the military command system and the national command authority. All elements of the NMCS, fixed and mobile, became increasingly vulnerable to sudden destruction. To maintain the same degree of positive control in the face of new submarine missile threats, a relaxation of negative control would have been necessary and vice versa. Reinforcing one meant undermining the other.

More extensive predelegation of nuclear release authority, for instance, would have facilitated retaliation in the event of the destruction of national command authority but increased the risk of unauthorized strikes by U.S. forces. Alternative measures to bolster positive control—especially those designed to achieve higher states of command readiness on shorter notice and plans to mobilize strategic forces at a lower crisis threshold—were also bound to erode negative control. Shortened decision time, earlier and more aggressive preparations to defend against attacks, more frequent and intense encounters with opposing forces in unfamiliar circumstances, and related conditions would have increased risks of miscalculation and overreaction.

The unclassified literature does not suggest that negative control practices were actually modified as a result of the new Soviet threats, but the increased vulnerability raised the level of tension between the conflicting principles. The trade-off between positive and negative control became a more salient feature of the strategic situation, whether or not it was recognized.

Force Components and Strategic Stability

In the mid-1960s an inverse relationship existed between the vulnerability of a given weapon and the vulnerability of its C³I system. Missile submarines were hard to locate and attack but easy to isolate from higher command authorities. Land missiles were more easily located and attacked but less easily isolated. Bombers ranked somewhere in between. This inverse relationship became more pronounced in the early 1970s. Missile submarines still found sanctuary at sea, while bombers and especially land missiles found themselves more exposed to attack. At the same time, investments in command structure had been disproportionately channeled into SAC, and land missile and bomber C³I proved clearly

superior to that of submarines. SAC took genuine strides toward survivable communications and command and control through reorganizing the
postattack command control system, deploying airborne launch control
centers, constructing hardened, underground low frequency antennas at
Minuteman launch control centers, and deploying the emergency rocket
communications system at a strategically located missile complex in Missouri. Although insufficiently robust by absolute standards, these systems
provided a degree of control over land missiles and bombers that far
surpassed that which could be exercised over submarines.

Reliance on Tactical Warning

By 1973 the U.S. command structure depended on early tactical warning of the launch of a strategic nuclear attack. With prompt notification,
NEACP and other essential command aircraft maintained on ground
alert stood some slight chance of escape, slight because the flight time of
submarine missiles launched from U.S. coastal waters was generally
shorter than the reaction time of command post aircraft on normal
ground alert. Prompt warning of surprise attack was thus insufficient by
itself to ensure aircraft survival, but without it targeted aircraft on ground
alert stood virtually no chance of escape. And without those aircraft, the
efficacy of the airborne command system was doubtful. Looking Glass
and the solitary TACAMO aircraft that were kept constantly aloft and
thus were not dependent on tactical warning lacked the capability by
themselves to keep U.S. retaliatory forces under effective control.

Policy Implications in Retrospect

Without exception the strategic issues considered important in the
early 1970s concerned nuclear weapons and delivery systems: the accre-
tion of Soviet strategic forces, the growing vulnerability of U.S. land-
based missiles, the emergence of a Soviet missile submarine threat to
ground-alert strategic bombers, the advent and deployment of MIRVs on
U.S. Minuteman and Poseidon missiles, and the imposition of SALT
ceilings and sublimits on offensive and defensive strategic deployments.
This emphasis was misplaced. In view of the continuing acute vulnerability of the U.S. strategic command system, the size and technical composition of the U.S. and Soviet force structures scarcely deserved the attention they received. The survival of the command structure, not the
vulnerability of Minuteman, ought to have been the focal issue.

David Packard and others recognized the skewed emphasis. But the distorted priorities stemmed from a deep-rooted perception of the strategic problem that together with entrenched institutional biases thwarted major departures from established policy. Packard and his coterie could not bring about the far-reaching conceptual and institutional change necessary to produce a sensible agenda. Packard could express only cautious optimism on the occasion of his resignation: his direction "in itself won't necessarily change anything but it will focus attention on the problem."[104]

Even the attention span proved short, however. The command problem did not receive the attention it deserved until the late 1970s; the decade was instead preoccupied with issues of force structure and attempts to refine the arcane science of force structure vulnerability. As a consequence the condition of the command structure deteriorated, culminating in a crisis of confidence in U.S. C^3I performance when the defense community realized that the price of past neglect was a deficient tactical warning system, a national command system that was enormously exposed to sudden destruction, a communications network that could effectively and reliably reach only a fraction of deployed retaliatory forces, and vulnerabilities that created powerful incentives to strike first or to launch on warning.

It is ironic that the idea of flexible response over a long time during and after a Soviet strike was promoted during the period between Packard's resignation and the late 1970s. The command system was fraught with deficiencies that cast fundamental doubt on U.S. operational capabilities to accomplish far simpler aims such as assured destruction, yet the fantasy of controlled, protracted strategic conflict captured the imagination of many strategists and assumed prominence in strategic policy. New demands would be imposed on a command system that could not even meet minimum essential requirements.

It is also ironic that the tactic of launch on warning became topical only after the demise of Minuteman survivability was perceived as imminent. Because of command vulnerability, strong incentives to use this tactic had existed for a long time.

104. *Congressional Record* (October 29, 1971), p. 38381.

CHAPTER SIX

Command Performance
in the Mid-1980s

FROM 1973 to 1985 arms competition did not radically alter the strategic balance, if standard measures are any indication. The potential second-strike capabilities in U.S. and Soviet force structures actually increased in many important respects. The U.S. command structure, however, remained defective. The resilience of aging command systems deteriorated, and new systems fielded from the early 1970s to the mid-1980s failed appreciably to improve overall performance. At the same time, Soviet modernization so greatly devalued some major U.S. innovations that deployment plans had to be canceled.

Ground Network Vulnerability

As of 1985, Soviet strategic forces could quickly overwhelm virtually all ground-based C³I. Although few observers thought that ground elements were very survivable in the early 1970s, modern Soviet forces have removed any lingering doubt. They can now obliterate those elements with greater efficiency, speed, and confidence. With several thousand additional warheads at their disposal, Soviet planners can afford to target not only the primary command centers and communication sites, but also such secondary targets as command aircraft ground-entry points and land-line switching centers. There are no more than 400 primary and secondary U.S. targets, including the 100 Minuteman launch control centers. With 7,000 deliverable weapons in their strategic arsenal, Soviet planners can easily commit two warheads to every U.S. C³I target.

182

Sanguine: A Case of Predeployment Obsolescence

One early casualty of Soviet strategic modernization, the Sanguine communications system, was intended to be a jamproof system for communicating with submarines. An underground grid in the United States composed of antennas and transmitters enclosed in concrete capsules had been designed to ensure survivability. Transmitting radio signals on frequencies below 100 cycles per second (an extremely low part of the spectrum), Sanguine communications was intended to be practically impervious to enemy jamming and immune to distortion caused by nuclear explosions in the atmosphere. Because signals propagated at that frequency can also penetrate water to a depth of several hundred feet before they dissipate, a missile submarine could have received messages from higher authority without trailing an antenna near the ocean's surface. Sanguine would also have eased restrictions on speed and depth of operation. Under current technical conditions, alert submarines must operate at shallow depths and slow speeds in order to deploy antennas that allow for continuous reception of broadcast traffic.[1]

The justification made most frequently during congressional hearings in the early 1970s touted Sanguine's relative invulnerability to physical and electronic attack. The system was promoted on the grounds that existing fixed VLF stations were not survivable, available radio signals were subject to atmospheric effects (such as sunspots and those generated by nuclear weapons) and to enemy jamming, satellites were vulnerable to jamming or direct attack, and the TACAMO system could be disrupted by mechanical failure or direct attack, or it could suffer severe range limitation under conditions of jamming. These and other arguments buttressed the conclusion that to reject Sanguine would be to rely on communications that were relatively vulnerable to attack and destruction.[2]

By 1975, however, the proposition that Sanguine could survive direct attack had been invalidated. "As the Soviet MIRVed missile threat grew, it became clear that neither Sanguine nor any other ELF [extremely low

1. See chapter 8 for further discussion of extremely low frequency (ELF) submarine communications.

2. *Fiscal Year 1975 Authorization for Military Procurement, Research and Development, and Active Duty, Selected Reserve and Civilian Personnel Strengths,* Hearings before the Senate Committee on Armed Services, 93 Cong. 2 sess. (GPO, 1974), pt. 6, pp. 3225, 3233, 3311.

frequency] transmitter would be able to survive a concentrated Soviet attack even by a small fraction of their force."[3] The main promise of Sanguine thus came to naught, and with its cancellation went the possibility of finding a near-term, high-confidence solution to the problem of survivable submarine communications. For the next decade U.S. planners were instead faced with the difficult task of revitalizing TACAMO, the obsolescence of which had reached an advanced stage because of its expected replacement by Sanguine.[4]

Emergency Rocket Communications Vulnerability

As part of an upgrading program implemented by SAC during the past decade, silos housing emergency communications rockets were hardened to withstand greater blast overpressure and surges of electromagnetic energy. Nevertheless, standard calculations of Minuteman silo vulnerability predict that only about 10 percent would survive attack if Soviet planners allocated two or more weapons to each silo. Emergency rocket communications silos located at Whiteman AFB have become equally vulnerable. A three-on-one attack would theoretically destroy the communications rockets (reportedly housed in eight silos) along with the nuclear-tipped missiles.

The questionable ability of ERCS missiles to ride out a full attack and their equally questionable ability to fly out through debris and dust during an attack cast doubts on their worth for communications during and after an attack. ERCS is not a highly survivable system, and thus a critical means of disseminating the go code to Minuteman launch control centers, bombers in flight, and alert missile submarines (via TACAMO) is not dependable.

Because ERCS can no longer carry out its postattack mission, the rockets can contribute to strategic communications only before the impact of nuclear weapons. This necessity has been recognized, suggesting that ERCS operations presently are being aligned with launch-on-warn-

---

3. *Fiscal Year 1978 Authorization for Military Procurement, Research and Development, and Active Duty, Selected Reserve, and Civilian Personnel Strengths,* Hearings before the Senate Committee on Armed Services, 95 Cong. 1 sess. (GPO, 1977), pt. 10, p. 6678.

4. *Department of Defense Appropriations for 1980,* Hearings before a Subcommittee of the House Committee on Appropriations, 96 Cong. 1 sess. (GPO, 1979), pt. 6, p. 144; and *Department of Defense Authorization for Appropriations for Fiscal Year 1980,* Hearings before the Senate Committee on Armed Services, 96 Cong. 1 sess. (GPO, 1979), pt. 6, p. 3345.

Table 6-1. *Vulnerability of Minuteman Forces to Soviet SS-9 and SS-18 Attack against Launch Control Centers under Selected Assumptions, 1978*

LCC hardness	Percent of Soviet missiles reliable	Percent of force incapacitated[a]					Percent of force impaired (expected)
		Expected	Risk ≥ 20%	Risk ≥ 10%	Risk ≥ 5%	Risk ≥ 1%	
500 psi[b]	75	70	80	85	90	100	30
	80	80	90	95	95	100	20
	85	85	95	100	100	100	20
	90	95	100	100	100	100	5
	95	95	100	100	100	100	5
1,000 psi[b]	75	50	60	65	75	80	35
	80	60	70	75	80	85	30
	85	65	75	80	85	90	30
	90	75	80	85	90	95	20
	95	80	85	90	90	95	20

a. Blast damage only. Assumes Minuteman force of 1,000 missiles.
b. No attack reprogramming.

ing tactics.[5] Even this limited mission could not be carried out with high confidence: as chapter 7 explains, modern Soviet strategic forces probably could prevent launch on warning by ERCS.

Launch Control Center Vulnerability

Underground launch control centers have also become increasingly vulnerable to ICBM attack. Table 6-1 estimates the expected damage to the land missile force resulting from a Soviet attack on underground centers in 1978.[6] The calculations are based on accuracy and yield combinations given for 1978 in appendix table A-3. It was assumed that Soviet attack strategy allocated two high-yield, single-warhead SS-9s or SS-18s to each launch control center. Such an attack would expend 14 percent of the total Soviet land missile force.[7]

5. *Department of Defense Authorization for Appropriations for Fiscal Year 1980,* Senate Hearings, pt. 6, p. 3296.
6. These are conservative estimates because the analysis excludes the possibility of airborne launch of isolated land missiles.
7. Two hundred Soviet land missiles out of a total force of 1,386 are assumed to be employed against 100 Minuteman launch control centers. Titan control centers are not struck. As was noted earlier, the model of a hypothetical attack on American missile silos in 1978 allocated one missile to each of the 1,000 targets (Minuteman only), expending 25 percent of the Soviet land missile force.

The results indicate that airborne launch control of the Minuteman missile force became essential long ago. Without that capability the damage from an attack on LCCs would have exceeded by a wide margin the damage from an attack aimed at missile silos.[8] And without the airborne launch system, the effects of blast damage from an attack on underground centers would have been about as severe in 1978 as the effects of blast damage projected for a Soviet attack on missile silos in 1985.[9] Because of the severity of the expected damage from blast effects alone, calculations omit possible damage from other effects such as electromagnetic pulse. It should be noted, however, that even moderate damage from those effects would compound the overall damage and further reduce Minuteman launch control capabilities.

Other Communications Nodes

Other ground-based communications nodes and systems could also be rapidly destroyed. Destruction of the fourteen ground-entry points, the connections between C^3 planes and land lines, would force aircraft to make direct radio contact with other air- and ground-based units.[10] Destruction of about thirty air force and navy fixed LF and VLF stations would force aircraft to deploy trailing antennas, which are neither as powerful nor as reliable as ground stations, in order to reach other command aircraft, TACAMO, Green Pine sites, underground launch centers, and submarines using the LF and VLF frequencies. The loss of fifty HF transmitters would eliminate systems that otherwise provide for ground-to-air communications to TACAMO aircraft and strategic bombers. Eliminating these transmitters would not be a great loss, however, because HF communications over long distance are not reliable in a nuclear environment.

Still other systems affect communications. The destruction of ERCS

8. In appendix table A-4 a Soviet attack on missile silos was expected to destroy 44 percent of the land missile force in 1978. This estimate assumed Soviet missile reliability to be 75 percent; higher reliabilities result in higher estimates of expected damage. As the number of targets increases, the damage associated with various levels of risk tends to converge on the expected value.

9. The projection for 1985 is that 80 to 88 percent of the Minuteman land missile force would be destroyed by blast effects.

10. These ground-entry points support NEACP and the SAC airborne command post; see *Department of Defense Authorization for Appropriations for Fiscal Year 1980*, Senate hearings, pt. 1, p. 390.

missiles in their silos would remove a critical link connecting command aircraft with TACAMO, strategic bombers, CINCPAC's airborne command post, and Green Pine sites. The loss of the Green Pine network would force command aircraft to use ERCS (vulnerable), HF radio (unreliable), or satellite UHF radio (susceptible to jamming and scintillation) to reach forward bombers. The destruction of two navy ground stations used as links for fleet satellite communications would sever key satellite connections with TACAMO, the only C^3 aircraft equipped with FLTSATCOM terminals, and submarines, the only force component equipped to receive these communications (the submarines cannot receive communications from any other satellite system). The destruction of ground stations that transmit over the Defense Satellite Communications System would eliminate all DSCS links. Presently, the E-4B is the only communications-control aircraft equipped with DSCS terminals (and none of the forces are so equipped). Finally, destruction of the main satellite control facility at Sunnyvale, California, would seriously impair the command and control of satellites. The additional loss of the handful of auxiliary satellite control facilities around the world would eliminate all operations that maintain satellites in proper orbit, orientation, and electromechanical working order. Communications satellites could begin to fail within hours following the loss of these facilities.

Other Command Nodes

The ground-based primary and alternate command centers that support national authorities, unified and specified commanders, and subordinate military commanders responsible for directing strategic operations cannot survive direct attack. Excluding Minuteman launch control centers, the number of key facilities totals about fifteen. Land communications interconnecting these facilities are equally vulnerable. The destruction of a few nodes in the land networks would disable large segments at a time. The critical vulnerability, however, lies with the command centers themselves.

Airborne Network Performance

The obliteration of the ground portion of the U.S. C^3I structure is a Soviet prerogative. The United States therefore depends totally on backup systems to maintain positive control. At present, the sole alternative system for authorizing and implementing retaliation is the airborne command network. The United States has staked its second-strike threat on that network.

The performance of the airborne command network—including NEACP, CINCPAC and CINCLANT airborne command posts, SAC airborne command posts, SAC communications relay aircraft, SAC airborne launch control centers, and TACAMO submarine communications relay aircraft—depends upon pre- and postlaunch vulnerability and communications effectiveness within the network and between the network and force components. Soviet nuclear modernization has adversely affected almost all aspects of these operations. Aircraft would operate in unprecedented levels of possible fallout, turbulence, dust, and other hazards. And the degree to which the atmosphere, and thus strategic communications, could be disrupted by nuclear effects has never been greater, given the Soviet Union's 7,000 deliverable strategic nuclear weapons.

Prelaunch Survival

Command and communications aircraft maintained on ground alert in the United States (including Hawaii) and Bermuda can be targeted by a larger, more modern Soviet submarine force than was the case in the early 1970s. Deployed Yankee-class submarines are more numerous and better armed, with SS-N-6 missiles that can launch multiple warheads at a range of 1,600 nautical miles. In addition, the Soviets have deployed thirty-three Delta-class missile submarines since the first of its kind entered service in 1973. The long-range SS-N-8 and SS-N-18 missiles carried by these submarines can reach targets as far away as 4,300 nautical miles, and SS-N-18 missiles can carry MIRVed warheads.[11] In 1984 Soviet Delta submarines began to patrol regularly in the Western Atlantic.

General Ellis, then commander in chief of SAC, testified in 1979 that the SS-N-6 missiles on board Soviet Yankee submarines patrolling off U.S. coasts were suited for attacks on soft C^3 sites; they could be ready within fifteen minutes of the launch order and all could be launched within the next two minutes. Ellis's testimony also suggests that Soviet missile submarines have made bold deviations from their routine patterns

11. See Robert P. Berman and John C. Baker, *Soviet Strategic Forces: Requirements and Responses* (Brookings, 1982), pp. 94, 107–08, 131.

of patrol, that normal deployment rates allow for a sizable attack, and that increasing deployments of MIRVed SS-N-18 missiles have expanded their coverage of U.S. targets.[12] Although Delta-class submarines primarily patrol in the Barents and Norwegian seas, some of these are also now positioned for short-range attack. There are normally at least five Yankee submarines on patrol near U.S. coastal waters.[13]

Half the 400 primary and secondary U.S. strategic C^3I targets could be struck by Soviet missile submarines on routine patrol. Of these targets, NEACP on ground alert at Andrews AFB was among the most vulnerable until 1983. Even if enemy submarines fired from positions near Bermuda, where they have been observed in the past,[14] the flight time of the SS-N-6 missile over the 800 nautical miles would have been a minute or two shorter than the time required for NEACP to escape its home base. The recent replacement of EC-135 with E-4 aircraft not only failed to mitigate this vulnerability, but increased it.[15] And although the 1983 relocation of NEACP to Grissom AFB, Indiana, did substantially improve its chances of survival, it continues to be exposed to sudden destruction.

Other elements of the ground-alert airborne command network are similarly vulnerable. The flight time of Soviet missiles launched from typical patrol stations in the Atlantic and Pacific is shorter than the fifteen-minute escape time of CINCLANT's command aircraft based in Virginia, CINCPAC's command aircraft based in Hawaii, and TACAMO ground-alert aircraft based in California, Hawaii, Bermuda, or Maryland. All other ground-alert aircraft in the PACCS network could also be destroyed if a small contingent of Yankee submarines crept within several hundred miles of the U.S. coasts before launch. Such movements might not be detected, and detection would not necessarily trigger an increase in aircraft readiness. In such circumstances, Soviet submarines would not

12. *Department of Defense Authorization for Appropriations for Fiscal Year 1980,* Senate hearings, pt. 1, pp. 367, 395-96.
13. Berman and Baker, *Soviet Strategic Forces,* p. 141, report that five is a high but normal patrol number.
14. Ibid., p. 96.
15. An EC-135 can be airborne about six minutes after startup, compared to about eight and one-half minutes for the E-4. The startup time for the E-4 is a minute faster, however (it takes about two minutes to start engines on an E-4 and about three minutes to start an EC-135). See *Hearings on Research, Development, Test, and Evaluation Programs for Fiscal Year 1973* before the House Committee on Armed Services, 92 Cong. 2 sess. (GPO, 1972), p. 11054.

only jeopardize the survival of NEACP but would also threaten such PACCS components as communications relay aircraft based at Rickenbacker AFB, Ohio, and Grissom AFB, Indiana; auxiliary airborne command posts based at Offutt AFB, Nebraska, and Ellsworth AFB, South Dakota; and launch control aircraft based at Ellsworth and at Minot AFB, North Dakota. Conservative U.S. planners cannot count on the survival of any ground-alert aircraft.

Measures that might be taken to protect aircraft during heightened tensions range from dispersal and increased readiness to full airborne alert. These measures should be generally effective against current Soviet forces, but any posture short of airborne alert is only as sound as the tactical early warning system. Because the sensors, communications to command centers, and communications from command centers to alert aircraft designed to support a positive control launch of command aircraft generally lack resistance to nuclear weapons effects and might cease to function with the first high-altitude explosion, aircraft might not be warned in time to survive.[16] Such an explosion could occur a scant few minutes after the first enemy submarine missile is fired. Nuclear missiles launched from a submarine stationed within several hundred miles of the U.S. coast could be detonated three or four minutes after breakwater, during the upward part of their trajectory, which would generate MHD effects and blanket the United States with a high-voltage EMP pulse. Either MHD or EMP could so severely disrupt land line communications that orders from SAC headquarters authorizing the launch of PACCS aircraft, orders from CINCPAC or CINCLANT headquarters authorizing the launch of their respective command post aircraft, and orders from national command centers authorizing the launch of NEACP might not get through. In fact, early warning communications might be disrupted before sensor data could be transmitted to the authorizing command centers. In the resulting confusion, ground-alert aircraft, regardless of their state of readiness, would be subject to destruction by followup SLBMs and perhaps even ICBMs.

Precursor EMP attacks could also directly damage aircraft on the ground or in the air. None of the PACCS EC-135 aircraft is protected against EMP. In fact, only two command post aircraft—the E-4Bs cur-

16. Efforts are under way to harden command centers themselves against EMP, at least NORAD headquarters in Cheyenne Mountain and selected SAC command posts; *Department of Defense Authorization for Appropriations for Fiscal Year 1983,* Hearings before the Senate Committee on Armed Services, 97 Cong. 2 sess. (GPO, 1982), pt. 7, pp. 4681, 4700.

rently assigned to NEACP—are hardened against these effects.[17] Thus the EC-135 airborne command posts operated by CINCPAC, CINCLANT, and SAC and all TACAMO aircraft lack protection.[18]

From 1973 to 1985, then, the vulnerability of command aircraft has not been remedied, although the United States has become totally dependent upon airborne command channels to execute a retaliatory strike. Given the substantial increase in the number of Soviet submarine deployments, the threat that most ground-alert command aircraft would be destroyed in the event of surprise attack or failure of tactical early warning is undoubtedly greater than it was in 1973.

Postlaunch Vulnerability

Command aircraft that manage to evade destruction on the ground or that become airborne during a crisis are not out of danger. Besides EMP, the airborne network, particularly the aircraft operating in U.S. airspace, must deflect the direct and indirect effects of a nuclear attack of almost unimaginable proportions, including radioactive fallout, severe turbulence, and dust clouds.[19] Damage resulting from any or all of these hazards defies exact calculation because the agents responsible are variable and largely unpredictable: the number and yield of attacking weapons, the target coordinates of the weapons, the height of bursts, fission-fusion ratios, weather conditions, the location and flight profile of command aircraft, and so forth.

It is safe to say, nonetheless, that lethal conditions might exist. For instance, Minuteman missile complexes are expected to be prime targets, and an attack on them would probably use ground bursts. Multiple ground bursts would produce high levels of radioactivity, turbulence, and dust. Many command aircraft, particularly airborne launch centers, would fly in the general vicinity of the attack and at some point would position themselves within about 150 miles of the Minuteman complexes in order to establish line-of-sight communications with launch control

17. *Department of Defense Authorization for Appropriations for Fiscal Year 1981,* Hearings before the Senate Committee on Armed Services, 96 Cong. 2 sess. (GPO, 1980), pt. 6, p. 3457.

18. *Department of Defense Authorization for Appropriations for Fiscal Year 1982,* S. Rept. 97-58, 97 Cong. 1 sess. (GPO, 1981), pp. 106–07; and *Department of Defense Authorization for Appropriations for Fiscal Year 1983,* Senate hearings, pt. 7, pp. 4696, 4718–19.

19. Testimony of the deputy under secretary of defense in *Department of Defense Authorization for Appropriations for Fiscal Year 1983,* Senate hearings, pt. 7, p. 4678.

centers and silos. Though aircraft presumably would be assigned orbits that are expected on the basis of wind pattern history to be upwind from the target complex, there is always an irreducible, significant risk that unusual (not necessarily aberrational) weather would blow fallout in the wrong direction. The dose administered could easily be lethal to the crew. If the chance of exposure to unacceptable levels of radioactivity (about 200 rads) is only 10 percent on average per orbit, then the chances are greater than even (57 percent) that at least one of the eight crews in the PACCS airborne network would be incapacitated. The risk that at least two crews would be incapacitated is 19 percent and that three crews would receive a lethal dose is 4 percent.

Lethal turbulence can persist for ten minutes over a distance of ten miles or more following a high-yield nuclear explosion. Though aircraft would presumably follow routes that circumvent high-risk areas such as Minuteman complexes, the boundaries of their assigned orbits would undoubtedly encompass other designated targets, and random flight profiles within those boundaries would be hazardous. Chance destruction of aircraft by turbulence is not a remote possibility.

Dust ingestion by engines could also destroy aircraft or cause sorties to be aborted. The experience of a DC-9, a C-130 transport, and two 727s that flew through the volcanic dust cloud produced by the eruption of Mount St. Helens suggests that this problem is potentially severe.[20] An engine would probably be damaged within one hour when the density of dust ingested was about ten milligrams per cubic foot, and the ingestion rate of some command aircraft would probably be that great following a large-scale nuclear attack involving thousands of ground bursts. The density of dust in the cloud of a single 200 kiloton surface burst is estimated to be about five milligrams per cubic foot; an aircraft that repeatedly flew into clouds of that density could be disabled within two hours.

U.S. aircraft thus remain very vulnerable after a nuclear attack. All command-network aircraft in the active inventory, except for two E-4B aircraft, lack adequate protection from EMP. In this respect the overall survivability of the airborne network has not been improved. In other respects—notably vulnerability to radioactivity, turbulence, and particulate matter—the survivability of command aircraft has decreased because of the large increase in the number of nuclear weapons in the Soviet arsenal.

20. The aircraft suffered wing, windscreen, and turbine abrasion after four minutes of exposure. In one case, two engines stopped in flight and remaining engines lost power after four minutes of exposure (three engines were totally destroyed).

Figure 6-1. *Airborne Network Minuteman Communications*

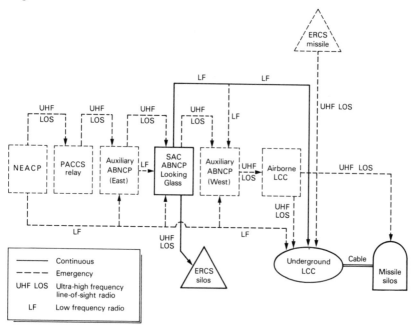

Postlaunch Communications Performance

Evaluation of communications capabilities within the airborne command network and between this network and force elements cannot assume any support from ground-based systems. Such systems could be impaired by EMP and MHD within several minutes of the launch of the first enemy missile. Following on the heels of this disruption would be blast destruction of ground-based command centers and communications by submarine-launched missiles. Followup attacks by ICBMs would result in wholesale destruction of primary, secondary, and tertiary ground-based systems. Virtually all ground support could be lost in the first thirty minutes.

Under the weight of a nuclear attack, strategic communications to airborne channels would thus collapse within thirty minutes. Potential channels are depicted in figures 6-1 to 6-5. Their establishment partly depends on the disposition of C³ aircraft at the time of enemy attack. Two dispositions are considered: day-to-day, with aircraft at normal levels of readiness, and airborne alert. Satellite radio links are excluded from this assessment, but satellites currently used for strategic communications would make only marginal contributions to airborne force management.

Figure 6-2. *PACCS Airborne UHF Network*

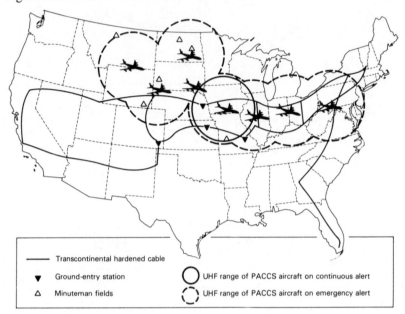

———	Transcontinental hardened cable	
▼	Ground-entry station	◯ UHF range of PACCS aircraft on continuous alert
△	Minuteman fields	◌ UHF range of PACCS aircraft on emergency alert

High-frequency radio links are also omitted because, as noted earlier, they are not expected to function in a nuclear environment.

COMMUNICATIONS WITH MINUTEMAN FORCES. The primary path running from higher authority to Minuteman forces consists of UHF transmissions among airborne units within line of sight of each other (figure 6-1). End-to-end communications involve a large formation of PACCS aircraft in series (figure 6-2). This aerial chain is only as strong as its weakest link. Loss of any one link because of aircraft destruction or UHF communications failure would break the UHF chain, forcing aircraft to activate backup LF or HF channels. Although these backup channels are supposed to provide for long-distance communications to bridge gaps in UHF line-of-sight coverage, high frequencies would be blacked out and the reliability of low frequencies is highly suspect. The importance of establishing an intact UHF chain is thus very great.

Unfortunately, the UHF chain is likely to be broken. The line-of-sight communications systems on board EC-135 aircraft are considered vulnerable to EMP,[21] and one or more aircraft in the chain is likely to be

21. *Department of Defense Appropriations for 1984*, Hearings before a Subcommittee of the House Committee on Appropriations, 98 Cong. 1 sess. (GPO, 1983), pt. 8, pp. 403–04.

destroyed on the ground if surprise attack occurs. Under day-to-day conditions, the reaction time of C³ aircraft on ground alert could be longer than the flight time of Soviet submarine missiles.

The implications of UHF radio failure or aircraft destruction for communications with Minuteman forces are very serious. If NEACP were lost, all Minuteman forces would be isolated unless authority for nuclear release resides with SAC's Looking Glass commander or other subordinate military commanders. The destruction of either the PACCS relay aircraft based in Indiana or the one in Ohio, or failure of their UHF radios, would disconnect NEACP from SAC unless LF communications could be established. Jamming, EMP, atmospheric disruption, trailing antenna breakage, and other problems prevent high-confidence LF communications from NEACP to Looking Glass. Direct LF transmission from NEACP to Minuteman launch control centers would be more doubtful because the centers themselves are subject to attack and because they are a greater distance away.

The destruction of airborne launch centers on ground alert in North and South Dakota or failure of their UHF radios would isolate the bulk of the Minuteman forces unless Looking Glass could establish LF communications with launch control centers on the ground. For reasons given above, high-confidence LF communications would not exist. Failure of UHF line-of-sight radio, moreover, could even prevent Looking Glass from reaching nearby launch control centers at the Minuteman complex in Missouri and using its equipment to fire isolated Minuteman missiles.

Under conditions of airborne crisis alert, reliable communications with Minuteman forces would depend upon the extent to which EMP, radioactivity, dust, and turbulence cause damage to radio equipment or the aircraft themselves. No one knows how much damage would be incurred, but conservative planners could expect that a sizable part of the Minuteman force would be isolated as a result. If UHF line-of-sight radios suffer extensive damage from EMP, Minuteman isolation could be total.

In the cases of both day-to-day and airborne alert, airborne communications with Minuteman forces would cease within a few hours because of limitations on aircraft endurance. Conservative planners heavily discount tanker support to extend flight time. If successful, refueling could, however, increase the endurance of NEACP and Looking Glass long enough that HF and satellite communications might be restored. It is possible though not probable that some aircraft could remain airborne for twenty-

Figure 6-3. *Airborne Network Bomber Communications*

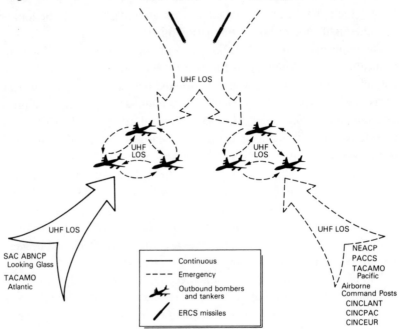

SAC ABNCP
Looking Glass
TACAMO
Atlantic

—— Continuous
- - - Emergency
✈ Outbound bombers
and tankers
／ ERCS missiles

NEACP
PACCS
TACAMO
Pacific
Airborne
Command Posts
CINCLANT
CINCPAC
CINCEUR

four hours or more, and the atmosphere might have healed enough by then to permit restoration of HF and satellite radio communications.

COMMUNICATIONS WITH STRATEGIC BOMBER FORCE. Airborne communication with bombers continues to be problematical. As depicted in figure 6-3 message delivery heavily depends upon UHF line-of-sight relay and ERCS, but both systems are unreliable. UHF provides the most reliable radio link with outbound bombers that fly within line-of-sight of Looking Glass and other PACCS aircraft (figure 6-4). Several factors, however, impose sharp constraints on the utility of this link.

The destruction of C³ aircraft or failure of their UHF radios would shrink the area of UHF coverage. In the worst case, in which surprise attack destroys C³ aircraft on ground alert, the UHF envelope would be reduced to a 400-mile radius around Looking Glass. Failure of Looking Glass UHF radios (or bombers' UHF radios) because of exposure to EMP would eliminate the effective UHF envelope.

The UHF link is further weakened because outbound bombers quickly fly out of range. Even aircraft based in the south would be beyond range three hours after takeoff. If a prompt NCA decision to retaliate could be

Figure 6-4. *PACCS Airborne UHF Network Bomber Communications*

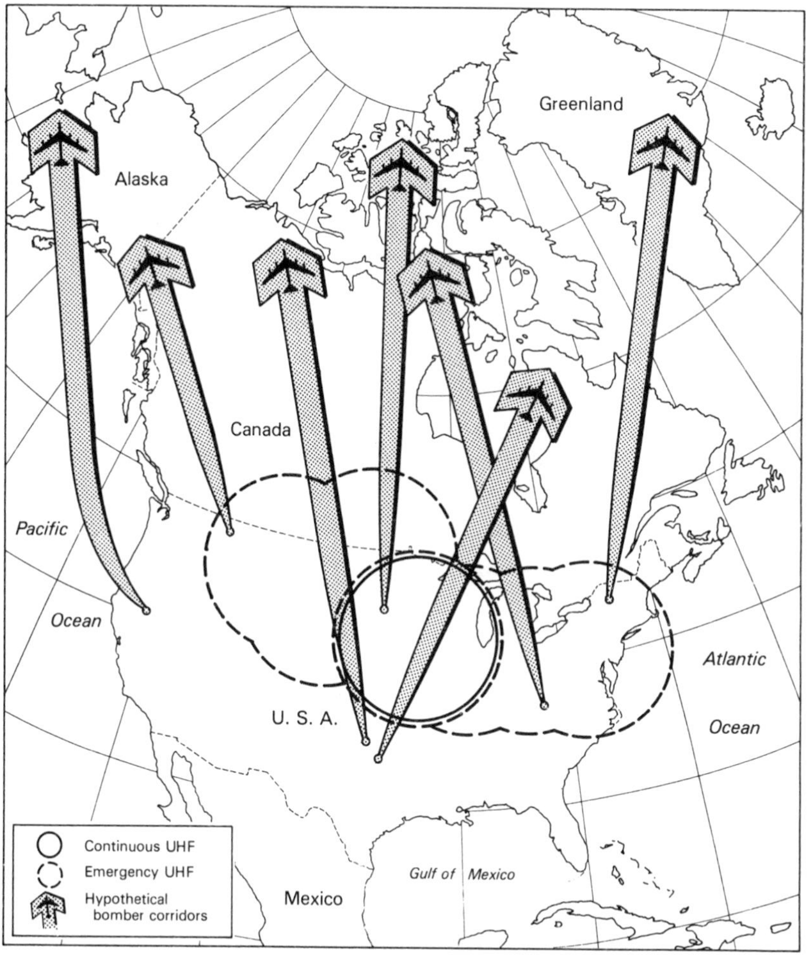

made and that decision communicated to the airborne command network, most bombers would stand a good chance of receiving the orders
either directly from C³ aircraft or from bombers or tankers following
behind unless their radios suffered EMP damage. If the decision were
delayed, or if it could not be promptly given to the airborne command
network, then bombers or tankers would put great distances between
themselves and C³ aircraft, reducing the timeliness and effectiveness of
UHF relay through other bomber or tanker units. Bombers loitering at
their positive control turnaround points, waiting for later arriving aircraft

to bring the orders, might fail to get the message in time to complete their assigned mission. In the event of an attack that destroys NEACP on the ground at Grissom AFB or that disrupts communications between the NCA and NEACP, bombers and tankers would probably be out of range of UHF communications by the time that C^3 aircraft were prepared to relay the NCA's decision. The destruction of bombers and tankers on ground alert would also reduce the ability of surviving units to relay the execution message to each other.

Emergency communications rockets, of course, represent an alternative means of reaching the dispersed bomber forces, and they are an especially important link to have if the airborne command network is not ready to disseminate the go code until after bombers have flown beyond UHF range. By this time, however, ERCS deployments would have been massively attacked. Even if they survived and were successfully launched, communications over this channel would be fleeting and tenuous.

The short-lived character of both UHF line-of-sight relay and ERCS puts pressure on decisionmakers to commit the entire bomber force without delay.

COMMUNICATIONS WITH THE SUBMARINE MISSILE FORCE. Communications with missile submarines still critically depend upon TACAMO aircraft, whose capabilities apparently do not impress even the chief of naval operations. Not mincing words, he stated flatly in 1981 that "the most serious deficiency in the navy's strategic nuclear posture . . . is the lack of reliable, survivable communications with SSBNs at sea."[22]

The single-thread TACAMO channel nearly disappeared during the 1970s, owing to anticipation of the deployment of Sanguine. Between 1971 and 1979 the navy drew down the Pacific-based fleet until only one aircraft was left in order to maintain continuous airborne operations in the Atlantic basin. The navy has since doubled the inventory of TACAMO aircraft, and continuous airborne alert in both oceans was instituted at the end of 1983, coinciding with the buildup of Trident submarine deployments in the Pacific.[23] At the same time, TACAMO aircraft have been equipped with improved VLF radio equipment for

22. *Department of Defense Authorization for Appropriations for Fiscal Year 1982*, Senate hearings, pt. 7, p. 4054.
23. *Department of Defense Appropriations for 1980*, Hearings before a Subcommittee of the House Committee on Appropriations, 96 Cong. 1 sess. (GPO, 1979), pt. 6, pp. 141–42; and *Department of Defense Authorization for Appropriations for Fiscal Year 1979*, Hearings before the Senate Committee on Armed Services, 95 Cong. 2 sess. (GPO, 1978), pt. 9, p. 6722.

one-way, low-data-rate communications to submarines. The navy has installed a jam-resistant, high-power (200 kilowatt) transmitter on each aircraft, extending the effective communications range between TACAMO and U.S. missile submarines. The aircraft now can operate close to the continental United States and still maintain reasonably good VLF communications to far-flung alert submarines.

This extension of range coincidentally alleviates the problem of delivering the message to TACAMO. In the 1970s a severe trade-off existed between TACAMO-to-submarine communications and higher authority-to-TACAMO communications. Ideally, the aircraft could receive the message and immediately relay it to submarines. In practice it was either on station to receive or on station to transmit. While this trade-off still exists, the problem is less severe, especially under alert conditions. As figure 6-5 indicates, the primary path to TACAMO Atlantic runs from NEACP through CINCLANT's airborne command post. This LF radio link probably could be established if a TACAMO aircraft is operating in the Western Atlantic, and TACAMO retransmissions over VLF probably could be received by most alert submarines in the Atlantic. Additional aircraft could be sent up in a crisis to reinforce the linkage; TACAMO-to-TACAMO relay would provide greater assurance that the most distant submarines would copy.

There are uncertainties, however, that reduce confidence in TACAMO's performance. Trailing antennas used in conjunction with VLF communications are prime collectors of EMP energy, and damage to sensitive electronic components could result, impairing VLF communications. The extension and operation of the five-mile trailing antenna core is unreliable, particularly in bad weather. Under day-to-day conditions, surprise attack might destroy all but SAC's Looking Glass aircraft and the TACAMO aircraft on twenty-four-hour airborne alert. High-confidence LF radio communications from Looking Glass to TACAMO do not exist, even when TACAMO is operating in the Western Atlantic. Furthermore, destruction of backup ground-alert TACAMO aircraft would reduce the likelihood that all alert submarines in the Atlantic would copy a message transmitted by a single aircraft stationed in the Western Atlantic.

In addition, because these aircraft cannot be refueled, their endurance could be as short as a few hours, depending on the fuel supply on board at the time of attack. Delay in the decision to retaliate could thus result in the loss of TACAMO support and the isolation of the alert submarine force.

Figure 6-5. *Airborne Network for Missile Submarine Communications*

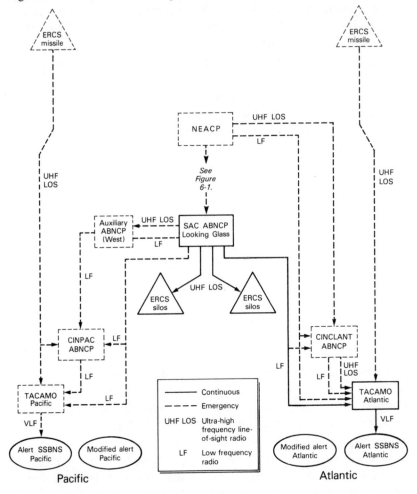

Finally, under day-to-day conditions, off-alert and modified-alert sub-marines at sea do not monitor communications on a continuous basis. Such submarines could fail to copy the go-code broadcast regardless of its source. In the Pacific, the risk is greater that submarines would be iso-lated, even under alert conditions. The primary path of communications runs from NEACP through SAC PACCS aircraft to Pacific-based TACAMO and CINCPAC's airborne command post (see figure 6-5). The LF channel used for this purpose does not offer high assurance of success-ful dissemination.

Emergency communications rockets offer a potential means of reaching Pacific-based TACAMO units as well as a redundant channel of communications with Atlantic-based aircraft. ERCS, however, cannot be counted on, for reasons discussed earlier.

In sum, communications with missile submarines are problematical under a wide range of plausible circumstances. Soviet surprise attack could immediately isolate a large number of them, and all would be isolated within a matter of hours even if Soviet attack is anticipated because TACAMO's endurance is very short. Despite the long endurance of the submarines themselves, the short-lived character of their supporting communications puts pressure on decisionmakers to commit the submarine force quickly and massively. In this respect, the submarine force is like the bomber force.

Satellite Communications

So far the analysis has discounted the contribution of satellites to strategic communications. Many observers, such as William J. Perry, former under secretary of defense for research and engineering, share this pessimistic assessment.

I see very significant command and control problems with all three legs of the Triad in that I do not envision that our fixed ground-based systems or our satellite systems would survive an attack. . . . In terms of enduring for a month or a week or even an hour after attack, we become essentially dependent on our airborne systems, those that survive an attack. That problem is really common to the three legs of the Triad.[24]

Conservative Soviet planners are doubtless more impressed with U.S. satellite capabilities and probably credit the United States with a significant capability for satellite communications with strategic forces during war. Current force deployments as well as C^3 aircraft are equipped with satellite receivers, and strategic communications satellites are fully operational. The capabilities and vulnerability of the operational systems deserve careful consideration.

The first successful military satellite communications program—called the Interim Defense Communications Satellite Program—was conceived in 1963 and put into operation in 1966. It was the forerunner of the Defense Satellite Communications System, first launched in 1971 and

24. *Department of Defense Appropriations for Fiscal Year 1980*, House hearings, pt. 3, p. 26.

managed by the Defense Communications Agency. DCA's mandate, and
the purpose of its satellites, is to provide two-way, long-distance communications between national command centers and military headquarters.
DSCS satellites now provide this capability using super high frequency
(SHF) channels.

A major disadvantage of current generation SHF satellite systems is
that large terminals and antennas are required. Except for jumbo-sized
vehicles such as the E-4 airborne command post, aircraft cannot accommodate the heavy, bulky equipment. Using current technology, exploitation of SHF satellite communications by EC-135 command aircraft, strategic bombers, TACAMO, and other small mobile units is impractical.

Terminals and antennas used in conjunction with UHF satellites, however, can be built small. Recognizing the varied military applications of
UHF satellites, the Defense Department conducted a series of experiments in the 1960s. In 1965, Lincoln experimental satellites demonstrated
the feasibility of UHF satellite communications. By 1970 a major military
experimental program known as TACSAT had proved the operational
usefulness of UHF satellites. In the early 1970s TACSAT UHF terminals
were installed on some EC-135 command aircraft. Using a transponder
carried by LES-6, an experimental satellite launched into geosynchronous
orbit in 1968, EC-135 command aircraft could for the first time communicate with other airborne command posts via satellite.

Extensive use of UHF satellite communications for military purposes
did not occur until 1976, when the navy leased the UHF portion of three
Communications Satellite Corporation satellites launched in 1976 (the
program was called Gapfiller; the satellites were called MARISATs). By
the end of the 1970s, 99 percent of the navy's fleet (some 430 ships including missile submarines) could copy fleet broadcast messages transmitted
from shore over MARISATs.

In part because of the weakening power of the LES-6, the navy
granted the national and unified and specified command aircraft access to
MARISATs. But the satellites were positioned to give maximum oceanic
coverage for navy operations, leaving a gap in coverage over the continental United States, and only NEACP and the CINCLANT airborne command post could be connected. The national command authorities could
also use LES-9, an experimental satellite launched in 1976 that provided
limited operational UHF communications between NEACP and the
CINCLANT, CINCPAC, and CINCSAC airborne command posts.

The key satellite program designed specifically for strategic communications—air force satellite communications (AFSATCOM)—achieved

Figure 6-6. *Air Force Satellite Communications (AFSATCOM) UHF Coverage*

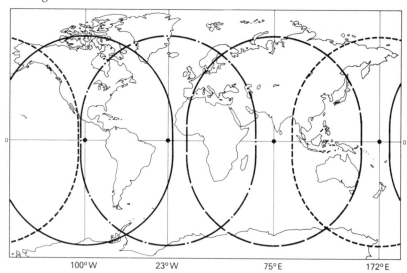

100°W   23°W   75°E   172°E

Source: *Hearings on Military Posture and H.R. 10929* before the House Committee on Armed Services, 95 Cong. 2 sess. (GPO, 1978), pt. 3, bk. 2, p. 1323.

initial operational capability in 1979. The space segment of this program consists of UHF transponders on board host satellites. The program is now merely a set of transponders on Satellite Data System satellites, fleet satellite communications satellites (the followup to MARISAT), and certain classified satellites. The operational ground and airborne segments of the air force program mainly consist of terminals at major military command headquarters, on E-4 and EC-135 command aircraft, on EC-130 TACAMO aircraft, on most B-52 bombers, and at Minuteman launch control centers. Missile submarines are not equipped.

The navy's FLTSATCOM satellites carry the AFSATCOM devices required for communications coverage of most ground and airborne locations (figure 6-6). All four satellites are now parked in geosynchronous orbit. The FLTSATCOM constellation provides worldwide coverage except in the polar regions. Two Satellite Data System satellites in elliptical polar orbits provide coverage for strategic bombers at the extreme northern latitudes.

The effectiveness of the Air Force Satellite Communications System appears very doubtful, however. Links to ground and airborne terminals are subject to severe weakening from signal absorption and scintillation.

A small number of high-altitude nuclear explosions could interrupt communications for long periods. According to then Assistant Defense Secretary Gerald P. Dinneen, testifying in 1979, "many of our communications satellites' links are blocked out because if they explode a nuclear bomb in the atmosphere that blacks out ultra high frequency communications to the satellites . . . we could not depend on the communications satellites because . . . blackouts in UHF last for a long period of time."[25] Absorption effects produced by a single high-altitude explosion can black out UHF satellite communications for nearly an hour, but the affected region is only a few hundred miles in diameter. Scintillation effects, on the other hand, can persist for many hours over large areas. By altering the electron density of the ionosphere, a single high-altitude burst over the center of the United States could induce sufficiently large fluctuations in signal amplitude and phase that reception would not be possible in most of North America. Scattered dust from multiple ground bursts would cause comparably extensive and persistent scintillation problems. As in the case of EMP effects and MHD, scintillation phenomena were belatedly recognized as a serious threat to strategic communications. Contrary to initial expectations, the performance of UHF satellites is very susceptible to disruption from the artificial auroras created by nuclear explosions.

AFSATCOM is also very vulnerable to jamming, a fact that has long been known and widely recognized. Jamming communications satellites is "the greatest threat," the "easiest thing for [the Soviets] to do."[26] AFSATCOM is said to possess modest antijam features,[27] but it is more vulnerable to jamming than is the Defense Satellite Communications System (E-4B aircraft are the only DSCS-equipped elements in the airborne command network), which itself is easily jammed.[28] According to Gerald Dinneen, current generation communications satellites, including AFSATCOM, have very little if any antijamming capability and would be effectively neutralized.[29]

In general, Soviet capacity to exploit the antijam shortcomings of U.S. communications satellites is greatest against those positioned within line

25. Ibid., pp. 98, 101.
26. *Hearings on Military Posture and H.R. 5068* before the House Committee on Armed Services, 95 Cong. 1 sess. (GPO, 1977), pt. 3, bk. 2, p. 1354.
27. *Department of Defense Authorization for Appropriations for Fiscal Year 1982*, Senate hearings, pt. 7, p. 3792.
28. *Department of Defense Appropriations for 1980*, House hearings, pt. 6, p. 62.
29. Ibid., p. 153.

of sight of Soviet territory, but satellites positioned out of range of high-powered jammers inside Soviet boundaries are also vulnerable. Jamming sources might include shipborne facilities, ground-based facilities in places like Cuba, or jammers covertly operated inside U.S. territory. These sources could probably neutralize key AFSATCOM channels, such as the one located at 100° west longitude (see figure 6-6). There is some consolation in the fact that Soviet nuclear attacks employing high-altitude EMP bursts might result in a form of fratricide in that they would impair the functioning of forward-based Soviet equipment used to jam U.S. communications.

Spoofing and other modes of electronic attack could also cause a host of problems. For instance, the orientation of satellites might be changed so as to impede user access despite efforts by ground-based control facilities to keep the satellites properly aligned.

Nuclear explosions in space may pose the greatest threat to strategic communications satellites because of the properties of the medium (outer space) and satellite design characteristics. Outer space permits the energy from nuclear bursts to travel unimpeded. Although energy intensity falls off as the inverse square of the distance from the burst location, targets hundreds or thousands of miles away could be exposed to high levels of gamma and X-ray energy. Hardening against nuclear effects currently ranges from essentially none to modest levels for operational satellites leased or owned by the Defense Department. Leased satellites have the least protection, while AFSATCOM and DSCS II reportedly have been hardened to some degree against some effects.[30] But military demand for satellite communications support of normal peacetime operations has risen so fast that channel capacity has taken precedence over wartime performance and survivability. Protective shielding and devices compete with the communications equipment itself for space and weight allocations. The inevitable compromises have historically favored capacity at the expense of survivability.

Table 6-2 summarizes the main nuclear effects that threaten satellites and gives associated damage thresholds and the range at which the

---

30. According to one source, "at present no U.S. communications satellites are specifically hardened against nuclear effects"; see Eric J. Lerner, "Strategic C³: A Goal Unreached," *IEEE Spectrum,* vol. 19 (October 1982), p. 53. Other sources report the existence of some protection. AFSATCOM space vehicles, for instance, are reportedly "hardened to electromagnetic pulse"; see *Department of Defense Authorization for Appropriations for Fiscal Year 1982,* Senate hearings, pt. 7, p. 3792.

Table 6-2. *Effects on Satellites of Nuclear Explosions*

Effects[a]	Assumed threshold for illustrative purposes[b]	Distance (km)
X-rays		
Ionization upset	1 rad (Si)	37,400
SGEMP upset	10^{-5} cal/cm^2	24,500
SGEMP burnout	10^{-3} cal/cm^2	2,450
Ionization burnout	10^4 rads (Si)	370
Thermomechanical shock	1 cal/g (Au)	270
Gamma rays		
Ionization upset	1 rad (Si)	550
Ionization burnout	10^4 rads (Si)	5
Neutrons		
Degradation	3×10^{11} n/cm^2	56

Source: Defense Nuclear Agency.
a. 1-megaton weapon, 10 keV blackbody, 30 nanoseconds prompt pulse.
b. Electronics behind 0.06-inch aluminum.

thresholds would be crossed. The fragility of unhardened satellites is such that an exoatmospheric explosion at a relatively low altitude might upset those in geosynchronous orbit (37,400 kilometers or about 22,400 miles altitude). The damage mechanism is referred to as ionization upset. Another mechanism capable of causing damage is known as system-generated electromagnetic pulse (SGEMP). As table 6-2 indicates, a 1-megaton explosion 7,700 miles above the earth could upset the electronics of geosynchronous satellites at a range of 24,500 kilometers. Appendix D demonstrates that a 25-megaton explosion only 60 miles above the United States (an event that simultaneously produces the ground and airborne EMP problems discussed earlier) could in theory generate a level of SGEMP sufficient to upset satellite electronics in geosynchronous orbit. A 25-megaton explosion 12,600 kilometers (about 7,600 miles) above the earth could in theory generate a level of SGEMP sufficient to burn up satellite electronics in geosynchronous orbit. A 220-megaton explosion (an order of magnitude greater than the highest yield of present weapons in the Soviet inventory) 60 miles above the United States could in theory burn up geosynchronous satellites.

These estimates may not be valid approximations of real satellite responses under actual conditions. They are meant to serve illustrative purposes only. High-yield, low-altitude exoatmospheric explosions, however, would almost certainly disrupt communications satellites. Moreover, to the extent that system-generated EMP can upset, damage, or destroy one geosynchronous satellite parked above the United States, it can simultaneously cause similar problems for others because such satellites tend to be clustered together.

Even if nuclear explosions in space merely upset satellite electronics, the resulting degradation is potentially serious. The impairment of communications would probably be temporary if satellite control stations on the ground were not attacked, but if they immediately came under attack, the necessary corrective actions could not be taken, and satellites could be rendered useless.

So far, the Soviet Union has not demonstrated an ability to intercept geosynchronous satellites. They have conducted a series of tests apparently aimed at developing the capability of disabling low-altitude satellites using an SL-11 booster to launch a space interceptor that maneuvers close to the target and detonates conventional explosives after one or two revolutions of the earth. But no interceptor satellite has flown higher than 2,328 kilometers during tests conducted since 1968. The public record also suggests that the Soviet Union has not demonstrated a capability of attacking AFSATCOM space vehicles with directed-energy weapons such as lasers. However, AFSATCOM vehicles in low orbit (for example, SDS, the perigee of whose highly elliptical orbit is about 400 kilometers) may not be immune from the effects of ground-based Soviet lasers.

The Strategic Situation: 1985

During the Carter and Reagan administrations, the command implications of large-scale nuclear deployments came into better focus. The relevance of command performance to basic national security purposes is now generally appreciated. C³I deficiencies have been cataloged, remedies have been intensively researched, and the need for a sound program of modernization is widely recognized. C³I modernization became a central theme of the Reagan administration's strategic agenda, and an improvement plan has begun to cohere under an umbrella of presidential endorsement and widespread approval. The depth of this comprehension and commitment, however, remains in doubt (see chapter 8). Command implications will need to be clarified, sharpened, and put into historical perspective before a modernization plan worthy of support can be crafted and implemented.

U.S. Second-Strike Capabilities

Analysis would support a judgment that U.S. strategic forces are adequately protected against Soviet attack. Although the vulnerability of land missiles, and to a lesser extent bombers, has grown, the United States possesses enough weapons that would survive even a massive surprise attack to strike back against an extensive enemy target base. They could inflict horrendous punitive damage in a retaliatory strike. The coherence of the U.S. strategic command system, however, is precarious in wartime. An attack on our command system could drastically reduce or even block retaliation, and such an approach continues to offer the most attractive military solution to the enemy planner's problem of limiting damage to the Soviet Union. A strategy designed to inflict as much damage as possible to U.S. C³I poses a much greater threat to U.S. second-strike capabilities than does a strategy designed to inflict maximum damage to the U.S. force structure.

Negative Control

Various unofficial sources suggest that negative control has been strengthened during the past decade by several programs. SAC reportedly installed new locks on Minuteman forces; launch control crews can now launch Minuteman missiles only when unlock codes are passed down from higher authority. Previously, launch crews possessed at all times the physical capacity to target, arm, and fire their forces.[31] Problems experienced by the U.S. early warning systems during 1979 and 1980 have led to procedural and technical changes that reduce the risk of false alarms. Erroneous warning indicators and the untoward reactions they trigger are less likely to occur during peacetime. Finally, the United States and the Soviet Union signed an agreement whose provisions require advance notification of certain weapons tests, maintenance of reliable, timely communications between the two countries' leaderships, and other steps designed to prevent accidental war.

31. For a discussion of safeguards against unauthorized launch of Minuteman missiles before the installation of new locks in the late 1970s, see Bruce G. Blair and Garry D. Brewer, "The Terrorist Threat to World Nuclear Problems," *Journal of Conflict Resolution,* vol. 21 (September 1977), pp. 379–403.

Crisis Stability

From the standpoint of force structure vulnerability, the stability of deterrence appears assured; the threat of retaliation cannot be removed by either side. The knowledge that opposing forces are partially vulnerable to a first strike is unlikely to affect superpower behavior in a crisis, however intense. That opposing forces are substantially invulnerable is the salient consideration.

Crisis instability is more likely to stem from command system vulnerability. The condition of the U.S. command structure creates a potentially severe penalty for delay in releasing weapons and thus encourages early release by U.S. authorities. By the same token the creaky state of our command system offers Soviet leaders potentially great rewards for prompt action; the situation discourages indecision and late release by Soviet authorities.

Command vulnerability not force vulnerability, then, is the main potential source of crisis instability. That this has been the situation throughout the missile era ought not to be drowned in the national debate over strategic modernization and arms control. Command vulnerability actually materialized long ago, only to be overshadowed by anticipated weapons vulnerabilities that never have fully materialized. Contrary to common belief, the United States is not entering a period of unprecedented danger.

Force Components and Strategic Stability

The inverse relationship between the vulnerability of a given force component and the strength of its supporting command system became more pronounced during the past decade. Land missiles are the most responsive to direction, but their vulnerability to a coordinated Soviet first strike is high relative to submarines and is growing. Submarine missiles are the most difficult to control, but their vulnerability to attack remains very low. Because submarines have become the mainstay of our strategic deterrent, failure to strengthen communications links with them caused further erosion of overall stability.

Reliance on Tactical Warning

From 1973 to 1985 the rapid annihilation of the ground segment of the U.S. command structure became a Soviet prerogative, and the backup airborne segment became increasingly exposed to attack from submarine missiles. The backup system depends critically upon early warning and rapid reaction to escape destruction by these missiles. Without strategic warning the ground-alert units that constitute most of the airborne network could be destroyed even if tactical early warning systems perform perfectly. Reliance on tactical and strategic warning has grown so that both are essential to the control of retaliatory forces.

Policy Implications

A variety of command deficiencies—the extreme vulnerability of the ground segment of C³I, the considerable prelaunch and postlaunch vulnerability of the airborne segment, deficient airborne communications, and the questionable performance of emergency rocket and satellite communications systems—undermine the ability of the United States to keep nuclear operations and national security objectives aligned during war.

Recent years have witnessed growing recognition of these deficiencies and growing appreciation of their implications for strategic policy and investment. A major breakthrough in this regard was the Reagan administration's unusual move to predicate force modernization on C³I repair. The administration expanded the scale of C³I research and development to create the most intensive, comprehensive effort to date. It also voiced a strong commitment to C³I modernization and indeed portrayed it as the linchpin of its overall strategic modernization program. C³I programs are supposed to compete, and fare well, against major weapons proposals.

This represents a notable first step toward balanced strategic priorities. Nevertheless, as later chapters will show, nuclear modernization under the Reagan administration has been a lopsided effort that has perpetuated imbalance and inconsistency. In stressing the need to lay the foundations of a strategy for protracted nuclear war, the administration has fostered the belief that the simple, traditional requirements of assured destruction were already satisfied and that future investment in both C³I and weapons systems would be devoted to removing the Soviet Union's purported advantages in protracted warfighting. This rhetoric has diverted attention from the fact that the basic C³I problem has not already been solved and that planned C³I upgrades have actually been designed to remedy weaknesses that might prevent the United States from responding at all to a Soviet first strike. At the same time, weapons modernization has been geared to the far more ambitious aims associated with a strategy of protracted nuclear warfighting. This effort is dubious indeed in view of the manifest inability of C³I systems—even after planned improvements are made—to support such a strategy. Doctrine and forces have become increasingly sophisticated, but C³I capability has remained rudimentary.

This disjuncture is conspicuous from even the most cursory examination. The specter of protracted nuclear war has nonetheless been raised and in due course it has become a standard scenario in assessing not only the future but also the present Soviet nuclear threat.

The next chapter explains why scenarios other than massive nuclear exchanges are not relevant to conditions in the 1980s.

Flexible Response in the 1980s

A STRATEGY of deterrence based on large-scale retaliation against a comprehensive enemy target base remains the cornerstone of U.S. nuclear policy. This strategy and the consensus behind it, however, have come under growing pressure to allow for a more flexible response. Massive retaliation, it is argued, should be one option, but the United States should be prepared for any contingency.

The idea of flexible response is appealing. It not only seems to answer the paradox of massive retaliation—that if deterrence fails it is not rational to carry out the threat of all-out retaliation—but also encourages healthy skepticism toward preconceptions about nuclear war. Nuclear planners begin to recognize that they can only speculate on the nature of nuclear conflict, on the preferences of national leaders, and on the appropriateness of attack options. However many options are programmed in advance, there is no assurance that one will correspond with the preference of national authorities. And however close the correspondence, their preference would represent, at best, a tentative, theoretical solution to conflict, the wisdom of which only experience could confirm or refute. In short, the highest form of rationality would be conscious trial and error. A strategy of flexible response sets up an elaborate experiment in conflict resolution, requiring an ability to tailor responses, to test and learn, and to adapt to changing circumstances.

Both the weapons and C³I programs of the Reagan administration can be understood as a continuation of America's effort to align its nuclear posture with the requirements of flexible response. In terms of C³I the stated goal is to create a system that allows for central, flexible direction of strategic forces throughout a protracted nuclear conflict. To this end the administration has said it would increase C³I endurance and provide

212

for its reconstitution to ensure continuing positive control over the forces for six months. The administration has also stressed the need to improve the timeliness, accuracy, and reliability of attack assessment to better inform the decision process and allow for selection of an initial response that corresponds to the scale of provocation. More accurate, timely, and reliable information would improve capabilities for postattack and post-exchange damage assessment, so that redirection or termination of force operations in progress might be more easily accomplished, and would also strengthen overall deterrence by allowing it to fail in stages. Last, the administration has also planned better communications systems for launch on warning to bolster Minuteman missile survivability.

Building a command system that fulfills current policy aspirations, however, is far easier said than done. To begin with, large strategic organizations are not very pliant. They operate according to established procedures that sharply limit opportunities the Pentagon claims would allow execution of ad hoc plans, even after repeated attacks.[1] The philosophy behind Reagan's strategy of flexible response and the operation of the actual organizations are based on fundamentally different principles of control. Improvisation and tailored response are incompatible with the especially rigid mechanisms that organize nuclear operations. Attempts to override programmed behavior and to induce innovative organizational behavior are more likely to disorder than reorder activity. Central decisionmakers would probably be forced to adapt to the organization and its established plans of action rather than be able to bend them to their will. Decisionmakers would, of course, still have some flexibility; they could select from among options of varying size and character. But as earlier chapters explained, rude surprises await those who imagine they could tune the options or impose significant conditions on their implementation, even without damage to the command system, or who imagine that military operations will conform exactly to the plan.

Strategic flexibility also depends on an extensive network of information channels, the protection of which presents a formidable challenge. Developers cannot exclude the possibility that Soviet planners would target whatever C^3I system is built. Designing a system to perform in the face of a carefully planned attack against it is, as previous chapters have shown, a difficult undertaking even when the demands on the system are

---

1. See "Fiscal Year 1984-1988 Defense Guidance" as reported by Richard Halloran, "Pentagon Draws Up First Strategy for Fighting a Long Nuclear War," *New York Times*, May 30, 1982.

modest. The United States has not yet succeeded in designing a system that fully meets the positive control requirements associated with a strategy of assured destruction. And if there is some doubt whether technical and economic considerations will allow meeting even this modest traditional goal, how much more difficult it will be to fulfill the ambitious aspirations now being advanced under the rubric of flexible response.

Most recent Western thinking and analysis related to nuclear war nonetheless slide past these difficulties. Scenarios that credit both sides with an impressive capacity for flexible response have replaced the specter of all-out attack and spasmodic retaliation. The most prominent of the scenarios imagines the Soviet Union manuevering into a position of bargaining dominance by means of a selected attack aimed at U.S. strategic forces. Such a scenario reflects a highly stylized Western view that emphasizes rational political choice and weapons technology and overlooks command-control limitations.

In the Western tradition, much analysis simply appeals to rational logic to justify the thesis that selective Soviet attack is as plausible and feasible as any. According to Benjamin S. Lambeth, who treated implementation of national decisions as a minor administrative detail, Soviet leaders would mount whatever attack "the exigencies of the moment warranted." He maintained that the Soviets, "like all reasonable men, will unhesitatingly cast aside their avowed doctrinal preconceptions in favor of real-time improvisation if a nuclear crisis (and U.S. behavior in it) should suggest that as an appropriate course of action."[2] Former Defense Secretary James R. Schlesinger reasoned similarly in describing the potential course of a limited U.S. strategic attack on the Soviet Union: in a conventional war in which NATO seemed on the verge of defeat, Minuteman missiles might be launched against remote oil refineries, but Soviet leaders would react rationally. Schlesinger foresaw Soviet nuclear retaliation; but while conceding their traditional aversion to limited war, he argued that all-out nuclear retaliation (avowed Soviet doctrine) would not happen because "when the existential circumstances arise, political leaders on both sides will be under powerful pressure to continue to be sensible."[3]

2. *Selective Nuclear Operations and Soviet Strategy*, P-5506 (Santa Monica, Calif.: Rand Corp., 1975), pp. 4, 18.

3. *U.S.-U.S.S.R. Strategic Policies*, Hearing before the Senate Subcommittee on Arms Control, International Law and Organization of the Senate Committee on Foreign Relations, 93 Cong. 1 sess. (GPO, 1974), p. 13.

These arguments state the obvious. Leaders would try to respond in a manner they feel would be most appropriate under the circumstances. The relevant question is whether preferences could be translated into appropriate action; the answer depends on specific details of Soviet command-control arrangements. Preparations for selective attacks on U.S. targets must have been made in advance, available options must have corresponded with preferences, and smooth execution of the plan must be accomplished.

In the same testimony cited above, Schlesinger justified his introduction of limited nuclear options into the U.S. nuclear war plan on the grounds that such options cannot be created on demand. He stressed that selective use of U.S. forces requires "the indoctrination and the planning in anticipation of the difficulties involved. It is ill-advised to attempt to do that under the press of circumstances."[4] In other words, when the existential circumstances arise, the course of action warranted by the exigencies of the moment had better be provided by plans already in existence. With complex organizations responsible for conducting a war, improvisation would be sharply constrained.

The vision of selective Soviet attack that has such a strong hold on most current assessments of nuclear war also reflects the Western tradition of treating flexibility largely as an issue of weapons technology (see chapter 2). Much Western analysis merely cites the sophistication of Soviet weapons as evidence of a capability for selective attack. Benjamin Lambeth, for example, argues that the characteristics of the newest weapons by themselves

portended an unprecedently rich Soviet menu of targeting options short of the all-out attack scenario envisaged by formal Soviet military doctrine. . . . To note only the most obvious of these potential targeting options, the Soviets are progressively moving toward the point where they may be able to implement a high-confidence disarming attack against the U.S. MINUTEMAN force solely with around 300 MIRVed SS-18s, leaving a residual force of 1,000 SS-17s and SS-19s (along with a fully alerted and undepleted SLBM fleet) for carrying out selective strikes against other targets in [the continental United States] and elsewhere or for providing a credible intrawar deterrent against U.S. countervalue retaliation with its surviving elements of the Triad.[5]

Carefully orchestrated, selective Soviet attacks cannot be inferred from weapons characteristics alone, however. Such a supposition must be

4. Ibid., p. 9.
5. *Selective Nuclear Operations and Soviet Strategy,* pp. 1, 18.

based on careful analysis of Soviet targeting doctrine and actual arrangements for command and control as well.

The view promoted by Western analysts would be more credible if Soviet nuclear doctrine appeared to mirror Western theories that nuclear weapons are instruments of nuclear diplomacy and that the potential bargaining advantage conferred by a selective attack is worth more than the additional military advantage conferred by a comprehensive attack. But there is not a shred of evidence that the Soviet Union values nuclear diplomacy over brute force to achieve its objective of limiting damage to the Soviet homeland. By all indications, Soviet planners have long believed that exploiting C³I deficiencies is the only route to significant damage limitation. The high priority assigned to command suppression in Soviet military writings strongly suggests that Soviet strategy has been designed to fracture the command system and disorganize counterattacks rather than to deter U.S. commanders from ordering a counterattack.

The scenario would also be more credible were the alternative strategy not easier to execute. An attack against command and control facilities would require relatively few strategic resources and less stringent timing and coordination than a limited counterforce attack. And the high level of damage that could be expected would not be terribly sensitive to aberrations in missile accuracy and reliability. A strategy that depended on inflicting a high level of damage on U.S. forces, however, would require a massive commitment of resources and surgically precise execution. Even if Soviet planners have devised a well worked out plan to do so, it seems unlikely that they are confident it is workable. According to Lambeth, they appreciate that "highly orchestrated war plans requiring careful coordination for mission effectiveness have had a rich record of becoming snarled beyond repair."[6] Prudent Soviet planners surely realize that compiling a plan requiring simultaneous operation of a large number of fixed procedures, all of which would depend on the cooperation and smooth interaction of all concerned, invites its frustration. Western strategists seem far less sensitive to the risks of attempting to implement a plan so intolerant of deviation.

To the prudent planner, human factors alone—limits on skills and motivation and errors in control systems—raise doubts about the viability of a plan that demands precise execution. Errors observed during

6. "Uncertainties for the Soviet War Planner," *International Security*, vol. 7 (Winter 1982/1983), p. 158.

training exercises in Minuteman control systems suggest the mistakes that forces on either side might make in a first strike. For instance, a single typographical error, the entry of a single wrong digit into a computer at a Minuteman launch center, could hurl missiles at the wrong targets, including cities. Though targeting errors may be discovered before actual launch, correcting them could easily throw off the coordination and timing of an attack.

Consider another example that suggests the way organizational constraints affect performance. In launching an attack, Minuteman crews are expected to complete the firing sequence within a couple of minutes after receipt of their orders. If actions within any given squadron cannot be completed within the time allotted, missiles assigned to that squadron must be withheld while missiles in squadrons that meet the time requirement are launched. The consequence is a loss of maximum coordination during the initial salvo. Although in simulation exercises crews usually meet the time requirements, prudent strategic planners know that such exercises fail to expose all the technical and procedural problems that may be encountered in real situations. They know there will be unforeseen problems in the established launch sequence and that these problems could substantially disrupt force coordination.

In the example of a Minuteman launch, any number of operating rules could have systematic adverse effects on timing. For instance, one rule requires crews to copy and react to the latest valid emergency action message, but while they are responding, the same message may arrive over any or all available means of communications—telephone, HF voice, UHF satellite teletype, ERCS voice, SACCS teleprinter, and SLFCS teletype. Actions undertaken in response to the initial message must be temporarily suspended while they copy and examine successive messages. The messages would probably be repeats, but rules dictate that crews examine them to be sure. This processing might disrupt activities and waste precious time (unless, of course, one of the messages does supersede the one currently being acted upon, the principal advantage of the rule), and crews could be hard pressed to complete the launch sequence in the time allowed. Some launches would probably be postponed. (Crews would resume launch activities at a time specified by a predetermined launch schedule.)

Small and often overlooked details such as the rule applied to message processing can have important ramifications, especially for attack strategies that depend on precise timing. Unanticipated procedural complications would probably result in the imperfect implementation of such strategies, yet Western planners still envisage smooth execution of elaborate Soviet war plans designed to inflict maximum damage on U.S. forces.

Indistinguishable Levels of Conflict

A selective Soviet attack against U.S. forces to deter reprisal and limit damage would also be more credible if levels of conflict were less difficult to distinguish. Soviet military writings on nuclear war barely acknowledge that such levels exist. The central, explicit, and persistent theme of these writings for decades has dismissed the possibility of limited nuclear war and stressed massive comprehensive attack at the outset. Apparent (one is tempted to say imputed) Soviet interest in conflict gradients leaves open the possibility, however, that Soviet war plans contain options for graduated response. Benjamin Lambeth noted that

Soviet writings now seem more disposed than before to admit threshold distinctions between theater and intercontinental nuclear war and between conventional and nuclear operations within the theater-war context. They also seem prepared to accept the possibility of threshold restraints within each of these categories as long as the Soviet side remains ahead and the U.S. has the good sense not to escalate.[7]

Threshold distinctions nonetheless remain highly abstract even in Western writings on nuclear strategy. Planners distinguish between theater and strategic nuclear war, limited and massive attack, and so forth, but their distinctions lack specificity. The categories form a typology in need of refinement along explicit dimensions such as the types of targets attacked, the types of weapons used, the scale of the attack, the identity of the nations and leaders undertaking hostile action, the location of combat or weapons detonation, and the damage and casualties suffered.

Much Western analysis of levels of conflict merely pretends that distinct thresholds exist and proceeds to treat escalation and deescalation as bargaining tactics. Upon the outbreak of war, such analysis envisions an endurance contest. Violence mounts and thresholds are crossed as part of a campaign of terror in which each side inflicts pain to show that more pain can come. Conflict intensifies until the side with the lowest threshold

---

7. *Selective Nuclear Operations and Soviet Strategy*, pp. 10–11.

of pain or the side unwilling to move a notch higher on the scale of conflict finally accedes to the opponent's demands.

Such imaginative formulations may be useful metaphors for speculations about the unthinkable, but for purposes of threat assessment and planning they offer no satisfactory working definitions of thresholds, they fail to address the question of whether force operations would actually embody rules of engagement implied by such definitions, and they beg the question of whether the opposing leaderships could accurately assess the situation.

To illustrate the conceptual and practical problems of distinguishing thresholds, consider the level of conflict commonly labeled "strategic." In what sense is this level distinct from "theater" nuclear warfare? A prevalent view is that the threshold between the two is crossed when either side or both employ strategic nuclear weapons. But both the United States and the Soviet Union deploy nuclear weapons that, although classified as strategic under the terms of SALT, have strong associations with theater nuclear war and regional defense. The Soviet Union probably has thousands of strategic weapons—ICBM and SLBM warheads as well as bomber forces—aimed at Western Europe and China. Similarly, the United States stands ready to launch, as part of a theater nuclear campaign, hundreds of warheads from strategic missile submarines, and some targets are probably inside Soviet borders. The American nuclear umbrella over Western Europe also provides for Minuteman strikes against targets in the Soviet Union. Do missile submarine launches or limited Minuteman strikes meant to prevent the collapse of NATO cross what Lambeth calls the threshold distinction between theater and intercontinental war, or do they relate to what he calls threshold restraints within a particular category? Answers to such questions are not obvious. Although most Western observers do not see implementing such options as tantamount to entry into the realm of strategic warfare, the Soviet Union may or may not share that vision. In any case, strategic warfare is indistinguishable from theater warfare in at least two key respects: the type of weapons employed and their use against targets in Soviet territory.

Other potentially important distinctions may disappear in the initial phases of conflict. For instance, it might seem desirable to refrain from attacking the opponent's strategic forces, especially if nuclear weapons remain leashed, in order to preserve this distinction as long as possible, but the ability to restrict activity that blurs this distinction seems questionable. U.S. Navy officials suggest that Soviet missile submarines would immediately become subject to attack in wartime[8] and that U.S. antisubmarine forces "would not be in a position of differentiating [Soviet] attack submarines from their SSBNs."[9] Moreover, U.S. military leaders apparently accept that "in a conventional war all submarines are submarines. They are all fair game."[10] At the outset of a major conflict, therefore, Soviet missile submarines in the open oceans, at launch stations near U.S. coasts, in transit, and in home waters would become targets, and there would be little likelihood of preserving the distinction between attacks on strategic and nonstrategic forces.

In conjunction with prosecuting an antisubmarine warfare campaign, there could also be an attempt to destroy targets inside Soviet borders. The chief of naval operations has testified that "our plan would be as the first line of defense to strike the airbases from which the Backfire bombers fly and the submarine bases from which the nuclear-powered submarines operate."[11] He gives no more particulars in this regard, but it is easy to infer that, as an early or opening move in a war, navy strategists contemplate an assault on missile submarines in Soviet home ports and on Backfire aircraft that some Western analysts insist are strategic bombers. Regardless of the type of munitions employed, a key distinction is blurred: the lower levels of conflict seem to be indistinguishable from the highest level—"strategic nuclear"—in a dimension that could be labeled "type of weapon system attacked." Attacks on strategic forces possibly would be mounted at an early stage, well before the employment of nuclear weapons.

In this same vein, one is led to ask whether Soviet military operations that reduce U.S. strategic capabilities necessarily take us across the stra-

8. See Bruce G. Blair, "Arms Control Implications of Anti-Submarine Warfare (ASW) Programs," in *Evaluation of Fiscal Year 1979 Arms Control Impact Statements: Toward More Informed Congressional Participation in National Security Policymaking*, prepared for the Subcommittee on International Security and Scientific Affairs of the House Committee on International Relations, 95 Cong. 2 sess. (GPO, 1978), pp. 103–19.

9. *Fiscal Year 1977 Authorization for Military Procurement, Research and Development, and Active Duty, Selected Reserve and Civilian Personnel Strengths*, Hearings before the Senate Committee on Armed Services, 94 Cong. 2 sess. (GPO, 1976), pt. 4, p. 1972.

10. *Fiscal Year 1978 Authorization for Military Procurement, Research and Development, and Active Duty, Selected Reserve and Civilian Personnel Strengths*, Hearings before the Senate Committee on Armed Services, 95 Cong. 1 sess. (GPO, 1977), pt. 10, p. 6699.

11. *Department of Defense Authorization for Appropriations for Fiscal Year 1979*, Hearings before the Senate Committee on Armed Services, 95 Cong. 2 sess. (GPO, 1978), pt. 5, p. 4321.

tegic threshold. Does Soviet antisubmarine warfare conducted during a conventional war constitute an act of strategic warfare if the result is some attrition among U.S. ballistic missile submarines or attack submarines whose nuclear cruise missiles constitute part of the strategic reserve force? Does Soviet electronic or physical attack on strategic command and warning elements constitute strategic attack? What about attacks on U.S. satellites, almost all of which serve both strategic and nonstrategic forces, including conventional forces? Some observers regard attacks on any of these elements as tantamount to strategic warfare, even though individual strategic weapons may not be targets. Testifying in 1963, Admiral Galantin concluded that Soviet attack on any one of the shore-based VLF stations used to broadcast messages to missile submarines "would probably mean an all-out war."[12]

Galantin's remark also reflects a subjective assessment of Soviet intentions and motives. There is a widespread belief that attack, however small, on U.S. C^3I elements would presage a large-scale missile barrage against U.S. targets. But while intentions are potentially a key distinguishing feature of levels of conflict, actual motives are often ambiguous. A range of different but equally plausible motives could be inferred from a limited attack against the command structure. For instance, an attack on U.S. reconnaissance satellites might be designed to impair the ability of the United States to assign targets to its strategic forces. But such an attack might instead be designed to send a political signal or demonstrate resolve while minimizing the scale of provocation. Antisatellite attack may be like some limited U.S. nuclear options in that demonstrating resolve is the primary objective.

In discussions of limited U.S. nuclear options, individuals have stressed the importance of conveying intentions through direct communications with the enemy to prevent misinterpretation. Former Defense Secretary Schlesinger, for example, considered escalation control and execution of limited nuclear options to be compatible provided the United States would "maintain continued communications with the Soviet leaders during the war, and [would] describe precisely and meticulously the limited nature of our actions, including the desire to avoid attacking their urban industrial base."[13] The importance of uninterrupted dialogue is quickly grasped. The proverbial fog of war would be closing in; along

12. *Department of Defense Appropriations For 1964,* Hearings before a Subcommittee of the House Committee on Appropriations, 88 Cong. 1 sess. (GPO, 1963), pt. 5, p. 819.
13. *U.S.-U.S.S.R. Strategic Policies,* Senate hearing, p. 13.

Figure 7-1. *Land-Based Ballistic Missile Warning Sites and Detection Sweeps*

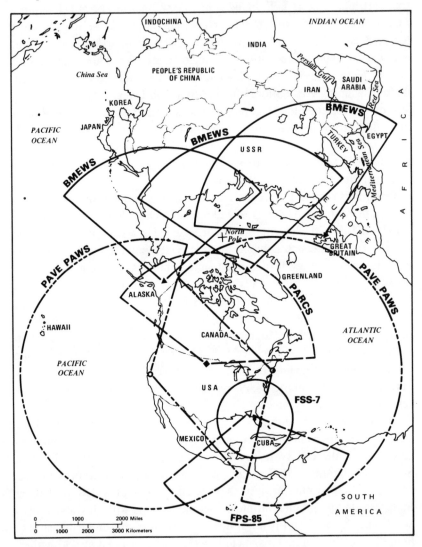

Source: Congressional Budget Office, *Strategic Command, Control, and Communications: Alternative Approaches for Modernization* (GPO, 1981), p. 35.

most perceptible dimensions, strategic warfare and lesser levels of conflict would fast become indistinguishable. Events leading up to and including execution of a limited nuclear option would blur most major distinctions. Strategic nuclear weapons have been employed, strategic nuclear weapons have come under attack, and strategic nuclear weapons have landed on the sovereign soil of the enemy. Except for the comprehensiveness and exact targets of the attack, few distinctions would remain to be drawn. And if it is thought that U.S. leaders must carry on a dialogue with Soviet leaders to prevent misperception of U.S. actions and objectives, there has to be some doubt about the opponent's ability to understand them by independent means.

The United States also lacks the capability to perform an independent accurate assessment of the scale and character of a Soviet attack. A selective counterforce attack could not be reliably distinguished from a comprehensive attack because of deficiencies in the U.S. tactical warning and attack assessment system. Figure 7-1 shows the tactical warning network, excluding early warning satellites and the Cobra Dane ground radar in the Aleutian Islands.[14] Of the ground radar sensors shown, only PARCS (the sole portion of the Safeguard ABM site in North Dakota still in service) gives accurate predictions of impact points for large numbers of reentry vehicles. But before describing its attack assessment capabilities and limitations, let me briefly discuss the capabilities of other early warning sensors.

Initial detection of Soviet ICBM and SLBM missile launches would occur within approximately one minute after booster ignition.[15] Three to four minutes later, the boosters would stop burning and the satellites would lose track of the missiles. During this brief period of powered missile flight, early warning satellites would estimate the approximate number of attacking missiles, their launch points, and their flight corridors, but they could not determine the missiles' destinations.[16]

The Ballistic Missile Early Warning System radars would confirm ICBM attack ten minutes later and begin transmitting predicted impact

14. Cobra Dane would be activated for attack early warning purposes at defense condition 3 or higher; see *Department of Defense Appropriations, Fiscal Year 1974,* Hearings before a Subcommittee of the Senate Committee on Appropriations, 93 Cong. 1 sess. (GPO, 1973), pt. 4, p. 483.

15. "Improved U.S. Warning Net Spurred," *Aviation Week and Space Technology* (June 23, 1980), p. 41.

16. *Department of Defense Appropriations for 1978,* Hearings before a Subcommittee of the House Committee on Appropriations, 95 Cong. 1 sess. (GPO, 1977), pt. 2, pp. 392, 418.

locations and the general class of targets under attack—nuclear retaliatory forces, command-control nodes, cities, and so forth—to NORAD. BMEWS predictions, however, would be suspect. This twenty-year-old system was originally designed to "detect a raid and say the 'missiles are coming' to support the national policy of massive retaliation in the 1960s."[17] In order to count thousands of modern reentry vehicles and predict their destinations, its vintage computers and tracking radars would have to be extensively upgraded.

PAVE PAWS, FPS-85, and FSS-7 radars would confirm SLBM attacks but would provide only marginal assessments of the character of the attack. Compared to the FSS-7 radars they replaced, the long-range, phased-array PAVE PAWS radars deployed in 1980–81 are better able to characterize SLBM attacks. The older FSS-7 radars, including the site currently operational, lack the accuracy needed to provide credible impact predictions.[18] But although PAVE PAWS radars represent an improvement, power upgrades would be required to achieve the tracking capacity and discrimination necessary for accurately counting MIRVs and predicting their impact. Two additional PAVE PAWS radars, furthermore, would be required to close gaps in the coverage of potential Soviet submarine launch stations. Without these additional radars, together with power upgrade, PAVE PAWS cannot provide the attack assessment capabilities required by the national command authority to select retaliatory options.[19] This expanded network would also eliminate reliance on the FSS-7 and FPS-85 radars still in use. The FPS-85 radar, which became operational in 1968, was originally designed to track satellites; it was modified to perform an SLBM warning function in 1975. Although it doubtless outperforms FSS-7 radar, FPS-85 probably cannot provide accurate attack assessment.

The PARCS radar is the most accurate attack-characterization sensor in operation. It can track hundreds of reentry vehicles and predict impact points within several thousand feet. Among other reports, PARCS can provide a raid count, an impact profile, and a target class summary (num-

17. *Department of Defense Authorization for Appropriations for Fiscal Year 1983,* Hearings before the Senate Committee on Armed Services, 97 Cong. 2 sess. (GPO, 1982), pt. 7, p. 4699.

18. *Department of Defense Appropriations for 1978,* House hearings, pt. 2, p. 390.

19. *Department of Defense Authorization for Appropriations for Fiscal Year 1983,* Senate hearings, pt. 7, pp. 4700, 4705; and *Department of Defense Authorization for Appropriations for Fiscal Year 1981,* Hearings before the Senate Committee on Armed Services, 96 Cong. 2 sess. (GPO, 1980), pt. 6, p. 3456.

ber of weapons expected to land on cities, missile fields, bomber or tanker airfields, command-control centers, and Washington, D.C.).[20] Located seventy-five miles northwest of Grand Forks AFB, North Dakota, PARCS provides radar coverage of SLBM attacks from near-arctic areas behind BMEWS as well as radar coverage of ICBM attacks.[21]

Its limitations, however, are considerable. Official statements indicate that accurate assessment is restricted to ICBMs aimed at the central United States.[22] The radar reportedly views most but not all trajectory "windows" that Soviet ICBMs would pass through in an attack against the United States. PARCS would be able to detect and track few SLBMs. The radar would also not lock on incoming weapons until late in their flight. Initial detection and assessment would occur only six to twelve minutes before impact, depending on the targets.[23] In fact, the U.S. command system, including PARCS, could be attacked and effectively destroyed by SLBMs before PARCS detected a single incoming missile. If the attack were comprehensive rather than limited, PARCS assessment would not be sufficiently timely.

Attack assessment capabilities are thus marginal at best because present sensors "track boosters or post boost vehicles, not reentry vehicles."[24] The MIRVed payloads of modern Soviet forces are practically invisible to all present U.S. sensors except for PARCS, which by itself cannot provide any assurance that Soviet weapons are aimed exclusively at strategic forces.

Additional information might be available after impact. Sensors designed for damage assessment have been deployed since the mid-1960s. A bomb-alarm system, deployed in 1966 and phased out in 1970, used visible light detectors to observe nuclear detonations at ninety-nine target areas (ninety-seven in the United States, including cities, Minuteman sites, and SAC bases).[25] Nuclear detonation sensors on board early warn-

20. "Improved U.S. Warning Net Spurred," pp. 38, 44.

21. *Department of Defense Authorization for Appropriations for Fiscal Year 1982,* Hearings before the Senate Committee on Armed Services, 97 Cong. 1 sess. (GPO, 1981), pt. 7, p. 4222.

22. *Department of Defense Appropriations for 1978,* House hearings, pt. 2, p. 389; and "Improved U.S. Warning Net Spurred," p. 44.

23. "Improved U.S. Warning Net Spurred," pp. 38, 44–45.

24. *Department of Defense Appropriations for 1978,* House hearings, pt. 2, p. 458.

25. *Department of Defense Appropriations for 1974,* Hearings before a Subcommittee of the House Committee on Appropriations, 93 Cong. 1 sess. (GPO, 1973), pt. 7, p. 1057. This testimony states, "Each detector was connected to a separate signal generating station which was installed in a smalltown Western Union telegraph office located 30 to 40 miles from the

ing satellites launched since the early 1970s have evidently replaced the bomb-alarm system. The public record contains scant information on the utility of these sensors, but comments on the improvements expected with the deployment of the next generation's system (IONDS) suggest that current sensors lack the coverage and accuracy needed to characterize enemy attack patterns.[26]

U.S. warning systems, then, are simply not adequate for assessing the scale and character of a Soviet attack. They would not be very helpful in guiding the choice of a flexible response option.

Insufficient Command-Control Endurance

Popular scenarios of selective Soviet attack, flexible U.S. response, and negotiated termination after protracted conflict also rest on the dubious assumption that U.S. and Soviet C³I systems remain viable for an indefinite period of time. This assumption may be partially justified on the grounds that the hypothetical attacks are concentrated, at least initially, on the respective force structures. But even in the event of attacks designed solely to inflict a high level of damage on opposing forces, each side's command system would be put under stress. At a minimum, these systems would be subject to collateral damage.

A Soviet attack designed to inflict maximum damage on U.S. forces— the possibility that underlies the principal perceived weakness of U.S. deterrence—would coincidentally produce extensive damage to the U.S. command structure. Many C³I elements would come under direct attack because of physical proximity to SAC bomber, tanker, and Minuteman bases (table 7-1). Among the command centers collocated with bomber and tanker bases are the air force headquarters located at Barksdale AFB and March AFB that double as alternate SAC headquarters. Other fixed command centers subject to direct attack include the underground launch

---

target area. The communication links that interconnect the detectors, the stations, the control centers, and the users were circuits routed over Western Union, Bell System, and railroad facilities."

26. See chapter 8. See also "Early Warning Satellite Picked Up Flash Over South Atlantic," *Defense Daily,* vol. 114 (February 23, 1981), p. 271; *Department of Defense Appropriations for 1974,* House hearings, pp. 1057–58; *Department of Defense Appropriations for 1978,* House hearings, pt. 2, pp. 386, 392; and *Department of Defense Authorization for Appropriations for Fiscal Year 1982,* Senate hearings, pt. 7, pp. 4205–06.

Table 7-1. *Collocated Strategic Command and Force Elements* [a]

Strategic command elements	Collocated SAC bases		
	Bomber bases	Minuteman bases	Tanker bases
Warning			
PARCS radar		Grand Forks AFB	
PAVE PAWS radars (2)	Westover AFB [b]		Beale AFB
FPS-85 radar	Eglin AFB [b]		
FSS-7 radar	MacDill AFB [b]		
Command-control			
2nd air force headquarters	Barksdale AFB		
15th air force headquarters	March AFB		
NEACP home bases	Blytheville AFB		Blytheville AFB Grissom AFB
West auxiliary ABNCP	Ellsworth AFB	Ellsworth AFB	Ellsworth AFB
Airborne LCC-1	Ellsworth AFB	Ellsworth AFB	Ellsworth AFB
Airborne LCC-2	Minot AFB	Minot AFB	Minot AFB
Airborne LCC-3	Minot AFB	Minot AFB	Minot AFB
All ground Minuteman LCCs		All six Minuteman bases	
Communications			
ERCS	Whiteman AFB	Whiteman AFB	
PACCS relay 1			Grissom AFB
PACCS relay 2			Rickenbacker AFB [b]
Short Order HF radio	Barksdale AFB March AFB Westover AFB [b]		

a. Partial listing.
b. Bomber/tanker dispersal bases.

centers in the Minuteman fields.[27] NEACP, stationed at Grissom AFB, EC-135 aircraft at Ellsworth AFB, Minot AFB, Grissom AFB, and Rickenbacker AFB, and emergency communications rockets at Whiteman AFB would also be struck—the ERCS system of last resort is interspersed

27. The missile silos nearest the launch centers are about three miles away. Attacks on silos would generate blast overpressures of sufficient magnitude (5 to 10 psi) to destroy land lines and exposed antennas around launch center complexes. Ground bursts would also generate EMP, which might severely damage VLF communications and the unhardened computers and electrical systems used by launch centers.

among Minuteman silos that in typical counterforce scenarios absorb the brunt of Soviet attacks. Because silos housing these rockets are supposed to be indistinguishable from other Minuteman silos in order to avoid preferential targeting, they are certainly subject to collateral damage; indeed, they would be attacked directly and massively. Among the tactical warning facilities that would be struck are the two phased-array PAVE PAWS radars located at Beale AFB and Otis AFB, the FPS-85 radar at Eglin AFB, and the FSS-7 radar in Florida. These sites constitute the entire radar network devoted to detecting a submarine missile attack. PARCS, situated near the Minuteman complex at Grand Forks AFB, which provides the most accurate attack assessment of SLBMs and ICBMs aimed at the central United States, probably would escape collateral damage, but its communications with external users would probably be destroyed.

If Soviet counterforce strategy employed high-altitude explosions to expose unhardened bombers and tankers to EMP, then virtually all C³I elements based in the United States would be incidentally exposed to the same pulses and most would suffer damage. In addition, networks such as land lines interconnecting sensors, NORAD headquarters, and national and major military command headquarters would be prone to collateral damage produced by blast effects from multiple and widely distributed ground explosions at the SAC bases.

Many C³I elements would also come under indirect attack because of various nonlocalized nuclear effects. Fallout, for example, would drift over C³I elements located hundreds or thousands of miles from targeted areas. Depending on prevailing weather conditions, fallout from a large-scale Soviet attack on the six Minuteman complexes and bomber and tanker bases could endanger virtually the entire PACCS airborne network as well as contaminate the airfields at which these aircraft must eventually land. At the same time, such major command facilities as SAC headquarters, NORAD headquarters, and the Eighth Air Force headquarters would be exposed. Major communications nodes—for instance, the Elkhorn control station near Omaha, which connects the SAC command center with Green Pine sites, and the SLFCS ground station at Silver Creek, Nebraska—would also be at risk. Early warning radar sites at all locations in the continental United States are situated close enough to targets to be exposed. The satellite control station at Sunnyvale, California, also falls into this category.

Attacks aimed at U.S. forces would also disrupt the transmission media used for strategic communications. Most long-distance strategic radio communications—especially HF and UHF (satellite and ERCS only)—would be considerably impaired even if the attack involved mostly surface and near-surface explosions.

Apart from the collateral damage sustained, surviving ground-based installations would remain under continuing threat of direct, deliberate assault by Soviet forces held in reserve. National officials, therefore, would have compelling reasons to adapt their decisionmaking to the exigencies of airborne command-control-communications. But although damage to the airborne network would be less severe than it would if the Soviets mounted an attack designed to neutralize it, collateral damage would also impair its performance.

Theoretically the airborne network could sustain considerable collateral damage and still function well enough to establish a line of communications to the strategic forces. The technical possibilities are such that despite damage to some circuits, a viable channel might be established and kept open; the network might even be able to absorb the complete loss of some aircraft. If an observer possessed a diagram of the interconnection possibilities within the network and knew which circuits had been damaged or destroyed, he could probably trace one or more complete paths over which information might flow.

In practical terms, however, communications channels would not be reestablished so easily. Airborne units obviously do not have the observer's omniscience. No up-to-date diagram exists for deciding which specific media, frequencies, and circuits need to be employed in order to establish a path through a damaged network. These things are discovered through trial and error. Establishing a path would be an epiphenomenal outcome produced when subunits could enact appropriate routines in concert. Technical redundancy in communications might be adequate, but operating procedures determine whether this potential can be realized. Organizational routines must be appropriate and consistent across the C³ and force units involved, and units must be geared to enact routines with speed and efficiency.

Organizational routines executed to establish communications consume a considerable amount of time, no matter how benign the environment. C³ aircraft must, in the first place, move into position; it takes at least thirty minutes just to set up the PACCS network.[28] Additional time is lost when units activate and adjust communications equipment once aircraft reach their preassigned orbits. In all, an hour or more may elapse before the network is prepared to receive, process, and transmit emergency war orders in any coherent way.

A damaged network would be even slower to establish communications, and programmed tasks would have to be frequently reaccomplished in order to keep a channel open in a fast-changing, unstable environment. Furthermore, reliance on backup channels of questionable effectiveness and reliability—for instance, HF radio and air force satellite communications UHF radio—would be substantially greater. There would be increased dependence on such relatively sluggish one-way channels as LF radio, and attempts at communications over certain channels, especially communications rockets (if available), would entail some elaborate and time-consuming procedures.

Other factors that might limit airborne communications capabilities during an attack against forces include EMP and partial destruction of SAC's tanker force. Exposure to EMP could substantially damage even UHF line-of-sight communications and might impair the critical avionics necessary to maintain flight. The status of the SAC tanker force is pertinent because EC-135 aircraft depend on in-flight refueling for endurance, and tanker support would probably be marginal. TACAMO aircraft are not configured for in-flight refueling, of course, which imposes a definite constraint on the endurance of the airborne network as a whole. That endurance would not exceed several hours, depending on the fuel load aboard TACAMO, Looking Glass, and other aircraft that happen to be airborne at the time of attack.

Furthermore, successful reconstitution of the airborne command network is unlikely. An attack aimed at SAC bomber or tanker bases would coincidentally destroy many runways, facilities, and logistics used by C³ aircraft. Off-alert C³ aircraft would be destroyed, and alert aircraft that survived could be denied the ground support needed for servicing and replenishment. Furthermore, aircraft landing at any undamaged home base or secondary base would put themselves in jeopardy. In all likelihood the early warning system on which ground-based aircraft depend

28. This estimate applies to day-to-day conditions with most PACCS aircraft on ground alert. With the transfer of EC-135 aircraft from Grissom AFB to Rickenbacker AFB in the late 1970s, the setup time for the network as a whole was reduced from one hour to thirty minutes.

for their survival would have suffered extensive collateral damage during the initial attack. It is also apparent that, regardless of the performance of early warning systems, aircraft undergoing maintenance could not react rapidly enough to escape destruction by incoming weapons. Finally, aircraft crews could receive lethal doses of radiation from fallout.

Other Constraints on Flexibility

Other technical and procedural limitations further undermine a policy based on graduated response and intrawar bargaining, among them a finite set of options for planned response. Available options for retaliation concentrate on a limited number of preconceived situations. The actual situation may recommend a tailored, unprogrammed response, but the ability to reprogram would be extremely difficult under current conditions.

Reprogramming bomber and submarine targets would not be practicable even without damage to the command system. Channels likely to be available for communicating with submarines could not handle detailed instructions because of their low data rate. Submarine location and disposition, which higher authorities may or may not know, might also impose missile-range and other constraints that sharply limit the choice of possible targets. And selective use of submarine missiles could compromise a boat's security. As Secretary Schlesinger said with respect to the submarine force's role in limited retaliation, "a submarine like the Poseidon is hard to adapt to . . . because you have so many MIRVs permissible and so many missiles per boat. As soon as you fire you expose the boat."[29]

Constraints on bomber flexibility are equally sharp. Replanning bomber attacks must take into account such considerations as home base, tanker rendezvous, flight path, navigation, Soviet defenses, penetration and defense suppression, aircraft recovery, and so forth. Detailed replanning of this sort could not be accomplished well, if at all, in wartime, and communications channels could not handle the information load necessary. Finally, radio emission control practices preclude bombers (and submarines) from acknowledging receipt of reprogramming instructions.

Minuteman forces are easier to retarget against unprogrammed targets, but the means by which this is accomplished—called command data buf-

29. *U.S.-U.S.S.R. Strategic Policies*, Senate hearing, p. 37.

fers—would not survive the collateral damage received during a limited attack aimed at nearby Minuteman silos. SAC relies on terrestrial communications to deliver detailed retargeting instructions to Minuteman launch control centers equipped with command data buffers. The link to these select centers would probably be severed at the receiving end.

Another deficiency that discredits the prevailing scenario is the lack of precise control over executing a plan. As discussed in earlier chapters, a partially damaged command system could produce all kinds of unexpected outcomes. Interactions among technical systems, standard operating procedures, and people can easily result in dramatic deviations from the intended plan. And central decisionmakers would not be quickly informed of such deviations and their consequences.

The lack of a reliable, timely method of terminating attacks in progress proves to be another limitation on strategic flexibility. By the time operations reached an advanced stage of execution, the airborne command network would not be coherent, and the forces themselves, particularly bombers, would be harder to reach. Under the best of postattack circumstances, termination instructions could not be reliably issued or received. And virtually none of the units that received the message could report that fact to higher authorities.

As a rule, technical systems and operating procedures are not geared for expeditious termination of offensive operations. ICBMs in terminal countdown to launch, for instance, are irrevocably committed; they cannot be stopped even though some of the missiles may be timed to lift off well after crews complete launch procedures. (Terminal countdown begins after two or more LCCs send the launch command to the missiles and may last from a second to more than an hour.) The launch of ICBMs in a preterminal, as opposed to a terminal, countdown technically could be stopped, but crews would not attempt to do so even upon receipt of war termination orders. (A preterminal countdown means that only a single LCC issued the launch command; this activates a long-term launch timer.) Canceling an authorized launch of a missile in preterminal or terminal countdown is prohibited, even though orders directing immediate termination might have been received. Similarly, missile-launching aircraft would not attempt to stop the launch of ICBMs after receipt of termination orders from higher authorities.

The questionable feasibility of directed termination of attacks in progress thus further reduces the scope for meaningful, productive bargaining and negotiations. Negotiated termination, moreover, critically depends on tenuous communication links between Washington and Moscow.[30]

All these factors interact to impose severe limitations on U.S. nuclear flexibility. In formulating a strategic response to a focused attack on U.S. forces, decisionmakers could not determine that the attack is indeed of this character. They would confront a situation in which there would be considerable damage to the ground portion of the command system, which would remain under threat of sudden and total destruction. Other relevant considerations are that the attack would trigger the launch of command aircraft and initiate an operation of relatively short endurance, that a coherent airborne network would be difficult to establish and maintain, that communications would be very difficult to establish, that reconstitution of the network would be highly improbable, that the capacity of communications channels would preclude delivery of detailed instructions, and that the communications subsystems that could be patched together would allow only one-way communication.

Under these conditions, a radical departure from any plausibly rational course of action seems a foregone conclusion. U.S. reaction could hardly be rational in either the subjective or objective sense. Subjective rationality, in its simplest version, is an attempt to specify objectives, calculate expected payoffs for alternative choices, and select the alternative with the highest payoff. Under conditions of nuclear attack, there would not be enough time and information for a subjectively rational decision process to run its course. The decision process is also unlikely to produce an objectively rational choice. Regardless of what calculations political leaders might make at the time, they would come under intense pressure to choose without delay an option that would provide for all that they would ever expect to accomplish in retaliation to an attack of uncertain dimensions. There would be strong incentives to order early and comprehensive retaliation, a response contrary to one that would correspond to the scale of provocation and extend deterrence into war itself.

Even if the response did correspond, there would be little if any scope for meaningful negotiation with the adversary. By the time the counterattack ended and negotiations ensued, U.S. strategic forces withheld

---

30. See Desmond Ball, *Can Nuclear War Be Controlled?* Adelphi Papers, 169 (London: International Institute for Strategic Studies, 1981), pp. 21–23.

would no longer be exploitable instruments of diplomacy. The airborne command network would have lost coherence, and the crippled ground network would remain vulnerable to sudden destruction. Inasmuch as the responsiveness of withheld U.S. forces would decline or hinge on Soviet restraint, U.S. bargaining leverage would be weak, and threats would not be very credible.

Thus, protracted war scenarios that project an attacker gaining a bargaining advantage by means of a selective counterforce attack are simply irrelevant to current realities.

Constraints on Launch on Warning

Instead of absorbing the full weight of a Soviet first strike, the United States might attempt to launch the Minuteman force before incoming warheads arrive. In the past this tactic—called launch on warning or launch under attack—was generally eschewed because it heightens the risk of accidental nuclear war. Now, because of diminishing confidence in the ability of land missiles to ride out enemy ICBM attack, the merits of launch on warning are being reconsidered. A higher risk of accidental war might be tolerated in order to reduce the risk that large numbers of Minuteman missiles would be destroyed in their silos.

The trade-off between force survivability and the risk of accidental war is much starker in the case of Minuteman missiles than it is in the case of bombers. Bombers and command aircraft on ground alert can be sent aloft upon receipt of even equivocal information from early warning sensors and recalled if the alarm proves false. There is substantial tolerance for human and technical error, and for this reason the authority to launch aircraft for survival has been delegated to military commanders. But ICBMs cannot be recalled or disarmed after they have received launch messages from the command centers. Missile launch on warning thus demands a quick decision and a practically foolproof filter against false or misleading indications of attack. The tactic is more difficult in part because the authority to fire cannot be responsibly predelegated to military commanders and in part because the exercise of this authority by national policy officials would be slower and more susceptible to enemy disruption.

Regarding the official position on launch on warning, Richard N. Perle, assistant secretary of defense, said that it

is not and never has been U.S. policy to rely on such a policy as a means of ensuring ICBM survivability. . . . As a practical and realistic matter, when one considers the amount of time available to a President to make a decision in such a situation as to whether or not to launch strategic nuclear weapons at the Soviet Union, it would put any President to a severe test to expect that a decision to launch nuclear weapons could be made.

I would hope that we could bear the burdens and pay the price to free our President, whoever he may be, from having to make a decision of that consequence in the small number of minutes available to him.[31]

How short is the time available to make the decision? Lieutenant General Kelly H. Burke reckons that in the very best of circumstances involving Soviet ICBM attack, the president has only a few minutes to decide not only to launch U.S. missiles but at what targets to launch them.[32] In the event of submarine missile attack, flight times could be as short as eight minutes.

Although a launch-on-warning attack option was programmed into the SIOP and Minuteman launch control centers in the late 1970s, most observers harbor doubts about its feasibility. Zbigniew Brzezinski commented that a "bolt out of the blue could create such initial disbelief among the U.S. decisionmakers that they would be unable to make a prompt response. Even without a special Soviet effort to disrupt or destroy U.S. decision makers, a sudden massive attack would put the American leaders under extraordinary psychological pressure, capable of inducing erratic behavior and hesitation."[33] General Burke stated flatly that with Soviet missile flight times as short as eight minutes, there "is just not enough time to do anything."[34] Richard K. Betts is equally skeptical:

Too many things have to happen within twenty-five minutes or less: tactical warning would have to be processed through the chain of command; the president would have to hear it, believe it, and authorize firing; the authorization would have to be transmitted back and confirmed to missile crews, who would have to believe it and then turn their keys. On paper, this can all be accomplished within

---

31. *Hearings on Military Posture and H.R. 5968* before the House Committee on Armed Services, 97 Cong. 2 sess. (GPO, 1982), pt. 2, p. 65.

32. *Department of Defense Appropriations for 1981,* Hearings before a Subcommittee of the House Committee on Appropriations, 96 Cong. 2 sess. (GPO, 1980), pt. 3, p. 1045.

33. "From Arms Control to Controlled Security," *Wall Street Journal,* July 10, 1984.

34. *Department of Defense Appropriations for 1981,* House hearings, pt. 3, p. 1045.

the time available; in the heat of crisis, with terrified people facing apocalypse, such a smooth-flowing rapid sequence is scarcely conceivable. . . . In one or more links of the chain of command, people are likely to disbelieve, panic, or wait and demand reconfirmation.[35]

More feasible, says Betts, is a modification: launch under attack. That is, authorize release of ICBMs immediately after Soviet warheads begin detonating. This plan is deemed feasible by the President's Commission on Strategic Forces, which in its report emphasized that Minuteman forces might be launched before they were struck but after other targets on U.S. soil had been hit. With respect to a simultaneous Soviet launch of ICBMs and SLBMs—a standard attack assumption—the commission noted that Soviet SLBMs would arrive more than fifteen minutes before Soviet ICBMs and that

in such a case the Soviets should have no confidence that we would refrain from launching our ICBMs during that interval after we had been hit. It is important to appreciate that this would not be a "launch on warning," or even a "launch under attack," but rather a launch *after* attack—after massive nuclear detonations had already occurred on U.S. soil.[36]

This common assessment is seriously flawed because it ignores the effects of massive nuclear detonations on the command and communications network. Psychological factors aside, the feasibility of any tactic that envisions the launch of Minuteman forces before their silos are hit by Soviet ICBMs is extremely doubtful if the U.S. command system is deliberately attacked by SLBMs arriving earlier, and it is very doubtful if the command system is subjected to only collateral damage.

In the case of deliberate attack, Richard Perle cites the vulnerability of U.S. warning sensors as one technical reason why launch under attack might be prevented:

As a practical matter, the ability to launch under attack depends on the security of one's warning systems. While we have succeeded to some degree in proliferating the number of weapons in order to make them more survivable, the vulnerability of warning systems would continue to be a problem. A well-designed Soviet attack might well deprive us of the realistic option of launching under attack in any case.[37]

What would a well-designed Soviet attack on the warning system look like? It would probably involve submarine missile attacks on the BMEWS

---

35. *Surprise Attack: Lessons for Defense Planning* (Brookings, 1982), p. 248.

36. *Report of the President's Commission on Strategic Forces* (Washington, D.C.: April 1983), p. 8.

37. *Hearings on Military Posture and H.R. 5968,* House, p. 65.

and PARCS radar sites that the United States relies on to distinguish Soviet ICBM attacks on Minuteman complexes. The radar systems could be destroyed by Soviet SLBMs before ICBMs penetrated their detection fans. Even if these radars were not attacked, their assessment reports would be submitted too late for launch on warning to be implemented. In the case of PARCS, initial ICBM detections would occur only six to twelve minutes before impact, which does not permit sufficient time to digest the information, render a decision, encode and transmit launch orders, and perform the launch sequence at the Minuteman control centers.

The president would therefore have to make a launch-under-attack decision on inconclusive, indeed ambiguous, data. The decision would have to be made long before a clear impression of the attack could possibly form. In effect, Minuteman launch under attack would be triggered by detection of an enemy missile salvo that *might* be directed at U.S. Minuteman complexes.

But even this hasty, untailored reaction could not be carried to fruition with high confidence under a wide range of circumstances. A well-designed Soviet attack probably could preclude Minuteman launch under attack altogether. It might even prevent SAC from flushing the bomber and tanker force and the PACCS fleet for survival. Using submarine missiles launched at close range, the Soviets would stand a good chance of destroying the national military command centers before a Minuteman launch-under-attack decision could be made. They could certainly disrupt the fast-data-rate communications channels used by national authorities to transmit launch orders to Minuteman and by SAC commanders to transmit orders to flush bombers, tankers, and PACCS aircraft. Submarine attack would depend on MHD and EMP to disrupt terrestrial communications, the only high-speed channels, within a few minutes of missile breakwater. It would also be based on blast effects to destroy national command centers as early as seven to ten minutes after breakwater.[38] Early neutralization of these elements would leave authorization of Minuteman and bomber launch under attack up to the airborne command network, which uses relatively slow-speed communications to transmit instructions. Except under the most favorable conditions, the airborne

---

38. Time estimates have been attributed to Donald Latham, deputy under secretary of defense. See *Department of Defense Appropriations for 1983,* Hearings before the House Committee on Appropriations, 97 Cong. 2 sess. (GPO, 1982), pt. 5, p. 47.

network could not deliver the necessary instructions before incoming ICBMs arrived.

This conclusion is especially firm in the case of surprise attack. The airborne network takes about thirty minutes to establish itself under day-to-day conditions in which most aircraft are on fifteen-minute ground alert. Soviet ICBMs would begin to strike by the time the airborne network could establish UHF line-of-sight communications among PACCS aircraft, Minuteman launch centers, and SAC bomber and tanker airbases. Furthermore, flushing PACCS aircraft on ground alert presupposes transmission of takeoff instructions from higher authority, a transmission that EMP or MHD effects could block in the first instance.

Generated alert is the only situation in which both Minuteman launch under attack and bomber, tanker, and EC-135 launch for survival might be effected successfully in the face of deliberate Soviet efforts to block these actions. With the airborne network fully generated, instructions possibly could be delivered and acted upon in time. But the time constraints are such that virtually no tolerances exist for indecision, equipment malfunction, or other performance lapses. The chances for success are low.

Launch under attack is arguably feasible if Soviet strategy conforms to the popular Western construction. If no deliberate attempt is made to interfere with U.S. C³I, the prospects of Minuteman launch under attack are improved. Whether there would be considerable improvement, however, depends on the specific character of the attack. An attack depending partially on EMP to impair bomber performance, for instance, would coincidentally disrupt the terrestrial communications channels. This collateral effect by itself could prevent rapid employment of Minuteman forces.

Regardless of the specific character of a Soviet counterforce attack and no matter how permissive the enemy attack is from the standpoint of launch under attack, a U.S. decision would have to be made on the basis of ambiguous sensor data. Technical and procedural limitations do not permit decisionmakers to wait until unambiguous data arrive. By that time it would be too late.

Summary

A minimalist's version of current U.S. nuclear policy aspirations might be this: in the event of a Soviet attack designed to cause maximum damage to U.S. forces, the United States should be able to retaliate against an appropriate part of the Soviet target base while retaining central direction of reserve forces for as long as necessary. Current policy is actually more ambitious; it calls for an enduring, sophisticated command system that can operate effectively in the face of a deliberate Soviet effort to neutralize it. But at a minimum, the system must be designed for extended deterrence and bargaining in the context of a limited nuclear exchange.

The postulated limited Soviet attack would carry a high risk of triggering an all-out nuclear war. Although decisionmakers might prefer a limited response, a technical-organizational bind would create strong pressure to respond massively: decisionmakers could not reliably determine if the attack were indeed limited, and in any case they could not expect to exercise positive control over whatever forces they decide to withhold.

At the onset of attack the burden of U.S. force management would shift to an airborne system of limited endurance. The system would strain just to carry out its basic mission of establishing a temporary command channel to trigger immediate implementation of the SIOP. Maintaining a functional airborne network more than a few hours after attack could not be reasonably expected, given the limited endurance of the aircraft, the complex coordination problems involved in operating a system with mutually dependent parts, the lack of experience in conducting such operations under realistic, adverse conditions, all the unpredictables that affect performance (ranging from the availability of tankers for in-flight refueling to the effects of turbulence, dust, and radioactivity on aircraft performance), and a host of human factors such as aircrew and battle staff fatigue. It is simply unrealistic to think that the present airborne network would be viable hours or days later when threatened or actual launch of reserve forces might be called for. In fact, the airborne network would probably disintegrate while some bombers were still en route to targets, some missile submarines were en route to launch stations, and some land missiles were being readied for launch. By the time negotiations ensued, the United States would depend on ground-based systems to manage strategic reserve forces, but these systems would have suffered extensive collateral damage and would remain under constant threat of attack and destruction by Soviet reserve forces.

These circumstances encourage comprehensive retaliation. A limited Soviet counterforce attack would not be unambiguously limited, and it would trigger preplanned operations that, in conjunction with extensive collateral damage to the command system, would create strong pressures for organizing retaliation around a single plan that releases most of the SIOP retaliatory forces. Regardless of what calculations political leaders might make at the time, they would have to select the plan that would achieve everything they would expect to accomplish in retaliation for the duration of the conflict.

A limited Soviet counterforce attack could also cause enough collateral damage to weaken capabilities for Minuteman launch under attack. Even under relatively favorable conditions, successful implementation of a launch-under-attack decision would be unlikely. Under unfavorable conditions involving a deliberate attack on C³I to prevent launch under attack, the chances of successful implementation would be low. In any case, current technological conditions force a decision before the character of an enemy attack can be accurately assessed and heighten risks of inadvertent war.

CHAPTER EIGHT

Command Modernization Issues and Programs

IMPROVEMENT in the nuclear control system is being promoted as the centerpiece of President Reagan's plan for strategic modernization. According to Reagan, modernization of the control system is crucial to the success of the overall plan; without dependable C³I, new weapons cannot be transformed into effective power. Support for this thesis runs deep and wide. The Scowcroft Commission expressed a representative opinion: "Our first defense priority should be to ensure that there is continuing, constitutionally legitimate, and full control of our strategic forces under conditions of stress or actual attack. . . . The Commission urges that this program continue to have the highest priority."[1]

Consensus on this priority masks a number of devisive issues, however, especially the proper aims of command system development, their technical feasibility, and their affordability. This chapter discusses these issues, which do not bode well for command modernization, before turning to assess specific programs in the modernization package.

Aims of Command and Control Modernization

National security officials, both uniformed and civilian, frequently emphasize flexibility and endurance through the postattack period in explaining the essence of modern deterrence and in attempting to fix the course of future C³I development. A flexible, enduring command system is a logical derivation of the postulates of extended deterrence, which

1. *Report of the President's Commission on Strategic Forces* (April 6, 1983), p. 10.

currently prevails over the strategy of deterrence based on assured destruction.

Extended deterrence and its implications for command system development are of course rejected or at least challenged by those who believe that the threat of swift and severe punitive retaliation in response to intercontinental nuclear attack is a sufficient deterrent. If deterrence works at all, they argue, it will work at this level. But there are also numerous observers who are at once sympathetic toward the administration's pursuit of flexible response and skeptical of heavy investment in C^3I systems designed to support that strategy. One reason given is that timely, reliable C^3I in the early phase of intercontinental conflict is needed in any case, and there is still ample room for improvement in this area. C^3I investment should therefore be channeled, at least for now, into programs that ensure high-confidence force execution in the initial stage of an intercontinental nuclear war. And that view has prevailed. General L. Allen, Jr., former air force chief of staff, said that programmed modernization of the command system is in fact

aimed at correcting deficiencies in survivability and performance of the glue that holds our systems together and permits us to control them in order to execute the forces.

The principal efforts in this area are aimed at improving the survivability for our warning and communications systems because we think that those initial communications are the most critical aspects to improve at the present time. In time, we will move forward with additional improvements that will permit some increased enduring survivability of our command and control systems to permit survival in the event of a protracted nuclear conflict.[2]

The lion's share of investment in strategic C^3I is indeed devoted to improving initial survivability. For all the rhetoric about gearing command and control systems for protracted conflict, remarkably little attention and few resources are actually being devoted to managing strategic weapons beyond the first few hours of a nuclear conflict. Resources allocated to this purpose, moreover, are concentrated in research and development, not deployment: "Over the next five years, we are proceeding with several programs that will improve the survivability of our strategic C^3 systems. We are also pursuing a comprehensive research and develop-

2. *Hearings on Military Posture and H.R. 5968* before the House Committee on Armed Services, 97 Cong. 2 sess. (GPO, 1982), pt. 2, p. 247.

ment program to ensure enduring communications connectivity during a nuclear war."[3]

This pursuit of "enduring connectivity" is just beginning. The challenge is not simply technological; a political consensus must also be formed. The solid support for improvements in initial C³I survivability does not by any means imply blanket approval for any C³I endeavor. The more ambitious goals, such as endurance, whose programmatic embodiments have found temporary refuge in R&D, will eventually surface to face aggressive scrutiny and certain resistance. It is open to question whether the political-bureaucratic support needed to buy and field enduring systems can be mustered, but there is little doubt that the abstractly stated aims of this administration have not yet been embraced in their entirety and that future endorsement of concrete measures to accomplish these wide-ranging aims will require very spirited promotion. No doubt many will insist upon the correction of basic C³I deficiencies as a condition of support for more ambitious undertakings.

Technical Feasibility

Defense officials seem keenly aware that a technological challenge of daunting dimensions accompanies the C³I goals laid out by the Reagan administration. As Secretary Caspar Weinberger stated in his 1984 annual report, "protecting a command, control, and communications system for nuclear forces is particularly difficult."[4] Although the administration remains convinced that C³I flexibility and endurance are realistic goals, skepticism runs deep in the defense community. Among others who do not share the administration's sanguine view are Desmond Ball and John D. Steinbruner. Ball concludes that "the capability to exercise strict control and co-ordination would inevitably be lost relatively early in a nuclear exchange. The allocation of further resources to improving the survivability and endurance of the strategic command-and-control capabilities cannot substantially alter this situation."[5] In this same vein, Steinbruner contends that a dependable technical solution to C³I endurance

3. *Department of Defense Annual Report for Fiscal Year 1984*, p. 229.
4. Ibid., p. 54.
5. "Can Nuclear War Be Controlled?" *Adelphi Papers*, 169 (London: International Institute for Strategic Studies, 1981), p. 37.

probably cannot be achieved at feasible cost.[6] Even Donald Latham, the administration official who is closest to current research and development activity, admits the magnitude of the problem.[7]

In the meantime, threats to the developing technologies could emerge. Because the deployment of new C³I systems will extend well into the 1990s, both the character of the Soviet threat and its impact on the performance of new U.S. systems are difficult to gauge. Not only are solutions to some problems not at hand, but in some cases the problems have not yet crystallized. It is nonetheless possible to anticipate some threats that might diminish the present value of certain key R&D programs.

U.S. R&D is concentrating on ground mobile units and advanced communications satellites to bolster endurance. The proposed satellite network will consist mainly of extremely high frequency channels provided by a constellation of MILSTAR satellites. These satellites would be an integral part of ground mobile operations because they would be programmed to be the primary communications link between ground mobile units. MILSTAR is also expected to connect these units with the individual forces. The promise of this R&D effort clearly hinges on future Soviet abilities to conduct antisatellite warfare. If MILSTAR could be destroyed, ground mobile units could be isolated from each other and from the forces. Although a threat to MILSTAR is not evident, the Soviets cannot fail to notice that the constellation will become the future backbone of the U.S. command system. It would be unreasonable to assume that they will not pursue antisatellite programs designed to counter it.

There are other future threats that diminish confidence in the technical feasibility of C³I systems under development. For instance, the vulnerability of ground mobile units to direct nuclear effects would depend on whether they could be detected, and if so, whether they could be safely relocated before enemy weapons arrive. There are no good answers to these questions.

Only in the narrowest sense of the term *technical feasibility* is any confidence in current R&D warranted. As pieces of equipment, many of the items under development will undoubtedly work. But such demonstrations will say little about wartime performance, much less the equipment's ability to satisfy operational demands such as endurance. Opti-

6. "Nuclear Decapitation," *Foreign Policy*, no. 45 (Winter 1981–82), p. 26.
7. *Department of Defense Appropriations for 1983*, Hearings before a Subcommittee of the House Committee on Appropriations, 97 Cong. 2 sess. (GPO, 1982), pt. 5, pp. 4, 24.

Figure 8-1. *Strategic C³I Budget Trends*

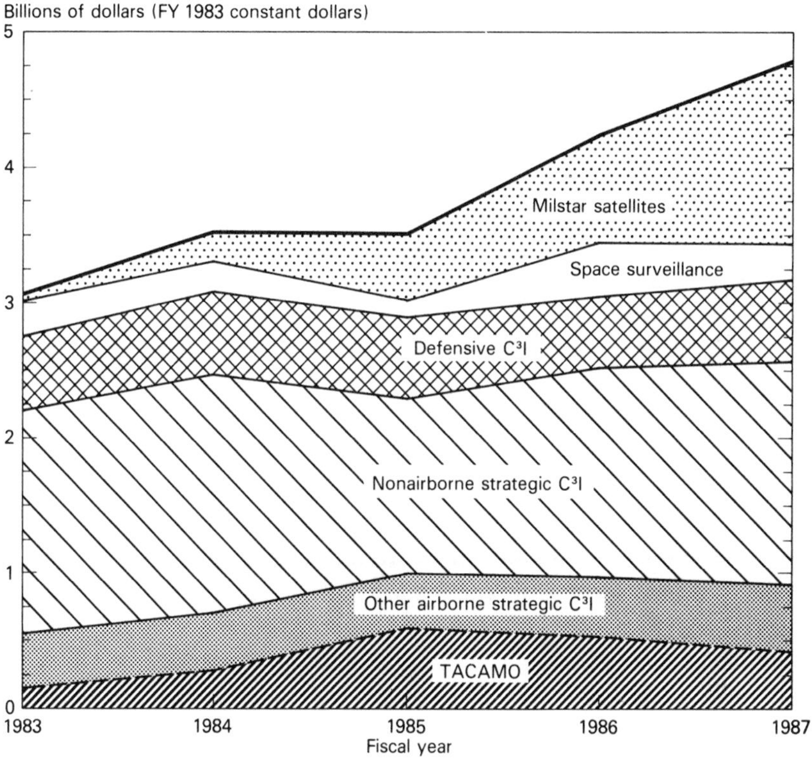

Billions of dollars (FY 1983 constant dollars)

Milstar satellites

Space surveillance

Defensive C³I

Nonairborne strategic C³I

Other airborne strategic C³I

TACAMO

1983 1984 1985 1986 1987
Fiscal year

mism is unwarranted, particularly in light of the potential of the Soviet Union to develop countermeasures.

Cost Control

Although strategic C³I programs are being trumpeted as the new centerpiece of U.S. strategic modernization, a massive infusion of new funds into the programs has not been forthcoming. Contrary to common belief, obligated funds will remain virtually constant in real terms in fiscal years 1983 to 1987 (figure 8-1) in almost every major category of interest. MILSTAR, which is an all-purpose system intended to serve a variety of users besides strategic units, is responsible for any substantial real growth in the strategic C³I budget. If its total cost is assigned to the strategic C³I

Table 8-1. *Rate of Real Growth in Strategic C³I as Projected in 1983*

	1983–84	1984–85	1985–86	1986–87	Average
Without MILSTAR	10.3	−7.8	10.9	0.9	3.6
With MILSTAR	15.3	0.4	17.5	14.5	11.9

Source: Author's estimates

account, that budget will grow in real terms at an average annual rate of 11.9 percent between 1983 and 1987 (table 8-1). If MILSTAR is not counted, the budget will grow at an average annual rate of only 3.6 percent. Allocations for strategic C³I represent a thin slice of the defense budget as a whole, and its share will not expand significantly. In fiscal year 1983, strategic C³I represented 1.3 percent of the defense budget. Whether or not MILSTAR costs are included, C³I will still claim the same small share of the total defense budget for the next five years (table 8-2). Because of the projected increase in investment in strategic offensive weapons, allocations for C³I will actually decrease in real terms as a fraction of the total strategic budget from about 12 percent in fiscal year 1983 to about 7 percent (excluding MILSTAR) or 10 percent (including MILSTAR) by fiscal 1987. Strategic weapons programs will take a larger and larger share of the total strategic budget at the expense of C³I. The all-important airborne segment of the strategic command system will continue to claim about 2 to 3 percent of the strategic budget, or about 0.3 to

Table 8-2. *Projected Strategic C³I Budget, Fiscal Years 1983–87*
Fiscal year 1983 constant dollars

Year	All strategic C³I programs (millions)		Percent of total strategic budget[a]		Percent of total defense budget[b]	
	MILSTAR included	*MILSTAR excluded*	*MILSTAR included*	*MILSTAR excluded*	*MILSTAR included*	*MILSTAR excluded*
1983	3,074	2,994	11.8	11.5	1.3	1.3
1984	3,544	3,301	11.8	11.0	1.4	1.3
1985	3,558	3,045	10.2	10.2	1.2	1.1
1986	4,179	3,376	10.2	8.2	1.4	1.1
1987	4,783	3,407	10.4	7.4	1.5	1.1

a. Based on estimated strategic budgets: 1983 ($26 billion), 1984 ($30 billion), 1985 ($35 billion), 1986 ($41 billion), 1987 ($46 billion).
b. Based on estimated Department of Defense budgets: 1983 ($240 billion), 1984 ($254 billion), 1985 ($289 billion), 1986 ($305 billion), 1987 ($317 billion).

Table 8-3. *Projected Budget for Airborne C³I Functions,*
Fiscal Years 1983–87
Fiscal year 1983 dollars unless otherwise noted

Year	Airborne WWMCCS (millions)	Percent of total strategic budget[a]	Percent of total defense budget[b]
1983	576	2.2	0.24
1984	704	2.4	0.29
1985	1,026	2.9	0.40
1986	1,005	2.5	0.39
1987	978	2.1	0.31

a. Based on estimated strategic budgets: 1983 ($26 billion), 1984 ($30 billion), 1985 ($35 billion), 1986 ($41 billion), 1987 ($46 billion).
b. Based on estimated Department of Defense budgets: 1983 ($240 billion), 1984 ($254 billion), 1985 ($289 billion), 1986 ($305 billion), 1987 ($317 billion).

0.4 percent of the total defense budget (table 8-3).

These figures raise some doubt as to whether the Reagan administration's pledge to overhaul the nuclear command system is genuine. Major C³I repair and a fundamental shift in strategic priorities are not supported by any significant shifts in the defense budget. There are of course better barometers of prevailing resolution, but the absence of strong economic support seems to belie the administration's contention that effort to revamp C³I is being redoubled, that weapons and C³I programs are competing for funds on an equal basis, and that C³I modernization is the key to a revitalized strategic posture. That weapons programs are the main preoccupation of the Department of Defense and the main beneficiaries of the administration's defense largess is further suggested by the fact that key C³I programs such as the E-4B airborne command post and ECX TACAMO replacement aircraft were scaled down or stretched out during Reagan's first term. And the prospects for deep commitment to strategies C³ modernization will remain dim during the coming years of significant cost growth in the weapons accounts. Indeed, we are likely to witness greater pressure, not less, on C³I expenditures and a continuing preference on the part of the services for weapons.

The Reagan administration, however, has stimulated a research and development program that could eventually summon a serious commitment to C³I development. Many embryonic programs promise to offer an expansive and expensive C³I system, one that would put commitment to an actual test. These programs could force the kind of hard choices that the administration has said it was prepared to make (indeed that have supposedly been made already).

The cost of deploying these programs cannot be precisely estimated, but a twofold increase over planned expenditures is not farfetched. Sustained investment on this scale would doubtless meet stiff and widespread resistance, however. The view that the United States can afford such investments is not likely to be advanced, and if it is, then it is unlikely to prevail given pressures cited above and the power over resource allocation that the services possess under the present budgetary process.

Programs

Virtually all of the programs examined in this section were begun before President Reagan took office. Most attempt to resolve problems of positive control during the initial phase of Soviet attack, initial decisions on targeting, and communications for executing the Single Integrated Operational Plan. Few of the solutions were designed to endure beyond a few hours or days; the Reagan administration is responsible for most of those systems designed to operate for weeks or months in a nuclear environment. In many instances, though, such systems are outgrowths of earlier concepts or prototypes. Under the Reagan administration, research and development of these concepts or prototypes was accelerated, but few solutions have been produced, and C^3I R&D today is mainly oriented to completing systems that improve upon current capabilities for executing the SIOP. In sum, the emphasis of the projects is to make certain that the threat of assured destruction cannot be removed by a Soviet attack on the U.S. command system.

The major modernization programs can be grouped as follows:[8]

Warning and Attack Assessment
— Improvements to increase the survivability of early warning satellites
— Mobile ground terminals for warning data readout

8. *Department of Defense Authorization for Appropriations for Fiscal Year 1983,* Hearings before the Senate Committee on Armed Services, 97 Cong. 2 sess. (GPO, 1981) pt. 7, pp. 4644–46.

— Two new PAVE PAWS radars
— Modernization of BMEWS radars
— Integrated Operational Nuclear Detonation Detection System
  (IONDS)
— Advanced warning concepts in R&D
Command and Decision
— Hardening airborne command posts against nuclear effects
— Mobile command centers
— Improvement in the survivability and capability of fixed
  command centers
— Other survivable command basing options under study
Strategic Communications
— Ground Wave Emergency Network (GWEN)
— New ECX aircraft for TACAMO
— MILSTAR EHF communications satellite system
— LF/VLF radio receivers on bombers
— DSCS-III satellite production
— ELF for communications with submarines
— Three additional fleet communications satellites
— Reconstructable communications concepts under study

These programs are intended to improve upon existing abilities to launch ground-alert bombers and command-communications aircraft during the early phase of Soviet attack, to make decisions at the national level, to disseminate retaliatory orders, and to manage reserve forces after a Soviet attack. As table 8-4 shows, the systems that support these functions cut across the three categories of modernization programs.

Positive-Control Launch

Because the entire bomber force and most command-communications aircraft are normally maintained on ground alert, measures must be promptly instituted to prevent their destruction before they can get airborne. Sensors must reliably and rapidly detect enemy missile launches, and their data must be transmitted to commanders. Decisions on protective launch must then be made and sent to the aircraft units on ground alert. The basic circuitry used to effect a positive control launch is depicted by the flow diagram in figure 8-2.

Table 8-4. *C³I Modernization Programs and Functions Affected*

Programs	Positive control launch	NCA decisionmaking (initial SIOP decisions)	Dissemination of SIOP initial execution message	Protracted-war force management
Warning and attack assessment				
Satellite survivability upgrades	x	x		
Mobile ground terminals	x	x		x
PAVE PAWS expansion	x	x		
BMEWS modernization		x		
IONDS		x		x
Advanced warning concepts	x	x		x
Command and decision				
Airborne command post hardening		x	x	
Mobile command centers				x
Fixed command center improvements	x	x	x	
Strategic communications				
Ground Wave Emergency Network	x	x	x	
ECX TACAMO aircraft			x	
MILSTAR satellites	x	x	x	x
Bomber LF/VLF minireceivers			x	
DSCS III satellites	x	x	x	
Extremely low frequency submarine communications			x	
FLTSATCOM satellites			x	
Reconstructable networks				x

Destruction of this circuitry by blast effects could begin as early as seven to ten minutes after the first launches of enemy submarine missiles.[9] Serious impairment could be experienced even earlier from sabotage, jamming, and various effects produced by high-altitude nuclear explosions. The Defense Department therefore plans "improvements that let us survive the first minutes of an attack, even before the destructive bursts on the ground come in, through the period of high-altitude burst with the electromagnetic pulse and various atmospheric disruptions and magnetic field interruptions, the jamming periods, and the destruction as the SLBMs begin to arrive."[10]

9. *Department of Defense Appropriations for 1983,* House hearings, pt. 5, p. 47.
10. *Department of Defense Authorization for Appropriations for Fiscal Year 1983,* Senate hearings, pt. 7, p. 4686.

Figure 8-2. *Positive Control Launch Circuits*

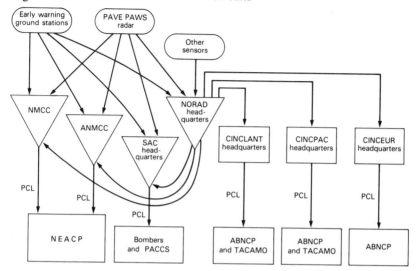

Because enemy missile launches are initially detected by early warning satellites—one over the eastern hemisphere and two over the western hemisphere provide the first warning of launches of ICBMs and SLBMs, respectively—considerable effort is being made to protect the satellites themselves, the ground readout stations, and the associated communications from sudden attack.[11] Additions to the satellites themselves include improved sensors that will be more sensitive to the infrared signature of Soviet SS-N-6 submarine missiles.[12] Features that protect the infrared detectors against laser attack are also being incorporated because Soviet ground-based lasers are currently a threat, and space-based lasers could pose a threat in the early 1990s.[13] Advanced-warning concepts might lead

11. "Improved U.S. Warning Net Spurred," *Aviation Week and Space Technology* (June 23, 1980), p. 41, reports that defense support programs will normally see the liftoff of a missile within about sixty seconds of ignition. It is also reported that DSP ground readout stations transmit warning messages to national authorities, NORAD, and SAC in near real time; see *Department of Defense Authorization for Appropriations for Fiscal Year 1983*, Senate hearings, pt. 7, p. 4701. For the stationing of satellites, see *Department of Defense Appropriations for Fiscal Year 1975*, Hearings before the Senate Committee on Appropriations, 93 Cong. 2 sess. (GPO, 1974), pt. 1, p. 116.

12. *Department of Defense Authorization for Appropriations for Fiscal Year 1982*, Senate hearings, pt. 7, p. 4234; and "Improved U.S. Warning Net Spurred," p. 40.

13. "Spacecraft Survivability Boost Sought," *Aviation Week and Space Technology* (June 16, 1980), p. 260; and *Department of Defense Appropriations for 1984*, Hearings before the House Committee on Appropriations, 98 Cong. 1 sess. (GPO, 1983), pt. 8, p. 502.

to a space-based sensor system to detect Soviet cruise missiles, which current sensors cannot reliably do.

Protecting ground readout stations is the primary focus of current effort. At present, the early warning satellite system is said to be vulnerable because the satellite data come to fixed ground stations for processing and dissemination.[14] In the official estimation, while the satellites themselves are relatively survivable,

the ground stations at Buckley Field, Colo., and Pine Gap/Alice Springs [Woomera], Australia, are the weakest link. These are now the only two fully operational DSP [defense support programs] ground stations, and early warning officials are extremely concerned about their vulnerability to acts of sabotage as well as to internal accident, which could cut by half, or even 100% in the case of coordinated sabotage, the front-line early warning capability.[15]

The loss of ground stations to sabotage, accident, or conventional or nuclear attack could have untoward consequences of two sorts. On one hand, failure to issue takeoff orders in response to an outage (of perhaps undetermined origin) would put bombers and command aircraft in jeopardy if enemy missile attacks were subsequently initiated. On the other hand, the launch of these aircraft in response to the loss of a ground station could be a dangerous overreaction. The director of the Defense Communications Agency once speculated, for instance, that the overseas ground station

could be neutralized or destroyed using a number of pretexts during a period of tension, depriving us of warning at a critical juncture. This could force the NCA to place a large proportion of the SAC bomber fleet on airborne alert, which in itself becomes a provocative action since it could be interpreted by an enemy as an intent to preempt and thus spark the very attack we are trying to deter.[16]

Transportable simplified processing stations were originally planned to augment and possibly replace the vulnerable fixed stations, and one such unit was actually developed. Testimony disclosed that the station was to be redeployed from the United States to an overseas location as a backup

14. *Department of Defense Authorization for Appropriations for Fiscal Year 1982,* Hearings before the Senate Committee on Armed Services, 97 Cong. 1 sess. (GPO, 1981), pt. 7, p. 4234; and *Department of Defense Authorization for Appropriations for Fiscal Year 1981,* Hearings before the Senate Committee on Armed Services, 96 Cong. 2 sess. (GPO, 1980), pt. 6, p. 3409.

15. "Improved U.S. Warning Net Spurred," p. 40.

16. *Department of Defense Appropriations for 1974,* Hearings before a Subcommittee of the House Committee on Appropriations, 93 Cong. 1 sess. (GPO, 1973), pt. 6, p. 1691.

to an existing ground terminal and was expected to be operational there in April 1982.[17] This deployment would add some readout redundancy but not survivability because the station becomes a fixed target once it is set up. It is transportable but hardly mobile in any practical sense.

Mobile ground terminals were therefore developed to augment the existing fixed readout stations. The Defense Department is procuring six of these truck-mounted terminals, which will receive early warning satellite data, process them, and relay the data through supporting communications to various users.[18] Because MGTs can be moved in a random manner, they are expected to present a very difficult targeting problem for Soviet planners. The terminals should be far more survivable than the existing fixed terminals.

Accompanying each MGT truck will be a communications van carrying a jam-resistant secure communications (JRSC) terminal. Described as providing a sensor data network and secure voice and graphics for tactical warning, JRSC terminals will operate with the Defense Satellite Communications System III (DSCS-III), a four-satellite constellation to be fully operational by 1986.[19] DSCS-III satellites were designed to withstand jamming and nuclear effects such as system-generated EMP and also to function autonomously for weeks or months without ground assistance for on-board maintenance.[20]

This combination of new systems—MGTs, JRSC vans, and DSCS-III satellites—will appreciably mitigate current vulnerability to jamming, sabotage, and direct attack. To the extent that they reduce reliance on leased terrestrial communications for data dissemination to users, they will also mitigate vulnerability to the effects of magnetohydrodynamic and electromagnetic pulses. They will not, however, solve the problem of scintillation effects, which could severely disrupt SHF transmissions over DSCS-III satellites.

Additional insurance against disruption of the aircraft launch circuitry

17. *Department of Defense Authorization for Appropriations for Fiscal Year 1983,* Senate hearings, pt. 7, pp. 4620, 4645.

18. Ibid., pp. 4645, 4692, 4701; see also *Department of Defense Authorization for Appropriations for Fiscal Year 1982,* Senate hearings, pt. 7, p. 4234.

19. For JRSC terminals, see *Department of Defense Authorization for Appropriations for Fiscal Year 1983,* Senate hearings, pt. 7, pp. 4618, 4699, 4701. For DSCS-III launch plans, see *Department of Defense Appropriations for Fiscal Year 1983,* House hearings, pt. 5, p. 59.

20. *Department of Defense Authorization for Appropriations for Fiscal Year 1981,* Senate hearings, pt. 6, p. 3449; and "Spacecraft Survivability Boost Sought," p. 261.

will be purchased in the form of the Ground Wave Emergency Network (GWEN). This system will consist of numerous unmanned LF radio sites hardened against electromagnetic pulse, which will ultimately connect warning sensors such as PAVE PAWS radars with NORAD, national command centers, SAC headquarters, and bomber and ICBM bases. The LF ground radio wave will permit secure low-data-rate communications in a nuclear environment. GWEN is being deployed in stages; at the end of 1984 a nine-node network connecting SAC headquarters, NORAD, and a few other units was operational. Figure 8-3 shows their locations. The other nodes in the diagram are being added to the network in the second stage of deployment. This so-called thin-line network becomes operational in 1985-86. In the third stage, a network composed of as many as 500 nodes might be deployed.[21]

Some contend that GWEN could convey minimum tactical warning information to national and senior military authorities along with the NORAD commander in chief's assessment of its validity; they also consider it able to carry takeoff instructions to the aircraft and even disseminate the SIOP execution message.[22] The system's initial capability is of course very limited; the thin-line network merely augments the EMP-vulnerable leased circuits that connect an early warning satellite ground station (Buckley AFB), NORAD, SAC headquarters, and the National Military Command System. This link is intended to withstand the effects of high-altitude explosions but not SLBM or ICBM attack. The thin-line network could in theory serve all the various purposes but only under a restricted set of circumstances. If directly attacked by even a relatively small number of nuclear weapons, the network would be readily severed. Its utility is therefore mainly limited to the period of high-altitude explosions and jamming that could precede weapons impact by several minutes. Full deployment of several hundred nodes would increase the chances that GWEN could continue to function during an SLBM attack and possibly during an ICBM attack, especially if the nodes were not attacked directly. This expansion is hard to justify, however, considering the high risk that the fixed C³I facilities GWEN serves would be struck and destroyed. Many of these facilities could be neutralized by SLBMs;

---

21. *Department of Defense Authorization for Appropriations for Fiscal Year 1983,* Senate hearings, pt. 7, pp. 4646, 4683; and *Department of Defense Appropriations for Fiscal Year 1984,* House hearings, pt. 8, pp. 339–40.

22. *Department of Defense Appropriations for Fiscal Year 1984,* House hearings, pt. 8, pp. 339–40.

Figure 8-3. *Ground Wave Emergency Network (GWEN) Thin-Line System*

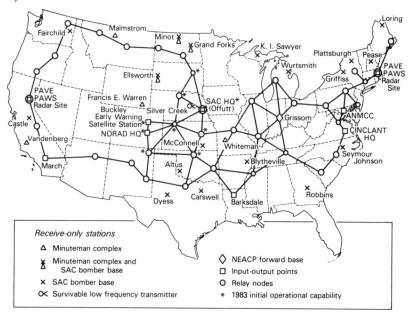

all could be destroyed by ICBMs. Although GWEN also serves airborne command aircraft and SAC forces on the ground, the network's post-attack role appears marginal considering that ICBM forces would be struck and destroyed and that bomber forces would presumably be already airborne. In short, the utility of GWEN lies primarily in its resistance to indirect nuclear effects produced during the short period that precedes weapon impact.

Two other programs that could improve U.S. capabilities for positive-control launch of bombers and command aircraft are PAVE PAWS and improvements to fixed command posts. (MILSTAR is also promising in this regard, but this is not its primary role.) PAVE PAWS are phased-array radar sensors designed to detect submarine missiles launched against the United States. Two radars, one on each coast (Massachusetts and California), are presently operational. Their range of 3,000 nautical miles extends coverage over a vast expanse of both oceans, but deployment of two additional radars is necessary to close gaps in coverage of potential launch stations to the southeast and southwest.[23] Although these

23. Ibid., pp. 4700, 4701, 4710.

areas are continuously monitored by early warning satellites, the Defense Department contends that space-based infrared and ground-based radar coverage of the same events increases the probability of detection while lowering the risk of false alarm. Without such "dual phenomenology," the United States might, for instance, hesitate to flush its bombers in the event of an actual attack. Alternatively, the bombers might be ordered into the air on the basis of false indications from a single detection source.

Decisions to launch aircraft to protect them require confidence in the performance not only of the sensors and communications channels but also of the decision centers themselves. Various improvements to fixed command posts have been proposed to increase this confidence. Protection against EMP is especially important. If such disruptions occurred during the first few critical minutes of an attack, fatal delays in NORAD and SAC decisionmaking, for example, could result. The commander in chief of NORAD is responsible for determining whether detected missile launches pose a threat to North America, and that assessment may well be the principal basis on which other commanders decide whether to flush their bombers or command-communications aircraft. At NORAD's Cheyenne Mountain complex—the hub of tactical warning and attack assessment—hardening against EMP is reportedly under way, as is a program to supply battery-based uninterruptible power. The SAC command post, where launch decisions are made, is also being shielded against the effects of EMP.[24]

Even if the details of these programs were open to public examination, it would still be premature to pass judgment on their impact. On the surface, they appear to be addressing critical deficiencies. In the end, however, they cannot alter the possibility that submarine-launched missiles could arrive at the same time aircraft would be taking off. As earlier chapters explained, some aircraft would react too slowly to survive, even if the warning sensors and launch circuitry performed perfectly. And in instances in which aircraft survival is theoretically expected, the margin of safety is thin. An unanticipated failure of some unknown component—technical or procedural—in this complex system could have catastrophic consequences for aircraft on ground alert. These programs also fail to address squarely an emergent near-term threat of major proportions:

24. Ibid., pp. 4681, 4683, 4700, 4705.

modern Soviet cruise missiles. Sensor systems capable of detecting them are a long way from being operational, while Soviet deployment of the missiles is imminent.

NCA Decisionmaking

As soon as initial detection of an attack is received at SAC and other selected headquarters, actions are taken to increase the readiness of the respective alert units. For instance, when indications of SLBM attack appeared on the SAC command post display on two separate occasions in June 1980, the SAC duty controller directed all alert crews to move to their aircraft and start engines in preparation for takeoff. If the NORAD commander determines the possibility of an attack, the next step is to convene a threat assessment conference, bringing the chairman of the Joint Chiefs and senior commanders at NMCC, ANMCC, SAC, and NORAD into the evaluation via communications link, while further steps to enhance the survivability of alert units are taken. In June 1980, for instance, a threat assessment conference was convened, and "as part of the ongoing reaction of the threat assessment conference, the Pacific Command airborne command post took off."[25]

If senior officers determine that an attack is actually under way, a missile attack conference, which brings in all senior personnel, including the president, is convened. During this time, NORAD "analyzes the attack, characterizes the threat, and provides the most current information available to Washington, D.C., and certain other locations."[26] This information is processed and displayed in common format at the NORAD, NMCC, ANMCC, and SAC command centers, which are equipped with computer-based displays.[27] The objective of the conference is to get to the national command authority "the information he needs to make a coherent, useful decision. . . . The purpose of that conference is to get a decision."[28] The NCA must digest the information, weigh it, and evaluate response options. A decision must be reached quickly; as SAC's com-

---

25. The incident was, of course, a false alarm; see *Recent False Alerts from the Nation's Missile Attack Warning System*, Hearings before the Senate Committee on Armed Services, 96 Cong. 2 sess. (GPO, 1980), Report October 9, 1980, pp. 5–7.

26. *Department of Defense Authorization for Appropriations for Fiscal Year 1983*, Senate hearings, pt. 7, p. 4683.

27. Ibid., p. 4717.

28. *Department of Defense Authorization for Appropriations for Fiscal Year 1982*, Senate hearings, pt. 7, pp. 4212, 4218.

mander in chief noted, "the time available . . . is critically limited due to the flight time of submarine-launched ballistic missiles,"[29] which could strike as early as seven to ten minutes after the first enemy missile breaks water.

Information forwarded to the president during this short period, assuming the president has by then been added to the missile attack conference, originates at the warning sensors. Besides providing greater assurance of early detection in order to effect aircraft launch actions, improvements to these sensors are meant to provide the president and his senior advisers a better picture of the character of the attack so that they would have a basis on which to select an SIOP option from the alternatives available. PAVE PAWS radars, for example, are scheduled for an increase in power that will improve their ability to observe MIRVs, estimate the size of an attack, and predict targets. BMEWS radars, which are oriented toward ICBM arrival corridors, are also scheduled for modernization; the Defense Department plans to replace pre-1960 computers and enhance the tracking radars.[30] The BMEWS system was designed in the 1960s to detect an attack consisting of twenty or more missiles arriving within a five-minute interval. The Defense Department now requires the ability to detect and characterize an attack involving thousands of reentry vehicles.[31] At present BMEWS cannot resolve objects well enough; it is prone to undercounts and can only determine whether an ICBM attack is headed toward the continental limits of the United States. The proposed improvement would allow better estimates of the size of the attack and the points of impact, estimates that should be sufficient to verify, for example, an attack on the Minuteman force: "If the NCA discovers that the attack is on him, he can transfer early to the succession of command. If he determines that it is headed toward the ICBM field, he can make one decision. If he determines it is headed toward New York City or Chicago, he can make another decision. This is what this is all about."[32]

    29. *Department of Defense Authorization for Appropriations for Fiscal Year 1983,* Senate hearings, pt. 7, p. 4683.
    30. Ibid., pp. 4699–4700.
    31. "U.S. Upgrading Ground-Based Sensors," *Aviation Week and Space Technology* (June 16, 1980), pp. 241–42.
    32. *Fiscal Year 1978 Supplemental Military Authorization,* Hearings before the Senate Committee on Armed Services, 95 Cong. 1 sess. (GPO, 1977), p. 81.

Several of the programs discussed in the preceding sections—upgrading the survivability of warning satellites, mobile readout terminals for the satellites, GWEN and DSCS-III communications for transmission of attack assessment information—will also expand the potential for an informed national decision on employing strategic weapons. In addition the early warning satellites are reportedly being redesigned to provide more refined calculations of missile launch azimuth and missile type to identify impact areas and country of origin.[33] Advanced warning concepts in R&D, however, offer the best hope of accurately assessing incoming missiles. The most promising concept involves applying new infrared sensor technology to early warning missions. Using current infrared technology, early warning satellites lose track of missiles after their booster rockets burn out because of a drastic decrease in the missiles' infrared emissions. The new technology, though in its infancy, could permit future early warning satellites to track reentry vehicles until ground radar can pick them up late in their trajectory. It could also provide tactical warning and assessment of a cruise missile attack. But this nascent technology will not be available in the near future when it is needed.

Aided by the NORAD and SAC commanders and other senior military commanders and civilian advisers, the president is supposed to reach a very quick decision on the basis of attack assessment information. In the extreme case of an SLBM attack in which weapons reach targets in less than ten minutes after breakwater, some information would be unavailable before ground command centers were destroyed. Sensors such as BMEWS and PARCS radars would not have detected a single ICBM before the principal users of sensor data began to come under attack. Disruption of the telecommunications missile attack conference could occur even earlier if some SLBMs were detonated at high altitudes during the upward portion of their trajectory.

As noted earlier, EMP-resistant communications such as GWEN, coupled with EMP shielding for major command centers, will help protect launch circuitry. But additional protected circuitry with higher channel capacity for voice communications is needed to support threat assessment and missile attack conferences. Two programs under development, DSCS-III and MILSTAR, could improve upon the existing MHD-vulnerable leased circuits for voice conferences and the blackout-prone air force satellite communications circuits for low-speed teletype conferences. Be-

33. "Improved U.S. Warning Net Spurred," pp. 40–41.

sides providing channels for relaying warning data to major command centers, DSCS-III satellites would provide a separate wide-band channel for voice conferencing among those centers. But because DSCS-III signals operate at super high frequencies, they are susceptible to scintillation caused by high-altitude nuclear explosions. The proposed MILSTAR constellation, however, will operate at the extremely high frequency band, which is less susceptible to blackout or scintillation. EHF also presents an opportunity to build a very high degree of jam resistance into the system.[34] The Defense Department reports that MILSTAR will incorporate features that effectively counter jamming threats postulated for the 1980s and 1990s. For this reason, and because satellite-to-satellite cross-links will interconnect the NCA and the commanders in chief without using intermediate ground stations,[35] MILSTAR could help ensure the participation of even CINCPAC and CINCEUR in the missile-attack conference during the critical period between launch detection and impact. According to Assistant Secretary of Defense Donald Latham, MILSTAR "will allow the President and his force commanders to voice-conference under any kind of EMP threats."[36] The statement assumes that this very expensive constellation of satellites can cope with future Soviet antisatellite capabilities. It is a large and arguably unjustified assumption.

None of these real or alleged improvements can relax the severe time limits under which the decision process must strain. It seems unreasonable to expect a rational decision on the employment of nuclear forces to be reached in less than ten minutes, with or without support from a sophisticated modern command system, the capabilities of which in the face of a reactive Soviet threat remain to be seen. During this short time the United States would be doing well just to flush the bomber force and the command aircraft and to transfer the SIOP decisionmaking function to airborne command centers. And after this transition the United States would be doing well if any rational decision on the employment of strategic forces could be reached.

As noted, the prelaunch survival of some command aircraft will be uncertain even after launch circuitry has been modernized. Doubtful sur-

34. *Department of Defense Appropriations for 1981*, House hearings, pt. 7, p. 438; and *Department of Defense Appropriations for 1983*, House hearings, pt. 5, pp. 64–68.

35. *Department of Defense Authorization for Appropriations for Fiscal Year 1983*, Senate hearings, pt. 7, pp. 4619, 4712; and *Department of Defense Authorization for Appropriations for Fiscal Year 1981*, Senate hearings, pt. 6, p. 3432.

36. *Department of Defense Appropriations for 1984*, House hearings, pt. 8, p. 1358.

vivors include aircraft normally maintained on ground alert within close range of enemy submarines: CINCLANT, CINCPAC, and CINCEUR airborne command posts and NEACP. The relocation of NEACP to Grissom AFB, Indiana, in 1983 increased its chances of survival but by no means assured it.

Transferring the authority to execute the SIOP could be relatively simple if NEACP is successfully launched on tactical or strategic warning. After the destruction or isolation of fixed national command centers, the airborne center could immediately assert release authority if a successor to the NCA were aboard—a possibility, given enough strategic warning. NEACP could also eventually assert release authority if communications with the NCA or a successor on the ground could be established. The transfer of authority to an airborne platform would be problematic, however, if NEACP failed to survive the initial SLBM attack or failed to make contact with the NCA or a successor.

Three of the programs listed in table 8-4, IONDS, MILSTAR, and hardening of airborne command posts, directly address problems of SIOP decisionmaking once that responsibility shifts to the airborne platforms. By 1988 the Integrated Operational NUDET Detection System (IONDS) will place nuclear explosion detectors on eighteen NAVSTAR navigation satellites intended to supply reconnaissance and strike forces with fixes on their positions and precise clock time.[37] The IONDS packages dispersed on this global system will provide real-time measurements of nuclear explosions anywhere in the world. The purpose, according to the Defense Department, is to provide damage assessments to the national command authority during and after an attack.[38] The system is reported to be accurate to less than 100 meters, but its most significant feature may be its ability to transmit reports directly to airborne command posts.[39] The "fusion" centers for collecting, analyzing, and disseminating pre- and poststrike assessment information are currently such major fixed facilities as NORAD. NEACP and other airborne command posts tie into this network via ground-entry points and leased terrestrial communications. By all indications, aircraft access to attack assessments could be perma-

37. *Department of Defense Authorization for Fiscal Year 1983*, Senate hearings, pt. 7, p. 4680; and *Department of Defense Appropriations for 1983*, House hearings, pt. 5, p. 16.

38. *Department of Defense Authorization for Appropriations for Fiscal Year 1982*, Senate hearings, pt. 7, p. 4206.

39. *Department of Defense Authorization for Appropriations for Fiscal Year 1983*, Senate hearings, pt. 7, p. 4624-25; and *Department of Defense Authorization for Appropriations for Fiscal Year 1982*, Senate hearings, pt. 7, p. 4206.

nently lost shortly after SLBM attack commences. Early destruction of the ground-entry points or the fusion centers or the interconnecting land lines would lead to early isolation of airborne command posts. They would lose access to intelligence data at the same time that responsibility for SIOP decisionmaking would devolve upon them. IONDS increases the chances that the airborne commanders will have continuing access to these data. Indeed, accurate information on the number and location of nuclear explosions as they actually occur seems essential to informed decisionmaking. Such information also seems far more reliable and definitive than prestrike assessments of the attack's apparent character. Unfortunately, the promise of IONDS in this regard is greatly diminished by the susceptibility of its radio transmissions to scintillation.

MILSTAR's contribution to airborne SIOP decisionmaking lies in its potential for providing direct voice communications channels among the NEACP, CINCLANT, CINCPAC, CINCSAC, and CINCEUR airborne command posts. At present, air force satellite communications provides the only means by which these aircraft could conduct a missile-attack conference in the absence of ground-entry points and access to distributed commercial lines. But AFSATCOM conferencing uses low-speed teletype and is very susceptible to jamming and scintillation; MILSTAR might permit officials in EC-135 and E-4 command aircraft to confer directly by EHF voice transmission, whose only major disadvantage is a susceptibility to interference from heavy rainfall, which normally could be overflown.[40]

Hardening airborne command posts against nuclear effects, particularly EMP, assumed higher priority after the Department of Defense decided in 1981 to deploy only four EMP-hardened E-4B command aircraft instead of the six originally planned for deployment in July 1987. As late as 1981 the department reported that no less than six aircraft were needed in order to support the NEACP and SAC Looking Glass missions, and SAC strongly recommended an accelerated delivery schedule and procurement of a seventh aircraft.[41] (With seven E-4B aircraft, the United States could simultaneously maintain a NEACP E-4B on twenty-four-

40. *Department of Defense Authorization for Appropriations for Fiscal Year 1981,* Senate hearings, pt. 6, pp. 3432, 3437; *Department of Defense Appropriations for 1981,* House hearings, pt. 6, p. 438; and *Department of Defense Appropriations for 1981,* House hearings, pt. 7, p. 438.

41. *Department of Defense Authorization for Appropriations for Fiscal Year 1982,* Senate hearings, pt. 7, pp. 4205, 4233; and *Department of Defense Appropriations for 1981,* House hearings, pt. 7, p. 417.

hour ground alert and a Looking Glass E-4B on twenty-four-hour airborne alert. With a fleet of six E-4Bs, SAC would need to retain two EC-135s as backup aircraft to support its Looking Glass mission.)[42] Although the E-4B was the only EMP-hardened airborne command post in the entire inventory,[43] its high cost led to a decision finally to deploy only four and thereby to continue to rely on unhardened EC-135 aircraft to fly Looking Glass missions. (Three E-4B aircraft are now operationally deployed in support of the NEACP mission. The fourth should enter service in 1985.) At the same time, the Defense Department proposed to spend $13.7 million to provide EMP hardening to elements of the EC-135 fleet; the figure closely corresponds with estimates of the cost of EMP hardening for all twenty-five EC-135s in SAC's Post Attack Command Control System (PACCS).[44]

IONDS, MILSTAR, and the hardening of command aircraft would improve airborne SIOP decisionmaking, but that capability is still far from adequate. First, hardening aircraft, particularly older aircraft, against EMP is more art than science—there are still uncertainties surrounding the resistance of the modern E-4B, which was deliberately shielded against EMP in the design stage.[45] Also, only partial protection of the EC-135s could be provided on a budget of $13.7 million; comprehensive hardening would exceed $100 million. And Defense Department plans to harden new and replacement components as they are phased in during normal aircraft modification will delay hardening critical systems such as the UHF line-of-sight radios on some aircraft until 1990, at least.[46] Second, MILSTAR will not be deployed until the early 1990s, and the terminals for airborne command posts will doubtless follow that deployment by several years. MILSTAR is also just being developed; considerable uncertainty exists about the final configuration of both the space and terminal segments. And because of past investments of billions

42. *Department of Defense Authorization for Appropriations for Fiscal Year 1981,* Senate hearings, pt. 6, p. 3447.

43. Ibid., p. 3457.

44. *Department of Defense Appropriations for 1983,* House hearings, pt. 5, p. 151; *Department of Defense Authorization for Appropriations for Fiscal Year 1983,* Senate hearings, pt. 7, p. 4690; and *Department of Defense Authorization for Appropriations for Fiscal Year 1982,* Senate hearings, pt. 7, p. 4234.

45. In particular, the crucial VLF trailing antenna on which the E-4B greatly depends for communications in a nuclear environment has not been EMP-tested; see *Department of Defense Appropriations for 1983,* House hearings, pt. 5, p. 162.

46. *Department of Defense Appropriations for 1984,* House hearings, pt. 8, p. 404.

of dollars in UHF terminals, the switch to full EHF operation will take years. During what could be a very long transition, a less capable hybrid system, part EHF and part UHF, will be necessary. MILSTAR will incorporate an EHF-UHF interlink to provide continuity of service with air force satellite terminals.[47] Reliance on UHF for part of the circuit, however, means that MILSTAR channels could be susceptible to jamming and scintillation. Third, IONDS probably could not communicate effectively in a nuclear environment. Finally MILSTAR (as well as IONDS platforms, early warning satellites, and DSCS-III satellites) might have to cope with unanticipated Soviet antisatellite capabilities. In light of intensifying military competition, it does not seem prudent to assume that space will be a sanctuary for the planned satellite systems on which the United States will rely during the 1990s and into the next century.

Dissemination of Orders to Retaliate

Senior defense officials hope that U.S. retaliatory orders can be disseminated before enemy missiles strike, while the U.S. command system is still intact and coherent. As the commander in chief of SAC put it in 1981, "The ultimate, of course, is to recognize that we are under attack, to characterize that attack, get a decision from the President, and to disseminate the decision to the forces prior to the first weapon impacting upon the United States."[48] Effective dissemination during this period presupposes minimal disruption of the ground command and communications network from high-altitude nuclear explosions. But both the fixed command posts and the leased terrestrial communications linking the NCA to the commanders in chief and the individual strategic forces are currently subject to serious disruption from such explosions. Hardening the command posts is supposed to mitigate this vulnerability, and the deployment of the Ground Wave Emergency Network is expected to reduce reliance on the leased lines—according to the Defense Department, GWEN could carry the initial SIOP execution message directly to the forces.[49] Actually, however, GWEN will not be able to carry the message directly to the submarine and bomber forces. Because it will be a terrestrial network of LF radios whose signals will travel short distances along the ground to

47. *Department of Defense Authorization for Appropriations for Fiscal Year 1983*, Senate hearings, pt. 7, p. 4618.

48. *Department of Defense Authorization for Appropriations for Fiscal Year 1982*, Senate hearings, pt. 7, p. 4213.

49. Ibid., p. 4683.

other radios and other fixed locations such as Minuteman launch control centers, the navy's shore-based VLF radio stations and other facilities will still be needed for communicating with missile submarines. Similarly, various radio systems will be needed to relay messages received via GWEN circuits to the bomber forces, whether those forces are still on the ground or en route to turnaround points.

It is of course a matter of considerable doubt whether an execution message would be ready for dissemination before the ground network began to sustain heavy blast damage. To the prudent planner the key links in the dissemination process as well as in the earlier decisionmaking process are the various aircraft that constitute the airborne command network. Several programs are intended to fortify the network's ability to communicate within itself and with the bomber, submarine, and land missile forces. Before examining these programs, it is useful to review present capabilities to send retaliation orders from command aircraft to various force components.

Bombers depend heavily upon air-to-air, line-of-sight UHF communications to receive war orders from command aircraft. Outbound bombers can receive instructions from PACCS aircraft as long as their corridors cross the PACCS orbits and as long as the transmissions start before the bombers have flown beyond UHF range (about 400 miles). If PACCS transmissions are delayed by difficulties in decisionmaking or in communicating the orders throughout the PACCS network, if bomber corridors do not traverse PACCS orbits, or if PACCS aircraft on ground alert do not survive SLBM attacks, dissemination would rely on the emergency rocket communications system, the AFSATCOM system, and HF radio. None of these links is reliable. If standard calculations are to be believed, the ERCS is increasingly vulnerable to early destruction because the rockets are housed in Minuteman silos that cannot ride out a coordinated attack by modern Soviet ICBM forces. AFSATCOM effectiveness is doubtful because of its susceptibility to jamming and scintillation. HF radio would be blacked out for hours and perhaps days. The major initiative designed to fortify the communications link between the airborne command network and the bomber force involves equipping bombers with LF/VLF receivers.

Alert submarines presently rely on TACAMO VLF communications for retaliation orders. Messages to TACAMO depend on precarious ERCS and AFSATCOM links and on LF/VLF transmissions from command aircraft such as Looking Glass. Looking Glass is the most survivable, but it lacks sufficient radio range to reach TACAMO with high confidence in a nuclear and jamming environment. And TACAMO itself is vulnerable to EMP and to VLF jamming and has limited endurance. Currently the ECX, a replacement for the EC-130 aircraft, is proposed to fortify TACAMO's link to the submarines. Other significant initiatives include MILSTAR and an ELF radio system being built in Wisconsin and Michigan.

The Minuteman force currently depends on the airborne launch control centers. Except for Looking Glass, all ALCC aircraft are normally maintained on ground alert. If, along with the rest of the ground-alert aircraft in the Post Attack Command Control System, they survive SLBM attacks, UHF radio links for transmitting launch commands to missile forces probably would be established. The links are line of sight and are not very susceptible to jamming or nuclear effects. There are no major plans to fortify the links to ALCC aircraft and Minuteman forces.

DSCS-III AND FLTSATCOM SATELLITES. All C^3 aircraft, most bombers, and all ground-based Minuteman launch control centers are equipped with AFSATCOM satellite communications terminals. The space segment of AFSATCOM is currently carried piggyback on FLTSATCOM host satellites, many of which will cease to be functional in the near future. The current FLTSATCOM constellation, for example, consists of four satellites launched between 1978 and 1980, each with an estimated life of six years. To extend full FLTSATCOM-AFSATCOM service until about 1992, the Defense Department plans to launch three additional FLTSATCOM satellites beginning in 1985. Additional redundancy in AFSATCOM will be acquired through the deployment of piggyback transponders on DSCS-III satellites, four of which will be operational by 1986. The so-called single channel transponders will permit only one-way communications to the forces but will feature better jam resistance than FLTSATCOM-AFSATCOM devices.[50] Because these programs basically serve to sustain existing communications, however, they do not offer substantial improvements in capabilities for disseminating attack orders.

MILSTAR. This system has been described as representing a new era in military satellite communications. As the centerpiece of the Reagan administration's plans for C^3I modernization, it is intended to reduce current dependence on vulnerable military and leased commercial communi-

---

50. *Department of Defense Appropriations for 1983,* House hearings, pt. 5, pp. 11, 59, 71, 154.

cations for SIOP execution, emergency action messages, warning information, and other strategic communications. The MILSTAR constellation will consist of eight satellites; three operational satellites and one spare will be placed in geosynchronous orbit, and four satellites will be placed in circular polar orbits. Coverage will extend to all areas of the earth except for the south polar region, with laser cross-links for satellite-to-satellite relay, eliminating vulnerable intermediate ground stations.[51] MILSTAR's EHF signal bandwidth will be highly resistant to nuclear effects and jamming and will permit use of short receiving antennas, thus enabling a variety of mobile users to be serviced. EHF will also permit transmissions to be focused along a narrow beam, which decreases the possibility of interception and increases covertness.[52]

The projected date of the first launch of a MILSTAR satellite is reported to be 1987 or 1988, and the constellation is scheduled to replace the AFSATCOM system on host FLTSATCOM and SDS satellites by the early 1990s.[53] MILSTAR purportedly will be immune to Soviet jamming and, because of its maneuverability, to antisatellite threats through the end of this century.[54]

But such assurances are surely difficult to offer without strong qualification. Arms competition in space appears to be intensifying. There are already semiofficial projections that the Soviet Union will develop weapons to attack satellites in geosynchronous orbit. According to one report, Soviet development of a large booster will threaten such satellites before the end of this decade.[55] In the absence of effective arms control, the Soviet Union might also field direct-ascent nuclear missiles, space mines, or space-based antisatellite lasers or neutral-particle-beam weapons. A qualitative improvement in Soviet antisatellite capability might emerge during the 1990s when the United States becomes heavily dependent on MILSTAR for strategic communications. MILSTAR's defenses against laser or particle-beam weapons could not be very formidable; instead, its

51. *Department of Defense Authorization for Appropriations for Fiscal Year 1983,* Senate hearings, pt. 7, pp. 4618, 4619, 4712.

52. *Department of Defense Appropriations for 1983,* House hearings, pt. 5, pp. 64, 68–69.

53. Deborah G. Meyer, "Strategic Satellites: Our Eyes in the Sky—Can They Save the World from Armageddon," *Armed Forces Journal International* (February 1983), p. 38; and *Department of Defense Appropriations for 1983,* House hearings, pt. 5, p. 70.

54. *Department of Defense Authorization for Appropriations for Fiscal Year 1983,* Senate hearings, pt. 7, pp. 4619 and 4712.

55. "Soviet Threat in Space Said to Be on Rise," *Aviation Week and Space Technology* (May 16, 1983), p. 47.

design appears to reflect a concern with lesser threats such as direct-ascent nuclear missiles and follow-on orbital interceptors launched by large boosters.

LF/VLF RECEIVERS FOR BOMBERS. After bombers leave the continental United States, they are beyond line-of-sight UHF communications from PACCS aircraft, and dissemination of attack orders to them by other means is unreliable. The Defense Department plans to strengthen communications by equipping bombers with LF/VLF terminals, designed for long distance reception of signals transmitted by EC-135 and E-4 airborne command posts. Effective communications over a range of 2,000 to 3,000 miles are predicted, a significant improvement over existing capabilities. Related improvements in LF/VLF airborne systems include a program to extend the reception range of EC-135 and E-4 aircraft by 1,000 to 2,000 miles and a program to increase the transmitting power of EC-135 aircraft and thereby extend the range by 1,000 miles.[56]

TACAMO ECX. The inventory of TACAMO EC-130 aircraft grew to eighteen in fiscal year 1983, and the Pacific TACAMO fleet is being transferred to a West Coast base.[57] With eighteen aircraft available, it should be possible to maintain continuous airborne coverage over both the Atlantic and Pacific submarine fleet operations areas.[58] Relocation to California reduces the distance between TACAMO and command aircraft and eases the communications problem.

A variety of deficiencies nevertheless plague the TACAMO fleet. The EC-130 aircraft lack adequate protection from EMP, their communications equipment needs to be modernized, and they are 10,000 pounds overweight, causing airframe stress and limiting endurance (they cannot be refueled while airborne).[59] Nine aircraft are on the verge of retirement, and an estimated fleet of twenty-nine is needed to fulfill mission requirements, according to the navy.[60] (Continuous airborne alert in both ocean

---

56. *Department of Defense Appropriations for 1980*, Hearings before a Subcommittee of the House Committee on Appropriations, 96 Cong. 1 sess. (GPO, 1979), pt. 2, p. 554; and *Department of Defense Authorization for Appropriations for Fiscal Year 1982*, Senate hearings, pt. 7, p. 4230.

57. *Department of Defense Authorization for Appropriations for Fiscal Year 1982*, Senate hearings, pt. 7, p. 4049; and *Department of Defense Appropriations for 1981*, House hearings, pt. 7, p. 403.

58. *Department of Defense Authorization for Appropriations for Fiscal Year 1981*, Senate hearings, pt. 6, p. 3458.

59. *Department of Defense Authorization for Appropriations for Fiscal Year 1982*, Senate hearings, pt. 7, p. 4048.

60. *Department of Defense Authorization for Appropriations for Fiscal Year 1983*, Senate hearings, pt. 7, pp. 4697, 4706-07.

areas, which requires eighteen EC-130s, is evidently only one of many mission requirements.)

The TACAMO ECX program addresses all of these deficiencies except for modernizing the communications equipment. The ECX has a Boeing 707 airframe like the one used in the E-3A Airborne Warning and Control System (AWACS). The Defense Department says it will eventually acquire fifteen such aircraft, with the first operational by 1987, the time that nine existing EC-130 aircraft must be retired.[61] The ECX will be EMP-hardened and employ fan-jet engines that provide twice the airspeed of the EC-130 aircraft. Aircraft endurance with refueling could be as long as several days, and maximum endurance without refueling could exceed fourteen hours.[62] Because of the lead time involved in ECX procurement and the imminent block obsolescence of existing aircraft, however, the navy has been forced to place orders for nine new EC-130s. They will be purchased by fiscal year 1985 at a total cost of $825 million; like the ECX, they will be hardened against EMP.[63]

A major unresolved problem with respect to future TACAMO performance concerns their aging, unreliable communications equipment. Present plans call for transferring the equipment and trailing wire antennas from worn-out EC-130s to the new EC-130 and ECX aircraft—because of budget constraints, ECX communications are not slated for replacement or modernization despite problems with reliability.[64]

The future of TACAMO also hinges on the procurement of replacement aircraft. Citing budgetary constraints, the navy decided against buying the first ECX in fiscal year 1985 as originally planned, a postponement that again raises doubts about the true priority of strategic C³I modernization and its ability to withstand budgetary pressures from the services. The program management and acquisition process described in chapter 3 continues to impede TACAMO modernization.

EXTREMELY LOW FREQUENCY COMMUNICATIONS. The planned ELF communications system is an austere version of the original Seafarer pro-

61. Ibid., pp. 4706–07, 4722; and Clarence A. Robinson, Jr., "Technology Key to Strategic Advances," *Aviation Week and Space Technology* (March 14, 1983), p. 29.

62. *Department of Defense Authorization for Appropriations for Fiscal Year 1982*, Senate hearings, pt. 7, pp. 4049–50; and *Aerospace Daily*, June 9, 1982, p. 210.

63. *Department of Defense Authorization for Appropriations for Fiscal Year 1982*, Senate hearings, pt. 7, p. 4207; and *Department of Defense Authorization for Appropriations for Fiscal Year 1983*, Senate hearings, pt. 7, pp. 4718–19.

64. *Department of Defense Appropriations for 1983*, House hearings, pt. 5, p. 6; *Department of Defense Authorization for Appropriations for Fiscal Year 1983*, Senate hearings, pp. 4694–95; and *Department of Defense Appropriations for 1984*, House hearings, pt. 8, p. 365.

Figure 8-4. *Coverage for Communications with Submarines*

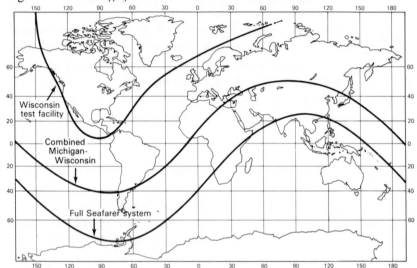

posal (see chapter 6). It will consist of a two-site system operated synchronously. The Wisconsin site already exists, and its transmitter and twenty-eight miles of antenna will be upgraded and EMP-hardened by 1985. At the same time, a transmitter and fifty-six miles of antenna will be installed in Michigan. Full operational capability is expected by 1987.[65]

Using the Wisconsin facility, the navy has conducted numerous successful tests of the basic concept; some U.S. SSBNs have been routinely patrolling with prototype ELF receivers for several years.[66] The range of ELF communications from the Wisconsin Test Facility is shown in figure 8-4, along with the coverage that could be expected for a hypothetical two-site system and for a full Seafarer system. (The two-site coverage shown assumes 130 miles of antenna in Michigan and thus somewhat exceeds the coverage of the planned two-site system. The full Seafarer system would have used 2,400 miles of antenna.)

The dissemination of SIOP attack orders is not the ELF system's primary purpose, which is to eliminate the possibility of intermittent Soviet

65. *Department of Defense Appropriations for 1983,* House hearings, pt. 5, p. 14; and Robinson, "Technology Key to Strategic Advances," p. 29.

66. *Department of Defense Authorization for Appropriations for Fiscal Year 1983,* Senate hearings, pt. 7, p. 4724; and *Hearings on Military Posture and H.R. 10929* before the House Committee on Armed Services, 95 Cong. 2 sess. (GPO, 1978), pt. 3, bk. 2, pp. 1314, 1323.

detection of conventional submarine antennas that could help narrow uncertainty about the location of SSBNs and thereby jeopardize their survival. Conventional antennas have numerous problems. At periscope depth, an antenna sticking above the surface will leave a trail if the submarine operates at any significant speed. A submarine at greater depth can deploy a trailing wire antenna about 2,000 feet long, but 200 feet of it must float on the surface for proper reception. One salty admiral testified that "I have looked through my periscope on the USS Will Rogers and have been horrified to find there are birds roosting on the doggoned wire back here. . . ."[67] A submarine can also use a buoyed antenna that floats fifteen to twenty feet below the surface, but if the submarine operates at significant speed or changes course, the buoy sinks and reception is lost. The towed buoy also has low reliability.[68]

With ELF receivers, however, SSBNs could patrol at a depth of 300 to 400 feet and could travel at speeds up to twenty knots without impairing reception. Still, the role of ELF will be extremely limited. First, it will be a peacetime system that will not withstand a major attack. Second, the rate that data can be transmitted is very low; the transmission of retaliatory instructions over ELF is technically possible, but it would take hours and therefore is not practical.[69]

ELF could send three-letter messages, perhaps simple coded references to more elaborate instructions stored in the submarine.[70] For instance, it could be used to deliver a short alerting message directing the submarine to change its communications posture so that it could continuously monitor TACAMO and other SIOP frequencies. Upon receipt of this instruction, the submarine would slow down, reduce its depth, and deploy a conventional antenna to receive emergency messages from TACAMO or other sources.

In the case of alert submarines, however, this capability is not exactly a virtue. Current arrangements, in fact, allow for more timely dissemination because alert submarines monitor TACAMO and other SIOP fre-

---

67. *Department of Defense Appropriations for 1980*, Hearings before a Subcommittee of the House Committee on Appropriations, 96 Cong. 1 sess. (GPO, 1979), pt. 6, p. 137.

68. For descriptions of antenna characteristics, see *Department of Defense Authorization for Appropriations for Fiscal Year 1982*, Senate hearings, pt. 7, pp. 4095–96, 4107.

69. *Hearings on Military Posture and H.R. 10929*, House, pt. 3, bk. 2, p. 1860; and *Department of Defense Authorization for Appropriations for Fiscal Year 1979*, Hearings before the Senate Committee on Armed Services, 95 Cong. 2 sess. (GPO, 1978), pt. 9, p. 6794.

70. *Hearings on Military Posture and H.R. 10929*, House, pt. 3, bk. 2, p. 1323.

quencies on a continuous basis. In the case of modified-alert or nonalert submarines, however, the virtue of ELF is clear: it could be used to order them immediately to assume continuous monitoring, instructions that cannot today be delivered so quickly. Attack submarines that now monitor communications as infrequently as once every twelve hours could also be notified. Such a capability will be valuable as attack submarines become armed with nuclear-tipped Tomahawk cruise missiles capable of hitting Soviet territory. Even if ELF were destroyed before any alerting message could be sent, the loss of the signal would implicitly send an alerting message: "The ELF system transmits at all times. . . . If, however, ELF were destroyed in a surprise attack, the loss of the ELF signal by the submarine would in effect tell the submarine to come to a shallower depth and copy other broadcasts; for example, the survivable TACAMO."[71] In the case of alert submarines, this feature of ELF again makes a virtue out of a liability, for it is the system itself that frees the submarine from having to monitor TACAMO broadcasts on a continuous basis. For modified-alert and other submarines that listen only periodically for message broadcasts, implicit ELF warning allows for unscheduled communications and thus improves upon existing capabilities.

Protracted War

Although the Reagan administration has stressed the need for strategic systems capable of operating for a long time in a nuclear environment, research and development efforts to attain the desired capability have been far less vigorous than the administration's rhetoric. The effort is, however, intensifying, with major programs being pursued in warning and attack assessment, command and decision, and strategic communications.

WARNING AND ATTACK ASSESSMENT. All missile-warning radar sensors are now fixed, and as such are subject to destruction within a few minutes after the launch of a missile attack. If the Soviet Union also targeted the fixed readout stations for early warning satellites, the existing warning network would be rapidly neutralized.

The mobile ground terminal readout stations for early warning satellites that are planned for deployment in the next few years probably could survive an initial attack. They might be able to operate for several

71. *Department of Defense Authorization for Appropriations for Fiscal Year 1982,* Senate hearings, pt. 7, pp. 4054–55.

days or longer, thus allowing tactical warning of follow-up Soviet missile attacks against withheld U.S. strategic forces. The Advanced Missile Warning System, however, appears to be the preferred long-term solution to the problem of enduring warning. Designed to ensure continued operation during a nuclear conflict, the system could eliminate all intermediate processing and relay nodes by incorporating on-board data processing so that warning messages could be transmitted directly to users. A decision on whether to undertake full-scale development of the system is expected in fiscal year 1987, with initial deployment possible in the 1990s.[72]

IONDS could also provide enduring attack assessment. It is being designed to furnish commanders with detailed information on above-ground nuclear detonations as they occur, information considered important for determining residual U.S. strategic capabilities and in targeting those forces for maximum retaliatory effect.[73] Such knowledge could also aid commanders in identifying areas that have escaped destruction so that they could direct bombers, tankers, and command post aircraft to them. Knowledge of detonations in enemy territory could aid in assessing enemy residual capabilities following the initial U.S. attack and in identifying targets to be covered in a second U.S. strike. Because IONDS sensors will be dispersed aboard eighteen satellites, the whole system is not expected to be destroyed by Soviet antisatellite attack.[74] Furthermore, the host satellites that will carry the devices are being designed to function autonomously for weeks so that the constellation could endure despite the loss of ground command-control-telemetry stations, some of whose functions may eventually be performed by mobile ground units.[75] The utility of IONDS remains doubtful, however, because of the susceptibility of its transmissions to nuclear scintillation and the potential vulnerability of the satellites themselves to advanced Soviet weapons.

Plans to reconstitute NORAD have also been drawn, especially the formation of a Rapid Emergency Reconstitution Team (RAPIER).[76]

72. *Department of Defense Annual Report for Fiscal Year 1984*, p. 230.

73. *Department of Defense Authorization for Appropriations for Fiscal Year 1983*, Senate hearings, pt. 7, p. 4645.

74. Congressional Budget Office, *Strategic Command, Control, and Communications*, p. 24.

75. *Department of Defense Authorization for Appropriations for Fiscal Year 1983*, Senate hearings, pt. 7, pp. 4692–93, 4700.

76. Ibid., p. 4700.

COMMAND AND DECISION. Existing strategic command posts lack appreciable endurance. No fixed command center stands much chance of weathering any deliberate attack by ICBMs, which could be delivered in a mere thirty minutes. Airborne command posts would be expected to remain in operation for much longer, but their initial airborne endurance could be as short as several hours, depending on the availability of tankers for in-flight refueling. Successful recovery and relaunch would then depend on the availability of usable runways, fuel stocks and maintenance, crew health, and exposure to follow-up enemy attacks. The utility of aircraft communication while grounded would be limited by the availability of external electrical power; radio range would be shorter and certain radio systems, for example LF/VLF radios with trailing antennas, could not be employed. The role of command aircraft in postattack battle management is further limited by their inability to store and process large amounts of data; force reconstitution and other management functions are presently performed by ground facilities such as SAC headquarters and the National Military Command Center.[77]

Two possible solutions to the general problem of command endurance have been given serious consideration. One still under study entails developing more versatile aircraft to replace the present fleet of EC-135s and E-4s. The replacement aircraft would be designed to permit operations from smaller airfields: current operations allow about 700 airfields to be used; 1,200 would be available if both long and short runways could be used. The new aircraft would also burn less fuel and require less maintenance.[78] A complementary system to aid these aircraft (or existing aircraft, for that matter) in identifying operating airfields following a nuclear attack has also been proposed. Locators would consist of radio beacon devices at an airfield that command aircraft could interrogate to determine its status (absence of a beacon signal would imply airfield destruction). This program has not been funded.[79] Neither have replacement aircraft.

77. *Department of Defense Appropriations for 1980,* Hearings before the House Committee on Appropriations, 96 Cong. 1 sess. (GPO, 1979), pt. 6, p. 192.
78. *Department of Defense Authorization for Appropriations for Fiscal Year 1983,* Senate hearings, pt. 7, p. 4683; and *Department of Defense Authorization for Appropriations for Fiscal Year 1982,* Senate hearings, pt. 7, p. 4013.
79. *Department of Defense Authorization for Appropriations for Fiscal Year 1982,* Senate Committee on Armed Services, 97 Cong. 1 sess. (GPO, 1981), Report 97-58, p. 108; and *Department of Defense Authorization for Appropriations for Fiscal Year 1983,* Senate hearings, pt. 7, pp. 4689-90.

The Defense Department favors an alternative approach that would field austere command centers in mobile vans. As described by the Congressional Budget Office, some vans would operate on a continuous basis; the rest could be mobilized in a crisis. Similar to truck-mounted mobile ground terminals for early warning satellites, the command vans would be deployed in areas away from major targets. Movement within operational areas would be random, covert, and frequent in order to avoid Soviet detection and attack. With prestored caches of fuel, food, and critical spare parts hidden in these areas, command vans might be able to operate indefinitely in a nuclear environment.[80]

Such mobile command centers could support the national command authority, the Joint Chiefs of Staff, and subordinate commands as a fourth element of the National Military Command System, which presently consists of two fixed facilities—the primary and alternate command centers at the Pentagon and Fort Ritchie—and the mobile National Emergency Airborne Command Post. The Defense Department considers this mix of elements as complementary, providing a strategic command system "capable of spanning the full spectrum of modern warfare, from crisis operations through execution of an initial nuclear exchange and conduct of a prolonged nuclear war to conflict termination."[81] Fixed centers would manage peacetime and crisis operations. Command aircraft would manage strategic operations during the initial stages of nuclear conflict. Mobile command centers would assume control over protracted engagements. In the words of Donald Latham, "the airborne command posts will endure long enough to ensure continuity of command through the transition from the initial phase to the follow-up phases, and then the covertly deployed MCCs could take over. . . ."[82]

A prototype ground mobile command center has been developed.[83] As presently planned, each unit will consist of two semitrailers, but this is only one of many possible truck-mounted options, and nonvehicular possibilities are also being considered. Deployment on ships has been proposed, as has a modular center that could be loaded on transport aircraft,

80. *Strategic Command, Control, and Communications*, p. 34.

81. *Department of Defense Authorization for Appropriations for Fiscal Year 1983*, Senate hearings, pt. 7, p. 4715.

82. Ibid., p. 4680.

83. Congressional Budget Office, *Strategic Command, Control, and Communications*, p. 34.

permitting airborne as well as ground operations.[84] The timetable report-edly calls for mobile command centers to be in full operation by the late 1980s; phased elements will come on line in 1985, 1987, and 1989 as part of an "evolutionary development toward modular command center capa-bility."[85]

The potential for mobile command centers to provide for command endurance in a nuclear environment is very difficult to gauge, given that physical configurations and concepts of operation are still being devel-oped. There are more questions than answers at this point. Would a strictly ground mobile version be susceptible to detection and direct at-tack? Would it be exposed to a lethal level of fallout? Could the Soviet Union identify which ships carried MCCs and successfully attack them at sea? Could transport aircraft safely launch and later find a usable runway to unload the MCCs?

STRATEGIC COMMUNICATIONS. Using existing systems, strategic com-munications would be marginal at best after C^3 aircraft were forced to land. Grounded aircraft, surviving ships at sea, and residual space-based assets might be able to support some limited communications once the atmosphere heals sufficiently to allow HF and satellite UHF radio trans-missions. High-confidence communications, however, would be nonexis-tent. Present systems were not designed to endure for weeks or months in a nuclear environment.

The Defense Department predicts that MILSTAR will dramatically improve U.S. capabilities for postattack strategic communications; it is the centerpiece of current aspirations for communications endurance. Apart from features noted earlier, MILSTAR's potential to support the management of strategic forces during multiple exchanges stems from its capacity to function autonomously. The department asserts that MILSTAR will not need to be constantly linked to major ground tracking stations for command-control-telemetry. It is being designed to operate for weeks without ground involvement and to accept command-control-telemetry data from multiple portable terminals, which might be able to

84. *Department of Defense Appropriations for Fiscal Year 1983,* House hearings, pt. 5, pp. 46–47; and Congressional Budget Office, *Strategic Command, Control, and Communica-tions,* p. 34.

85. Robinson, "Technology Key to Strategic Advances," p. 27. See also Philip Taub-man, "U.S. Command Seeks Mobility to Elude Attack," *New York Times,* February 25, 1983.

provide the essential telemetry, tracking, and mission data needed to keep it in operation.[86] DSCS-III was also designed to function for long periods without ground assistance for on-board systems maintenance.[87]

The role of MILSTAR in a protracted strategic campaign would be further enhanced by its ability to transmit EHF signals with a low probability of interception, which translates into covertness and hence greater survivability for mobile users.[88] A low probability of interception would also help prevent the Soviet Union from locating bombers and submarines that break communications silence. One of the touted advantages of MILSTAR is that strategic missile submarines will be able to use its communications for replies.[89] Covert, two-way communications are considered essential for battle management, force retargeting, and related postattack operations. It is especially important for control of the strategic reserves that today consist of submarines and that in the future probably will be largely constituted of Trident SSBNs.[90]

To avoid complete dependence on MILSTAR for enduring communications, the Defense Department is also exploring possibilities for postattack reconstitution of communications. The idea is to rebuild communications as needed in the event that MILSTAR, which would be operational at the start of hostilities, failed to survive during a protracted conflict. The investment in reserve communications, however, is negligible. The fiscal year 1980 budget requested a total of $21 million for reconstitution initiatives in communications, surveillance and warning, and command-control combined.[91] This request covered, for example, the cost of testing the ground mobile command center prototype. As of 1980, many ideas had been proposed but not seriously acted upon, and the Defense Department conceded that "there is insufficient technical data available to assess performance or cost risk of these potential alternatives." It did not envision any operational deployments before the early 1990s.[92]

86. See *Department of Defense Authorization for Appropriations for Fiscal Year 1983*, Senate hearings, pt. 7, p. 4692; and "Spacecraft Survivability Boost Sought," p. 261.

87. Robinson, "Technology Key to Strategic Advances."

88. *Department of Defense Appropriations for 1983*, House hearings, pt. 5, pp. 68–69.

89. *Department of Defense Authorization for Appropriations for Fiscal Year 1982*, Senate hearings, pt. 7, p. 4095.

90. *Department of Defense Appropriations for 1984*, House hearings, pt. 8, pp. 274, 365.

91. *Department of Defense Authorization for Appropriations for Fiscal Year 1981*, Senate hearings, pt. 6, p. 3422.

92. Ibid., p. 3406.

In 1982, reconstructable communications concepts were still under study, and fiscal year 1983 funding requests for concept development totaled $2.4 million.[93] Options considered in recent years include the following:

—Postattack launch of communications satellites, which would require survivable launch facilities. Submarines were among the candidate systems, but because of budgetary considerations, the Defense Department is not pursuing any program of satellite reconstitution.[94]

—An ELF grid transportable by mobile van has been proposed as a reconstructable means of submarine communications.[95]

—Land-mobile vans could be equipped to transmit VLF radio signals using a tethered balloon or an erectable tower as antennas.[96]

—High-altitude balloons with trailing wire antennas could be launched, perhaps with the assistance of rockets, from aircraft, surface ships, submarines (via torpedo tubes), or land mobile units. Once deployed, their utility and endurance would be determined by wind drift and on-board battery power (approximately two to seven days).[97]

—Reconstructable communications based on "adaptive HF" and "meteor burst" technologies could be versatile enough to support operations during as well as after attack.[98] They would lend themselves to a variety of purposes besides reconstitution. "Adaptive HF" refers to long-range HF radio communication using one of two general techniques to avoid signal blackout caused by nuclear-disturbed ionosphere. One technique tests different HF frequencies, selects the best from those sampled, and adjusts transmitter power to attain proper signal-to-noise ratio. The alternative technique simply repeats messages across the frequency band. Rapid repetition in different frequencies would eventually allow receivers to piece

93. *Department of Defense Authorization for Appropriations for Fiscal Year 1983*, Senate hearings, pt. 7, pp. 4646, 4690.

94. *Department of Defense Authorization for Appropriations for Fiscal Year 1981*, Senate hearings, pt. 6, p. 3422; and *Department of Defense Appropriations for 1984*, House hearings, pt. 8, p. 505.

95. *Department of Defense Authorization for Appropriations for Fiscal Year 1982*, Senate hearings, pt. 7, p. 4098; and *Department of Defense Authorization for Appropriations for Fiscal Year 1983*, Senate hearings, pt. 7, p. 4729.

96. *Department of Defense Authorization for Appropriations for Fiscal Year 1983*, Senate hearings, pt. 7, p. 4729.

97. Ibid.

98. *Department of Defense Authorization for Appropriations for Fiscal Year 1982*, Senate Report 97-58, p. 108.

together the message. "Meteor burst" refers to long-range (600–1,200 miles) VHF radio communications using the microscopic ionized trails of meteoroids in the upper atmosphere to reflect signals between users. Such trails occur at altitudes of roughly 60 miles. They last only a fraction of a second but appear very frequently (approximately every second). During their brief appearance, useful burst transmissions could be sent between small, widely spread units such as mobile command centers and surfaced submarines. The data rate would be low and the message probably would have to be repeated several times (the rapid degeneration of trails could prevent a given message from getting through), but the technology has been proved. In fact, several systems are already in operation. The Department of Agriculture routinely uses such communications to collect data from 500 remote stations located in 11 western states.

Among these concepts the most developed and the strongest candidates for actual deployment are, in order of readiness, free-floating VLF balloons, adaptive HF radio, and meteor burst communications.

Summary

Current plans for modernizing C³I are ambitious and wide-ranging, but numerous problem areas compete for attention and resources. One concerns the initial few minutes of enemy attack. Improvements are being made so that emergency orders can be formulated and disseminated before the impact of Soviet missile warheads. The improvement plan is funded and technically defined, but it is not comprehensive and slides past the issue of whether a responsible, considered decision is humanly and organizationally possible when there are only a few minutes to decide.

Another area receiving attention concerns command performance during the first several hours of enemy attack. Improvements are being made to the backup airborne network, which might be called upon to assume responsibility for initial SIOP decisionmaking and dissemination. These improvements are only partially funded, because many extend over a period of ten years. Most seem likely to be financed, however, because it is widely accepted that a viable airborne system capable of performing SIOP execution functions is an essential hedge against a decapitating attack on the ground network. The improvements are fairly well defined in technical terms, but they are neither comprehensive nor uniformly promising. Modernizing TACAMO communications equipment, for example, is not planned at all, and thorough overhaul of the airborne command network has not been undertaken.

The weeks and months following an initial strategic exchange also present problems. Planners have been instructed to develop an enduring command system for managing strategic forces through subsequent exchanges of indefinite duration. With some notable exceptions—for example, IONDS—this pursuit is neither technically defined nor financially authorized. Cases in point are mobile command centers and MILSTAR, the costly core elements of the system envisaged. The $3 billion MCC program is undefined in technical and operational respects, while the more developed $10 billion MILSTAR system may require redesign to cope with future antisatellite weapons and faces an uphill battle for financial support. Both programs are being promoted for their potential contribution to the management of a protracted nuclear campaign, a justification of dubious merit to many observers who wield authority over the defense budget. And they would have to be augmented by C³I, logistics, and other programs costing tens of billions of dollars in order to establish a credible technical capacity for protracted nuclear war.

CHAPTER NINE

Summary and Recommendations

STRATEGIC analysis has long suffered from a methodological affliction known as the law of the instrument, which states that problems must be tailored to the tools at one's disposal. Because available tools are generally honed for problems that can be readily quantified, rigorous assessment has steadily advanced, but in narrowly circumscribed areas of interest: the size, technical composition, and economics of nuclear weapons. Progress toward assessing the central question—command system performance—has not been commensurate. Standard calculations, in fact, have obscured the problem of force management, a subject that generally defies meaningful quantification.

Nor does the theory of rational decisionmaking throw adequate light on the subject. Nuclear organizations do not behave like the highly abstract models of rational decision commonly used to explain and prescribe nuclear operations. The organizations instead operate according to built-in decision rules that link information to preprogrammed responses. These diffuse rules serve two basic purposes: to prevent unauthorized launch of nuclear forces and to ensure that fully authorized launches will be carried out.

Such effective negative and positive control requires appropriate rules and adequate information, but neither requirement is easily met. The appropriateness of rules is especially uncertain because they are untested. No amount of rehearsal and exercise can eliminate this uncertainty, which would manifest itself in unintended consequences if modern nuclear organizations attempted to institute crisis alert or wartime procedures. In the absence of experience and learning, the diffuse rules governing emergency operations are bound to produce untoward surprises.

The adequacy of information is uncertain because it flows through complex networks that evolved piecemeal and remain subject to severe damage from attack. The current vulnerability of these networks creates a particularly knotty problem because it brings positive and negative control into sharp conflict. Negative control cannot be tightened to a point where all activities of nuclear units require the direct personal approval of the president. Not only would that degree of centralization be immobilizing, but it would also invite a carefully planned attack against the national command authority that could neutralize the entire U.S. arsenal. Yet the decentralized arrangements necessary to reduce the risk of such decapitation and ensure positive control also heighten the risk of accidental or unauthorized use of nuclear weapons. Neither centralization nor decentralization can eliminate the potential for discontinuity between national objectives and force operations.

The inherent tension that exists between the two control priorities has created a situation in which they are neither equal nor static. In peacetime, negative control is predominant. In wartime, positive control takes precedence. Somewhere in between these circumstances a transition occurs. The transition may or may not be centrally directed, orderly, or complete.

This simple construction offers a basis for historical perspective on three important questions with major C³I dimensions: the strategic balance, crisis stability, and negative control.

The Strategic Situation from the Mid-1960s to the Present

Since the mid-1960s the Soviet Union has possessed the military strength needed to disrupt the process by which the United States would organize strategic forces for coordinated attack. Before coordinated retaliation could be accomplished, the vehicle for its implementation—the C³I network—could be severely impaired by a relatively limited attack. A Soviet first strike could disrupt positive control on a massive scale by blocking the flow of information that would alert U.S. nuclear units to an impending attack, initiate SIOP decisionmaking, and trigger retaliation by the dispersed forces. Such an attack could isolate almost all U.S. forces and sharply reduce coordination among those remaining.

Transition to effective positive control has been especially vulnerable to a surprise attack. The predominance of negative control in peacetime means that C³I readiness is relatively low; the network could not simply ride out the attack. To mitigate this high vulnerability, nuclear organizations are primed to shift rapidly to a state of high positive control once an attack is detected. But accomplishing this aim before enemy missiles strike is extremely difficult when negative control is predominant at the start of the attack. Initial organizational reactions, though largely decentralized and automated, are unlikely to be as rapid and coherent as the situation demands. In all likelihood the brunt of an attack would be felt before measures protecting C³I (for instance, the launch of command aircraft) could be implemented. And it is virtually certain that thousands of megatons of explosive power would be delivered before authorization to retaliate could be passed to the forces.

The risk that attack could block retaliation would be lower under crisis conditions because the transition to positive control could begin much earlier, and a high state of C³I readiness could be reached before the opponent attacked. Nevertheless, even the theoretical optimum performance of past and present C³I networks has not been sufficient to ensure positive control. Deficiencies in communications that have plagued the airborne network have by themselves greatly undermined U.S. capabilities for retaliation. A Soviet first strike on an alert U.S. command system could still isolate most forces and severely reduce the effectiveness of the rest.

Cautious Soviet planners probably credit the U.S. command system with greater resilience than this book does. They could hardly fail, however, to appreciate that their only chance to block retaliation would be to paralyze U.S. C³I. And even if it did not succeed, such an attack could still serve to blunt retaliation. Compared to a strategy designed to knock out Minuteman missiles, bombers, or submarines, strikes against C³I would better serve to limit damage to the Soviet Union that U.S. forces could inflict in retaliation. This has been the situation throughout the missile age.

Soviet planners must be wary of the standard calculations that weigh the strategic balance by pitting Soviet weapons against U.S. weapons in formal statistical models of combat. Such calculations are simplistic. They not only mask the operational difficulties and risks involved in attacking U.S. forces but also overstate the potential to produce exploitable bargaining dominance from counterforce attacks. Today, as in the past, a

Soviet attack against U.S. forces would be practically indistinguishable from an all-out assault and would inflict such heavy collateral damage to the U.S. command system that American reaction would surely focus on a one-time plan of retaliation. Instead of producing bargaining leverage that would coerce concessions and restraint, a counterforce attack would create almost irresistible pressure on the U.S. command system to commit all its forces before greater C³I disruption could take place. At the same time, Soviet planners, anticipating a spasmodic U.S. response to the attack, could hardly fail to realize that it would be advantageous to fracture the U.S. command system at the outset.

The general historical implication is that the overall strategic balance has been relatively unaffected by changes in the size and technical composition of the U.S. and Soviet nuclear arsenals. The state of C³I has been the primary determinant of overall strategic capabilities, and thus the United States (and doubtless the Soviet Union) has lived with enormous vulnerability for a long time. Exposure to potentially incapacitating attack against command facilities has been the salient feature and central problem of the strategic situation for nearly two decades. Major developments in the areas of perceived importance—size and technical composition of strategic force deployments—have not had nearly as much effect on the strategic balance as many have believed or alleged.

Two decades of development in force deployment have had as little effect on crisis stability as on strategic balance. Although both standard indicators and command structure analysis agree that the parameters of stability have been relatively constant, they disagree on the amount of stability that has existed.

According to standard indicators, nuclear modernization has created some problems of deterrence—notably a counterforce asymmetry stemming from unequal ICBM vulnerability—but has not created any strong incentives to strike first in a crisis. The number and characteristics of survivable weapons in the respective inventories since the mid-1960s have firmly established that a nuclear first strike risks a devastating counterattack. Crisis stability has been high because neither side could confidently remove the opponent's threat of retaliation by means of first strike against his forces.

According to command analysis, however, while strategic modernization has not created any new incentives to strike first, strong incentives have existed all along. The Soviet Union has long possessed the capability to destroy the U.S. command system, and Soviet command vulnerability probably has been comparable. Inherent in such mutual vulnerability is an appreciable degree of latent instability. Command deficiencies weaken crisis stability because of the heavy penalty incurred by the side struck first and the tremendous advantage gained by the side that initiates attack. Fortunately, an occasion for this instability to surface has not arisen, but the fact remains that it has existed as a potential combustible in a crisis.

That the programmed emergency operations of nuclear organizations are geared for launch on warning is symptomatic of this instability. Mutual command vulnerability creates strong incentives to initiate nuclear strikes before the opponent's threat to C^3I could be carried out. Launch-on-warning tactics are nonetheless very difficult to implement given the short flight times of the attacker's missiles. For this reason, both sides would come under increasing pressure to mount a preemptive attack in a crisis of increasing gravity.

These instabilities are again not new. The U.S. posture at least was geared to launch on warning long before the problem of Minuteman vulnerability drew attention to it. Command vulnerability has virtually dictated a philosophy of early use, and it is this broad instability rather than the narrow one resulting from Minuteman vulnerability that should be underscored in historical assessments of crisis stability. Even though political leaders possibly have not recognized the hair-trigger posture of our nuclear control system, military planners have long appreciated the need for this posture and have devised operations plans accordingly.

Policy advisers aware of this broader instability would hesitate to recommend raising the alert level of strategic forces merely to send diplomatic signals to the adversary. To flex military muscle as part of crisis diplomacy is to transform a latent instability into a salient one. This muscle has an Achilles heel—command vulnerability—that could assume prominence in a confrontation even though increases in nuclear alert levels would lend some protection against decapitation.

We must also be sensitive to the great potential for mobilized, agitated strategic organizations to cause unintended consequences during a crisis. All too frequently, policy officials evidence an exaggerated sense of control over organizations that are inherently decentralized. To flex military muscle as part of crisis diplomacy is to trigger organizational responses that national policy officials cannot fully grasp or manage.

Despite the chronic weaknesses that have plagued the U.S. system of positive control, negative control has gradually been tightened over the past twenty years. The physical capacity to fire nuclear weapons has been further centralized, and signs point to further centralization of nuclear release authority. Additional safeguards designed to reduce the risk of accidental war have also been introduced, at the significant expense of positive control.

Although firm conclusions are not warranted given the paucity of public information, the high priority assigned to negative control would seem to warrant high confidence in peacetime safeguards against accidental or unauthorized use of nuclear weapons. But in circumstances of crisis or war, these safeguards would be harder to maintain as military organizations become more active and decentralized and have more frequent and intense encounters with opposing forces. In the event of a Soviet nuclear attack, the demands of positive control would further weaken negative control. A logical solution to these demands would be to permit military commanders to exercise release authority under some circumstances, especially verified nuclear attacks on U.S. territory coupled with a loss of communications with national authorities. Such delegation necessarily compromises negative control, however, and it carries troublesome political implications. Unambiguous delegation of nuclear authority has the potential for eroding the effective power of the president or a successor who might wish to retain release authority. Ambiguous devolution of authority might facilitate the national command authority's effort to maintain or reassert control, but it too raises questions about the integrity of safeguards.

One of the most severe tests of negative control would be a situation in which enemy attacks isolate subordinate units from the president or his successors and communications could not be expeditiously restored. But in a real sense the command system is primed to avoid this test. The weaknesses in positive control that risk such isolation create strong pressures to issue authoritative instructions while the command system is still intact. A potentially severe strain on negative control is thus ameliorated by virtue of a bias to transmit nuclear release orders at the earliest possible moment. In other words, command deficiencies, insofar as political authorities recognize them, work to force an early decision that makes unauthorized retaliation a moot issue. Even if political authorities are not aware of the implications of these deficiencies, cognizant military planners would be inclined to devise procedures that incorporate this bias for early release.

A command system primed for early NCA release of nuclear weapons, however, increases the scope for miscalculation and accidental war. This risk, though negligible in peacetime, increases considerably during a crisis; the priority of positive control could become so high so quickly that a false alarm might trigger nuclear release.

The Prognosis for the Future

The Reagan administration's version of nuclear diplomacy led to plans to modernize the U.S. command system so that it could support a lengthy war. The context of the administration's plans is an image of nuclear conflict that begins with a large-scale Soviet counterforce attack and an immediate U.S. counterattack against time-urgent military targets. Unless and until a bargain to end the war is struck, the campaign is prolonged with follow-up exchanges and escalation to attacks against population centers among the possibilities. In this context an effective program for strategic modernization would introduce both new weapons capable of prompt hard-target attack and new command networks capable of supporting a variety of aims ranging from launch on warning to managing strategic reserve forces. It would also have to address the sharpened conflict between negative and positive control that would result from the necessity for maintaining strict control over forces withheld during nuclear exchanges.

Several pertinent points may help put the current program in proper perspective. First, the existing command structure cannot begin to support a doctrine of extended nuclear flexible response. Second, standard calculations of a Soviet advantage in protracted counterforce exchanges bear no relation to actual circumstances because they presuppose a command structure that does not exist. Third, the technological and procedural foundations of such a structure have scarcely been defined, much less conceived. Fourth, procurement of such a structure has not been funded, is bound to be costly, and would compete with force modernization programs for scarce resources. Fifth, preparing forces and command networks for protracted intercontinental nuclear war is not palatable to significant segments of the defense community, a fact that dims the out-look for financial authorization. Sixth, even if the large outlays required for extensive command modernization are ultimately approved, the in-vestment surely would stimulate aggressive Soviet development of coun-termeasures.

A final point, and one of key significance, is that pressures for pre-emptive attack or immediate retaliation would remain strong even if sub-stantial improvements in the versatility, survivability, and endurance of the command structure were realized. Although such improvement would allay fear of a sudden collapse of command-control, decisionmak-ers would still come under other pressures to unleash forces without de-lay. Because effective counterforce attack depends on the rapid delivery of weapons against time-urgent military targets, for instance, incentives to initiate offensive operations at the earliest possible moment would still be powerful.

Time and information constraints on nuclear decisionmaking would thus remain onerous under the strategy pursued by the Reagan adminis-tration. Today, in the event of Soviet first strike, national officials have at most several hours in which to weigh options and reach a decision. Stra-tegic organizations actually expect to receive retaliatory authorization within minutes after initial detection of missile launches. That expecta-tion is so deeply ingrained that the nuclear decision process has been reduced to a drill-like enactment of a prepared script, a brief emergency telecommunications conference whose purpose is to get a decision from the national command authority before incoming weapons arrive.

Those who doubt whether a responsible decision on employing nuclear weapons can be made within minutes or even several hours will find in the president's modernization program little improvement over the pres-ent situation. Provisions for command endurance and the operations of the strategic reserve force are marginal and in any case do not relax the constraints that exist during initial counterforce operations. Planned in-vestment in weapons for prompt counterforce attack together with an increasing inclination to rely on launch on warning for ICBM protection will in fact exacerbate these constraints. Already strongly institutional-ized predispositions to respond quickly and massively to enemy nuclear provocation would be reinforced by the president's program. The SIOP decision process will remain drill-like.

A long-term goal of nuclear modernization should be to adopt a policy that allows for no immediate second use. The basic justification for this policy is that nuclear decisionmaking should not be reduced to reflexes and brief drills, but should instead be regarded as a careful deliberative exercise of national leadership that could take days or longer. A moment's reflection would suggest that a decision on nuclear retaliation should not be forced on officials before they have had a chance to assess actual damage, evaluate Soviet political and military objectives, define U.S. security interests, and determine the role of nuclear weapons in promoting those interests. These matters cannot be given adequate consideration in a matter of minutes or hours.

The general aim of the proposed doctrine would be to create an option to extend strict negative control over all nuclear forces well into the period after an enemy attack and then to provide for an orderly transition to effective positive control if and when national officials authorize retaliation. But to accomplish this aim, radical adjustments to the U.S. nuclear posture would have to be made.

The Long-Term Goal: No Immediate Second Use

The response to impending or actual Soviet nuclear attack would initially be geared to ensuring the survival of the forces and command structure. Under current arrangements, protective dispersal and other survival actions are related organically to preparations for immediate retaliation. Under a doctrine of no immediate second use, survival actions would be separate from and would take strong precedence over counterattack coordination during and after a Soviet first strike. Authority to conduct offensive operations would be withheld for at least twenty-four hours, and military units would be programmed to operate accordingly.

Because retaliation would be eliminated as an organizational priority during an attack, the main purpose of early warning systems would be to alert units to an impending strike and trigger preprogrammed responses that would minimize their exposure. Because early warning systems would not be required to support an early decision to retaliate, the United States could design them to meet the narrower requirements of organizational survival. Planned improvements in early warning sensors, computers, communications, and so forth would be judged solely on the basis of their potential contribution to this objective.

To reinforce defensive reaction and suppress the offensive impulses of military organizations, negative control would have to be tightened. Conditional authority to release nuclear weapons could not be predelegated to military commands. If arrangements of this kind presently exist, they would have to be revoked. Physical, mechanical, and procedural restraints on nuclear weapons would also have to be strengthened. Mechanical locks would have to be installed on all weapons, including submarine missiles, to prevent their launch until enabling codes could be transmitted by higher authority. Positive control activities in general would have to require explicit approval from central authorities, reducing the scope for decentralized preparation for immediate counterattack.

At the same time, activities associated with force and command survival could be highly decentralized. Because these activities would be purely defensive, nuclear units at all levels, including the lowest echelon, could be programmed for rapid dispersion and could be granted unprecedented authority to take whatever unplanned steps would be necessary for their continuing survival. Various information channels, particularly tactical warning circuits, would have to be modified to provide maximum support for this decentralized activity. Direct links between warning sensors and individual units, for instance, could be installed. Sensor outages or other failures would have to trigger extensive defensive responses on the part of affected units.

Among the three force components, bombers would be most affected by this reposturing. Under current arrangements, alert bombers with traditional SIOP missions launch on tactical warning and fly toward loiter orbits on the periphery of enemy territory in anticipation of the imminent dissemination of retaliatory orders. Under the proposed doctrine, bombers would launch on tactical warning, but they would not leave the continental United States until retaliation had been authorized; they would thus operate like strategic reserve bombers. Bomber takeoffs, flight profiles, tanker rendezvous, and recovery would have to be designed to ensure the continuing survival and coherence of the force and could not be offensive.

The survival of bombers over a prolonged period is of course an objective of questionable feasibility. Despite careful planning, attrition could be very high: airborne endurance is inherently limited, usable runways could be scarce, fuel could be in short supply, and the exposure of crews to radiation could be very high. Deep reductions in the Soviet nuclear arsenal might have to be negotiated and a bomber capable of landing at austere airfields might have to be built for the future of this force to be bright under the proposed doctrine.

The same problems plague the airborne segment of the U.S. command structure. While it is a vital part of current strategy, it is ill suited to a doctrine of delayed response. Unless more versatile aircraft are developed and deep reductions in nuclear weapons deployments are achieved, reliance on the airborne command network probably would be reduced greatly if a doctrine of no immediate second use is adopted. Along with bombers, command aircraft might even be phased out entirely in favor of force and command elements that can endure for long periods or that lend themselves to reconstitution.

The role of fixed land-based missiles might also be diminished. These forces could not ride out a well-coordinated Soviet missile attack, and they could not be afforded the putative protection of launch on warning. Survivors could not endure very long given existing provisions for supplying backup power and other essential logistical support. On the other hand, the coordination of a Soviet attack could well fall short of conservative expectation, and additional steps could be taken to increase the endurance of surviving forces. The development of mobile land-based missiles such as Midgetman could expand the potential contribution of this leg of the triad to the proposed policy.

Missile submarines would undoubtedly play the pivotal role in the proposed strategy by virtue of their invulnerability and capacity to endure. Submarine operations would require only minor adjustment.

But regardless of the ultimate composition of the force structure, the command system that stands behind the forces would have to possess attributes that the existing system lacks. More enduring or reconstructable command, control, communications, and intelligence systems must be provided if effective delayed retaliation is to succeed.

The existing intelligence system cannot be relied on to assess damage caused by a Soviet attack. Its worth mainly derives from the tactical warning before impact and the attack assessment it could provide to reduce exposure to initial Soviet strikes. Preimpact information would be too fragmentary and unreliable to be a sound basis for strategy and policy formulation after an attack. The United States needs to develop intelligence systems that can generate reliable, accurate, and current reports as the damage occurs. IONDS is the only system being developed for this purpose.

Command centers that can withstand a massive attack and can continue to function long afterwards are also needed. Current arrangements place too much reliance on airborne command posts. Alternative arrange-

ments under study envisage a major change in crisis relocation plans for
national authorities and senior military commanders as well as the introduction of mobile command centers that would provide for eventual reconstitution of essential command functions regardless of events. Part of
the system would have to be independent of strategic or tactical warning
for protection. The rest would have to be designed for rapid dispersal
during an emergency. The merits of the planned system depend on details
that have not been publicly disclosed. The level of effort devoted to it,
however, is clearly insufficient. Programs that show promise ought to be
accelerated, and alternative technical options ought to be pursued more
vigorously. One alternative that deserves serious consideration is the development of undersea command posts, perhaps using Trident submarines or retired Polaris submarines.

Technical options for strategic communications after an attack also
need to be pursued more vigorously. Virtually all of the present networks
are subject either to direct attack or to sharp constraints on endurance,
and planned networks appear to offer only marginal improvement. MIL-
STAR holds some promise as a partial solution, but other capabilities
enjoying high confidence need to be developed. Communications between
national authorities and missile submarines, for instance, are now vastly
inferior to communications with bombers and land-based missiles, yet
this is the force component on which the United States relies most heavily. If the proposed doctrine is adopted, reliance would grow.

The backbone of postattack communications ought to be constructed
from elements that can be reconstituted, including meteor-burst communications, adaptive HF, and mobile HF, LF, VLF, and ELF radio. A
dedicated network of these elements could support ground mobile and
undersea command posts as well as missile submarines and other strategic forces. Various units such as submarine command posts and designated mobile missiles could be equipped for launching austere communications satellites into orbit.

The United States should also reexamine the technological feasibility
of survivable ELF submarine communications using railroad tracks or
the geological formations of the continental shelf. The Defense Department investigated these promising technical possibilities in the early
1970s but did not pursue them vigorously because of technological risks
and high cost. They ought to be seriously reconsidered.

The development of virtually all these technical options is presently underfunded. Substantially higher investment and accelerated delivery schedules are warranted.

Although a doctrine of no immediate second use is theoretically neutral with respect to targeting principles, certain practical ramifications would affect target selection. Adopting the proposed doctrine would lead to greater reliance on missile submarines and low-data-rate communications and would substitute delayed response for prompt retaliation. The aggregate effect of these changes would be to deemphasize counterforce targeting, especially strikes against time-urgent military targets. The presumed value of such targets would be diminished, and the generally high hardness of most of them would not normally permit judicious targeting by submarine-launched weapons.

Deploying the D-5 missile on submarines could compensate for the decline in capabilities for prompt hard-target attack that would otherwise result from changes in U.S. force composition. The time delay in retaliation, however, would by itself reduce greatly the worth of weapons for prompt hard-target attack. In general, adopting the proposed doctrine would dampen pursuit of capabilities for attacking Soviet missile silos and emphasize targeting military and economic infrastructure.

The doctrine would promote crisis stability in several ways. Insofar as it fosters deployment of a more survivable C^{3}I network, it might reduce incentives for preemptive attack and relieve pressures for early employment of U.S. forces. By the same token, it would establish that the U.S. threat of retaliation could not be removed by a sudden attack on its command system and thus alter Soviet calculations of the military advantage of first strike, reducing their incentive to initiate attack in a crisis. The command modernization resulting from adoption of the proposed doctrine would work to dispel any belief that rapid suppression of the U.S. command system would deliver a decisive military blow.

By emphasizing defensive response the United States would also be able to take military precautions in a crisis without signaling aggressive intent. At present, any increase in strategic readiness associated with crisis alert could work to heighten tensions and make the possibility of nuclear war seem less remote. Peak readiness represents an especially serious offensive threat that could engender Soviet fear of imminent attack and provoke rather than deter a first strike. The defensive orientation of the doctrine of delayed response, however, should dampen escalation. Increases in strategic readiness would be less provocative and more apt to raise the psychological threshold of the imminence of nuclear war.

The proposed doctrine would also inhibit the development of first-strike counterforce capabilities that conventional wisdom regards as destabilizing. Because weapons would be less useful for prompt attack against time-urgent military targets, less would be invested in them. The technical composition of the resulting force would not pose a first-strike threat and thus would not undermine crisis stability. At present, confidence in second-strike capability is declining on both sides because of sustained parallel investment in first-strike weapons. Although the implications of this trend for stability are exaggerated because they slide past the more serious issues of C^3I vulnerability to a first strike, they are significant. If present trends in weapons technology continue, a further erosion of crisis stability will be perceived. The proposed doctrine would work to channel investment into less destabilizing weapons.

Finally, efforts to strengthen command performance and hence crisis stability are more likely to succeed if they are dissociated from war-fighting and war-winning doctrines. Protracted war-fighting in order to prevail does not appeal strongly to traditional strategic principles and constituencies, and programs advanced under such a label are apt to be strongly resisted. At the same time, command preparations for prevailing in protracted nuclear war are apt to stimulate vigorous Soviet countermeasures. Command preparation for delayed response is less provocative and is not at variance with the component of U.S. declaratory policy that remains the cornerstone of U.S. deterrence strategy and the focus of broad consensus: assured destruction. The aims of the proposed doctrine require substantial adjustments to U.S. operational posture, but they do reemphasize the inadmissibility of intercontinental nuclear war and the negligible military utility of nuclear weapons.

Critics may argue that the doctrine of no immediate second use undermines crisis stability because the Soviet Union would perceive a defeatist attitude and an opportunity to prosecute an offensive campaign without the interference, disruption, and devastation that a prompt U.S. counterattack would produce. But such criticism misses the key point that the certainty of retaliation is more important for deterrence than is its timing. At present, notwithstanding a strong inclination to administer punishment swiftly, the state of U.S. C^3I casts fundamental doubt on the ability of the United States to respond at all to Soviet nuclear attack. It is the chronic imbalance in force and command structure development that has created this state of affairs. By channeling more resources into C³I programs, the proposed doctrine would build confidence in the ability of the United States to exercise a minimum essential degree of positive control under a wide range of adverse conditions while blocking the most plausible route to Soviet victory in a nuclear war. Retaliation might not be swift, but it would be sure and would be better aligned with coherent national purposes. Such a prospect would surely not invite aggression; it would instead bolster deterrence.

The Near-Term Goal: Assured Retaliation

The immediate concern of C³I planners is to create a system that will not collapse under the weight of a Soviet first strike and will provide for prompt, comprehensive retaliation. To accomplish this, budgetary support for the development and deployment of programs in the five-year defense plan must be sustained and new programs must be initiated.

The necessary C³I improvements already planned and funded are too exposed to service efforts to delay or eliminate them. A prime example is the navy's decision in fiscal year 1985 to postpone the initial purchase of TACAMO ECX replacement aircraft (while vigorously pursuing a 600-ship fleet) that is the key to modernizing communications with submarines. A fleet of fifteen ECX aircraft is planned, but such plans have historically tended to be sidetracked during service budgetary deliberations and not to be reinstated. The E4-B NEACP program met a similar fate.

The case for strategic C³I modernization needs to be reiterated by the president, and stronger advocacy and power must be exercised on its behalf. Under the current budgetary process, vigorous and conscientious representation of this interest at high levels of the defense bureaucracy is essential to sustained progress. The Office of the Secretary of Defense, the Defense Resources Board, and the Joint Chiefs of Staff must be vigilant and persistent in the face of inevitable service pressures to divert funds from C³I accounts. The assistant secretary of defense for C³I ought to possess the authority to create a special national C³I account that is exempt from control by the service budgets. Among the key C³I programs that ought to be fenced off in this account are the TACAMO ECX program, LF receivers for the bomber force, ground mobile command centers, and mobile ground terminals for satellite early warning sensor readout. And these programs should be expanded. ECX procurement should be accelerated, LF terminals should be installed on all tankers and C³I aircraft as well as bombers, and ground mobile command centers should be bought for the unified and specified commanders as well as for the Joint Chiefs of Staff and the national command authority.

The C³I budget must also be expanded to accommodate other important adjustments to current modernization plans. A substantial increase is needed to replace the outdated EC-135s with modern EMP-hardened aircraft, such as the Y-17, which is also capable of using runways that are not suitable for EC-135 operations. Additional funding is also needed to replace or upgrade the old, unreliable radio systems and associated trailing antennas carried by EC-135s and EC-130s and scheduled for transfer to TACAMO ECX aircraft. New EMP-hardened and jam-resistant radio systems, particularly LF systems, should be installed on old and new aircraft alike as soon as possible. Other needed improvements to the airborne command network include modern automatic data processing equipment and onboard sensors for detecting airborne nuclear radiation and turbulence. Sensors to identify and locate usable runways should also be developed. Dedicated tanker support for refueling in flight should be substantially increased. Operating procedures of ground-alert aircraft need to be designed so that threats to prelaunch survival from close-in Soviet submarines are offset by relocation to inland bases or instituting airborne alert. Two-way radio links between airborne launch control centers and missile silos should be provided.

Current funding levels for hardening ground facilities and terrestrial communications are also inadequate. The entire commercial landline network is vulnerable to collateral nuclear effects and could be hardened considerably by simple modifications or the use of fiber optics. The planned near-term solutions—the Ground Wave Emergency Network and jam-resistant secure communications—provide very slow communications as an alternative to reliance on leased commercial networks. The latter, if upgraded at a cost of several billion dollars, could provide reliable, fast communications resistant to EMP and MHD.

Two emergent threats to future C³I systems—modern Soviet cruise missiles and advanced antisatellite weapons—have not been adequately addressed. The development and deployment of sensors capable of detecting cruise missiles should have higher priority and more funding. Future Soviet antisatellite weapons should be anticipated even if they are not projected and key U.S. satellites designed accordingly. Some plausible weapons such as space-based lasers or neutral-particle-beam weapons could pose major threats to satellites during the 1990s, yet the satellites on which the United States will heavily rely are apparently not being designed to cope with such threats. MILSTAR, for example, could probably not survive attack and should not become the centerpiece of our future strategic C³I system in the absence of effective antisatellite arms control agreements. New, more survivable satellite systems should be developed, but in any event the United States should not stake as much C³I capability on satellites as present plans do.

Other unfunded or underfunded items worthy of support include NORAD's Rapier unit and SAC's headquarters emergency relocation team unit, which provide relocatable backup ground command posts to the existing fixed facilities. The Emergency Rocket Communications System is vulnerable and should be replaced, preferably by a mobile launcher and missile like the Pershing II or the Midgetman mobile ICBM. An undersea command post and mobile reconstitutable communications units on land should also be deployed.

The above list does not exhaust the possibilities. Dozens upon dozens of smaller improvements that would significantly fortify positive control for assured retaliation have also been identified yet remain unfunded. And although the aggregate cost of these fixes is high, it is not exorbitant given the stakes involved. The total additional expense of major and minor improvements that could create a system capable of supporting traditional SIOP missions would roughly equal the cost of any of the major weapon systems under development—$30 billion to $50 billion. This investment would be consistent with the stated aims and priorities of the Reagan administration. Whether it could survive the fiscal pressures on the defense budget and the rigors of internal Defense Department review is another matter, however. If history is any guide, C³I modernization is destined to fare poorly in the competition for scarce resources. Fundamental changes in the perception of the strategic problem and in the legal and institutional mechanisms that govern programs and budgets are probably necessary to bring about the kind of nuclear control system that the United States deserves and needs.

Arms Control

By accentuating the command problems of strategic stability, these near- and long-term goals encourage consideration of C³I topics in arms control negotiations. An agenda could include a wide range of prospective measures intended to lend protection to the respective command structures and reduce risks of misperception in time of crisis. The following are among the items worthy of consideration.

Ban Antisatellite Testing and Deployments

The United States suspended antisatellite negotiations with the Soviet Union after the invasion of Afghanistan in 1979. These talks are being resumed in Geneva and will perhaps produce a mutual moratorium on antisatellite launches that could lead to a total ban on antisatellite testing and deployment.

Although the United States is conducting initial tests of a weapon based on the F-15 that is superior to antisatellite weapons in the Soviet inventory, the long-term costs of unrestrained competition could vastly outweigh any near-term advantages that could be gained. Space-based assets are important, in some instances vital, to national defense. Both sides have a strong interest in preserving the accepted legitimacy of such activities as worldwide communications and intelligence collection, but the stakes are especially high for the United States. Its strategic forces are far-flung and hence dependent on satellite communications; the Soviet Union relies to a far greater extent on land-based missile forces, which in turn depend less on satellites for communications. Furthermore, the United States is becoming increasingly dependent on satellites for strategic communications and tactical early warning. Under the provisions of the current C³I plan, MILSTAR communications satellites and early warning satellites will form the backbone of our C³I network. The emergence of an antisatellite threat to these systems could derail plans for command modernization. An antisatellite treaty is strongly in the U.S. interest.

Soviet compliance with a moratorium on testing and deploying antisatellite weapons would not prove difficult to verify, assuming an agreement that remains in force for a year or so. The ease of verification stems in part from the fact that the Soviet Union does not now possess any weapons that could be based in space and will not have such a capability for at least several years. Indeed, there is no solid evidence of any Soviet plans to base weapons in space, though that of course could and probably would change if space becomes an arena of intensifying superpower military competition. Furthermore, the United States can closely monitor tests of virtually all Soviet ground-based weapons that are now or might soon be available for use against U.S. satellites. Testing could be difficult to monitor in a few cases, but the United States could develop passive countermeasures that greatly reduce most such threats.

Arguments against a moratorium focus on weaknesses in monitoring high-energy lasers, antiballistic missiles, and residual Soviet antisatellite capabilities that could remain despite full compliance with a moratorium. Verification of laser and antiballistic missile tests could be enhanced through cooperative measures. In this context, however, it is well to keep in mind that the most critical U.S. space assets are deployed at geosynchronous altitudes well beyond the range of antiballistic interceptors and the effective range of ground-based lasers (if prudent measures are taken to protect satellites against laser beams). In addition, using antiballistic interceptors armed with nuclear warheads is not plausible except during nuclear war, in which case the loss of low-altitude satellites would not matter very much. One must concede that some antisatellite capability resides in Soviet ICBMs, SLBMs, ABMs, and standard space-launch vehicles, even if they are never tested for this purpose, although Soviet planners could not be confident in their performance if they were not tested. Finally, other residual antisatellite capabilities are either not very plausible (a manned Soviet spacecraft ramming a U.S. satellite) or not very threatening if the United States prudently invests in satellite survivability (protection against jamming, for example).

Soviet compliance with a permanent ban on testing and deploying antisatellite weapons would be harder to verify than a moratorium because of the eventual possibility of Soviet weapons actually based in the vast expanse of space. Still, if present projections of Soviet capabilities and plans for space-based weapons in the more distant future are reasonably accurate, then our ability to negotiate a mutually verifiable ban should be very strong. There are grounds for optimism. High-energy lasers are the only Soviet weapons that are expected to be deployed in space in this century (they would be operational by the early-to-mid 1990s), and their presence could be detected with high confidence. Most other potential space-based weapons would be more difficult to detect, but for technical, operational, or economic reasons they are far less promising. These low-probability, hypothetical threats include radio frequency/electronic damage weapons and space mines. They are not expected to be deployed at all and not before the end of this century if they are. A possible exception is a miniature homing vehicle, which the Soviet

Union might develop. Covert tests and deployments of aircraft-based homing vehicles would be difficult to monitor. Another possible exception is a neutral-particle-beam weapon tested and based in space. Like space-based lasers, it could appear by the early 1990s, and covert tests and deployments might prove difficult to monitor.

Considering these potential verification problems, the strongest counterargument is simply that the Soviets are much more likely to pursue space-based lasers and that this weapon system will not be difficult to monitor. At the same time, it should be stressed that nuclear mines in space are already banned by the Outer Space Treaty of 1967, that our ability to monitor the more problematic weapons including space mines would be good enough to deter large illicit programs involving extensive testing, and that the United States has ample time to improve its monitoring capabilities. Many potential verification problems can also be avoided by careful drafting of a treaty, and cooperative measures and other innovative responses could resolve any remaining problems of verification. The importance of space to U.S. C³I is so great that antisatellite competition ought to be dampened to the extent possible.

Prohibit Stationing Missiles Close to Enemy Borders

Both the Soviet Union and the United States currently operate nuclear ballistic missile forces at forward locations from which quick strikes against enemy command facilities could be launched. Both U.S. and Soviet submarines are poised for short warning attacks. From a Soviet standpoint, Pershing II deployments in Western Europe aggravate the problem because they can strike key command facilities to the west of Moscow ten minutes after launch. An arms agreement restricting nuclear deployments to zones that preclude short-range attack would mitigate the threat of such sudden command decapitation and thus promote crisis stability. Because the pertinent deployments to be traded off—Pershing II and SSBNs, to cite the prominent examples—would involve both INF negotiations and START, the talks would have to be bridged for this purpose.

Prohibit Tests of SLBM Depressed Trajectories

The flight time of SLBMs can be substantially reduced by lowering the missiles' trajectory. To date, neither side has conducted tests of depressed trajectories, but were they to do so, the threat of sudden decapitation would become more pronounced and crisis stability would be undermined. An agreement prohibiting such tests should be negotiated.

Ban Forward Deployment of Cruise Missiles

Although cruise missiles are much slower than ballistic missiles, they are much less susceptible to detection. They could therefore be used in a decapitation attack, especially if launched from delivery systems in close proximity to the targets, and represent the most serious emerging threat to U.S. C^3I systems, one that planned modernization scarcely addresses. To mitigate the threat, the parties could agree to prohibit close-in deployment of ships, submarines, aircraft, and ground bases armed with nuclear cruise missiles. Because of the extreme difficulty of verification, however, a better solution, albeit a politically infeasible one, would be to ban cruise missile deployments altogether.

Create Undersea Command Posts and Ocean Sanctuaries for SLBMs

Undersea command posts and ocean sanctuaries for SLBMs might be created to prevent inadvertent or deliberate engagements between antisubmarine warfare forces and central strategic forces and command units. As reliance on sea-based strategic systems grows, the value of measures that increase confidence in the survival of these systems also grows. One such measure is to prohibit antisubmarine forces from operating in designated ocean areas.

Establish Risk-Reduction Centers

Senators Sam Nunn and John Warner have proposed that the two superpowers establish jointly manned centers in each country to deal with acts of nuclear terrorism, nuclear explosions of ambiguous origin, accidental or unauthorized nuclear attacks, and so forth that could trigger a nuclear war.

Improve the Hot Line between Washington and Moscow

Timely emergency communications between the leaders of the United States and the Soviet Union depend on the so-called hot line, which provides for teletype communications only, is accessible from few locations, and is routed through circuits having little redundancy. The system should be expanded to include a satellite voice channel with greater accessibility and more redundancy. A direct satellite link between NEACP and alternative Soviet command facilities would be potentially very useful.

Conclusion

The Reagan administration not only formally acknowledged the importance of command performance for national security but defined command modernization as the overriding aim of U.S. nuclear policy. For the first time in twenty-five years, the government asserted that C^3I has been elevated to the top of the strategic agenda. Underneath the encouraging rhetoric, however, lies the sobering reality that the United States is not much closer to a solution to the basic problem than it was a decade ago. The outlook for genuine progress in rectifying command deficiencies is therefore not as hopeful as one might initially imagine.

It is also open to question whether command modernization can remain a high priority of U.S. security policy. The government still has to contend with analytic, technical, economic, and bureaucratic conditions that detract from this goal. These conditions have historically favored other priorities, and the Reagan administration in its first term neither confronted them squarely nor devoted the necessary attention and resources to command modernization. Problems of nuclear control were overshadowed by other pressing security matters: deadlocked arms control negotiations, political hostilities with the Soviet Union, and continuing involvement in conflicts in Central America and the Middle East. Even in matters of nuclear security, officials spent more time and energy on weapons development and deployment and on such matters as Soviet compliance with arms control treaties than they did on problems of command-control. In practical terms, and contrary to official contention, command modernization does not appear to enjoy high priority, and the administration's handling of the issue to date has the earmarks of another false start and faltering commitment that result in little or no improvement in command performance.

The crucial first step that has yet to be taken involves major legal and institutional changes. Implementing any plan that gives command development the same priority as weapons systems requires a powerful C^3I advocate in the defense bureaucracy. Sponsors of command modernization wield too little program and budget authority to prevail over advocates of force modernization. Unless a countervailing power base is created, weapons programs will continue to take precedence, regardless of the prominence of command modernization themes in presidential oratory and defense guidance.

Nevertheless, the climate for new concepts and initiatives for this issue has never been more favorable. Defense professionals must now emphasize that effective command performance is central to national security and intensify the search for answers. This search needs to be conducted without the emotional extremes of despair or wildly inflated expectations. With redoubled effort, the United States could at least begin to come to grips with one of the most important security dilemmas of our time.

Trends in ICBM Vulnerability

IT IS possible to show the adverse trend affecting ICBMs by using standard equations that combine technical characteristics of targets and attacking land missiles to estimate the probability of target destruction. The target attribute of primary importance, missile silo hardness, is expressed in pounds per square inch (psi) of maximum blast overpressure that can be safely tolerated. Primary weapons characteristics include the number of attacking weapons and their yield, accuracy, and reliability. A standard mathematical relationship between these factors and the probability of target destruction by a single attacking warhead is

$$TKP = OAR \times (1.0 - 0.5^{8.41\,(Y^{2/3})/H^{0.7}\,(CEP)^2})$$

where TKP is the terminal kill probability, OAR is the overall reliability of the attacking missile, Y is the explosive yield of the attacking warhead, H is the silo hardness in psi, and CEP is the accuracy of the attacking warhead. For attacks by two warheads with identical attributes, the probability of silo destruction is $1.0 - (1 - TKP)^2$.

These formulas and assumptions, given in table A-1, were used to calculate the results of hypothetical missile attacks on opposing land missile forces between 1962 and 1974. As figure A-1 shows, the technical trend ran in favor of U.S. ICBM forces during the initial period and began to be reversed about 1965. The trends reversed again about 1970, reflecting a leveling out of Soviet ICBM deployments (see table A-2), the increased hardness of U.S. missile silos, and the U.S. deployment of MIRVs.

The trendlines changed again about 1975, however. The U.S. threat to Soviet ICBMs leveled out, while the Soviet threat increased sharply with

Table A-1. *U.S. and Soviet Land Missile Force Characteristics, 1962–73*

Year	Launchers	Type	Yield (mt)	CEP[a] (mi)	Hardness (psi)
1962					
United States	120	Atlas	3	1.0	5
	30	Titan I	4	1.0	100
Soviet Union	30	SS-7	5	1.5	5
1963					
United States	120	Atlas	3	1.0	5
	54	Titan I	4	1.0	100
	54	Titan II	5	0.7	300
	186	Minuteman I	1	0.7	300
Soviet Union	100	SS-7	5	1.5	5
1964					
United States	120	Atlas	3	1.0	5
	54	Titan I	4	1.0	100
	54	Titan II	5	0.7	300
	630	Minuteman I	1	0.7	300
Soviet Union	150	SS-7	5	1.5	5
	50	SS-8	5	1.5	100
1965					
United States	54	Titan II	5	0.7	300
	800	Minuteman I	1	0.7	300
Soviet Union	150	SS-7	5	1.5	5
	70	SS-8	5	1.5	100
	42	SS-9	25	0.7	100–300
1966					
United States	54	Titan II	5	0.7	300
	800	Minuteman I	1	0.7	300
	80	Minuteman II	1	0.3	300
Soviet Union	150	SS-7	5	1.5	5
	70	SS-8	5	1.5	100
	110	SS-9	25	0.7	100–300
	10	SS-11	1	1.0	300
1967					
United States	54	Titan II	5	0.7	300
	700	Minuteman I	1	0.7	300
	300	Minuteman II	1	0.3	300
Soviet Union	150	SS-7	5	1.5	5
	70	SS-8	5	1.5	100
	162	SS-9	25	0.7	100–300
	178	SS-11	1	1.0	300
	10	SS-13	1	1.0	300
1968					
United States	54	Titan II	5	0.7	300
	600	Minuteman I	1	0.7	300
	400	Minuteman II	1	0.3	300
Soviet Union	150	SS-7	5	1.5	5
	70	SS-8	5	1.5	100
	192	SS-9	25	0.7	100–300
	426	SS-11	1	1.0	300
	20	SS-13	1	1.0	300

Table A-1 (continued)

Year	Launchers	Type	Yield (mt)	CEP[a] (mi)	Hardness (psi)
1969					
United States	54	Titan II	5	0.7	300
	500	Minuteman I	1	0.7	300
	500	Minuteman II	1	0.3	300
Soviet Union	150	SS-7	5	1.5	5
	70	SS-8	5	1.5	100
	228	SS-9	25	0.7	100–300
	550	SS-11	1	1.0	300
	30	SS-13	1	1.0	300
1970					
United States	54	Titan II	5	0.7	300
	490	Minuteman I	1	0.7	300
	500	Minuteman II	1	0.3	300
	10	Minuteman III	3 × 0.17	0.2	300
Soviet Union	150	SS-7	5	1.5	5
	70	SS-8	5	1.5	100
	288	SS-9	25	0.7	100–300
	751	SS-11	1	1.0	300
	40	SS-13	1	1.0	300
1971					
United States	54	Titan II	5	0.7	300
	390	Minuteman I	1	0.7	300
	500	Minuteman II	1	0.3	300
	110	Minuteman III	3 × 0.17	0.2	300
Soviet Union	139	SS-7	5	1.5	5
	70	SS-8	5	1.5	100
	288	SS-9	25	0.7	100–300
	956	SS-11	1	1.0	300
	60	SS-13	1	1.0	300
1972					
United States	54	Titan II	5	0.5	300
	290	Minuteman I	1	0.7	(80% at 300
	500	Minuteman II	1	0.3	psi, 20% at
	210	Minuteman III	3 × 0.17	0.2	1,500 psi)
Soviet Union	139	SS-7	5	1.5	5
	70	SS-8	5	1.5	100
	288	SS-9	25	0.7	100–300
	970	SS-11	1	1.0	300
	60	SS-13	1	1.0	300
1973					
United States	54	Titan II	5	0.5	300
	140	Minuteman I	1	0.7	(60% at 300
	510	Minuteman II	1	0.3	psi, 40% at
	350	Minuteman III	3 × 0.17	0.2	1,500 psi)
Soviet Union	139	SS-7	5	1.5	5
	70	SS-8	5	1.5	100
	288	SS-9	25	0.7	100–300
	970	SS-11	1	1.0	300
	60	SS-13	1	1.0	300

a. Circular error probable (CEP) is the diameter of a circle around the target within which 50 percent of attacking weapons will strike.

Figure A-1. *Results of Massive Attack Aimed at Opponent's ICBM Force, 1962–74*

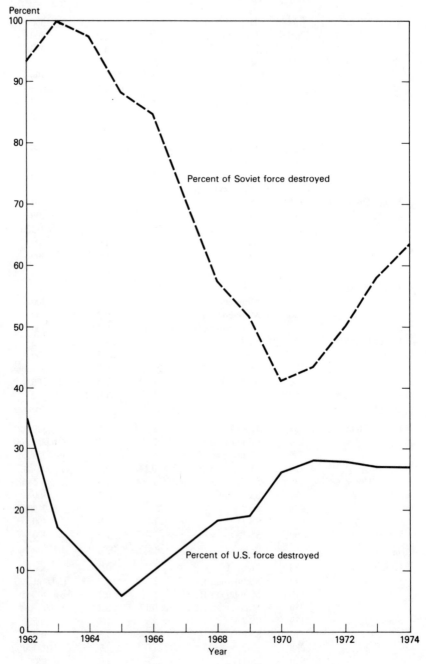

Percent

Table A-2. *U.S. and Soviet Strategic Nuclear Delivery Vehicles,*
Selected Years 1962–83

| | United States | | | Soviet Union | | |
Year	Land missiles	Submarine missiles	Strategic bombers	Land missiles	Submarine missiles	Strategic bombers
1962	294	144	600	75	some	190
1964	834	416	630	190	107	175
1966	904	592	630	292	107	155
1968	1,054	656	545	858	121	155
1970	1,054	656	460	1,513	304	140
1972	1,054	656	401	1,527	500	140
1974	1,054	656	397	1,618	720	140
1976	1,054	656	387	1,477	845	135
1978	1,054	656	366	1,400	1,028	135
1980	1,054	656	338	1,398	1,028	156
1982	1,052	520	316	1,398	989	105
1983	1,045	568	272	1,398	980	143

Source: International Institute for Strategic Studies, *The Military Balance, 1983–84* (London: I.I.S.S., 1983) and earlier annual issues.

the deployment of SS-17, SS-18, and SS-19 land missiles. Many of these ICBMs were designed to carry MIRVs, and they were credited with higher accuracy than their predecessors.[1]

These improvements produced a large increase in the lethal index of the Soviet missile force, a quantitative measure reflecting the size, yield, and accuracy of nuclear inventories. Table A-3 compares the pertinent statistics for the beginning of 1975 and 1978.[2] By themselves, lethality statistics do not measure the ability of a missile force to attack military targets. Nor do marginal increases in lethality necessarily imply any improvement in this ability. To transform lethality into a meaningful measure, a set of targets must be specified, target hardness estimates supplied, and the probability of target destruction computed. But this caveat notwithstanding, the calculations do indicate a definite decline in U.S. land missile survivability. Although there has been a sustained U.S. effort to give missile silos added protection against the effects of nuclear explosions, it has not been enough to offset increases in the lethality of Soviet

1. *Fiscal Year 1978 Authorization for Military Procurement, Research and Development, and Active Duty, Selected Reserve and Personnel Strengths,* Hearings before the Senate Committee on Armed Services, 95 Cong. 1 sess. (GPO, 1977), pt. 1, p. 584.

2. The lethal index, or K, of U.S. missile forces is shown for comparison. It should be noted that K is more sensitive to accuracy than weapon yield. U.S. warheads, even though usually smaller in yield than Soviet warheads, have had greater accuracy. Soviet deployment of fourth-generation ICBMs erased this edge.

Table A-3. Lethality of U.S. and Soviet Strategic Missile Forces, 1975 and 1978[a]

Missile	Explosive yield of warhead (mt)		Accuracy of reentry vehicle (nautical mi)		Lethality per reentry vehicle (K)[b]		Number of reentry vehicles per missile		Total number of missiles		Total lethality of missile force (K × N)	
	1975	1978	1975	1978	1975	1978	1975	1978	1975	1978	1975	1978
United States												
Minuteman III	0.17	0.17	0.20	0.15	7.7	13.6	3	3	550	550	12,705	22,440
Minuteman II	1.00	1.00	0.30	0.30	11.1	11.1	1	1	450	450	4,995	4,995
Titan	5.00	7.40	0.50	0.35	11.7	31.0	1	1	54	54	632	1,674
Poseidon	0.04	0.04	0.30	0.25	1.3	1.9	10	10	496	496	6,448	9,424
Polaris	0.20	0.20	0.50	0.50	1.4	1.4	3	3	160	160	672	672
Total											25,452	39,205
Soviet Union												
SS-9	25.00	25.00	0.70	0.50	17.4	34.2	1	1	288	183	5,011	6,259
SS-11, SS-13	1.00	0.5–1.50	1.00	0.55–1.50	1.0	0.8–2.1	1	1–3	970	778	970	2,187[c]
SS-17, model 1	...	0.80	...	0.35	...	7.0	...	4	0	70	0	1,960
SS-18, model 1	...	25.00	...	0.30	...	95.0	...	1	0	40	0	3,800
SS-18, model 2	...	2.00	...	0.25	...	25.4	...	8–10	0	55	0	12,573
SS-18, model 3	...	15.00	...	0.25	...	97.1	...	1	0	30	0	2,913
SS-19, model 1	...	0.60	...	0.30	...	7.9	...	6	0	230	0	10,902
SS-N-6	1.00	1.50	1.50	0.55	1.0	4.3	1	1	528	384	528	1,651
SS-N-8	1.00	2.00	1.50	0.50	1.0	6.4	1	1	80	344	80	2,202
SS-N-17	...	2.00	...	0.30	...	17.6	...	1	0	70	0	1,232
SS-N-18	...	0.20	...	0.30	...	3.8	...	3	0	60	0	684
SS-7, SS-8	5.00	...	1.50	...	1.3	...	1	...	209	...	270	0
Total											6,859	46,363

a. Estimates for 1975 and 1978 differ in some cases because of different data sources rather than missile improvements over the three-year period.

b. K is the yield of a warhead in megatons to the two-thirds power divided by the square of the CEP.

c. Sum of 48 SS-13s (1 megaton, 1.1 nautical miles CEP, 1 reentry vehicle), 490 SS-11s, model 1 (1.5 megaton, 1.25 nautical miles CEP, 1 reentry vehicle), and 240 SS-11s, model 3 (0.5 megaton, 0.55 nautical miles CEP, 3 reentry vehicles).

Table A-4. *Estimated Results of Surprise Attack against Opponent's Strategic Forces, 1973, 1978, and 1984*

Year	United States				Soviet Union			
	Land missiles[a]	Submarine missiles[a]	Strategic bombers[a]	Total	Land missiles[a]	Submarine missiles[a]	Strategic bombers[a]	Total
Percent of delivery vehicles destroyed								
1973	24	45	68	n.a.	56	85	100	n.a.
1978	44	45	77	n.a.	41–63	85	100	n.a.
1984	80	45	78	n.a.	50–58	80	100	n.a.
Warheads survive								
1973	1,293	2,160	850	4,303	667	76	0	743
1978	1,016	2,960	904	4,880	1,666–2,238	172	0	1,828–2,410
1984	429	2,834	740	4,003	1,863–1,976	365	0	2,395–2,508
Total yield of surviving warheads (equivalent megatons)								
1973	742	373	579	1,694	2,106	76	0	2,182
1978	558	400	357	1,315	2,218–3,260	185	0	2,503–3,445
1984	257	446	264	967	2,002–2,115	393	0	2,395–2,508

n.a. = Not applicable.

a. Assumptions for characteristics of land missiles in 1973 are given in table A-1. Statistics for 1978 are given in table A-3. Estimates for 1984 are based on table A-3 and *The Military Balance 1983-1984* (London: International Institute for Strategic Studies, 1983). Silo hardness in 1978 and 1984 was assumed to be 1,500 psi for U.S. Minuteman silos and 300 psi for Titan silos. In 1978 and 1984, Soviet silos for newer missiles (SS-17s, SS-18s, and SS-19s) were assumed to be hardened to 1,500 psi. Silos for older missiles (SS-9s, SS-11s, and SS-13s) were assigned a minimum hardness of 300 psi and a maximum of 1,000 psi. The ranges that appear under the Soviet columns reflect this uncertainty.
   In the analysis, only land missiles were targeted against opposing land missiles. All U.S. land missiles were assumed expended in the attacks in 1973, 1978, and 1984. All Soviet land missiles were assumed expended in a Soviet first strike in 1973. In 1978 it was assumed the Soviet first strike allocated only one warhead to each of the 1,054 American silos. This strategy expended only 25 percent of Soviet land missiles (183 SS-9s, 125 SS-18s, including 55 model 2 SS-18s with ten warheads each, and 43 SS-19s with six warheads each). The remainder were assumed to be not allocated against U.S. missile silos because the U.S. hardening program had rendered the missiles ineffective in this role. In the 1984 first strike, two warheads were allocated to each of the U.S. silos. This hypothetical strategy expended only 15 percent of the Soviet land missile force. The remainder were not allocated against U.S. silos because their marginal contribution to increasing damage expectancy would have been low even in the absence of fratricide.
   b. All submarine missiles at sea were assumed to have survived an opponent's first strike. The fraction of U.S. missile submarines at sea in 1973, 1978, and 1984 was assumed to have been 55 percent of the total force (22 out of 41 in 1973 and 1978, and 18 out of 33 in 1984). The analogous alert rate for Soviet missile submarines was assumed to have been 15 percent in 1973 and 1978 (5 out of 34 in 1973, and 8 out of 56 in 1978). An increased alert rate of 20 percent was assumed for 1984 (11 out of 57). Characteristics of U.S. and Soviet submarine missiles are based on table A-3, *The Military Balance 1983-1984*, and earlier annual issues of *The Military Balance*.
   c. Because of the low readiness rates of Soviet long-range bombers, the entire Soviet bomber force of Tu-95s and Mya-4s was assumed to have been destroyed in a surprise U.S. attack for all years considered. By contrast, a significant portion of the U.S. strategic bomber force was maintained on five-minute ground alert in 1973, 1978, and 1984. The analysis assumed that 40 percent of the U.S. strategic bomber force (397 B-52s and 66 FB-111s) was alert in 1973, that a Soviet surprise attack destroyed all off-alert bombers and 10 percent of the alert force, and that Soviet air defenses destroyed 10 percent of the bombers that survived the initial missile attack. In 1978, 30 percent of the total force (266 B-52s and 56 FB-111s) was assumed to be alert, and 90 percent of the alert bombers survived the initial strike. Of these, Soviet air defenses destroyed 20 percent (see the following table).

Type	Alert			Survive			Warheads			Total yield (mt)		
	1973	1978	1984	1973	1978	1984	1973	1978	1984	1973	1978	1984
B-52 G/H	102	77	72	83	59	52	498	708	624	332	236	208
B-52 D/F	57	24	7	46	19	5	184	76	20	184	76	20
FB-111	26	20	17	21	15	12	168	120	96	63	45	36
Total	185	121	96	150	93	69	850	904	740	579	357	264

missiles. Theoretically, a Soviet ICBM attack in 1978 could have destroyed nearly half the U.S. ICBM force.[3] Five years earlier, before the introduction of the fourth generation of Soviet ICBMs, only about one-fourth of the ICBM force was vulnerable to attack (table A-4).

Refinements in Soviet missile accuracy after 1978, coupled with further MIRVing of missile payloads (increasing the number of warheads that can be allocated to each target, thus raising the kill probability above that which could be realized if only a single warhead were allocated) moved the Soviets still closer to what many consider to be one of their prime strategic objectives: the capability of destroying virtually the entire U.S. ICBM force. If standard calculations are to be believed, Soviet missiles threatened four-fifths of the U.S. ICBM force (table A-4). (The United States is not standing still in this regard and will theoretically pose an analogous threat within ten years.)

3. This estimate assumes force characteristics shown in table A-3. Minuteman silos were assigned a hardness of 1,500 psi. SS-17, SS-18, and SS-19 ICBMs were assigned a silo hardness of 1,000–1,500 psi, and SS-9, SS-11, and SS-13 missiles were assigned a hardness of 300–1,000 psi. By comparison, U.S. ICBMs launched in a first strike could have destroyed between 40 and 60 percent of the Soviet land missile force, depending on Soviet silo resistance to blast overpressure.

Minuteman Command
Vulnerability, 1966

TABLES B-1 through B-9 estimate the vulnerability of Minuteman forces to Soviet missile strikes against launch control centers in 1966. The results vary with the assumptions about Soviet missile accuracy, attack strategy, reprogramming capabilities, and the hardness of Minuteman launch control centers.

Table B-1. *Vulnerability of Minuteman Forces to Soviet SS-9 Attack against Launch Control Centers, Scenario A* [a]

Percent of Soviet missiles reliable	Percent of force incapacitated [b]			
	Expected	Risk ≥ 20%	Risk ≥ 10%	Risk ≥ 5%
Reprogrammed attack				
70	47–71	59–77	65–82	71–82
75	59–77	65–82	71–88	77–94
80	65–77	77–88	77–94	82–94
85	71–82	82–94	88–94	88–100
90	82–88	88–94	94–100	94–100
95	88–94	94–100	100	100
100	100	100	100	100
Nonreprogrammed attack				
70	18	29	35	35
75	24	35	41	47
80	35	47	53	53
85	47	59	65	71
90	59	71	77	82
95	77	88	88	94
100	94	100	100	100

a. Assumes LCC hardness of 50 psi, SS-9 accuracy of 0.7 nautical miles CEP, and SS-9 yield of 25 megatons; one-on-one attack against 18 Minuteman squadrons
b. Minuteman force of 880 missiles.

313

Table B-2. *Vulnerability of Minuteman Forces to Soviet SS-9 Attack against Launch Control Centers, Scenario B*[a]

Percent of Soviet missiles reliable	Percent of force incapacitated[b]			
	Expected	Risk ≥ 20%	Risk ≥ 10%	Risk ≥ 5%
Reprogrammed attack				
70	47–65	53–71	59–77	65–77
75	53–71	65–77	65–82	71–88
80	59–71	71–82	77–88	77–88
85	65–77	77–88	82–88	88–94
90	77–82	82–88	88–94	94
95	82–88	88–94	94	94–100
100	94	100	100	100
Nonreprogrammed attack				
70	18	24	29	29
75	24	29	35	41
80	29	41	47	47
85	41	53	59	59
90	53	65	71	77
95	71	82	82	88
100	94	100	100	100

a. Assumes LCC hardness of 100 psi, SS-9 accuracy of 0.7 nautical miles CEP, and SS-9 yield of 25 megatons; one-on-one attack against 18 Minuteman squadrons.
b. Minuteman force of 880 missiles.

Table B-3. *Vulnerability of Minuteman Forces to Soviet SS-9 Attack against Launch Control Centers, Scenario C*[a]

Percent of Soviet missiles reliable	Percent of force incapacitated[b]			
	Expected	Risk ≥ 20%	Risk ≥ 10%	Risk ≥ 5%
Reprogrammed attack				
70	41–53	47–65	53–65	59–71
75	47–59	53–71	59–77	65–82
80	53–65	59–71	65–77	71–82
85	59–65	65–77	71–82	77–88
90	65–71	77–82	77–82	82–88
95	71–77	82	88	88–94
100	77	88	88–94	94
Nonreprogrammed attack				
70	12	18	24	29
75	18	29	29	35
80	24	35	41	47
85	35	47	53	53
90	47	59	65	65
95	59	71	77	82
100	77	88	88	94

a. Assumes LCC hardness of 150 psi, SS-9 accuracy of 0.7 nautical miles CEP, and SS-9 yield of 25 megatons; one-on-one attack against 18 Minuteman squadrons.
b. Minuteman force of 880 missiles.

Table B-4. *Vulnerability of Minuteman Forces to Soviet SS-9 Attack against Launch Control Centers, Scenario D*[a]

Percent of Soviet missiles reliable	Percent of force incapacitated[b]					Percent of force impaired[b] (expected)
	Expected	Risk ≥ 20%	Risk ≥ 10%	Risk ≥ 5%	Risk ≥ 1%	
75	33	44	44	50	56	22
80	39	50	50	56	56	17
85	44	50	56	56	61	22
90	50	56	61	51	61	11
95	56	61	61	61	61	6

a. Assumes LCC hardness of 250 psi; SS-9 accuracy of 0.7 nautical miles CEP; and two-on-one attack against eleven Minuteman squadrons, seven squadrons not attacked, and no reprogramming.
b. Minuteman force of 880 missiles.

Table B-5. *Vulnerability of Minuteman Forces to Soviet SS-9 Attack against Launch Control Centers, Scenario E*[a]

Percent of Soviet missiles reliable	Percent of force incapacitated[b]					Percent of force impaired[b] (expected)
	Expected	Risk ≥ 20%	Risk ≥ 10%	Risk ≥ 5%	Risk ≥ 1%	
75	22	28	33	33	39	38
80	22	28	33	39	44	28
85	28	39	39	44	50	22
90	33	39	44	50	56	22
95	33	44	50	50	56	22

a. Assumes LCC hardness of 250 psi; SS-9 accuracy of 0.9 nautical miles CEP; and two-on-one attack against eleven Minuteman squadrons, seven squadrons not attacked, and no reprogramming.
b. Minuteman force of 880 missiles.

Table B-6. *Vulnerability of Minuteman Forces to Soviet SS-9 Attack against Launch Control Centers, Scenario F*[a]

Percent of Soviet missiles reliable	Percent of force incapacitated[b]					Percent of force impaired[b] (expected)
	Expected	Risk ≥ 20%	Risk ≥ 10%	Risk ≥ 5%	Risk ≥ 1%	
75	17	22	28	28	33	33
80	17	28	28	33	39	39
85	28	33	39	44	50	39
90	33	44	50	50	61	39
95	44	56	61	67	72	39

a. Assumes LCC hardness of 250 psi; SS-9 accuracy of 0.7 nautical miles CEP; and one-on-one attack against eighteen Minuteman squadrons, no reprogramming.
b. Minuteman force of 880 missiles.

Table B-7. *Vulnerability of Minuteman Forces to Soviet SS-9 Attack against Launch Control Centers, Scenario G*[a]

Percent of Soviet missiles reliable	Percent of force incapacitated[b]					Percent of force impaired[b] (expected)
	Expected	Risk≥20%	Risk≥10%	Risk≥5%	Risk≥1%	
75	11	17	22	22	28	22
80	17	22	28	28	33	22
85	17	28	33	33	39	28
90	22	28	33	39	44	28
95	28	39	39	44	50	22

a. Assumes LCC hardness of 1,000 psi; SS-9 accuracy of 0.7 nautical miles CEP; and two-on-one attack against eleven Minuteman squadrons, seven squadrons not attacked, and no reprogramming.
b. Minuteman force of 880 missiles.

Table B-8. *Vulnerability of Minuteman Forces to Soviet SS-9 Attack against Launch Control Centers, Scenario H*[a]

Percent of Soviet missiles reliable	Percent of force incapacitated[b]					Percent of force impaired[b] (expected)
	Expected	Risk≥20%	Risk≥10%	Risk≥5%	Risk≥1%	
75	17	22	28	28	33	17
80	22	28	28	33	33	17
85	22	28	33	33	39	11
90	28	33	33	39	39	11
95	28	33	39	39	39	11

a. Assumes LCC hardness of 1,000 psi; SS-9 accuracy of 0.7 nautical miles CEP; and three-on-one attack against seven Minuteman squadrons, eleven squadrons not attacked, and no reprogramming.
b. Minuteman force of 880 missiles.

Table B-9. *Vulnerability of Minuteman Forces to Soviet SS-9 Attack against Launch Control Centers, Scenario I*[a]

Percent of Soviet missiles reliable	Percent of force incapacitated[b]					Percent of force impaired[b] (expected)
	Expected	Risk≥20%	Risk≥10%	Risk≥5%	Risk≥1%	
75	6	11	17	17	22	17
80	11	17	17	22	28	17
85	11	17	17	22	28	17
90	11	17	22	22	28	17
95	17	22	22	28	33	17

a. Assumes LCC hardness of 1,000 psi; SS-9 accuracy of 0.9 nautical miles CEP; and three-on-one attack against seven Minuteman squadrons, eleven squadrons not attacked, and no reprogramming.
b. Minuteman force of 880 missiles.

Sample Computations: Nonreprogrammable Attacks

This section of the appendix derives the results entered in the third row of tables B-4 and B-6. The results in this row correspond to an assumed Soviet missile reliability of 85 percent and to other assumptions given in the table notes.

Table B-6 assumes that the Soviets allocate one SS-9 missile to each of the eighty-eight launch control centers. Based on the formula given in appendix A, the probability that any LCC would have remained functional following the attack was 24 percent. Calculated next is the probability that zero, one, two, three, four, or five centers would have survived in any squadron, given that the probability of survival is 24 percent for an individual control center. This set of probabilities was derived as follows:

> None survives $C(5,5)(0.76)^5 = 25$ percent
> One survives $C(5,4)(0.24)(0.76)^4 = 40$ percent
> Two survive $C(5,3)(0.24)^2(0.76)^3 = 25$ percent
> Three survive $C(5,2)(0.24)^3(0.76)^2 = 8$ percent
> Four survive $C(5,1)(0.24)^4(0.76) = 1$ percent
> Five survive $C(5,0)(0.24)^5 = 0$ percent

where $C(n,r) = n!/r!(n-r)!$ and $n = 5$ and $r = 1, 2, 3, 4,$ or 5.

The expected number of Minuteman squadrons with zero, one, two, three, four, or five surviving launch control centers was obtained by multiplying each of these probabilities times the total number of squadrons deployed (eighteen).

> No centers survive in four or five squadrons
>   because $(0.25)(18) = 4.5$
> One center survives in seven squadrons because
> $(0.40)(18) = 7.2$
> Two centers survive in four or five squadrons
>   because $(0.25)(18) = 4.5$
> Three centers survive in one or two squadrons because
> $(0.08)(18) = 1.44$
> Four centers survive in zero squadrons because
> $(0.01)(18) = 0.18$
> Five centers survive in zero squadrons because
> $(0)(18) = 0$

Table B-10. *Sample Risk Calculations for Table B-6*

Squadrons destroyed[a]	Formula	Results (probability)	
0	$C(18,0)(0.75)^{18}$	0.01	
1	$C(18,1)(0.25)(0.75)^{17}$	0.03	
2	$C(18,2)(0.25)^2(0.75)^{16}$	0.10	
3	$C(18,3)(0.25)^3(0.75)^{15}$	0.17	
4	$C(18,4)(0.25)^4(0.75)^{14}$	0.21	
5	$C(18,5)(0.25)^5(0.75)^{13}$	0.20	
6	$C(18,6)(0.25)^6(0.75)^{12}$	0.14	Risk of six or more destroyed $= 0.27$[b]
7	$C(18,7)(0.25)^7(0.75)^{11}$	0.08	Risk of seven or more destroyed $= 0.13$[c]
8	$C(18,8)(0.25)^8(0.75)^{10}$	0.04	Risk of eight or more destroyed $= 0.05$[d]
9	$C(18,9)(0.25)^9(0.75)^9$	0.01	Risk of nine or more destroyed $= 0.01$
10	$C(18,10)(0.25)^{10}(0.75)^8$		
11	$C(18,11)(0.25)^{11}(0.75)^7$		
12	$C(18,12)(0.25)^{12}(0.75)^6$		
13	$C(18,13)(0.25)^{13}(0.75)^5$		
14	$C(18,14)(0.25)^{14}(0.75)^4$		
15	$C(18,15)(0.25)^{15}(0.75)^3$		
16	$C(18,16)(0.25)^{16}(0.75)^2$		
17	$C(18,17)(0.25)^{17}(0.75)$		
18	$C(18,18)(0.25)^{18}$		

a. Squadrons in which all five launch control centers are destroyed or deprived of communications based on previous estimate that the probability of destruction was 25 percent for any single squadron.
b. Sum of 0.14 + 0.08 + 0.04 + 0.01.
c. Sum of 0.08 + 0.04 + 0.01.
d. Sum of 0.04 + 0.01.

This arithmetic indicates that four or five squadrons, or 200 to 250 land missiles, or 22 to 28 percent of the total Minuteman force, would have been deprived of launch control. In the analysis, estimates were rounded to the nearest unit (full squadrons). In this example, the expected number of destroyed squadrons was rounded to five, which represented 28 percent of the American land missile force. This estimate is shown under the column headed "Expected" in table B-6, row three.

The next step in the quantitative treatment of this case was to compute the probability that more than the expected number of squadrons would have been destroyed. The risks of losing all five control elements in zero to eighteen squadrons were estimated as shown on table B-10.

Risks were calculated by reading up from the bottom of the column headed "Results," summing the probabilities at each step, and reading off the corresponding number in the column headed "Squadrons destroyed." The cumulative percentage represents the risk that N or more squadrons would have been destroyed in 1966. For example, 27 percent (the sum of

1 percent, 4 percent, 8 percent, and 14 percent) represents the risk that six or more squadrons would have been disabled. Because 27 percent fell within the first risk category (headed "Risk $\geq$ 20 percent") of table B-6, the number of missiles deprived of launch control in six squadrons was converted to a fraction (33 percent) of the total number of Minuteman land missiles and then entered in table B-6. The same procedure was used to fill in the other risk categories in the third row.

The Soviet Union could have increased the expected damage from an attack on the launch control centers by adopting a different attack strategy. With a force of 110 SS-9 missiles, they could have allocated 2 missiles to each of the control centers in 11 squadrons (55 control centers in all). Table B-4 shows the results of the alternative attack strategy using SS-9 missiles with an assumed reliability of 85 percent. When the results were derived, it was found that this attack strategy decreased the probability from 24 percent to 6 percent that any individual LCC would have survived. This probability is the simple product of the probability of an LCC surviving the first missile times the probability of that same center surviving the second missile, or 24 percent times 24 percent.

The expected number of LCCs that would have survived in any of the squadrons attacked was estimated by the procedure used previously:

$$\text{None survives } C(5,5)(0.94)^5 = 73 \text{ percent}$$
$$\text{One survives } C(5,4)(0.06)(0.94)^4 = 23 \text{ percent}$$
$$\text{Two survive } C(5,3)(0.06)^2(0.94)^3 = 3 \text{ percent}$$
$$\text{Three survive } C(5,2)(0.06)^3(0.94)^2 = 0 \text{ percent}$$
$$\text{Four survive } C(5,1)(0.06)^4(0.94) = 0 \text{ percent}$$
$$\text{Five survive } C(5,0)(0.06)^5 = 0 \text{ percent}$$

In the seven squadrons that were not attacked, five centers survive with communications capabilities intact. In the other squadrons

No centers survive in eight squadrons because
$(0.73)(11) = 8.03$

One center survives in two or three squadrons because $(0.23)(11) = 2.53$

Two centers survive in zero squadrons because
$(0.03)(11) = 0.33$

Three centers survive in zero squadrons because
$(0)(11) = 0$

Table B-11. *Sample Risk Calculations for Table B-4*

Squadrons destroyed[a]	Formula	Results (probability)
0	$C(11,0)(0.27)^{11}$	0
1	$C(11,1)(0.73)(0.27)^{10}$	0
2	$C(11,2)(0.73)^2(0.27)^9$	0
3	$C(11,3)(0.73)^3(0.27)^8$	0
4	$C(11,4)(0.73)^4(0.27)^7$	0.01
5	$C(11,5)(0.73)^5(0.27)^6$	0.04
6	$C(11,6)(0.73)^6(0.27)^5$	0.10
7	$C(11,7)(0.73)^7(0.27)^4$	0.27
8	$C(11,8)(0.73)^8(0.27)^3$	0.26
9	$C(11,9)(0.73)^9(0.27)^2$	0.24
10	$C(11,10)(0.73)^{10}(0.27)$	0.13
11	$C(11,11)(0.73)^{11}$	0.03

a. Squadrons in which all five launch control centers are destroyed or deprived of communications based on previous estimate that the probability of destruction was 73 percent for any single squadron.

Four centers survive in zero squadrons because
$$(0)(11) = 0$$
Five centers survive in zero squadrons because
$$(0)(11) = 0$$

The expected destruction of eight squadrons would have rendered 400 Minuteman missiles unusable. This represents 44 percent of the total Minuteman land missile force, which was entered in table B-4 in the third row under the column headed "Expected."

Finally, the risk categories were filled in using the procedures explained above and the computations in table B-11.

Sample Computations: Reprogrammable Attacks

The Soviets were assumed to possess modest capabilities to reprogram reserve missiles to replace known launch failures. The method used is described by Davis and Schilling[1] and in effect produces new inputs for the statistical calculations described above.

1. See Lynn Etheridge Davis and Warner R. Schilling, "All You Ever Wanted to Know about MIRV and ICBM Calculations But Were Not Cleared to Ask," *Journal of Conflict Resolution*, vol. 17 (June 1973), pp. 218–22.

Electromagnetic Pulse

THE PEAK electric field strength of electromagnetic pulse generated by high-altitude nuclear explosions is estimated using theoretical models that have not been empirically validated. Different models produce estimates that range from a low of several kilovolts per meter to a high of 100 kilovolts per meter. A standard assumption in EMP vulnerability assessment is that the Soviet Union detonates a one-megaton weapon at an altitude of 300,000 feet that produces a peak EMP field of 50 kilovolts per meter. This peak field would blanket a significant portion of the area circled in figure 4-1. The field strength throughout most of this area, however, would be half the peak amount or about 25 kilovolts per meter.[1]

Despite its high field strength, electromagnetic pulse is like a brief pulse of sunlight in that it must be focused on a small area to cause damage. This focusing and damage are especially likely in the case of long electrical wires connected to sensitive equipment: "A prime example here would be a radio receiver, connected to a long antenna and to the A.C. power line. The wires pick up the energy in the electromagnetic field over a large area and then deliver it in the form of current and voltage pulses to the attached equipment."[2]

1. See *DNA EMP Awareness Course Notes,* DNA 2772T (Chicago: I.I.T. Research Institute, September 1973); Samuel Glasstone and Philip J. Dolan, *The Effects of Nuclear Weapons,* 3d ed. (Department of Defense and Department of Energy, 1977), pp. 537–38; *Hearings on Military Posture and H.R. 12604* before the House Committee on Armed Services, 92 Cong. 2 sess. (GPO, 1972), pt. 2, p. 10781; and *Fiscal Year 1973 Authorization for Military Procurement, Research and Development, Construction Authorization for the Safeguard ABM and Active Duty and Selected Reserve Strengths,* Hearings before the Senate Committee on Armed Services, 92 Cong. 2 sess. (GPO 1972), pt. 3, p. 1945.

2. David B. Nelson, "EMP Impact on U.S. Defense," *Survive,* vol. 2 (November-December 1967), p. 4.

Metallic objects collect and focus EMP energy because they are sensitive to the radio frequency region of the spectrum, and EMP energy tends to be concentrated in that region. For a high-yield, high-altitude explosion, the EMP energy is concentrated at the high frequency radio band. EMP produced by a surface burst tends toward lower frequencies, depending upon the weapon yield. The higher the yield, the larger the ionized sphere surrounding the burst point and the lower the principal frequency. For example, the radius of the ionized sphere generated by a high-yield surface burst can be as large as five miles. The principal frequency for this (or any other) burst is given by

Frequency (cycles per second) = speed of light/diameter of sphere.

Thus the principal frequency in this case is 18 to 19 Khz (very low frequency).

The vulnerability of launch center computers is a concern. This analysis assumes a high-yield burst above the atmosphere and calculates the voltage surge at the ends of a hypothetical buried cable connecting a missile silo with a launch center computer. Soil only partially insulates buried cables from the energy of electromagnetic pulse. Dry, sandy soil, such as that found in many areas where Minuteman missiles are deployed, permits the very low frequency component of EMP to penetrate about 500 feet.[3] The low frequency component penetrates 150 feet. About one-half of the strength of the high frequency component penetrates 30 feet.

This analysis assumes the presence of dry, sandy soil and an EMP of 50,000 volts per meter. The time required for the pulse to decay from 50,000 volts to 18,400 volts is assumed to be one-millionth of a second. The underground cable connecting a hypothetical missile silo and launch control center is two inches in diameter, tubular, shielded with a lead sheath one hundred mils thick, and five kilometers or three statute miles long.

The voltage surge at the ends of the buried cable would vary with the direction of the incoming pulse. The direction of arrival (elevation and angle of incidence) of the EMP at the earth's surface depends on the dip angle of the magnetic field below the burst location. In this analysis the direction of arrival is limited to vectors that apply to bursts anywhere

3. Assumptions and method of calculation are taken from L. W. Ricketts, J. E. Bridges, and J. Miletta, *EMP Radiation and Protective Techniques* (New York: John Wiley, 1976).

Table C-1. *Exterior Current and Interior Voltage Surges of EMP under Various Direction Vectors*

Azimuth angle (degrees)	Elevation angle (degrees)				
	10	20	30	60	90
	Exterior sheath current (amperes)				
10	86	171	257	428	542
30	228	428	684	1,140	1,340
50	399	684	912	1,710	1,995
70	456	855	1,197	2,280	2,850
90	485	912	1,368	2,337	2,850
	Interior voltage surge (volts)				
10	35	71	106	177	224
30	94	177	282	470	553
50	165	282	376	705	823
70	188	353	494	941	1,176
90	200	376	564	964	1,176

over the continental United States. Assuming the worst-case direction of arrival, EMP generates an estimated peak current of 2,850 amperes on the exterior sheath of the cable. This current penetrates into the cable and a voltage surge propagates to the ends. A peak inside surge of about 1,200 volts occurs at the ends, rising from 10 to 90 percent of this value in about 1.3 millionths of a second.

Such a worst-case surge exceeds the voltage damage threshold of components used in modern computers by a factor of one hundred. The direct coupling of this surge into a modern computer, which typically has an interference threshold of about two volts and a damage threshold of ten volts for a pulse lasting one millionth of a second, would be expected to disable it.

Other possible angles of arrival should be considered. Table C-1 gives the estimated exterior current surge and interior voltage surge at the ends for various direction vectors applicable to targets in the United States. As shown, voltage surges in excess of the tolerances of computer components are predicted. An average surge might be on the order of 1,000 amperes and 400 volts. This exceeds the damage threshold by a factor of forty.

These calculations identify a potential threat. Validation, however, requires experimental testing and simulation. In general, such tests have established that because of the extensive use of sensitive semiconductors,

Table C-2. *Soviet SS-9 Attack against Minuteman Launch Control Centers, Scenario A, 1966*[a]
Percent

Soviet missile reliability	EMP kill probability[b]	Minuteman missile force incapacitated[c]				
		Expected	Risk ≥ 20%	Risk ≥ 10%	Risk ≥ 5%	Risk ≥ 1%
75	0	18	24	29	29	35
75	10	18	24	29	35	47
75	20	24	29	35	41	53
75	30	29	35	41	47	59
75	40	35	47	53	53	65
75	50	41	53	59	65	71
75	60	53	65	71	77	82
75	70	65	71	77	82	94
75	80	77	82	88	94	100
75	90	88	100	100	100	100
85	0	29	35	41	47	53
85	10	29	41	47	53	59
85	20	35	47	53	59	71
85	30	41	53	59	65	71
85	40	47	59	65	71	82
85	50	59	65	71	77	88
85	60	65	71	77	82	94
85	70	77	82	88	94	100
85	80	82	88	94	100	100
85	90	94	100	100	100	100

a. Blast and electromagnetic pulse damage from surface bursts only.
b. The probability that a surface burst would disable a launch center by EMP effects alone.
c. Minuteman force of 880 missiles.

transistors, and integrated circuits, modern communications and electronics equipment is highly susceptible to damage from EMP-induced currents and voltages. Without special design considerations, this equipment usually cannot handle the voltage and current surges that result from EMP coupling.[4] A study sponsored by the Defense Nuclear Agency notes, "old cable systems remain a focal point of EMP concern."[5]

Because quantification of the EMP threat to computer and communications equipment in Minuteman launch control centers is prone to serious error, analysis should consider a wide range of threat levels. Tables C-2 and C-3 reflect EMP threat levels ranging from 0 to 90 percent probability that an LCC would be disabled by a single pulse. Using the same

4. Edwin J. Gaul, "Electromagnetic Pulse," *Military Review,* vol. 55 (March 1975), p. 16.
5. *DNA EMP Awareness Course Notes,* p. 124.

Table C-3. *Soviet SS-9 Attack against Minuteman Launch Control Centers, Scenario B,* 1966[a]
Percent

Soviet missile reliability	EMP kill probability[b]	Minuteman missile force incapacitated[c]				
		Expected	Risk ≥20%	Risk ≥10%	Risk ≥5%	Risk ≥1%
75	0	18	24	29	29	35
75	10	24	29	35	41	53
75	20	35	41	47	53	65
75	30	47	53	59	65	77
75	40	59	65	71	77	88
75	50	71	82	88	88	100
75	60	82	88	94	100	100
75	70	88	100	100	100	100
75	80	100	100	100	100	100
75	90	100	100	100	100	100
85	0	29	35	41	47	53
85	10	35	47	53	59	71
85	20	47	59	65	65	77
85	30	59	65	71	77	88
85	40	65	77	82	88	94
85	50	77	88	94	94	100
85	60	88	94	100	100	100
85	70	94	100	100	100	100
85	80	100	100	100	100	100
85	90	100	100	100	100	100

a. Blast and electromagnetic pulse damage from surface bursts and a single exoatmospheric burst.
b. The probability that a surface burst by itself would disable a launch center by EMP effects alone, and the equal probability that an exoatmospheric burst would disable a launch center by EMP effects alone. Assumes independent but equal kill probabilities for each pulse.
c. Minuteman force of 880 missiles.

basic method of calculation explained in appendix B, these threat levels were combined with expected blast damage to estimate the vulnerability of Minuteman forces to a Soviet missile attack against launch control centers.

Table C-2 summarizes one set of calculations. The results are far from the worst case because the centers are credited with a blast hardness of 250 psi, and the attacker is not credited with any reprogramming capability. The underlying assumptions are identical to those that apply in Table B-6 above, though of course the earlier treatment ignored electromagnetic pulse effects. It might be useful to recapitulate the key assumptions: (1) the Soviets targeted eighty-eight SS-9 missiles at eighty-eight Minuteman launch control centers, (2) SS-9 accuracy was 0.7 mile, (3) LCCs could have withstood up to 250 psi of blast overpressure, (4) each LCC received a pulse of electromagnetic energy in addition to some overpressure, (5) the damage from blast and electromagnetic pulse was uncorrelated. Table C-3 shows the expected damage when it is further assumed that the Soviets would have exploded a single high-yield warhead above the atmosphere, generating another pulse which simultaneously struck all eighty-eight launch control centers.

Satellite Vulnerability to System-Generated EMP

WHEN the radiated energy from a nuclear explosion in space strikes a satellite, several interactions occur. The likelihood of damage from each interaction increases the closer the weapon is to the target at the moment of detonation. This relationship holds because impinging X-ray energy—the source of the interaction effects—falls off as the inverse square of the distance between the weapon and target.

The effect of primary interest in this appendix is called system-generated electromagnetic pulse (SGEMP). Two other prime causes of satellite damage are thermomechanical shock and ionization burnout (see table 6-2). Thermomechanical shock is simply an overheated state produced when satellite materials absorb X-ray energy. Although satellites are very sensitive to it, damage from ionization burnout is likely to occur first.

High-energy X-rays, particularly gamma rays, cause ionization burnout.[1] Incident X-rays penetrate the outer structures and internal electronic boxes, exposing semiconductor components to a direct dose of radiation. The rate of exposure (dose rate) and the total exposure (bulk dose) are both responsible for damage. A bulk dose on the order of 10^4 rads (silicon) alters the threshold voltage of transisters, for example, resulting in damage to communications equipment.

These two effects are generally thought to be weak damage mechanisms as long as weapon detonation occurs far away from the target. At relatively close range—a few hundred kilometers—the effects are consid-

1. A nuclear explosion releases most of its energy in the form of X-rays, whose energies range from relatively low to very high energy gamma rays.

ered lethal to satellites (see table 6-2). Because U.S. communications satellites cluster in geosynchronous orbit, in all likelihood a few weapons detonated at close range would cripple strategic communications. However, positioning nuclear-armed spacecraft within close range of the satellites would take two to six hours; it might alert the United States to impending attack, and it would carry a significant risk of technical failure because it has never been done.

An alternative, less demanding strategy would be to detonate high-yield weapons at relatively low altitudes, perhaps sixty miles—a land missile such as the SS-9 could be the delivery vehicle. An explosion at this altitude would generate strong electromagnetic effects that could impair command elements on the ground or in the atmosphere. Thus the strategy would entail a simultaneous electromagnetic attack on both satellites and ground and airborne command networks. The attack on ground and airborne systems would take advantage of the Compton effect, produced when the weapon's gamma rays collide with air molecules. The resulting electrical field would interact with the earth's magnetic field to blanket the United States and surrounding airspace with an intense electromagnetic pulse. From the same weapon but traveling in the other direction would be low- and high-energy X-rays that would encounter no air molecules and thus would experience neither absorption nor collision. Consequently, a large fraction of the energy emitted by a nuclear explosion in space would travel unimpeded until it struck an object like a satellite. About 80 percent of the total energy of a nuclear explosion would escape into space in the form of X-ray energy, which, though not absorbed, would spread out radially in accordance with the inverse square law.

SGEMP is simply a current flow on the surface of a satellite; it is the product of the photoelectric effects generated when X-rays strike a satellite. Photoelectric effects occur when incident X-rays transfer all their energy to the electrons of atoms in satellite materials—aluminum, for example. Energized electrons are then ejected from the atoms, especially those at the surface where exposure to X-rays is most intense. When negatively charged electrons that are ejected from the surface escape permanently into space, the satellite is left with a positive charge. SGEMP is this positive photocurrent. It tends to spread evenly across all external surfaces—skin, antennas, solar arrays—where it couples into electrical cables that run along the surface. These cables feed the energy into electronic components inside internal boxes.

SGEMP strength cannot exceed a certain limit. The greater the number of ejected electrons, the greater the positive charge left behind, and the harder it becomes for ejected electrons to escape the rising potential. Some of the ejected electrons are so strongly attracted by the positively charged satellite that they return to the surface. This dynamic process that limits the permanent escape of electrons and hence the strength of the photocurrent is called space-charge limiting.

SGEMP damage is likely to occur if a nuclear explosion produces a surface current of sufficient magnitude to feed into satellite electronic boxes more energy than internal components can tolerate and space-charge limiting allows surface current to reach or exceed this threshold. According to the Defense Nuclear Agency, surface currents on the order of 50 to 100 amperes per square meter would be a matter of concern for communications satellites having little or no protection from SGEMP effects.

The following calculations demonstrate that a high-yield weapon detonated sixty miles above the earth could generate 350 to 700 amperes per square meter on the surface of representative satellites in geosynchronous orbit. These estimates are necessarily based on simplifying assumptions—the geometry of actual satellites is too complex and varied to permit precise calculation, and the response of electronic components to different SGEMP currents defies prediction. Nevertheless, they may provide reasonable approximations. Derivations are given below. The first computation is used to estimate the current on the surface of a satellite that is produced by a one-megaton burst at an altitude of 17,950 kilometers, or half the distance between the earth and satellites in geosynchronous orbit. The same steps were followed to estimate SGEMP from a low-altitude (100 kilometer) SS-9 ICBM explosion with a yield of twenty-five megatons. The representative satellite material is aluminum three mils thick.

Step 1. Convert weapon yield to joules. Because 1 kiloton equals 4.18×10^{12} J, 1 megaton equals 4.18×10^{15} J.

Step 2. Compute the amount of joule energy that is emitted as X-ray energy. Because 80 percent of the total yield of an exoatmospheric burst is emitted as X-ray energy, X-ray joule energy equals $0.8 \times 4.18 \times 10^{15}$ J, or 3.34×10^{15} J.

Step 3. Apply inverse square law to obtain X-ray energy on target at a distance r (meters) from the weapon at the moment of detonation:

X-ray joule energy $\div\ 4\ \pi\ (r^2)$. Since r = 17,950,000 meters, X-ray joule energy incident equals

$$\frac{3.34\ \times\ 10^{15}\ \mathrm{J}}{12.57\ (3.22 \times 10^{14}\ \mathrm{m}^2)} = 0.83\ \mathrm{J/m}^2$$

Step 4. Convert J/m² to Cal/cm² by dividing results at step 3 by 4.18×10^4.

$$\frac{0.83\ \mathrm{J/m}^2}{4.18\ \times\ 10^4} = 2.00\ \times\ 10^{-5}\ \mathrm{Cal/cm}^2$$

Step 5. For a range of plausible weapons characteristics (so-called black-body temperatures), estimate the electron yield, in coulombs per calorie, ejected at the surface of 3-mil aluminum because of X-rays incident at 1 Cal/cm². (I am indebted to the Defense Nuclear Agency for these estimates.)

Blackbody temperature (keV)	Electron Yield (C/Cal)
2	2.80×10^{-6}
5	5.72×10^{-7}
8	2.16×10^{-7}
10	1.32×10^{-7}
12	8.00×10^{-8}

Step 6. Multiply previous results (step 5) by 2.00×10^{-5} Cal/cm² (step 4 result), giving product in C/cm². Convert results to C/m² by dividing by 10^{-4} (coulombs/m² equals amperes/m²/second).

Blackbody temperature (keV)	C/cm²	C/m² (a/m²/s)
2	5.60×10^{-11}	5.60×10^{-7}
5	1.14×10^{-11}	1.14×10^{-7}
8	4.32×10^{-12}	4.32×10^{-8}
10	2.64×10^{-12}	2.64×10^{-8}
12	1.60×10^{-12}	1.60×10^{-8}

Step 7. Step 6 results give currents over a one-second interval. Nuclear weapons yield energy much faster. Analysts use a summary measure of

energy emission time known as the full half width maximum (FHWM) shown as Δt on the diagram below.

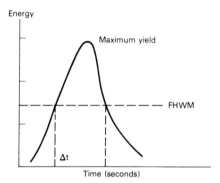

Divide step 6 results by a range of plausible Δt measures expressing final results in A/m², or SGEMP photocurrent.

The final results in table D-1 indicate that a one-megaton weapon exploded half the distance between the earth and a satellite in geosynchronous orbit could generate SGEMP currents as high as fifty to one hundred amperes per square meter.

Following the steps outlined above, one can see that the estimates for a twenty-five-megaton bomb detonated only one hundred kilometers above the United States are about six times greater.

Table D-1. *SGEMP Photocurrents Generated by Nuclear Explosion*
Amperes per square meter unless otherwise designated

Yield of explosion	Blackbody temperature (keV)	FHWM			
		$\Delta t = 5 \times 10^{-9}$ sec	$\Delta t = 1 \times 10^{-8}$ sec	$\Delta t = 2 \times 10^{-8}$ sec	$\Delta t = 4 \times 10^{-8}$ sec
1 megaton	2	112	56	28	14
	5	23	12	6	3
	8	9	5	2	1
	10	5	3	1	1
	12	3	2	1	...
25 megatons	2	694	347	174	87
	5	142	71	36	18
	8	53	27	13	7
	10	33	16	8	4
	12	20	10	5	3

Index